MW00629472

WOMEN OF FAITH
IN THE LATTER DAYS

WOMEN OF FAITH IN THE LATTER DAYS
Previously Published Volumes

Volume One, 1775–1820
(2011)

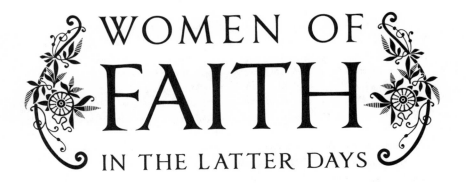

WOMEN OF FAITH

IN THE LATTER DAYS

VOLUME TWO, 1821–1845

RICHARD E. TURLEY JR. AND
BRITTANY A. CHAPMAN, EDITORS

DESERET
BOOK

SALT LAKE CITY, UTAH

Except as noted below, all images are courtesy of the Church History Library, The Church of Jesus Christ of Latter-day Saints, Salt Lake City, Utah. Used by permission.

Page 15: Image of Sarah Maria Mousley Cannon courtesy of Roxanne Davis. Used by permission.

Images of Cordelia Calista Morley Cox, page 45; Mary Goble Pay, page 243; courtesy of Patricia H. Stoker. Used by permission.

Images of Janetta Ann McBride Ferrin, page 61; Mary Minerva Dart Judd, page 167; Susanah Stone Lloyd, page 183; Julia Sophia Raymond McKee, page 229; Emmeline Blanche Woodward Wells, page 384; Catherine Elizabeth Mehring Woolley, page 413; courtesy of International Society Daughters of Utah Pioneers, Salt Lake City, Utah. Used by permission.

Page 76: Image of Lucy Hannah White Flake courtesy of David F. Boone. Used by permission.

Page 136: Image of Ann Prior Jarvis courtesy of McQuarrie Memorial Museum, International Society Daughters of Utah Pioneers, St. George, Utah. Used by permission.

Page 196: Image of Rosa Clara Friedlander Logie from Marjorie B. Newton, "Australia's Pioneer Saints," *Ensign,* February 1997, public domain.

Page 149: Image of Jane Cadwalader Brown Johnson courtesy of Patricia Lemmon Spilsbury. Used by permission.

Page 288: Image of Emeline Grover Rich courtesy of Rosaland Thornton. Used by permission.

Page 315: Image of Margaret Condie Sharp courtesy of Emily B. Farrer. Used by permission.

Page 333: Image of Rachel Emma Woolley Simmons courtesy of Laura F. Willes. Used by permission.

© 2012 Richard E. Turley Jr. and Brittany A. Chapman

All rights reserved. No part of this book may be reproduced in any form or by any means without permission in writing from the publisher, Deseret Book Company, P. O. Box 30178, Salt Lake City, Utah 84130. This work is not an official publication of The Church of Jesus Christ of Latter-day Saints. The views expressed herein are the responsibility of the authors and do not necessarily represent the position of the Church or of Deseret Book Company.

DESERET BOOK is a registered trademark of Deseret Book Company.

Visit us at DeseretBook.com

Library of Congress Cataloging-in-Publication Data
Women of faith in the latter days. Volume 1, 1775–1820 / edited by Richard E. Turley Jr. and Brittany A. Chapman.
    pages cm
    Includes bibliographical references and index.
    ISBN 978-1-60641-033-2 (hardbound : alk. paper; v. 1, 1775–1820)
    ISBN 978-1-60907-173-8 (hardbound : alk. paper; v. 2, 1821–1845)
    1. Mormon women—Biography. I. Turley, Richard E. (Richard Eyring), 1956– editor. II. Chapman, Brittany A., editor.
    BX8693.W66 2011
    289.3092'52—dc23   2011035215

Printed in the United States of America
Malloy Lithographing Incorporated, Ann Arbor, MI

10 9 8 7 6 5 4 3 2 1

FOR THE WOMEN WHO
CONSECRATED ALL

CONTENTS

INTRODUCTION TO THE SERIES

Although approximately half the people in the history of The Church of Jesus Christ of Latter-day Saints have been women, their lives of faith and dedication are just beginning to receive the attention they merit. This series, *Women of Faith in the Latter Days*, aims to enhance awareness of these women through inspirational accounts written for a general readership.

The seven volumes projected for the series will be arranged as follows:

Volume 1: Women born between 1775 and 1820

Volume 2: Women born between 1821 and 1845

Volume 3: Women born between 1846 and 1870

Volume 4: Women born between 1871 and 1895

Volume 5: Women born between 1896 and 1920

Volume 6: Women born between 1921 and 1945

Volume 7: Women born between 1946 and 1970

Within each volume, the chapters are arranged alphabetically by the last name of each woman of faith.

We have sought to balance the preferences of general readers with the needs of scholarship by following common editorial conventions that enhance ease of reading but preserve the accuracy of historical sources and the personalities of the subject women. Briefly stated, in the historical sources we have preserved the original spelling and grammar, using square brackets [ ] to expand, correct, or clarify when necessary for readability. We have silently added punctuation and capitalized the first words of sentences, using our best interpretive judgment to discern the writer's intentions. We have also altered capitalization when failure to do so might prove distracting to readers.

We have included chapters written by a range of authors, from well-established scholars to beginning writers. Some chapters adopt a scholarly approach, often quoting the subject woman's own words at length. Others follow a more popular approach, avoiding long quotations from the subject and replacing them with the author's own prose.

Some of the subject women left few or no writings behind, making it difficult or impossible to quote them. Our goal has been to feature a diverse group of women, both those well known to readers and those who lived lives of faith in comparative anonymity. We hope both scholarly and popular audiences will find value in these volumes. Our intent in producing them is to plant seeds for future work. If our series leads to better scholarly and popular works, we will feel rewarded for our efforts.

We invite you to join with us in celebrating the many Latter-day Saint women whose lives are an inspiration to readers in the present generation and in generations to come. We hope these volumes will prompt readers to write about their own lives and will lead to longer works about past and present women of faith in the latter days.

PREFACE

Volume 2 of *Women of Faith in the Latter Days* features women of The Church of Jesus Christ of Latter-day Saints born from 1821 to 1845. Persecution followed members of the Church from their roots in New York state through settlements in Ohio, Missouri, and Illinois. Seeking a haven of peace and rest, Latter-day Saints found refuge in the Rocky Mountain West, a region they called Zion. The women whose stories are told here lived during an age when Latter-day Saint leaders emphasized the literal gathering of Israel spoken of in the Church's tenth article of faith. For that reason, this volume includes accounts of the trek to Utah and the settlement of new communities in the west.

The gospel spread internationally, and thousands of converts from the British Isles and Scandinavia made their way to Zion. The most tragic story of gathering was that of the last two handcart companies of 1856, the Willie and Martin companies, and the two wagon trains that supported them. This volume includes first-person accounts of that tragedy.

When the Saints arrived in their land of promise, they experienced the strength of being among like-minded believers but also endured the hardship of taming uncultivated land and starting new settlements. Eventually, Mormon colonies spread through Utah and into Idaho and Canada in the north and Arizona and Mexico in the south.

As with volume 1, during much of the period covered by volume 2, some Latter-day Saints practiced polygamy, or plural marriage, as it was also known. Many of the women featured in these volumes experienced this form of marriage, wrestled with their feelings about the practice, and recorded their experiences. Because plural marriage is no longer practiced in the Church, their experiences may seem foreign to modern Latter-day Saints. Yet the way the women dealt with this challenge in their lives may have application to other challenges faced by readers today.

Several people aided in the preparation of this volume. We thank Hillary Schmutz, Betsy Crane, Eleanor C. Jensen, Kevin P. Searcy, Angela B. Wagner, Carly M. Jakins, Elizabeth Miles, Amanda Brown, and Shannon Armstrong Smith for their invaluable assistance. Again we thank Sheri Dew and Cory Maxwell of Deseret Book, who encouraged us throughout this project, and our ever-patient editor, Suzanne Brady, whose skills have made this volume more readable.

We thank the authors who have contributed chapters to this volume. Most of all, we express our undying gratitude to the women who are the subject of these chapters and whose lives are a monument to their faith and sacrifice.

Timeline

Spring 1820	Joseph Smith receives First Vision in Palmyra, New York.
April 6, 1830	Church of Christ is organized in Fayette, New York.
1831–38	**Saints in Kirtland, Ohio.**
July 20, 1837	First missionaries arrive in Britain.
1831–39	**Saints in Missouri.**
1831–33	Independence, Jackson County.
1834–36	Clay County.
1836–39	Far West, Caldwell County.
April 26, 1838	Revelation declares the name of the Church to be The Church of Jesus Christ of Latter-day Saints.
October 27, 1838	Extermination order is issued, demanding that the Saints leave Missouri.
April 1839	Missouri settlements have been abandoned by the Saints.
1839–46	**Saints in Nauvoo, Illinois.**
April 1841	First plural marriage in Nauvoo is performed.
March 17, 1842	Female Relief Society of Nauvoo is organized.
June 27, 1844	Joseph and Hyrum Smith martyred in Carthage, Illinois.
December 1845	Nauvoo Temple endowments and sealings begin.

February 4, 1846	Nauvoo Saints begin crossing Mississippi River for the West.
1846	**Most of the Saints leave Nauvoo and trek across Iowa,** living in such temporary camps as Sugar Creek, Bloomfield, Garden Grove, and Mt. Pisgah, as well as in semipermanent posts at Council Bluffs, Iowa, and Winter Quarters in what became Nebraska.
July 16, 1846	Mormon Battalion organized in Council Bluffs, Iowa.
July 24, 1847	Brigham Young, leader of the first pioneer company, arrives in Salt Lake Valley.
1847–69	**Saints migrate to Utah by wagon or handcart.**
Fall 1849	Perpetual Emigrating Fund established.
August 29, 1852	Plural marriage is publicly announced in Utah.
October–November 1856	Willie and Martin handcart companies and the Hunt and Hodgetts wagon companies are rescued.
1857–58	Utah War occurs between the Utah territorial militia and a United States Army expedition led eventually by Colonel Albert Sidney Johnston. Settlements in northern Utah are temporarily abandoned until the conflict is resolved by negotiation.
1868	Reorganization of Relief Society begins.
1869	Transcontinental railroad completed.
1870	Utah women receive the right to vote.
1876	First colonies established along the Little Colorado River in Arizona.
January 7, 1876	First missionaries arrive in Mexico.
April 6–8, 1877	St. George Temple dedicated by Daniel H. Wells under direction of Brigham Young.
August 29, 1877	Brigham Young dies in Salt Lake City, Utah.
August 25, 1878	Primary Association for children organized.

June 19, 1880	Eliza R. Snow sustained as second Relief Society general president, Elmina S. Taylor as first general president of the Young Ladies' Mutual Improvement Association, and Louie B. Felt as first Primary general president.
October 10, 1880	John Taylor sustained as third Church president.
1882	Edmunds Act passed, intensifying legal action against polygamists.
1885	First Mormon colonies established in Mexico.
1887	Edmunds-Tucker Act further intensifes legal action against polygamists, dissolves the Perpetual Emigrating Fund, and revokes the right of women in Utah to vote.
December 5, 1887	Eliza R. Snow dies in Salt Lake City, Utah.
April 8, 1888	Zina D. H. Young sustained as third Relief Society general president.
April 7, 1889	Wilford Woodruff sustained as fourth Church president.
September 24, 1890	Wilford Woodruff issues Manifesto, leading to the discontinuance of the practice of plural marriage.
April 6, 1893	Salt Lake Temple dedicated by Wilford Woodruff.
September 2, 1898	Wilford Woodruff dies in San Francisco, California.
September 13, 1898	Lorenzo Snow ordained and set apart as president of the Church.
August 28, 1901	Zina D. H. Young dies in Salt Lake City, Utah.
October 10, 1901	Lorenzo Snow dies in Salt Lake City.
October 17, 1901	Joseph F. Smith ordained and set apart as president of the Church.
November 10, 1901	Bathsheba W. Smith sustained as fourth Relief Society general president.
September 20, 1910	Bathsheba W. Smith dies in Salt Lake City.

October 3, 1910	Emmeline B. Wells sustained as fifth Relief Society general president.
November 19, 1918	Joseph F. Smith dies in Salt Lake City.
November 23, 1918	Heber J. Grant ordained and set apart as president of the Church.
April 2, 1921	Emmeline B. Wells released as Relief Society general president.
April 2, 1921	Clarissa Smith Williams sustained as Relief Society general president.
April 25, 1921	Emmeline B. Wells dies in Salt Lake City.

Chapter 1

"THE HAND OF GOD WAS WITH ME"

PATIENCE LOADER ROZSA ARCHER (1827–1921)
Andrea Ventilla

BIOGRAPHICAL SKETCH

Patience Loader Rozsa Archer's life spanned nearly a century. She was born in Aston Rowant, Oxfordshire, England, on August 23, 1827. Her father, James Loader, was the gardening foreman on a large estate, which provided him with a comfortable cottage. Her mother, Amy Britnell Loader, took care of their home and their children, who eventually numbered thirteen. Patience left her parents' house at age seventeen and worked as a maid and seamstress in various parts of eastern England, including Watlington, Ramsgate, and greater London. Vivacious and social by nature, Patience moved to the city of London in 1853 to take full advantage of its "worldly pleasures."[1] Shortly thereafter, she went home to visit her parents and

---

1. Patience Loader Rozsa Archer, "Reccolections of Past Days: Autobiography," Photocopy of holograph, p. 60, private possession. Photocopy of holograph also available at L. Tom Perry Special Collections, Harold B. Lee Library, Brigham Young University, Provo, Utah.

several siblings, all of whom had joined The Church of Jesus Christ of Latter-day Saints in 1851. Patience learned more of the gospel and, despite her initial doubts, was baptized in June 1853.

Her life changed completely after she joined the Church, and within two years the family decided to gather with the Saints in the United States. Their voyage in December 1855 was a difficult one, but they arrived safely in New York City in 1856. That summer they joined the Martin Handcart Company to cross the plains to the Salt Lake Valley. After enduring the death of her father, James, in Nebraska and starvation and exposure to intense winter storms in Wyoming, Patience, her mother, and their remaining family members reached the Salt Lake Valley in November 1856. Patience was twenty-nine years old and unmarried.

Patience moved south to Lehi, not far from Camp Floyd, where she met her future husband, John Eugene Rozsa, a Hungarian immigrant who was stationed there as a sergeant in the Utah Expedition of the United States Army (later known as Johnston's Army). John joined the Church, and the couple was married on December 8, 1858. When the Civil War broke out in 1861, John's infantry unit was ordered to Washington, D.C., and Patience moved east with her husband and their baby son. In 1865 the family was transferred to Fort Leavenworth, Kansas, and in 1866 John was sent west as a military unit clerk at Fort Douglas, Utah.

The couple started the journey back to Utah with their three little children. Once again, Patience crossed the plains, this time with a wagon instead of a handcart. John did not reach their destination but died of consumption in Nebraska. Patience arrived in Salt Lake City widowed with three young sons and pregnant with a daughter. Shortly after their arrival, one of her sons followed his father to the grave.

Patience undertook any work she could find to support her family. In 1872, for example, she cooked for sixty miners at a mining camp in American Fork Canyon. Sometime after 1878 she married John Bond Archer, an acquaintance from England who had also migrated to Utah. Although they did not have children together, Patience and John adopted a relative's baby, Ruth, and raised her as their own.

Patience spent the rest of her life in Pleasant Grove, Utah, where she served as one of the first Relief Society presidents and was city treasurer. She died on April 22, 1921, a faithful member of the Church who left a great legacy of faith and indomitable courage.[2]

LIFE EXPERIENCES

Patience's autobiography recounts the story of her conversion and the mighty change in her heart:

> While I was living here [in the outskirts of London], Mormonsm came to My Fathers home. At that time I had never heard of a Mormon Elder. But Miss Henderson had been to her meeting one evening, and she came home and called me into her room and said do you know anything about the Mormons? I answered no. Well, she said, I have heard that your father and mother have joined them and said she was sorrey for them. I told the her I did not think it was so. I wrote home to enquire of father and mother and I found it was true that thay had been baptised and said thay was Latter day Saints. . . .
>
> I went home to visit my parents . . . and there was two Elders came to my fathers house to preach. I did not pay any great attention to there preaching, but on the Sunday morning my father ask me if I would accompany him to aplace called Benson as he was going there to visit a Br[other John] Archer who was also in the Church.[3] . . . I staid there

2. Drucilla Smith, interview by Andrea Ventilla, Pleasant Grove, Utah, August 1, 2011.

3. John Bond Archer (1820–1909) and Patience married twenty-five years later; he was her second husband, and she was his third wife. See Sandra Ailey Petree,

untill Tuesday. I had quite a pleasant visit with Mrs. Archer on Monday, but not so pleasant with Mr [John] Dalling for he set about to try to convert me to the Mormon faith. Of course this was his Mission he was sent out to do, but he was to[o] tiresome. He done nothing but preach to me all the time, and at that time I did not want to be troubled so much about religion, and Mrs. Archer seeing I did not like it came to my rescue. And she said to Mr Dalling, I think you had better stop your preaching to Miss Loader. She dont like so much of it; you are enough to tire her out. From this he did not talk so much of religion to me but commenced upon the Subject of marrage and let me know that he was without a wife in the world and that he would like to get a companion before he returned to Utah.

Monday evening Mr Archer returned home from Oxford. We all spent a pleasant evening together. Mr Archer and Mr Dalling Sang several Mormon Songs, and thay talked upon the principles of Mormonsm. We had prayer and retiard to rest for the night. . . .

In the morning . . . we had breakfast and Mr Dalling and myself took leave of our friends, Mr. & Mrs Archer, and started for a long walk eleven miles to my Fathers home where I anticipated staing for a few more days before I returned to the city of London. . . . It seemed in this matter as in many other that man or woman can make apointments but God can dissapoint and in my case I am willing to acknowledge that his watchfull care was over me and he knew what was best for me to do before I left my Fathers home again and his Spirit worked upon me and opened my eyes and my understanding to and shoed me the necessity of baptism for the remission of our Sins and true repentance and

ed., *Recollections of Past Days: The Autobiography of Patience Loader Rozsa Archer* (Logan: Utah State University Press, 2006), 159, 202n37.

obedince to the Gospel of Jesus Christ would bring everlasting joy and happeyness, but the pleasures of this world was
only for a short time. It seemed that I had the two Spirits
to contend with the good and the bad. I did not feel that I
realy could settle down to live a religious life as the world
beleived allways going to religious meetings and gatherings
and there faces allways looking so Sad and Searious and thay
think it a sin to Sing a laughable Song or go to a dance or
Theater. This way of living was so contrary to my Nature
that I could not think of living this way and mope my life
away. But I found the Latter day Saints did not doctering
was verey different to the religion of the world and I could
see that in the Gospel of Christ there was true happeyness
and true enjoyment. And before I left my parents roof I was
led by the Spirit of God to chuse the good part, and I went
fourth and was baptised and into the Church of Jesus Christ
and in two days after returned back to London rejoicing but
in a different way to which I had intended to rejoice when
I left London two weeks previous to my going home. The
hand of God was with me and his Spirit was around me to
teach me the way to real happeyness and I am thankfull I
accepted it just at the right time. It was a safe guard to me at
a time when I was young and full of life and needed aguard-
ian angle around me in the midst of the worldly pleasurs I
was Surrounded with in while an Hotell life. So much company and pleasure of all kind belonging to the world and
the many invitations I had to join in with them it was no
temptation to me. I fealt satisfied that I had found the true
way to pleasure and happeyness and when I refused to join
my young friends to go to a ball or Theater thay woundered
what was the matter with me and said I was become so settled down. Of course thay did not know that I was enjoying

myself at home when thay was out or perhaps I would go to a Meeting and there have a time of rejoicing.[4]

Desiring to join the Saints in Utah, Patience, her parents, and five of her siblings boarded the ship *John J. Boyd* on December 10, 1855, and arrived in New York on February 15, 1856.[5] That summer they joined the Martin Handcart Company and began their twelve-hundred-mile trek from Iowa City at the end of July. In her writings, Patience recollected the experiences she and other members of her pioneer company underwent and the hardships they endured while crossing the plains.

One month into their journey, the Loader family fell behind the main company when one of Patience's sisters gave birth on August 27, and another was very ill. They were able to catch up with the company by trekking into the night for several days in a row. Having little to eat and little sleep, this sprint was "quite hard on us," wrote Patience.[6]

Perhaps as a result of this exertion, Father James Loader, who had been so ill in Florence that he could hardly walk, became

---

4. Archer, "Past Days," 38, 53–54, 56–61.

5. Patience traveled with siblings John (thirty-five) and his wife, Harriet King Loader, and their two children; Maria (eighteen); Jane (fourteen); Sarah (twelve); and Robert (nine). Biographer Sandra Ailey Petree writes: "Ann Loader Dalling was already in Salt Lake City with her husband John. . . . Her sisters Tamar (22), Zilpha [Zilpah] (25), with her husband John Jaques and infant daughter, would remain in Liverpool until July and then join the rest of the family for the overland journey from Iowa to the Wasatch Mountains." Patience's brother John and his family remained in Iowa until 1866, when they joined the Roszas on their second journey to Utah. Petree, *Recollections,* 61, 204n2; "Edward Martin Company," Mormon Pioneer Overland Travel Database, 1847–68, The Church of Jesus Christ of Latter-day Saints, accessed September 14, 2012, http://mormontrail.lds.org; "Patience Loader," Mormon Migration Database, Brigham Young University, accessed February 6, 2012, http://lib.byu.edu/mormonmigration/index.php. See also Patience Loader Archer, "Autobiography," in *Our Pioneer Heritage,* comp. Kate B. Carter, vol. 14 (Salt Lake City, UT: Daughters of Utah Pioneers, 1971), 260–61, 263.

6. Archer, "Past Days," 145.

increasingly weak but struggled to carry on. He walked seventeen miles on September 23, 1856, but was too ill to walk the next day. "Poor dear father realizing he had to leave us he was to weak to talk to us he looked on us all with tears in his eyes then he said to Mother with great diffulcuty he said you know I love my children then he closed his eyes thees was the last words he ever said."[7] He died that evening, September 24. Patience wrote:

> This was a severe trial. Here we had to rap my dear father in a quilt, all we had to lay him in. No nice casket to lay him away in comfortable but put into the grave and the earth thrown in upon his poor body. Oh that sounded so hard. I will never forget the sound of that dirt being shoveld onto my poor fathers boday. It seemed to me that it would break every bone in his body. It did indeed seem a great trial to have to leave our dear father behind that morning, knowing we had looked upon that sweet smiling face for the last time on earth but not without a hope of meeting him again in the morning of the resurection, for he had been afaithfull servant of God and bore testimony to the truth of the Gosple of Jesus Christ numbers of times. And we know if we his children follow his example that we will meet our dear father again and be reunited with him, to dwell in unity and love all through eternity. And so our dear Mother and we girls traveled that day; it was a verey Sorrowfull day and we all greeved greatly.[8]

Early in October the company reached Fort Laramie, in what is now Wyoming, but found no provisions waiting, and they were forced to cut back their rations. An early winter storm overtook them at the Platte River on October 19. After nine days' exposure to ice, deep snow, and freezing winds, the surviving members of the

7. Archer, "Past Days," 149–50.

8. Archer, "Past Days," 153–55.

Martin company faced starvation. The handcart company was still in Wyoming, about four hundred miles from Salt Lake City, when express riders Joseph A. Young, Abel Garr, and Daniel W. Jones found the company on October 28, 1856. After distributing what food they could, the rescuers departed to direct additional relief wagons, forty-six miles away, to the handcart group. Patience recalled:

> After the Breathren had left us, we fealt quite encuraged. We got our flour and beef before night came, and we was all busy cooking. And we fealt to thank God and our kind brothers that had come to help us in our great disstress and miserey, for we was suffering greatly with cold and hunger. When night came we went to bed. We slept pretty comfortable, more so than we had done for some time. We fealt arenewed hope. We was all glad to make a moove from this place.[9] It Seemed that if God our Father had not sent help to us that we must all have perished and died in ashort time, for at that time we had only very little provisions left and at the request of Br [Edward] Marten we had come on four ounces of flour a day for each one to make the flour last us as long he could. I dont know how long we could have lived and pulled our handcart on this small quantity of food. Our provisions would not have lasted as long as thay did had all our breathren and sisters lived, but nearly half the company died[10] and caused our provisions to hold out longer

---

9. The Martin Handcart Company was camped at Red Buttes near the Hodgetts wagon company. They were several miles ahead of the Hunt wagon company, which was still camped near the last crossing of the Platte River.

10. The mortality rate of the Martin Handcart Company is estimated to have been between 18 and 26 percent. Of the 575 members of the company, there were 103 documented deaths; the exact number is unknown because not all deaths were recorded. Andrew D. Olsen, *The Price We Paid* (Salt Lake City, UT: Deseret Book, 2006), 401–2; Howard A. Christy, "Weather, Disaster, and Responsibility: An Essay on the Willie and Martin Handcart Story," *BYU Studies* 37, no. 1 (1997–98): 53, 71.

accordingly. We struck tents in the Morning and packed our carts and started on our journy again. It was anice bright Morning but very cold and clear. The Snow was very deep in places; it was hard pulling the cart.

I remember well poor Brother [David] Blair. He was afine taul man; had been one of Queen Victorias life guards in London. He had awife and four small children.[11] He made a cover for his cart, and he put his four children on the cart. He pulled his cart alone. His wife helped by pushing behind the cart. Poor Man. He was so weak and wourn down that he fell down Several times that day. But still he kept his dear little children on the cart all day. This poor man had So much love for his wife and children that instead of eating his Morsel of food himself he would give it to his children. Poor Man. He pulled the cart as long as he could. Then he died, and his poor wife and children had to do the best thay could without him to help them. The poor children got frozen. Some parts of there bodys was all sores, but thay all got in to Salt L[ake] City alive but suffering. . . .

I will say we traveld on all day in the snow, but the weather was fine, and in the midle of the day the sun was quite warm. Some time in the after noon, astrange man appeard to me as we was resting. As we got up the hill he came and looked in my face. He sais, Is you Patience? I said, yes. He said again, I thought it was you. Travel on. There is help for you. You will come to a good place. There is plenty. With this, he was gone. He dissapeared. I looked but never

11. David Blair and his wife, Deborah Jane Rushnell Blair, were the parents of three children: Deborah Louisa, age eight; Elizabeth, age five; and David, an infant. "Edward Martin Company (1856)," Mormon Pioneer Overland Travel Database, 1847–68, The Church of Jesus Christ of Latter-day Saints, accessed February 6, 2012, http://mormontrail.lds.org; "David Blair," Mormon Migration Database, Brigham Young University, accessed February 7, 2012, http://lib.byu.edu/mormonmigration/index.php.

saw whare he went. This seemed very strange to me. I took this as some one sent to encourage us and give us strength.[12]

On November 4, the Martin Handcart Company reached the final crossing of the Sweetwater River:

> There was three brave men there in the water pack-
> ing the women and children over on there backs Names
> William Kimble Ephrem Hanks and I think the other was
> James Furgeson.[13] Those poor breathren was in the water
> nearly all day we wanted to thank them but thay would not
> listen to my dear Mother felt in her heart to bless them for
> there kindness she said God bless you for taking me over
> this water and in such an awfull rough way oh D_m that
> I don't want any of that you are welcome we have come to
> help you. Mother turned to me saying what do think of that
> man he is arough fellow. . . . I am told thay are all good men
> but I daresay that thay are all rather rough in there manners,
> but we found that thay all had kind good hearts.[14]

After crossing the Sweetwater, the handcart company camped at Martin's Cove for several days. Patience recorded:

> That night was a terrable cold night. The wind was
> blowing, and the snow drifted into the tent onto our quilts.

---

12. Archer, "Past Days," 173–75.

13. In her recollection of events, Patience has confused details here. In actuality, "William Kimball, Ephraim Hanks, and James Ferguson were not with the Martin Company on the day it crossed the Sweetwater. At the time of the crossing, Kimball was assisting the Willie Company while Hanks and Ferguson were still en route." The three men typically associated with the Sweetwater crossing are C. Allen Huntington, George W. Grant, and David P. Kimball; however, fifteen additional rescuers have been positively identified as having participated in the Sweetwater crossing on November 4. Chad M. Orton, "The Martin Handcart Company at the Sweetwater: Another Look," *BYU Studies* 45, no. 3 (2006): 13n13, 8, 12.

14. Archer, "Past Days," 182–83.

That morning we had nothing to eat if we got up, not untill we could get our small quantity of flour. Poor Mother called to me, Come Patience; get up and make us afiar. I told her that I did not feel like geting up. It was so cold, and I was not feeling very well. So she ask my sister Tamar to get up, and she said she was not well and she cauld not get up. Then she sais, Come Maria; you get up. And she was feeling bad and said that she could not get up. With this Mother sais, Come Girls. This will not do. I beleive I will have to dance to you and try to make you feel better. Poor dear Mother. She started to Sing and dance to us, and she slipt down as the snow was frozen, and in a moment we was all up to help our dear Mother up, for we was afraid she was hurt. She laugh[ed] and said, I thought I could soon make you all jump up if I danced to you. Then we found that she fell down purposely, for she knew we would all get up to see if she was hurt. She said that she was afraid her Girls was going to give out and get disscuraged, and she said that would never do to give up.[15]

The Loaders arrived in the Salt Lake Valley at last on November 30, 1856. Reflecting on her journey years later, Patience said:

It seemed we did not suffer with hunger it seemed the Lord fitted the back for the burden every day we realised that the hand of God was over us and that he made good his promices un to us day by day as we know God our Father has promised us thees blessings if we will call on him in faith we know that his promises never fail and this we prooved day by day we knew that we had not strength of our own to preform such hardships if our heavenly Father had not help us and we prayed unto God continuely for his help and we allways acknowledged his goodness unto us day by

---

15. Archer, "Past Days," 173–75, 186.

day. Sometimes in the morning I would feel so tiard and feel
that I could not pull the cart the day through. Then the still
small voice would wisper in my ear as thy day thy strength
shall be. This would give me new strength and energy and
thus we traveled on day after day week after week and for
four Month before we reached the valley.[16]

After reaching Utah, Patience worked as a seamstress on a ranch
at the Jordan River, which also happened to be where the Tenth
Infantry of the United States Army was stationed. There Patience
met her first husband, Sergeant John Rozsa, whom she married
in 1858. John died in Nebraska on May 24, 1866, while he and
Patience and their three young sons were returning to Utah after his
Civil War service in the east.

Shortly afterward, Patience and her sons arrived at her mother's home in Pleasant Grove, Utah, where Patience gave birth to a
daughter. Five months later, her four-year-old son became ill:

When my little daughter was one month old, my
Second little son Frank Loader Rozsa was taken very Sick
with sore throat and in three days he died. . . . Poor deer
boy it seemed after his father died he greeved and pined
away. . . . I tried in every way to console him and make him
feel to forget his father, as it hurt my feelings to see how he
had changed since his father died, and whenever he would
see me greive or cry he would come and whipe my tears
away and he would do some little kind act for me. Then he
would put his dear little arms around me and say, Dont cry
any more for my papa. I will take care of you Mama. . . .

He was such aloving affectionate child, to[o] good to
stay here very long, and God took him home to dwell with
him. This was another severe trial. . . . When he was near
dieing . . . I said, Oh my dear Frank. You dont want to die

---

16. Archer, "Past Days," 145–46.

and leave poor mama like your dear father did. He looked at me and said, Yes I do. I want to go to my papa. I dont like this home. Of course this made me feel bad. He said, When it gets dark can I go in your bed with you? I told him he could, and as the day was closing and it began to get dark, he called to me, Now, Mama, it is dark. Put me into your bed, and you come and sleep with me. Before going to bed I was siting by the fire trying to warm his dear little feet as thay was cold. I could not think that my dear boy was so near death. . . . I took [him] in my arms and laid him in my bed. He Said, Now, Mama, come to bed with me. . . . He looked at me and Smiled and was So pleased to Sleep with me. He put his dear little arm around my neck and went to Sleep for nearly an hour quite comfortable. Then he awoke and called, Oh Mama. Mama, lift me up quick, Mama. And he died instantly. I called to Mother to come, Sa[y]ing, My Frank is dead. She came to me. She did not think he was dead, but I knew he was. I Said, Surely God is not going to take all away from me that is So near and dear to me. My greif was So great that it seemed more than I could endure, as it was only five Months since My dear husband died. My dear Mother Said, God will be Mercifull unto you, I hope, and Spare your other children unto you and give you Strength to indure this trial.[17]

This hope was fulfilled. She remained certain that God would be merciful to her and give her strength to endure these trials. Patience remained a strong member of the Church and shared her testimony of the gospel whenever an opportunity arose, often bearing witness of the Lord's assistance in her journey with the Martin Handcart Company: "We was blessed with health and strength day by day to endure the severe trials we had to pass through. . . . I can say we put

---

17. Archer, "Past Days," 304–7.

our trust in God. and he heard and answerd our prayers."[18] Despite the many difficulties and trials Patience had to overcome, she was not indignant, nor did she complain. God had proven His watch care, and Patience knew by experience that His hand would sustain her in all things.

---

18. Archer, "Past Days," 185.

Chapter 2

"Joyful Were My Feelings"

S A R A H   M A R I A   M O U S L E Y   C A N N O N (1828–1912)
Madelyn Stewart Silver Palmer

B I O G R A P H I C A L   S K E T C H

Sarah Maria Mousley was born July 21, 1828, in Centreville, Newcastle County, Delaware, the sixth of ten children born to Titus and Ann McMenemy Mousley. Sarah accepted the restored gospel and was baptized into The Church of Jesus Christ of Latter-day Saints on April 14, 1842.[1] Her mother and four siblings also joined the Church. Sarah's father, Titus, was "popular and well respected" and, though not baptized himself, was generous in hosting missionaries and supportive of his family's chosen religion.[2]

---

1. "Sarah Maria Mousley," *Membership of The Church of Jesus Christ of Latter-day Saints, 1830–1848,* ed. Susan E. Black, Microfiche no. 59, Church History Library, The Church of Jesus Christ of Latter-day Saints, Salt Lake City, Utah, hereafter cited as Church History Library.

2. Marian Cannon Nelson Warner, "In Search of the Mousley Heritage, 1884–1900," in "In Search of the Mousley Heritage," comp. Angus M. Cannon Reunion Committee (unpublished manuscript, 1990), pp. 13–14, Church History Library.

Devoted to her faith, Sarah later broke off her engagement when her fiancé refused to join the Church. She was about twenty-seven years old and still unmarried when a young missionary named Angus M. Cannon caught her eye.[3] He became acquainted with the Mousley family, and an attachment developed between them. After parting, Angus corresponded with Sarah and her younger sister Amanda for the next two years.

The members of the Mousley family who had joined the Church were eager to gather with the Saints in Utah.[4] Titus, still not baptized, chose to migrate west with his family. In 1857, Sarah journeyed with her parents and siblings across the plains to Salt Lake City. Ten months after arriving, having previously decided to share their lots in plural marriage, both Sarah and Amanda married Angus on July 18, 1858, a few days before Sarah's thirtieth birthday.

In 1861 the Angus M. Cannon family moved to southern Utah for six years to help settle the St. George area. They returned to Salt Lake City in 1867, and Sarah and Amanda continued to share

---

3. Angus, the fourth child of George and Ann Quayle Cannon, was born May 17, 1834, in Liverpool, England. He migrated to the United States at age seven and became orphaned at age ten in Nauvoo. He spent his youth in the Parowan-Cedar City region of Utah's Iron Mission and began serving in the Eastern States Mission in 1854 at age twenty. His elder brother was George Q. Cannon (1827–1901), a counselor in the First Presidency to Brigham Young, John Taylor, Wilford Woodruff, and Lorenzo Snow. Donald Q. Cannon, "Angus M. Cannon: Pioneer, President, Patriarch," in *Supporting Saints: Life Stories of Nineteenth-Century Mormons,* ed. Donald Q. Cannon and David J. Whittaker (Provo, UT: Brigham Young University, Religious Studies Center, 1985), 369–401; George M. Cannon, "A Brief Sketch of the Life of Angus Munn Cannon," in *Angus Munn Cannon, President of Salt Lake Stake, 1876–1904,* comp. Angus M. Cannon Reunion Committee (unpublished manuscript, 1991), pp. 2–9, Church History Library; Warner, "Mousley Heritage," 17.

4. Two of Sarah's brothers had already migrated to the Salt Lake Valley. Other Church members in Sarah's family included one married sister, Margaret Jane Foreman, and her family; a third brother, George; and Sarah's mother and grandmother. Warner, "Mousley Heritage," 23.

the same home, as they had done since the beginning of their marriage. In 1872 their homes were built next door to each other, so each could have her own home and still be close to her sister and her sister's children.[5] Sarah had six children, four of whom lived to adulthood.[6] She supported her husband as the president of the large Salt Lake Stake for twenty-eight years (1876–1904). When the federal government intensified its efforts to stamp out polygamy, Sarah moved to a farm in Bluffdale in southern Salt Lake County, residing there from about 1880 to 1881. Angus was imprisoned in 1885 for six months for practicing plural marriage.

Around age sixty, Sarah suffered a broken hip and was lame for the next twenty-four years. Living with daughter Ann M. Cannon, Sarah kept a positive spirit and exerted a strong influence in the lives of her children and grandchildren. She died March 12, 1912, in Forest Dale, Utah.

LIFE EXPERIENCES

Sarah Maria Mousley was twenty-eight years old when she left Delaware and journeyed toward an unknown Zion in the American West.[7] Her family boarded a train in Baltimore in May 1857 and

---

5. Warner, "Mousley Heritage," 69, 72.

6. Sarah's children were Maria Cannon (1860–1860), George Mousley Cannon (1861–1937), John Mousley Cannon (1865–1917), Ann Mousley Cannon (1869–1948), Henry Mousley Cannon (1872–1873), and Leonora Mousley Cannon Stewart (1874–1961).

7. In Sarah's middle name, Maria, the *i* is pronounced like the word *eye* and is the accented syllable. The surname is often pronounced with the "Mous" sounding like "Mos" in *Moses*. Descendants of Sarah, however, pronounce the "ou" in her last name like *mouse,* which is how Sarah's daughter Ann Mousely Cannon was taught to pronounce her name. Elizabeth Silver Clawson, interview by Madelyn S. Palmer, July 14, 2011, Highlands Ranch, Colorado; Sarah Maria Mousley, "Delaware to Utah, 1857," in *Covered Wagon Women,* ed. Kenneth Holmes, vol. 7 (Glendale, CA: Arthur H. Clark, 1988), 157.

rode to Iowa City, where they joined other Latter-day Saint immigrants in outfitting for the trek to Utah.[8]

As Sarah traveled, she carried feelings for former missionary Angus M. Cannon close to her heart. Family tradition holds that

> when in Centreville [Delaware, Angus] asked [Sarah] to marry him, she hesitated; he asked permission to place his picture in her locket, saying if he got it there, he'd take chances on her marrying anyone else. She finally let him take it; he had the picture placed in it and she wore it across the plains.[9]

The Mousleys joined the Jacob Hofheins–Matthew McCune Company and left Iowa City on June 6, 1857.[10]

1857 Trail Diary

While traversing the trail from Iowa to Utah, Sarah kept a near-daily journal of her experiences. Sarah's love of nature, upbeat personality, and faith in the gospel surface in various entries in her journal, which she began writing in Iowa City. In the first lines, she describes events since leaving her home in Delaware:

> Left home or rather my former home on the [blank] day of May for Utah, landed in Philadelphia the afternoon of the same day & started for Baltimore through Wilmington as President Taylor had made arraingements for our going by that line of railway. Friday the [blank] and on the following Tuesday landed in Iowa City, Iowa. Stoped at the Irving house kept by Mr Stanton for near three weeks at

---

8. Warner, "Mousley Heritage," 23, 28.

9. Warner, "Mousley Heritage," 19.

10. "Jacob Hofheins/Matthew McCune Company (1857)," Mormon Pioneer Overland Travel Database, 1847–68, The Church of Jesus Christ of Latter-day Saints, accessed April 11, 2012, http://mormontrail.lds.org.

which time our goods having all came to hand we started for the Camp of the saints with the view of starting across the plains and making the camp our home untill such times as we should start, being very much detained on account of a remarkable Late spring, cattle not coming &c.

I never knew or appreciated the merits of mormonism as since in the wisdom of Gods providence I have been thrown so continuelly amidst the enemies of truth and consequently I am not priviledged to withdraw from there society. joyful were my feelings although many privations in view when the time rolled on to again mingle with the people whose aim was to do the will of God and obey his commands.

Saturday afternoon [June 6] we made a start for Florence [in Nebraska Territory] with very wild cattle inexperienced drivers &c our journey consisted of five miles. the following day which was Sunday in the afternoon we started again. the cattle were something better than the first day. the next morning Monday took an early start but did not travel far on account of inexperienced cattle and drivers. Tuesday morning started again after a very pleasant night's rest. . . .

Thursday [June] 11. started about half past eight detain by the broken wagon of yesterday. passed through the most beautiful country some handsome houses were to be seen an evidence of good taste. passed through a handsome villiage called Brooklyn [Iowa] at which place Pa's carriage stopd. We entered a store and were soon asked where are you travelling—Pa told them to Utah. . . . they said you had better stay and assist in building our villiage to which Pa replied, no indeed he did not sell his former home to allow his means to benefit the gentiles he intended to do all he could for the interests of mormonism. encamped about two miles from the villiage above named. . . .

Friday 12 Started at half past six the morning not very clear but a prospect of rain cleared away and proved a splendid day. Stoped for dinner as usual. The company travelled better than usual they seem to be improving in experience encamped ~~near~~ on the open plain. There was water near but no fuel—we all seemed lost on that account but the goodness of God provided for our want and as an old gentleman was passing with a wagon load of wood he called to the children to come to him and he then gave them wood sufficient for cooking supper and breakfast, which kindness will never be forgotten by me. numbers came to see us and ask questions with a request to stay for our evening's meeting accordingly Jos Foreman spoke to them for a considerable time. Had good attention from sensible person's.

Saturday 13. started early and travelled within one or two miles of a handsome town called Newton encamped near the banks of a handsome stream just in sight of a camp of Kansas emigrants who had kept either just before or behind us. . . .

Monday 15. Started at six Oclock travelled ten miles. At noon encamped on the banks of mud creek where we found a splendid spring. Started again after dinner and travelled ten miles encamped on the banks of a beuatiful stream. Had a violent thunder storm rained violently could make no fire on account of the wet. . . .

Saturday 20. . . . Had early supper and just about sunset we beheld four missionarys from the valley their names were [blank]. Supper was prepared for the weary travellers as they had crossed the plains to Florence by hand cart's.[11] Our

___

11. After the tragic experiences of the Willie and Martin companies in 1856, Latter-day Saint emigrants hesitated to use handcarts. To restore confidence in handcart travel, Church leaders in 1857 asked some seventy newly called

meetings was joyful and yet sorrowful for seperating they to labour among the gentiles, how rejoyced were their hearts when on raising a hill they beheld the Mormon Camp at its foot; retired to rest at nine, &c. . . .

Monday 22 Started at the appointed time travelled well being cool the cattle were lively and got along first rate. Passed through the town of Lewistown quite a pretty place and rapidly improving the people crowded round to hire some of our folks offering great wages if they would stay some were almost ready to stay. Travelled about twenty four miles and encamped just out of the town.

Tuesday 23. . . . passed ~~through~~ over some great hills and pleasant vales beautiful flowers to improve the appearance of the prospect, diversifing and beautifing the surronding object—travelled about seventeen miles and encamped near the river called ~~Jordo~~ Little Jordon—had quite a shower to cool the air and the evening passed maraculously away as there was no gentiles to infringe upon our rights which was a treat to us as we have almost become tired answering questions people have no business to ask. After a pleasant meeting retired at ten to rest. . . .

Thursday 25 Again started at six cooler than yesterday more pleasant for travelling encamped for dinner on the Missourie bottom near the spot where the mormon [Battalion] soldiers were drafted in forty six. viewed the spot where a few short years ago in compliance with the contrys call men left their

missionaries to pull handcarts during their journey east from Salt Lake City to Florence, Nebraska Territory. LeRoy R. Hafen and Ann W. Hafen, *Handcarts to Zion: The Story of a Unique Western Migration, 1856–1860* (Glendale, CA: Arthur H. Clark, 1960), 143–48; John Taylor, "Editorial Correspondence," *The Mormon,* July 18, 1857.

weeping familes to fight for that contry that had exiled them from its protection on account of the religion of heaven. . . .

Friday 26 Started at six and travelled over some of the steepest mountains I ever could have thought it possible to pass met Br John Taylor who came from Florence to meet the camp and whose happy smile illumed our way and whose presence is ever a joy and comfort [to] those who are honoured with his society.[12] encamped on the bank of the mighty missourie but feared it to[o] late to ferry our wagons across the river. . . .

Mon 29. Were very busy washing ironing cooking &c clear and warm just as we were about to retire we were soluted by a splendid seranade from the citizens the music was splendid, the evening beautiful and every thing delightful, President Taylor, P[hineas] Young and two other bretheren took supper with us.

Tuesday 30 Finished washing and ironing were busy preparing to start on the morrow. Pa and ma visited Omaha city found it really beautiful retired to rest after survise [service].

Wednesday July 1st we bade adieu to civilazation and started across the plains in company with some of the St. Louis saints. . . .

Thursday 2 Bade adieu to President Taylor and those associated with him. . . . We seperated praying mutually for each others safty and prosperity not only untill we meet in the peaceful home of the saints but through life. . . .

---

12. John Taylor (1808–1887), who would later become president of the Church, had been serving a mission in New York, where he had edited *The Mormon,* a Latter-day Saint newspaper. With the advent of the Utah War, Brigham Young called missionaries home to Utah in 1857. B. H. Roberts, *The Life of John Taylor* (Salt Lake City, UT: Deseret Book, 2002), 235–36; John Taylor, "Editorial Correspondence," *The Mormon,* July 18, 1857.

Sat [July] 4 rested from travelling washed ironed & baked. Attended two meetings and a musical entertainment consisting of dancing singing &c. Prayer by President Hart benediction by Jos Foreman. Retired to rest at eleven and refreshed our self by sleep. . . .

Monday 6 started at seven and travelled about fifteen miles encamped early which gave the sisters a chance to bake and cook which by the bye is quite necessary for comfort and convenience. . . .

Tuesday 7 . . . we have seen no Indians ~~since~~ for the past four or five days. An incident connected with the indians I will here relate as they have been very friendly with us we returned the compliment in the same manner. They called at our table for refreshment and accordingly I was making lemonade which I offered to one who had watched the process of preparing and to whom I had handed a chair. He seated himself with great dignaty and took in his hand the cup I offered but would not touch the drink untill I would drink with him. I began to drink from another cup but he handed his to me as much as to say drink from this. I took it drank and returned it. He drank, said good squaw with many gestures of satisfaction he drank exclaiming good good. . . .

Friday 10 . . . A difficulty arose between Br Taylor teamster and the Captain. I never witnessed such a struggle which ended by the Captain tore the mans cloths out of the wagon and left him on the plains alone the last the camp seen of him he was kneeling in prayer. . . .

Thursday 23 . . . encamped near the cool spring which is really beautiful and so refreshing to the thirsty traveller. The water boils up from a bed of sand so as to afford drink plenty for the cattle. Surely our God is good for his mercys to us in our unworthyness in causing the fountain to burst forth as it were on the sandy desert. I feel to say Lord we will praise the[e] whilst life and thought and being last or immortality endures. . . .

Monday 27 Started early and travelled well our cattle very quiet to all appearance but on the afternoon of this day I was called to witness the most terrific of all scenes a stampeed on the plains. The cattle started all most all together and Oh my father my heart sickens as I recall the scene and my soul is grievd in memory of the painful occurrance I beheld men thrown woman leaping from their wagons children screaming as team after team ran on in wild confusion dashing headlong on the wild parari without power to impeed their progress in the wild scene of apparent death God gave me presence of mind sufficient to remain in my wagon which I did and alone except the unseen guardian who in God's wisdom did not leave me alone but shielded me from the shafts of the destroyer. I set or remained unhurt and beheld the cattle stoped and their affright calmed in answer to my fervant prayer after the wagon in which I had been riding was stoped and my driver who had been knocked down and allmost knocked senceless had overtaken me I alighted from the wagon only to witness the most terrific of all scenes—my sisters loved and dear had all jumped from the wagon and Nellie [Martha Ellen] and Willie [Wilhelmina] were badly injured—in their fright they jumped from the wagon and weather some of the cattle had steped in our dear Willie face and on the side near her heart and streaming with blood and crying for help. . . . And yet in the all my heart exclaimed Lord we will praise thee for thy goodness thou has shielded us from death thou hast taught us a bitter lesson on the power of saten and his designs to overthrow thy saints.—thou hast stood by in the hour of triel and thy arm has protected us in a maraculous manner—and now Oh Father we pray thee through thy son to accept the heartfelt gratitude of all and enable us to serve thee faithfully in time and eternity. . . .

Tuesday 28 Arose not very well from excitement and anxiety remained all day in camp were visited by Indians noble and true. They deeply sympathised with us in our bereavement or distress. . . . One wept and said he loved the pale faces of those by whom he was surrounded and would pray to the good Spirit for their recovery. . . .

Wed 29 . . . remained in camp and were visited by a tribe of young Indian children Oh how I love their society and although so ignorant of their language I love to behold them. The tribe is the Siou[x].

Wed [August] 5 . . . came in sight of chimney Rock [Nebraska] and indeed passed some of the most splendid edifices apparently my eye ever beheld. Oh how I wish mine were a painters pencil or poets pen—I would portray if possible the beauty of the scenes through which we have been called to pass. . . . .

Wed 19 . . . we regret being on this side [of the river] as the roads are awful—scarcely passable with our weakened teams—an express arrived from the valley for those in the settlements as well as the camps to hasten home Oh how I wish for the wings of the morning to fly away to the saints of light. . . .

Tue 25 Arose early had breakfast soon and all necessarily arrangements made for visiting Indepdance Rock. Mounted its towering summitt and viewed the surrounding objects but I feel my pen or thoughts inadequate to the task of portaying a true picture of the awful grandure and beauty of these scenes. . . .

Wed [September] 2 Arose all well travelled fast as the weather is now cool and pleasant for travelling. . . . get along well under the special care of our Father in Heaven—my heart rejoices in prospect of so speedy a meeting with those from whose lips flow the words of life. . . .

Sun 6 This morning a beautiful chance for a prosperous journey and may God our Father speed us home in peace and prosperity. Started but found we had taken the California road and was consequently obliged to retrace our steps this we found out through the kindess of a Mountaineer who directed us aright. . . .

Sat 12 Travelled 12 miles to Fort Bridger . . . met many saints and remained in camp all night. . . .

Tue 15 arose and started at seven Oclock . . . passed the Cache cave two miles and Camped making 18 or 20 miles

Wed 16 Had a very heavy rain last night cloudy morning and started down Echo Kanyon some dreadful places to pass[13]

The entry of Wednesday, September 16, was the last one Sarah made in her trail journal. The Mousleys arrived in the Salt Lake Valley five days later, September 21, 1857.

Sharing a Husband

Sarah and Amanda agreed as young women "to share with each other, their lot in marriage."[14] Twenty-four-year-old Angus Cannon finished his mission in the eastern states and arrived in Salt Lake

---

13. Sarah M. Cannon, Journal, May–September 1857, Holograph, Church History Library.

14. Warner, "Mousley Heritage," 29.

City in June 1858.[15] Decades later, he recorded a decision he had made as a young man about the principle of plural marriage:

> It was in September of 1854. I was called . . . to fill a mission in the Eastern States. . . . It then occurred to my mind that if I married one wife and loved her as my heart was capable of loving, could I afterwards take another wife, as it was evidently a requirement of God in the doctrines taught by Joseph Smith, that faithful men should marry each more than one wife. I concluded that it would be more consistent if I proposed to practice celestial marriage, not to marry until I found two women who were willing to marry me at one time, and so establish my abiding faith in a principle revealed from God. I concluded it would be more acceptible unto the Lord for me to furnish two families with the common necessaries of life, teaching my children to toil for their support and be subject unto the counsel and approval of the Lord, than to take one wife and indulge her in luxury while her sister was left out in the cold without even the common necessaries of life.[16]

Despite his ideal to love his wives equally, Angus was especially fond of Amanda and planned to marry her as his first wife and Sarah his second on the same day. Ann Cannon, daughter of Angus and Sarah, recalled a story her father related when he went to Titus Mousley to ask permission to marry his daughters:

> He said he approached "Father Mousley" with trepidation as the latter had not joined the church, and would

---

15. Angus traveled in the John W. Berry Company. *Mormon Pioneer Overland Travel Database, 1847–68,* The Church of Jesus Christ of Latter-day Saints, accessed April 11, 2012, http://mormontrail.lds.org.

16. Angus Munn Cannon, "Statement of an Interview with Joseph Smith, III," 1905, Typescript, pp. 8–9, Church History Library; Warner, "Mousley Heritage," 19.

therefore not understand the principle of "Plural Marriage." Hence Father asked only for the privilege of marrying "your daughter." Grandfather understood this to mean Aunt Amanda and consented. Mother . . . [Sarah] had decided to defer her marriage.

Upon their arrival [to Brigham Young's office to be married], President Young took Mother aside and said: "Why aren't you being married today?" To her indecision he said: "Do you ever intend to marry Angus?"

She answered, "Yes."

He then said: "Do you believe I am a prophet?"

"Yes, I know you are!"

Then he continued: "In the name of the Lord I tell you if you ever intend to marry him, now is the time to do it."[17]

Perhaps following biblical precedent, Brigham Young "decided that Sarah, being the eldest, should become the first wife."[18]

In the fall of 1861, Angus Munn Cannon was called to help settle St. George in the Dixie Cotton Mission. Soon after their arrival, Sarah gave birth to her first son, George Mousley; she had lost an infant daughter the year before. She bore Angus six children, four of whom lived to adulthood.[19] In 1867, Angus M. Cannon moved his family back to Salt Lake. He was called as president of the Salt Lake Stake on April 6, 1876, and served in that position for twenty-eight years. Shortly after becoming stake president, he was asked to marry widow Clarissa Cordelia Moses Mason, which he did on June 16, 1876. He married Dr. Martha "Mattie" Hughes on October 6, 1884; Maria Bennion on March 11, 1886; and Johanna Cristina Danielson on March 21, 1887.[20]

---

17. Warner, "Mousley Heritage," 29–30.

18. Cannon, "Angus M. Cannon," 388.

19. Cannon, "Brief Sketch of the Life of Angus Munn Cannon," 3–4.

20. Cannon, "Angus M. Cannon," 369–401.

During the time when the federal government was prosecuting polygamists, Sarah lived for a year, from about 1880 to 1881, in Bluffdale, Utah, at one of Angus's four homesteading farms, a place kept secret from all except a few family members.[21] Sarah spent fourteen years in the same home with Amanda and then lived in a house next door to her sister on Folsom Avenue in Salt Lake City, being dear aunts to each other's children. Sarah and Amanda lived peacefully as sister wives, even though Amanda was Angus's favorite, his first sweetheart, and the wife he presented in public and as hostess of many social affairs.[22]

Sarah's daughter Ann, with whom she lived, reported an accident that occurred when Sarah was nearly sixty years of age and described her mother's final years:

> About six o'clock one morning . . . [Sarah] started the fire in the kitchen and stepped out on the platform that led from the door to the coal house. . . . As she stepped briskly along, her feet slipped, she fell and broke her hip. Physicians were not so skillful then as now and she was in bed many months and lame for the remainder of her life.
>
> She spent the next twenty years sitting down. This must have been almost unbearable to a woman as active as she had been, but through it all she remained cheerful, mentally active and in her home there was still peace. She had a wonderful sense of humor which must have helped a great deal and she developed a keen sensitiveness for other people in trouble. . . .
>
> Mother expected or demanded nothing and this seems to have been the secret of her receiving much. Her timely admonitions ring in my ears often: "Never cry over spilt milk"; "Blessed are the merciful"; "Pride goeth before destruction"; "Let him who stands take heed lest he fall."

21. Warner, "Mousley Heritage," 31–32.
22. Cannon, "Angus M. Cannon," 388–89; Warner, "Mousley Heritage," 69, 72.

Only once in all my acquaintance with mother did I know her intrepid spirit to falter . . . and I thank God that he gave me strength to help her.

I[t] was toward the end of her days on earth. . . . She said, almost to herself, as she looked at me, "Oh, I shouldn't be afraid to go if only you could go with me." . . .

Here on March 12, 1912, after a few days of failing strength, about two o'clock in the morning . . . her breath grew fainter till the pulse in her throat was stilled. Out upon the vast unknown path, yet lighted by faith, her spirit passed, undaunted and courageous to the end.[23]

---

23. Ann M. Cannon, "My Mother, Sarah Maria Mousley Cannon," in "In Search of the Mousley Heritage," comp. Angus M. Cannon Reunion Committee (unpublished manuscript, 1990), pp. 69–70, Church History Library.

Chapter 3

"Contentment with My Lot"

HANNAH LAST CORNABY (1822–1905)
Craig C. Crandall and Cathleen C. Lloyd

Biographical Sketch

From the youngest of ages, Hannah Last Cornaby lived with her heart fixed on the Supreme Being. Born on March 17, 1822, in Beccles, Suffolk, England, Hannah was the eldest of six children born to William and Hannah Hollingsworth Last. She may be most noted today for writing the words to the hymn "Who's on the Lord's Side?"[1] She was taught to love the words of the Bible and therefore had great reverence for "that Being who rules in the heavens above, and on the earth beneath."[2]

Around age twenty-six, Hannah met a young man named Samuel Cornaby, and it was immediately impressed on her mind

---

1. *Hymns of The Church of Jesus Christ of Latter-day Saints* (Salt Lake City, UT: The Church of Jesus Christ of Latter-day Saints, 1985), no. 260.

2. Hannah Cornaby, *Autobiography and Poems* (Salt Lake City, UT: J. C. Graham, 1881), 11–12.

that he was to be her future husband. On January 30, 1851, they married and began their life's journey together.

Soon after their marriage, Samuel and Hannah were taught by missionaries of The Church of Jesus Christ of Latter-day Saints and were converted through their message. Samuel was baptized on February 21, 1852, and Hannah in May 1852, after the birth of their first child.[3] Many former friends no longer desired to associate with them. The Cornabys desired the fellowship of the Saints, and so in January 1853, they said their good-byes to beloved parents and family members and embarked on their journey to Utah.

Hannah and her family arrived in the Salt Lake Valley on October 12, 1853.[4] With joyful hearts they settled there for three years, during which time they received their temple ordinances in the Endowment House.[5] In October 1856, they left Salt Lake City to nurture the budding community of Spanish Fork, Utah.

Hannah gave birth to seven children, but only two, Edith Hannah and Samuel Last, lived to adulthood. One daughter, Mary

---

3. Their daughter Edith Hannah was born on March 3, 1852. "Hannah Last," "Samuel Cornaby," and "Edith Hannah Cornaby," New FamilySearch, The Church of Jesus Christ of Latter-day Saints, accessed April 14, 2012, http://new .familysearch.org.

4. The Cornabys traveled by chartered packet ship from Liverpool to New Orleans, then by riverboat to Keokuk, Iowa, which had been chosen to be the staging area for Latter-day Saint companies in 1853. As members of the Cyrus H. Wheelock Company, they departed from Keokuk between June 1 and 3, 1853, on their overland journey. Rulon A. Walker, "The Voyage of the *Ellen Maria,* 1853," *BYU Studies* 27, no. 1 (1987): 57–65; "Cyrus H. Wheelock Company (1853)," Mormon Pioneer Overland Travel Database, 1847–68, The Church of Jesus Christ of Latter-day Saints, accessed April 18, 2012, http://mormontrail.lds.org.

5. Before the Salt Lake Temple was completed in 1893, several buildings were used for the administration of temple ordinances. In Salt Lake City one such building was the Endowment House, which was in operation on Temple Square from 1855 to 1889. LaMar C. Berrett, "Endowment Houses," in *Encyclopedia of Mormonism,* ed. Daniel H. Ludlow, 4 vols. (New York: Macmillan, 1992), 2:456.

Ann Amelia, died at age fifteen, and four other children died in infancy.

Hannah was a woman of faith who lived a life of service to God and family. She suffered years of ill health, witnessed healing miracles, endured famine, and grieved over the death of her precious babes. She was known for her delightful poetry, which gladdened hearts and graced the lives of many.

Hannah passed away on September 1, 1905, in Spanish Fork, Utah, at the age of eighty-three. Her autobiography, from which the following excerpts are taken, is a testament to her lifelong commitment to her Maker.

LIFE EXPERIENCES

Autobiography, 1881

Surely "goodness and mercy have followed me all the days of my life,"[6] I am compelled to acknowledge, as from the grave of the buried past, I seek to bring forth some events in my life, which, for the glory of God, and the good of my fellow creatures, ought not to be lost in oblivion. I realize that if I have received but one talent, I am accountable to the Giver for the proper use of the same, which consideration has induced me to write a short history of my life. . . .

I was early taught by [my parents] to love that Being, who has made the earth so beautiful, and provided so much for His creatures dwelling thereon; thus I was early led to admire and reverence the Creator through His works; and especially from my mother's teaching, learned my duty to Him, as revealed in the Bible. This sacred book was my mother's companion by day and by night; and before able to read, I had committed to memory, under her tuition, many of its holy precepts. . . .

6. Psalm 23:6.

As the years passed on, there seems nothing to record, except that my religious desires deepened and my anxiety to understand the plan of human redemption increased. I attended public worship with my parents, who began to be dissatisfied with the religious tenets they had espoused. . . .

One day I was in the town on business . . . when I met a young man, an entire stranger to me. Now this was nothing remarkable in a busy town like Beccles, nor was there anything remarkable in the appearance of this stranger; but something whispered, "That is your future husband." Surprised at this, I turned to take a look at him, and, to my annoyance, he had also turned to look at me. Ashamed of myself for this breach of street etiquette, I hastily resumed my way, and this stranger, who had thus attracted my attention was lost to sight. Business was for the time forgotten; I walked aimlessly on, thinking of this strange event, when I was met by my sister Amelia, who asked what had happened to make me look so pleased. I told her frankly of the singular circumstance just recorded. She smiled, and said, "Oh, my romantic sister." I replied, "Do not make fun of me; I shall marry that man, or I shall never marry on this earth." . . .

Months rolled on . . . when, apparently by the merest accident, at the house of a friend, I met, and was introduced to Mr. Cornaby. . . . Accidental meetings with Mr. Cornaby frequently happened after this. Our acquaintance ripened into friendship; and a sympathy, which neither of us understood, was making that friendship a necessity.

Three delightful years followed. . . . [At length] he told his love . . . If I had expected this consummation to my long cherished hopes would bring entire happiness, I was doomed to disappointment. Mr. Cornaby was not a believer, although he attended meeting punctually, and led a strictly moral life. I had refused other suitors on this very ground, and I keenly felt the inconsistency into which love was now leading me; especially as it was pointed out by friends, including my minister and adviser, who, in kindly earnestness, told me, that "loving him would take me to hell." In an instant, the words seemed put into my mouth, "If loving him will take me to hell, I shall go." . . .

. . . On January 30, 1851, we were married in St. George's Church, a venerable structure, celebrated for its antiquity and architectural beauty.

Among the current literature of the day that, in the way of business, passed through our hands, was a series of tracts . . . one of which, entitled, "Religious Impostors," attracted our attention. After giving an account of various religious impostors, it concluded by giving a brief history of Joseph Smith. . . .

This was our first introduction to Mormonism. Soon after this, another book came in our way, entitled, "The Mormons, Illustrated." . . . It contained copious extracts from Col. Kane's Lectures before the Historical Society of Pennsylvania; also from Joseph Smith's teachings. Although the book was written to show the fallacy of "Mormonism," it made a deep impression on my mind. My husband and I read it together carefully and thoughtfully, and we arose from its perusal satisfied of the divine mission of Joseph Smith. . . .

It was the beginning of February '52, on a cold stormy evening, that . . . I saw a man sheltering under the awning in front of our store. I invited him to come inside for better protection from the weather, which he did, expressing his thanks, but assuring me that if I knew who he was I probably would not welcome him under my roof. I was startled at this, but replied that I had only done what was my duty to any fellow-creature under the circumstances. He then introduced himself, as George Day, a Latter-day

Saint Elder, who had been sent to preach the gospel in that town. I remarked, that I thought we had ministers enough already to preach the gospel; he replied, none of them had authority to preach; but he had been sent with authority as the Saviour sent his disciples. I then hastened to call my husband, who received him courteously, and invited him to supper. After supper, he spent the evening with us, telling of the Latter-day work; we listened with great interest until bed-time. We procured lodging for him at a hotel near by, and he breakfasted with us next morning. Before he left, he made an appointment, at our request, to call again that evening and preach to us, we promising to call in our near neighbors to hear him.

All day emotions of hope and fear were battling in our bosoms. Could this wonderful news be true? Was God about to answer our prayers for guidance in this manner? . . . We scarcely dared to hope, yet dared not to doubt. Evening came, and with it Elder Day and the friends we had invited. He preached and we believed, and thought it impossible for any one who heard it to do otherwise; but with our neighbors, it was different; they could scarcely refrain from abusing him and us, and called us fools for listening to such lies. We were astonished beyond measure at this, thinking they would be so glad; but we were too happy to be angry at such strange conduct. . . . It was such a sudden turn of affairs, we hardly knew what to do; our friends became enemies; we were persecuted and annoyed in many ways. Before this, we were respected and esteemed by many. Now, if we walked along the streets, we met no kindly greeting, but were pointed out as "Saints," and sometimes stoned. . . . Elder Spencer removed a few lingering doubts from my husband's mind, and he was baptized and confirmed. I, too, desired baptism, but the birth of our first child delayed it for a time. . . . As soon as my health would admit, I renewed my request for baptism. A time was appointed to attend to this ordinance. I . . . proceeded to a house near the sea-side, where we met to make preparations. We found the house surrounded by a mob, through which we with difficulty made our way, amid oaths and threats of what would be done if any attempt were made to go into the water. We waited until near midnight, hoping the crowd would disperse; but it had all this time been increasing, until it numbered many hundreds, and we feared violence, not only to ourselves, but to the family, under whose roof we were waiting.

Wearied of the delay, the master of the house thought of a ruse. He went to the door, and asked permission for his son to pass through the crowd to his boat, as he was a fisherman, and it was necessary that he should sail with the outgoing tide. My husband, previously dressed in the son's clothes, stepped out, and I followed in the darkness unnoticed. They soon discovered that their prey had escaped, and before we reached the water's edge, the whole horde was upon us; and my husband baptized me amid a shower of stones, and shouts of "duck him! duck him!" and such cries. . . . We then made our way back, as best we could, followed by the mob; and, although the stones whizzed around us thick as hail, not one touched us, and we reached home in safety, thanking God for our miraculous deliverance; determined, more than ever, with the assistance of the holy spirit, to adhere—through evil, as well as good report—to the principles we had embraced. At the next meeting of the saints, I was confirmed, and knew for myself that the work was of God. . . .

Now, we were identified with [the latter-day work], and our names cast out as evil for its sake; but oh! how happy we felt, as we journeyed on; how unspeakably dear we were to each other! The trials through which we had already passed, purified our faith and increased our love. . . .

. . . [We] caught the spirit of gathering and felt that England was no longer our home; but this thought brought with it a severe pang. . . . My husband went and advised our parents of the intended departure; and they, although believing us deluded, yet gave us their blessing and their prayers, with many substantial proofs of their undying affection. . . .

. . . On the ninth day of January, 1853, we left Norwich. . . . I often think that the weeks spent crossing the plains were as full of instruction and interest as any part of our lives.

When at length, from the top of the Little Mountain, we caught a first glimpse of the "Valley," our delight and gratitude found vent in tears of unfeigned joy, and when, on the morning of the 12th of October, 1853, we emerged from the mouth of Emigration Canyon and beheld the "City of the Saints," we felt more than repaid for the nine months of travel, and all the hardships we had endured. . . .

As our camp life was over, my husband went in search of a house, and rented one near where he had obtained employment. . . . Everybody seemed so kind that we thought of the promise of the Savior, "There is no man that hath left house, or brethren, or sisters, or father, or mother, or wife, or children, or lands, for my sake, and the gospel's, but he shall receive a hundred fold now in this time . . . and in the world to come, eternal life." . . . [7]

[In October 1855,] famine was creeping on, making itself felt. It was a gloomy time, even bread becoming scarce. . . .

. . . Our beloved president, Brigham Young, encouraged the saints to faithfulness and dependence on our Father

---

7. Mark 10:29–30.

in Heaven; promising them in the name of Israel's God, that none who would live their religion should die of starvation.

We believed this, and in the weeks following, found that our daily bread was given us; though sometimes in a manner as miraculous as the feeding of Elijah by the ravens. . . .

On the twenty-first of March [1856], we passed through the Endowment House. Those who have enjoyed the privilege, can appreciate the blessing it was to us at this time. Having left all for the gospel's sake, we were repaid a hundred fold. I recollect how happy we felt next morning, as we joined a company going to dig roots. The warm rays of the spring sun seemed to diffuse gladness all around; everybody seemed cheerful; I was as free from care as the birds; and like them, wanted to praise the Creator for all His goodness. . . .

. . . The children, sometimes hungry, and beginning to understand the value of prayer, would coax me to pray to our Father in Heaven to send us bread; and I, feeling most anxious that my darlings should not lose confidence in prayer, would plead with great earnestness, they lisping the words after me. Many times the prayer was answered almost immediately. . . . I could relate many . . . circumstances of . . . how wheat had been increased in the bin, and flour in the sack. . . .

On the 26th of October, 1856, we left Salt Lake City, with all its advantages, to "rough it" in the country. For a time we felt the change very much; and especially did our children, who would cry to be taken home. Spanish Fork was a new settlement, having been but recently surveyed for a town site, and at this time, consisted principally of large wheat stacks, temporary dwellings, and houses in course of erection. . . . We rented a house, purchased a good building site, and built a small room in which to winter.

A Miraculous Healing

[In 1864] I was suddenly prostrated by sickness, the like of which I had never known. . . . We did all that wisdom dictated, and all that the love and affection of my family and friends could devise. . . . During all this time I was only able to attend public worship three times. This absence was a sorrow to me, as I feared to lose the spirit of God, but the assurance came, "My grace is sufficient for thee; for my strength is made perfect in weakness;" and like Paul I could say, "Most gladly, therefore, will I rather glory in my infirmities, that the power of Christ may rest upon me."[8] . . . My suffering was so great, that I could not sleep, but during the night I had a vision.

A heavenly personage stood by me and asked: "Are you willing to suffer for your own good, and for the glory of God?" I answered that I was. He then said: "Thou shalt come out of this sickness unscathed in body, sound in mind, and thy hair shall not be changed." . . . I believed every word he had spoken, and during the years of sickness which followed, seldom lost hope of recovery, although, through the weakness of the body, sometimes feared I should not hold out. . . .

On one occasion, to my great delight, [my bishop] came accompanied by Apostle Orson Pratt. . . . Brother Pratt drew me into conversation, in which I told him the sorrows that were weighing down my spirit, and asked why I had not been healed. He answered my questions by referring me to many passages in the Old and New Testaments, Book of Mormon, and Doctrine and Covenants; conversing a long time as I had never heard any one else.

His words, though very gently spoken, came with such

---

8. 2 Corinthians 12:9.

power that I knew they were the words of God to me; and have comforted me ever since. Before leaving, he asked if I wished him to administer to me, which, of course I was most anxious for. . . .

He told me I should yet arise from my bed, and stand upon my feet . . . that I should again walk in the garden and enjoy the beauties of nature; that I should visit my neighbors, and enjoy their society; that I should again walk to the house of the Lord, join in the singing, and speak of the goodness of God in the congregation of the saints. . . .

He said he knew by the spirit that all he had promised would be fulfilled, but did not know when, as the spirit did not testify—the promised blessing might come soon, or I might have to wait—meanwhile he counselled us to continue to pray and to call upon the Elders as often as wisdom dictated. . . .

After this, though my health did not materially improve, my mind was calm and happy; and if at any time I felt like yielding to doubt, reminders would come of the promised blessing. Although it was fifteen months after this when the Lord in His mercy saw fit to restore me to health, the time of waiting passed hopefully, knowing as I did that the words of the servants of God would not fall to the ground. . . .

In the spring of 1874, President Brigham Young taught the principles of the United Order. The beauty and perfection of this heavenly order was shown to me with all the benefits it would confer upon those who lived in accordance with it.

In May, a company of young men was called to work at a saw mill, in the United Order. My son was among the chosen ones for this labor. I knew that if I desired it, he would be excused, but I was too glad to find him willing to obey the presiding priesthood, to raise any objection. . . .

Sunday came, I felt very feeble in body and depressed in

mind, when brother William H. Darger, our block teacher,[9] came to administer the sacrament to me. He noticed that I was not as well as usual, and asked if I wished to be administered to before he left. My husband anointed my head with consecrated oil, after which they placed their hands upon my head, and as nearly as I can remember, Bro. Darger uttered the following words. "Thus saith the Lord thy God, inasmuch as thou hast received the United Order, with all thine heart, and hast not withheld thy son, even thine only son, thy faith is tried, even as was Abraham's, thou shalt arise from thy bed, and shalt stand upon thy feet." In an instant I felt the healing power in every part of my body. Several persons were present at the time, who also testified to the power that attended the words.

When brother Darger was leaving, he said; "You will soon be well." I replied that I knew I should. . . . As it was late in the evening I did not say much, I was so astonished at this wonderful event, that I seemed overpowered by the greatness of the blessing that had come upon me.

Next morning, when alone with my daughter Mary, I told her I was well, and requested her to bring my clothes that I might dress and arise from my bed. . . . I then got out of bed, and with one hand laid upon her shoulder, walked six times the length of the bed. My darling child was so overjoyed, that she exclaimed with uplifted hands, "Oh! mother, give the glory to God, give all the glory to Him, for it is all His work!" and she wept for joy. My husband coming in at the time, was astonished, and joined us in thanksgiving to God.

Thus, after being confined to my bed four years [with six years of illness previous], I realized the promise made to me at the commencement of my sickness. I arose from my

---

9. Equivalent to a home teacher.

bed unscathed in body, sound in mind, and my hair was not changed. Although the sickness had left me, I was quite feeble, but strength returned gradually. . . . In less than a month from the time of my recovery, I walked to the house of God, and attended the fast meeting—thus verifying the words of Elder Orson Pratt. . . .

It is more than six years since I was healed by the power of God; and if not robust, my health has been measurably good, enabling me to some extent to attend to my domestic duties, and in the summer time to enjoy myself in the cultivation of flowers, raising silk, and assisting in our apiary. . . .

Much of my life has seemingly been wasted by sickness; still the years I had fondly hoped to have spent in active service in promoting the Latter-day work, have not, I trust, been altogether unfruitful, I having had opportunities at home to testify to those who have visited me, of the sustaining power of God. One thing I have learned, and prize it more than gold or silver; it is contentment with my lot. I have never known a time in my life when I could supinely sleep, or waste a moment in hopeless sorrow. . . .

. . . My way has indeed been hedged up, and I have been led in a way which I knew not, yet I am satisfied that it has been the right way. . . .

The memory of the famine, and other privations through which I have passed, serve to enhance the happiness of the years of comfort and plenty I have since enjoyed, and which still crown my path; forcibly reminding me of the words of Moses to the children of Israel; in the 8th chap. Deut., 2nd and 3rd verses. "Thou shalt remember all the way which the Lord thy God led thee, these forty years in the wilderness, to humble thee, and to prove thee, to know what was in thine heart, whether thou wouldst keep His commandments or no. And He humbled thee, and suffered thee to hunger, and fed thee with manna, which thou knewest not, neither did thy fathers know, that he might make thee know that man doth not live by bread only, but by every word that proceedeth out of the mouth of the Lord doth man live."

In conclusion, I would say it is now twenty-nine years since in my native land, I heard and obeyed the Gospel as restored by an angel to Joseph Smith, the prophet of this dispensation, and gathered to this land that I might hear a living prophet make known the will of God to His people. And have I been disappointed? No, a thousand times, no. Though Joseph was slain, and Brigham Young, his successor, has gone behind the veil, a living prophet still leads and guides the Latter-day Saints.

This Gospel with all the keys, gifts, and blessings of former dispensations is worthy the acceptation of every creature under heaven. To establish this great truth, our Prophet, Patriarch and many others have sealed their testimony with their blood. Many of our Elders are traveling without purse or script, bearing their testimony and gathering the honest in heart to Zion; others are laboring at home in the interest of the Kingdom of God.

Women, whose names are widely known as champions for our faith, are earnestly working in the same cause, and many others equally zealous, whose names are comparatively unknown are working for the same end.

I desire to add my humble name to the great cloud of witnesses to the truth of this Latter-day Work.

HANNAH CORNABY.

Spanish Fork, Utah, January 17th, 1881.[10]

---

10. Cornaby, *Autobiography,* 9–10, 12, 18–26, 28–29, 33, 35–36, 38–40, 42, 44, 53–59, 62–64.

Chapter 4

"THE LORD HAS BEEN MY GUIDE"

CORDELIA CALISTA MORLEY COX (1823–1915)
Patricia H. Stoker

BIOGRAPHICAL SKETCH

Cordelia Calista Morley was seven years old in February 1831 when Joseph and Emma Smith came to live with the Morley family in Kirtland, Ohio.[1] She was born November 28, 1823, the fifth of nine children born to Isaac and Lucy Gunn Morley, two of the earliest converts to The Church of Jesus Christ of Latter-day Saints in Kirtland, Ohio.[2] While the Smiths lived with the Morleys,

---

1. Joseph and Emma arrived in Kirtland, Ohio, on February 1, 1831. They first lived with the Newel K. Whitney family and then lived in the Morley home "through the winter." Cordelia Morley Cox, "Collection of Biographies, ca. 1880," Photocopy of holograph, n.p., L. Tom Perry Special Collections, Harold B. Lee Library, Brigham Young University, Provo, Utah; Richard Lyman Bushman, *Joseph Smith: Rough Stone Rolling* (New York: Vintage Books, 2005), 145–46.

2. Accounts differ as to the total number of Morley children. Cordelia recorded that nine children, counting stillborn twins, were born to her parents, Isaac and Lucy, in 1821. Her sister Calista died at the age of two, four months prior to

a small frame home was built for Joseph and Emma on the Morley farm. Joseph and Emma were living in that home when their twins were born and died only hours later.[3] The Morley farm became a gathering place for new Church members moving to Kirtland and was also the location of the fourth general conference of the Church.[4]

The Church became the center of the lives of the Morley family. In June 1831, Isaac was sent to Missouri, where he was asked to remain. He sent word for his family to sell all and join him.[5] When the Morley family arrived in Missouri during the bitter cold of winter, Cordelia, now eight, was eager to be baptized by her father despite the cold, and he cut through the ice in the river to baptize her.

As a young girl growing to adulthood, Cordelia experienced the devastation of mobs and their attacks against Church members in Missouri and Illinois that finally forced them to move west. She watched her father and later her own husband be taken captive by mobs and saw those around her suffer. Yet even with the turmoil, Cordelia found joy and comfort as she strove to overcome their dire situations and put her trust in the Lord.

Cordelia's birth. Cordelia Morley Cox, "Sketch of Cordelia Morley Cox," *Woman's Exponent* 41, no. 5 (January 1, 1913): 33; Isaac and Lucy Morley Family Group Record, FamilySearch, The Church of Jesus Christ of Latter-day Saints, accessed October 17, 2011, http://familysearch.org. Isaac, Lucy, and their three children over the age of eight were baptized on November 15, 1830, by Parley P. Pratt. See Richard Henrie Morley, "The Life and Contributions of Isaac Morley" (master's thesis, Brigham Young University, 1965), 10.

3. "The 'gentle Morley girls' assisted with the delivery and helped with the housework." Linda King Newell and Valeen Tippetts Avery, *Mormon Enigma: Emma Hale Smith* (Garden City, NY: Doubleday, 1984), 39.

4. A conference of the Church was held June 3–6, 1831, in the log schoolhouse on the Morley farm. Karl Ricks Anderson, *Joseph Smith's Kirtland: Eyewitness Accounts* (Salt Lake City, UT: Deseret Book, 1989), 107; J. Christopher Conkling, *A Joseph Smith Chronology* (Salt Lake City, UT: Deseret Book, 1979), 24.

5. Doctrine and Covenants 52:23; Cox, "Biographies."

In 1844 Joseph Smith asked the consent of Cordelia's parents for twenty-year-old Cordelia to become his wife, and her parents introduced the principle of plural marriage to her. At the time, Cordelia had a sweetheart she expected to marry; so although she admired and respected Joseph, she declined.[6] After Joseph's death, Cordelia became the third wife of Fredrick Walter Cox in a ceremony in the Nauvoo Temple on January 27, 1846. They were married for time, and with her husband's permission, Cordelia was posthumously sealed to Joseph Smith.[7]

The Cox family was forced to leave Nauvoo in 1846 with other Church members, and for some years they lived first in Mt. Pisgah, Iowa, and then farther west in Iowa, across the river from Winter Quarters, Nebraska, as they worked to be able to gather with the Saints in the Great Basin. Finally in 1851 they made their way to Manti, Utah, where Isaac Morley, Cordelia's father, and other family members had been sent by Brigham Young to settle.

After her husband's untimely death in an accident in 1879 at the age of sixty-seven, Cordelia spent the next three decades living among her seven children,[8] recounting for her grandchildren the stories of her youth and married years—always emphasizing her love of

---

6. Family tradition holds that Cordelia's intended was eventually "left by the wayside" because "he could not endure the persecutions and hardships." "Cordelia Morley Cox Autobiography [Biography]," Orville Sutherland Cox Website, accessed February 1, 2011, http://oscox.org/fwcox/cordeliaccox.html. The autobiography is actually a later family compilation of Cordelia's writings.

7. Frederick Walter Cox (1812–1879) was a carpenter, chair maker, and musician. He was known as Walter.

8. Cordelia and Walter had eight children. One son, Isaac (1856–1856), died shortly after his birth, and of the seven living children—Lavina Emeline (1846–1935), Theressa Emmerett (1849–1933), Sarah Ann (1851–1931), Francis Morley (1853–1937), Calista Cordelia (1857–1933), Arletta Marie (1861–1947), and Evelyn Amelia (1867–1965)—five married before Walter's death. John Clifton Moffitt, *Frederick Walter Cox, Sr.: Frontiersman of the American West* (privately printed, [1972]), Church History Library, The Church of Jesus Christ of Latter-day Saints, Salt Lake City, Utah, hereafter cited as Church History Library.

family and her testimony of the gospel. Her personal writings detail her experiences as she faced fear, destruction, and loss. Her determination to obey gospel principles she knew to be true has become an example of strength and given hope to the generations of her family that have followed.

LIFE EXPERIENCES

Cordelia spent her early childhood in a comfortable home in Kirtland, Ohio, with forested hills and green fields on the large family farm where she and her siblings explored and played as children. In the autumn of 1831 when the Prophet Joseph Smith asked her father to move his family and sell his farm, they began a new life of pioneering in the frontier settlements of Missouri. Cordelia wrote several autobiographies, one of which was a polished version published in the *Woman's Exponent,* and others were preserved in handwritten records.[9]

Beginnings

Cordelia's autobiography published in the *Woman's Exponent* begins with a description of her parents' background and early experiences in the Church:

> My parents were born in Montague, Franklin, Mass.; my father, Isaac Morley,[10] March 11, 1786, and my mother, Lucy Gunn Morley, January 24, 1786.

---

9. There are at least two handwritten autobiographies extant, but it cannot be confirmed that they are in Cordelia's handwriting.

10. Isaac Morley was a counselor to Bishop Edward Partridge from 1831 to 1840, serving in both Kirtland and Missouri. He was ordained a patriarch by Joseph Smith in 1837 and gave patriarchal blessings throughout the rest of his life. He was stake president in Lima, Illinois, and led the initial settlement of Sanpete Valley, Utah, in 1849. "Isaac Morley," in Andrew Jenson, *Latter-day Saint Biographical Encyclopedia,* 4 vols. (Salt Lake City, UT: Andrew Jenson History Company, 1901–36), 1:235; Dean C. Jessee, Mark Ashurst-McGee, and

Here they grew to manhood and womanhood and were married in the year 1812. During this year they left their homes of wealth and comfort for the wilderness of Ohio, where they built their cabin homes. It being a quarter of a mile from any white neighbor, [they] cleared the lands near which later became the city of Kirtland.

For twenty years father lived here surrounded by his father's family, who had followed him.[11]

Trials in Missouri

Cordelia's published autobiography describes how her family came to leave Ohio and relocate in Missouri:

In the spring of 1832 [1831], Joseph Smith called Edward Partridge's family and father's family to go to Missouri to find a location for the Saints.[12] A place was found near the town of Independence, Missouri.

Here father's family and the Partridge family, who had become life-long friends in traveling from Kirtland, Ohio, to Jackson, Missouri, moved, father giving up his home, father, mother, sisters and brothers for the Gospel's sake. . . .

Richard L. Jensen, eds., *Journals, Volume 1: 1832–1839,* vol. 1 of the Journals series of *The Joseph Smith Papers,* ed. Dean C. Jessee, Ronald K. Esplin, and Richard Lyman Bushman (Salt Lake City, UT: Church Historian's Press, 2008), 425.

11. Cox, "Sketch," 33. Isaac's parents, Thomas and Editha Marsh Morley, along with his eight other siblings, joined Isaac in the Kirtland, Ohio, area three years later in 1815. Only one of Isaac's siblings, Lucy Diantha Morley Billings, joined the Church. See Catherine Wheelwright Ockey, "'Rejoice Notwithstanding the Trials': Diantha Morley Billings," in *Women of Faith in the Latter Days, Volume 1: 1775–1820,* ed. Richard E. Turley Jr. and Brittany A. Chapman (Salt Lake City, UT: Deseret Book, 2011), e-book edition, chap. 36.

12. Doctrine and Covenants 52:23.

Father never after had a home of any pretensions, just a place of shelter for his family.[13]

After moving to Missouri to establish a location for Church members to gather, Cordelia and her family were caught in unrest and mob violence. In a handwritten autobiography, Cordelia recorded:

People began to threaten to drive us out of the country, they were determin the mormon people should not settle there. It soon got so that we were threatened day & night. They told us they would burn our hous down over our heads if we did not leave the country. We got so we were afraid of them. One night some of the mob came to my Father's house & through a large rock throu our window smashing it to pieces I was sleeping with my little sister on a trundle bed under the window, the glass filled our faces & bed full, woke us up & we were crying & frightened almost to death.

The mob gave us no peace. They were threatning the people & telling them they had to leave their homes or they would kill them. We took our thing[s] out of the house three different times, expecting each time our home would be burnt to the ground. We would leave at night & go away to sleep. The men had to stand guard at night, the women & children would go to a house away in the woods to sleep, back home again before breakfast in the morning. . . . There was no protection or safety for us in the Country & we had to leave—

In the month of November, we started out again. We went from Jackson Co to Clay Co Missourie, where the Church settled again. This place was call Far West. Here was built a nice town with comfortable homes & good farms & all enjoying life once more. This enraged the mob &

13. Cox, "Sketch," 33.

they began to threaten the mormons again. They burnt our houses, destroyed & burnt the stacks of wheat, drove off our cattle & sheep untill we were left destitute. Nothing was safe with the people. Not even there lives.

I have seen hundred of wicked men ride into town with guns & bayonets upon their shoulders threatning to kill who they pleased & plunder our houses. The mob took a great many prisoners amongst them was my Father. . . . Father beged the privilege to see his family before leaving. They gave him a few moments to see us; two of the mob came with him when he came to bid us good bye, told us he was a prisonor & they were going to put him in jail, but said, he did not know what it was for, neither did he know when he would see us again. Father called us children around him, told us all to be good & he would come back sometime. He than took us one by one in his arms & kissed us, said good bye, than he was gone, you cannot imagin the scene that followed, all were crying as tho he had gone from us forever.[14]

In November 1838, after three weeks' incarceration, Cordelia's father was acquitted and returned home to his family. The experience was "so hard for him," Cordelia penned, that "he did not look natural & we hardly new him. . . . All seemed to be against us, And we were compeld to leave our homes again. We went from Missouri to the state of Illinois Hancock co."[15]

Morley Settlement, Hancock County, Illinois

After the Saints arrived in Commerce, renamed Nauvoo, in 1839, Isaac was sent to establish and preside over a satellite community about twenty-five miles south of Nauvoo named Yelrome

14. Cordelia Morley Cox, "Grandma Story," 1893, Photocopy of holograph, n.p., Betty K. Anderson Papers, 1989, Church History Library.

15. Cox, "Grandma Story."

(*Morley* pronounced backwards), also called the Morley Settlement.[16] After the years of violence the family had endured, they cherished times of peace with family and friends before violence set in again. Cordelia remembered:

> I attended school whenever and wherever I had the opportunity, amidst all our moving, mobbing and driving, until at the age of sixteen father built a small schoolhouse where I taught in the summer and went to school in the winter to a larger school.
>
> This was at the place known as the Morley Settlement, where my father was president and F. [Walter] Cox and Edwin Whiting his counselors. Here we lived five years of blessed peace and prosperity.
>
> In my father's home at this time were four grown sisters. Our house was small, but there was room for love, friends and merriment.
>
> A cooper by trade, father's shop was adjoining the house. Our beaus being plentiful, they made themselves both useful and agreeable in the cooper shop; they would come, and out the barrels and rubbish they'd send, start the fiddle and the fun began. We danced; how we danced. For a change, we played chase the squirrel and thread the needle, sailing the boat, whirl the plate. Forfeits were taken up which led to many other games.
>
> We had dancing and spelling schools, husking bees, house raisings. At this time we made fun out of everything, and with us it was the one gleam of sunshine for many years to come.
>
> Though so many years have passed since this change of scene, it is with a pang at the heart and quivering lips I recall

---

16. Clare B. Christensen, *Before and After Mt. Pisgah* (Salt Lake City, UT: privately printed, 1979), 99.

them. The pen and hand fail to paint the emotions of the heart. May I not pass them by, as well as the martyrdom?

A year later, September, 1845, the Morley Settlement was burned.[17] The labor and toil of years was ruthlessly destroyed; homes and stacks burned, cattle taken possession of and driven away. Helpless old people, women and children robbed of even a shelter and the necessaries of life. Oh, the inhumanity of our own countrymen, for they left ruin and desolation where had been a happy, prosperous people. Now they scattered wherever they could find a shelter or friend, or a crust of bread.[18]

Reflecting on these experiences more than seventy years later, Cordelia wrote: "All the years of my youth were years of mobbing, and hardships of every conceivable kind for my parents. . . . And it was from year to year, persecution which increased our faith in our Creator."[19]

Plural Marriage

Cordelia wrote candidly about her introduction to the principle of plural marriage in terms that can be understood by all who read them. Despite her initial reaction, two years later she became a plural wife to Frederick Walter Cox and accepted the principle devotedly. Throughout her entire life, she spoke of her sincere love for her husband, for his other wives, and for the family of each of them.[20]

My father spent the winter in Nauvoo and here I want to bear my testimony, no matter by whom it is denied.

---

17. William G. Hartley, *The 1845 Burning of Morley's Settlement and Murder of Edmund Durfee* (Salt Lake City, UT: Primer Publications, 1997; repr. 1999), 1.

18. Cox, "Sketch," 33–34.

19. Cox, "Sketch," 33.

20. Cox, "Biographies."

The Prophet Joseph Smith taught and practiced polygamy, himself having five wives whom I was acquainted with.
It was just as much a trial to us to those days as it would be
to this people today. But we tightened our armor and made
ready to overcome our selfish desires.[21]

In the spring [of] 'forty-four, Plural marriage was introduced to me by my pearents from Joseph Smith—asking
their consent & a request to me to be his wife. Imagine if
you can my feelings [to] be a plural wife. Something I never
thought I ever could. I new nothing of such religion and
could not except it neither did I.

In June 1844 Joseph Smith was martyred. It was a time
of mourning for all. After Joseph Smith death I was visited
by some of his most intimate friends who new his request
& explained to me this religion counseling me [to] except
his wishes for he now was gone & could do no more for
himself. I excepted Joseph Smith desire—in 1846 January
27 I was ~~sea~~ married to your Father [Walter] in the Nauvoo
Temple. While still kneeling upon the alter my hand clasped
in his now his wife, he gave his consent and I was sealed to
Joseph Smith for eternity.

I lived with your Father and loved him. I was satisfied
with the course I had taken. I had three little girls, with
them I took comfort born under the new and everlasting
covanant.[22]

From Nauvoo to Winter Quarters

The Cox family lived one year in Mt. Pisgah, Iowa, after Church
members left Nauvoo in 1846 and then settled close to Winter

---

21. Cox, "Sketch," 34.

22. Cox, "Biographies."

Quarters on the Iowa side of the Missouri River.[23] Four years later, a few Saints residing there were threatened by the courts with imprisonment if they did not renounce their plural wives. To her grandchildren, Cordelia wrote:

> Your Grandfather Cox did not have means to travel any further to-ward Utah so we went five miles from Winter Quarters & made another home. This place was called Cutlers Branch.[24] Built another house, cleared & fenced land & raised corn & potatoes but not any wheat—Had to go down into Missouri for bread stuff, There was no grist mill with in fifty miles of where we lived, so your Grandfather fell a large tree, dug out the center of the tree, fixt a spring pole to it & pounded the corn for our bread. In this way we lived for four years. . . .
>
> By the time we were comfortable in our home the Gentiles began to buy the places that were vacated by the Mormons & began to move in. It was soon found out your Grandfather had more than one wife for which he was arrested & brought in to court & informed that he would have to send his plural wives away, or he would have to leave the Country, so we had to go.[25] My husband had the courage of his convictions and stood up to them, saying, "I will

---

23. Cordelia Morley Cox, "History [of] Grandpa Cox," 1896, Photocopy of holograph, p. 1, Church History Library. This source is a manuscript reflecting Cordelia's perspective but differs in handwriting from her other documents written later in life. Her handwriting may have changed over time, or the document may be a copy of her original. See also Christensen, *Before and After Mt. Pisgah,* 178.

24. Cutler's Camp, also known as Silver Creek, was located about twenty miles southeast of Council Bluffs. Danny L. Jorgensen, "Cutler's Camp at the Big Grove on Silver Creek: A Mormon Settlement in Iowa, 1847–1853," *Nauvoo Journal* 9, no. 2 (Fall 1997): 39–51.

25. Cox, "Grandma Story."

never forsake these wives and their little ones, so help me
God."[26]

But to gain time and to keep peace he put Aunt
Jemima,[27] myself and our children into a wagon [on January
15, 1852][28]. . . . Through the cold we traveled into another
country. He hunted for a house, but could not find a house
of any kind. A stable was found about fourteen feet square,
without doors or windows; no place for a fire; not a friend
or an acquaintance; called spiritual wives, looked down
upon by every passerby with suspicion and distrust. At this
time Aunt Jemima had two children and was in a delicate
condition [pregnant], needing a loving husband's care.

I had three little ones, the oldest was five years old.
Nervousness was my ever present companion.[29]

It was dark when we got there to our journey end. Who
can discribe our feelings on reaching our new home cold &
hungry no place to make down beds for our tiered Children
& our selfs to rest.[30]

Our husband took up the loose boards, scraped the
floor and replaced them. Made two pole bunks, cut a little
wood and left us alone, yes, alone amongst a town full of

---

26. Walter had three wives and was serving as a counselor to branch president
Alpheus Cutler. When brought before the same courts, Alpheus chose to abandon
his plural wives and eventually left the Church to form one of his own. Cordelia's
older sister Philomena and her husband, Chauncey Whiting, also left to join with
Alpheus Cutler and his newly organized church. Christensen, *Before and After Mt.
Pisgah*, 178, 183.

27. Jemima Losee and Cordelia were married to Walter on the same day, January 27, 1846.

28. Cox, "History," 2.

29. Cox, "Sketch," 34.

30. Cox, "History," 2–3.

people.[31] Alone when we could not help but feel that He who knows when even a sparrow falls.[32]

I had no one to go to for knowledge or for Comfort. I began to worry & to wonder if I had in these years been so deceived. I longed for a testimony from my Father in Heaven to know for myself whether I was right or wrong. I was called a fallen woman—the finger of scorn was pointed at me. I felt that it was more than I could endure. In the humility of my soul I prayed that I might have a testimony from Him who knows the hearts of all.[33]

February came and went, we had made no acquaintances. Father Cox did not come as we expected. I was scared, for I know Jemima was trying to keep her trouble to herself. Suddenly there was a knock at the door. I timidly opened it after asking who was there. A lady walked in, an entire stranger to us. Who had sent her here this wintry night so unexpected, yet so welcome, so necessary, for it was not long before a newborn babe came to that stable and was laid in its mother's arms, Feb. 29, 1852.[34]

Well, all this was just a little too much. This over, I just dropped every feather and wept. Oh, but was not this a God-given testimony; we ever since have felt so. Who could have expressed a keener sympathy. He did not send to us an earthly doctor, whose every look and action would seem to cut us as a knife, but a poor hunted being who, like ourselves, must be kept out of sight, keeping our troubles to ourselves.

She had accidentally heard that we were here and came

---

31. Walter moved Cordelia and Jemima over the county line to Carterville, Pottawattamie, Iowa. Christensen, *Before and After Mt. Pisgah*, 183–86, 269.

32. Cox, "Sketch," 33–34.

33. Cox, "Biographies."

34. Esther Phelena Cox was the third child born to Jemima and Walter Cox.

to us or I can only feel that she was sent and I don't doubt that she went her way comforted, as she left us as soon as her work was done. We have never seen her since.[35]

A Home in Manti, Utah

Eventually, Cordelia and her family journeyed west to Utah Territory and then south to settle the community of Manti. She recounted:

[Father] Cox was making every preparation he could to take us to Utah. every thing being ready we started on our wearysome Journey the 20th of June 1851 [1852],[36] we had three wagons five yoke of cattle & a yoke of cows. [Father] Coxs family consisted then of three wives & ten children, we were four months on the way. Arived in Manti on the fourth of October [and were welcomed by my father and a score of relatives and friends[37]]. . . . By the time we reached Manti it was cold weather, & we were without a home again. We lived in our wagon untill a house could be found that we could rent, found a little log house where we could stay for the winter.

In the Spring the Indians became hostile, & it was dangerous every where. Men could not put in there Crops or go in the mountains for Timber to Build without going in Companies. The Indians were so trouble some they were Obliged to Build a Fort. When it was finished, every Family

---

35. Cox, "Sketch," 34.

36. The Cox family was part of the John B. Walker Company, which arrived in the Salt Lake Valley on September 28, 1852. Cox, "Sketch," 34; "John B. Walker Company (1852)," Mormon Pioneer Overland Travel Database, 1847–68, The Church of Jesus Christ of Latter-day Saints, accessed February 4, 2012, http://mormontrail.lds.org.

37. Cox, "Sketch," 34.

moved in. Our family moved in on the 27th of July [1853]. Here we lived nine years. In this time [Walter] was working to . . . build another home for his family. He was seven years in building & before it was finished we moved in.[38]

We had now a good home, A Farm & a Flock of Sheep & thought we were well fixed. The boys could work on the farm and hurd the Sheep. The girls & their mothers, Spin & weave. [39]

And though the next twenty years were filled with hardships and danger, still they were happy years.

Everything we had to wear was made in our home; our summer shoes, our hats, bonnets, dresses and underwear, by our own busy hands.[40]

CORDELIA'S TESTIMONY TO HER CHILDREN

A decade after a two-year mission to England and later service as a special missionary to the Indians, Walter died in 1875 from a logging accident.[41] His wives found they had to sell their wonderful home and rely on their children for support. During her remaining years, Cordelia used every opportunity at family gatherings and reunions to speak of her life experiences and those of the family. Cordelia was a widow for thirty-six years; she died on June 9, 1915, at the age of ninety-two. Her writings have become the basis of biographies and

---

38. The Cox home was completed in 1861 and is located at 98 North 100 West, Manti, Utah. "Its oolite exterior was quarried from the same hill as the Manti Temple . . . Each wife had their own separate room with a fireplace and outside entrance. . . . The second floor had a partition in the center that could be opened and used as a multi-purpose room [where] dance lessons . . . silk and wool spinning, classroom instruction, public dances, weddings, and other community events" were held. "Historic F. Walter Cox Home in Manti, Utah," Heritage Realty Group, accessed February 4, 2012, http://www.waltercoxhome.blogspot.com.

39. Cox, "History," 3–4.

40. Cox, "Sketch," 34.

41. When he died, Walter had five wives and thirty-eight children.

family stories for the entire Frederick Walter Cox family. Most important to her descendants, she left behind her testimony:

> [I] must say the Father of us all watched over and
> blessed us for striving to obey His will. I am not denying the
> wavering of my will, for when you feel the finger of scorn
> pointed your way and know you are against all the teachings
> of your youth, a strong faith must be yours to be able to
> overcome this feeling.
>
> Many were the nights of weeping. I must have some
> assurance of a higher source to be able to go on with any
> degree of comfort. I went to bed praying earnestly to have
> the right made known to me. I then seemed to be one of
> the multitude of people who evidently were sorrowing. I felt
> that a glorious personage was moving among them whis-
> pering words of inspiration and comfort. Soon he came to
> me and in startling distinctness these words he said: "Never
> change your condition or wish them otherwise." Today I am
> thankful I obeyed that voice, it was so real to me that I felt
> strengthened and comforted.[42]
>
> The Lord has been my guide—in Him I put my trust.
> I am thankful that I have been true to the covanants I have
> made with my Father in Heaven. I am thankful for my chil-
> dren that has been given to me. I pray that God will except
> us all & blessed to come fourth through a glorious reserec-
> tion & receive a crown of eternal life in His kingdom.
>
> CORDELIA COX[43]

---

42. Cox, "Sketch," 34.
43. Cox, "Biographies."

Chapter 5

"All Kinds of Trials and Hardships"

JANETTA ANN MCBRIDE FERRIN (1839–1924)

Rebekah Ryan Clark and Marcus Patrick Ryan

BIOGRAPHICAL SKETCH

We went through all kinds of trials and hardships of pioneer life on the frontier," Janetta Ann McBride Ferrin[1] told her granddaughter just a few months before she died.[2] This early British Saint

---

1. Although some sources employ other spellings of her name, "Janetta" is the spelling used in her personal histories and engraved on her headstone in Pima, Arizona.

2. Ethel Ferrin Davis [granddaughter], "Story of Janetta Ann McBride Ferrin," ca. 1924, Typescript, p. 11, private possession. Janetta apparently dictated her oral history to various children and grandchildren, resulting in multiple versions. See also Janetta McBride Ferrin, "Autobiographical Sketch," 1924, Typescript, p. 1, private possession; Janetta A. McBride Ferrin, "Personal History," 1924, Typescript, private possession; Janetta Ann McBride Ferrin, "My Life with My Husband," dictated to daughter Sarah Elizabeth Ferrin Lines, available at Pioneer Memorial Museum, International Society Daughters of Utah Pioneers, Salt Lake City, Utah, hereafter cited as DUP; Janetta A. McBride Ferrin, "History of Janetta A. Ferrin," dictated to granddaughter Elizabeth Lamb Crockett, 1924,

had survived her journey across the ocean and plains, braved hunger and fear of war as she settled in the unknown wilderness of Zion, and raised a large family alone in the midst of heartbreak. Her grand-daughter records, "Janetta's life was stricken with sorrow in the un-timely death of her husband who was killed by Indians . . . , and the family had to take up the threads of life and go it alone."[3] Janetta's pio-neer spirit of faith persisted throughout her long and industrious life.

Janetta Ann McBride was born in Churchtown, Lancashire, England, on Christmas Eve 1839, when The Church of Jesus Christ of Latter-day Saints was just beginning its rapid expansion into the British Isles. At a Sabbath meeting held in her parents' home, Brigham Young gave baby Janetta her name and blessing.[4] Her par-ents, Robert McBride III and Margaret Ann Howard, had been firmly rooted in their new faith from the Church's earliest moments on British soil.[5] Janetta's youth was marked by close associations with early Church leaders. Her father had been baptized by Orson Hyde just days after the first missionaries arrived in England.[6] Heber C. Kimball then baptized Janetta's mother, befriended the family, and later urged them to join the Saints in Utah.

When she was sixteen years old, Janetta and her family made the long-awaited journey as part of the ill-fated Martin Handcart

---

Typescript, DUP; Elizabeth Lamb Crockett, "A Sketch of the Life of Jacob Samuel and Janetta McBride Ferrin," Typescript, private possession.

3. Davis, "Story of Janetta," 11.

4. Ferrin, "Autobiographical Sketch," 1.

5. See Anna T. Rolapp, "'The Lord Will Provide': Margaret Ann Howard McBride," in *Women of Faith in the Latter Days, Volume One, 1775–1820: Bonus Chapters,* ed. Richard E. Turley Jr. and Brittany A. Chapman (Salt Lake City, UT: Deseret Book, 2011), e-book, 148–60.

6. Phyllis Barker Van Wagenen, "Margaret Ann Howard McBride Ferrin," p. 1, DUP. See also Bruce L. McBride and Darvil B. McBride, *Against Great Odds: The Story of the McBride Family* (Anaheim, CA: KNI Book Manufacturers, 1988), p. 15, available at the Family History Library, The Church of Jesus Christ of Latter-day Saints, Salt Lake City, Utah.

Company. After her mother grew too sick to walk and her father died after carrying others across an icy river, the burden fell mainly on young Janetta and her next-younger sibling, Heber, to lead their family to Zion. Leaving footprints of blood in the snow, she forged ahead in faith.

Soon after arriving in Salt Lake City, Janetta settled in Ogden, Utah. In 1861, she married Jacob Samuel Ferrin, with whom she had a thriving family of eleven children. When they were called upon to settle in Arizona, Janetta drove a wagon all the way from Ogden with her youngest baby in her arms. Mourning her husband's murder just months later, she rallied her strength and raised all of her children to be faithful Latter-day Saints. Her devout life of eighty-five years left an enduring legacy of perseverance, industry, service, and sacrifice.

Life Experiences

How Firm a Foundation:
Childhood among the First British Saints

Born on December 24, 1839, Janetta Ann McBride was among the first children outside the United States to be born into the fledgling Church of Jesus Christ of Latter-day Saints. Her father, Robert McBride III, had attended the meeting in which Heber C. Kimball first preached the restored gospel in England,[7] and Janetta's parents had quickly accepted the teachings as the true gospel of Jesus Christ. As one of the original twenty-seven British converts confirmed as members of the Church, Robert was a founding member of the first branch in England, which was organized the following Sunday, August 6, 1837.[8] During Janetta's early years, her family remained at

7. James B. Allen, Ronald K. Esplin, and David J. Whittaker, *Men with a Mission, 1837–1841: The Quorum of the Twelve Apostles in the British Isles* (Salt Lake City, UT: Deseret Book, 1992), 31–32.

8. Bruce L. McBride and Darvil B. McBride, *Against Great Odds*, 16–17.

the heart of Church activity in the British Isles and interacted closely with the apostles. "The elders used to stay with my parents and missionary meetings were held in our home," she recalled. "My mother would make the bread for the sacrament for the meetings."[9]

In describing her childhood, Janetta preserved a rare glimpse of what life was like for a Latter-day Saint child during these formative years of Church history in the region:

> We moved to Southport, England, where I lived until I was about five years old, then I went to Scotland with my father to stay with my grandparents. I was poor in health and they thought the change would do me good as they lived close to the sea. My mother came the next year. There was no branch of the church there [on the Isle of Bute] but we belonged to the Glasco [Glasgow] Conference. We were the only Mormons on the Island, but the elders from Glasco came to visit us often and I used to go to Glasco to the conferences with my parents. I was in Glasco at the time that the Cholera was so bad and I slept in the house where there were four or five cases and got up and waited on them although I was only a little girl, but the Lord blessed us and we didn't take it. I got most of my schooling there. When I was eight years old I went to the School of Industry and graduated from there when I was eleven years old. The school was under the Presbyterian Church, but our studies were the Bible and my Father always instructed me if I formed any wrong ideas. I had to learn their Catechi[s]ms. When I was nine years old, I was baptized in the river Clyde on New Years Eve. There was ice on the edge of the river, for we had to go in the night.[10]

---

9. Quoted in Davis, "Story of Janetta," 8.

10. Ferrin, "Autobiographical Sketch," 1.

Life seems to have been good for adventurous young Janetta, who was an accomplished swimmer and rower. She once rowed so far out to sea that she was almost hit by a large steamer.[11] Tragedy first struck in 1853, when her grandmother Janetta Sharp McBride died from burns she suffered after her dress caught fire during one of Janetta's frequent visits.[12] Her death must have been especially traumatic for Janetta, who had grown particularly close to her namesake during the years she lived near her grandmother in Scotland.

Around this time, the McBride family moved back to England, where they remained dedicated to the growth of the Church. Janetta recounted:

> Then we moved back to South Port where there was a branch of the Church and we were in the Liverpool conference, but we had to go several miles along the shore to a house to hold meeting. I went to school for about a year and myself and some of the girls used to spend our Sunday mornings taking [missionary] tracts where the[y] would receive them. My father was secretary of the Branch and our house was the home of the elders.[13]

At the age of fourteen, Janetta was apprenticed to a dressmaker for two years, learning a trade that would prove essential much later in life.

Come to Zion: "No Tongue Nor Pen Could Tell the Sorrow"

About the time of Janetta's first birthday, her father received a letter from family friend Heber C. Kimball urging the McBrides to gather with the Saints when their circumstances permitted. More than a decade and a half passed before gathering became a reality for

---

11. Crockett, "Sketch," 4.

12. McBride and McBride, *Against Great Odds,* 12.

13. Ferrin, "Autobiographical Sketch," 1.

the family.[14] Janetta described how eager the family was to make the journey, not fully realizing the great sacrifice that would be required:

> We had always looked forward to the time when we could go to Utah, and in the Spring of 1856 we received word that we could go by the Emigration Fund, if we would go with the Hand Cart Company. . . . By going this way we could travel from Liverpool to Salt Lake City, Utah for forty-five dollars. This was a big savings, but for the seven of us, my parents and five children, it was still quite a bit.[15]

On May 25, 1856, the McBride family set sail aboard the *Horizon* and arrived at Boston's Constitution Wharf on June 30, 1856. Robert and Margaret traveled with their five children: Janetta Ann, age sixteen; Heber, age thirteen; Ether, age eight; Peter, age six; and Maggie, almost three. Janetta recalled:

> While traveling from Boston to Iowa we passed through Buffalo on the 4th of July. The people were celebrating while we poor emigrants were packed into box cars. While at Chicago we went swimming in the lake.
>
> When we arrived in Iowa, everything was to be ready for us to travel on, but through some mistake nothing was

---

14. Heber C. Kimball to Robert McBride, December 17, 1840, Holograph, Church History Library, The Church of Jesus Christ of Latter-day Saints, Salt Lake City, Utah, hereafter cited as Church History Library. This letter is addressed to "Brother Robert in Christ and to all the Saints in Church town and South port," indicating the position of authority that Janetta's father held in that area. Elder Kimball advises Robert: "It is not wisdom to go with out your SercumStances [circumstances] will admit of it. You know of your own situation. . . . Go a head and in this way, the way will be opened fore you to go to [America]. It is your privledg to go when you can."

15. Ferrin, "Personal History," 3.

ready. We walked in heavy rain and waded creeks in mud. Three weeks later the handcarts were ready.[16]

The delay would soon prove fatal for many of these Saints who, undaunted by the inadequate preparations, steadfastly built handcarts themselves. Janetta's account alludes to two critical turning points that would dramatically affect their fate:

> At last we left with our handcarts on the 300 mile journey to the Missouri River, which we crossed by ferry and camped at Florence, Nebraska [Winter Quarters] until the 25th of August. We made up the Fifth Hand Cart Company and Edward Martin was our leader. [Some of] the Missionaries tried to talk us into staying until Spring, since it was a month later than we should have started, but we voted to go on.
>
> We had disposed of all our bedding and clothing that we could spare, and we left Florence on the 25th day of August on the 1000 mile journey to Utah.[17]

The company's vote to continue to Utah despite the late start and its decision to discard extra supplies to lighten the load showed the Saints' confidence and optimism at the outset. Janetta described how quickly their hardships became more severe:

> We had a very good time as there were pretty good roads part of the time, but my mother got sick and we had to haul her on our carts part of the time and as we got near the mountains the roads got worse and provisions got scarce and the people began to die of hunger and fatigue and we had to wade the rivers and it was getting cold and the people

---

16. Davis, "Story of Janetta," 8, 10.

17. Ferrin, "Personal History," 4.

were getting discouraged, so we did not have our good times singing and dancing.[18]

Her father's health also quickly failed. Sixteen-year-old Janetta and her younger brother Heber pushed the family's supplies on their handcart while their parents alternated riding on the cart with little Maggie.[19] Heber struggled to depict the burden he and Janetta shouldered:

> [N]o toung [tongue] nor pen could tell what my Sister [Janetta] and me passed through. Our parients both sick and us young. It seemed as though death would be a blessing, for we used to pray that we might die to get out of our misery for by this time it was getting very cold weather and our clothing almost worn out and not enough of bedclothes to keep us warm. We would lay and suffer from night till morning with the cold. . . . [W]e used to cry and feel so bad. We did not know what to do but we would never get into camp till away after dark and then we would have to hunt something to make a fire.[20]

Despite her trials, Janetta pressed on with faith and perseverance beyond her years, often singing "for some must push and some must pull" with her family to lift their spirits.[21] Janetta's role in her

---

18. Ferrin, "Autobiographical Sketch," 2.

19. Heber explained: "My older sister [Janetta] and I pushed the handcart most of the way. . . . The handcart was so heavy and father and mother were so sick that we would get behind the main group and not reach camp until after dark." Heber McBride to Zelma McBride Ririe West, May 13, 1923, in "Heber McBride: From the Personal History of Zelma McBride Ririe West," Typescript, p. 1, DUP.

20. Heber Robert McBride, "Autobiography," ca. 1868, Typescript, pp. 10–11, Church History Library.

21. See Laura McBride Smith [Peter's daughter], "The Story of My Grandfather: Peter Howard McBride," Typescript, p. 4, DUP.

family's survival became nothing short of heroic as they reached the banks of the North Platte River on October 19, 1856. She recalled:

> When we got to the upper c[ro]ssing of the Platt River, it was freezing and the river was very wide. I crossed it with my hand cart and had to go back and haul my mother across, and get the children across and it was getting dark and very cold and my clothes were wet.[22]

While young Janetta dodged dangerous chunks of ice and braved the chest-deep river to pull her family across, her starving father rallied strength beyond his own and "worked all day pulling, pushing, wading through the icy river," making "about twenty five trips across the river helping to get all the people and carts across."[23] In an effort that cost him his life, her father "never stopped until the last person and all carts were accross."[24]

Janetta pushed her handcart the remaining mile to camp, her wet dress freezing on her body in the biting winds of the early winter snowstorm. Despite her exhaustion, Janetta gathered wood for the fire and "cooked what [they] had," only "[o]ne half pound of flour a day and nothing else."[25] Heber related another act of heroism: "With cold wind blowing and snow drifting, my sister [Janetta] and I let our parents have our blanket and we would lie down without any covering."[26]

Janetta poignantly described her father's abiding faith even in his final hours:

> When we camped that night my Father was very sick and said he was very cold. . . . He revived a little and began

---

22. Ferrin, "Autobiographical Sketch," 2.

23. Smith, "Story of My Grandfather," 5.

24. Gladys McBride Stewart, "Peter Howard McBride," Typescript, p. 2, DUP.

25. Ferrin, "Autobiographical Sketch," 2.

26. McBride to West, May 13, 1923, in "Heber McBride," 1.

to sing the hymn, 'O Zion.' I think he sang the song thru and then we led him to the wagon. That was the last I saw of him alive. He died in the wagon the next day and they buried him that night with 14 others, all in the same grave.[27]

Young Janetta now took the lead in caring for her family. She struggled to pull her handcart through the deepening snow and desperately coaxed on her starving younger siblings with biscuit crumbs saved from her own meager rations.[28] Her brother Peter remembered:

My mother was sick all the way and my sister Jennetta Ann had all the worries of taking car[e] of us children. She carried water from the river for cooking purposes, her shoes gave out and she walked through the snow bare foot, actually leaving bloody tracks in the snow.[29]

Janetta recalled the suffering she witnessed on the dismal journey to the Sweetwater River, where she "cried for joy" upon seeing the rescuers' fires at Devil's Gate.[30]

[A]bout one fourth of the company left their bones on the trail, and of the ones left some of them were disabled, fingers and toes frozen and a lot were sick. Their movements became mechanical and they pulled their carts from force of habit with no hope for the future. . . . But help came, and

---

27. Ferrin, "Personal History," 3. Janetta's father "had ch[a]rge of the singing in [the] company." Smith, "Story of My Grandfather," 5. His final hymn was particularly meaningful on the frozen plains of Wyoming: "O Zion when I think of thee, I long for pinions like the dove, And mourn to think that I should be so distant from the land I love."

28. Laura McBride Smith, "The Life of Janetta Ann McBride Ferrin," Typescript, p. 1, DUP.

29. Smith, "Story of My Grandfather," 5.

30. McBride to West, May 13, 1923, in "Heber McBride," 2.

the Saints were glad to get what provisions that were available. It was only a drop in the bucket to what they needed.[31]

Even after the rescue wagons arrived, Janetta walked the rest of the way "up the steep mountain, barefoot with snow two or three feet deep."[32] Janetta recorded that the "survivors of the fearful journey" arrived in Salt Lake City on November 30, 1856.[33]

I'll Go Where You Want Me to Go: Pioneering New Frontiers

Janetta's surviving family members rejoiced in their long-awaited arrival in Zion. They were immediately sent to Ogden, where widower Samuel Ferrin kindly provided for them in exchange for help with cooking and cleaning. The dirt roof in their small one-room home leaked mud, and the family continued to suffer sickness, hunger, and privation throughout the winter. Janetta's brother Ether asked, "Is this Zion to live in such a place as this?" Despite all the trials they had passed through, however, their mother faithfully responded, "Never mind, the Lord will provide."[34]

Springtime brought new beginnings. Romance quickly blossomed between now seventeen-year-old Janetta and Samuel's son Jacob, and they were married on March 29, 1857. Janetta's widowed mother married Samuel shortly thereafter. Janetta recalled their tumultuous life in the wake of the Utah War later that year:

---

31. Davis, "Story of Janetta," 11.

32. Davis, "Story of Janetta," 11.

33. Ferrin, Personal History," 11; "Arrival," *Deseret News [Weekly],* December 3, 1856.

34. Ether Enos McBride, "Autobiographical Sketch," Typescript, p. 4, DUP. Incomplete holograph available at DUP. Ether further wrote: "What were the thots of mother who had always lived in comfort and good homes[?] . . . In all her trials and hardships I never knew of, or heard of her complaining. . . . Our diet was corn meal, squash and salt with little else. My baby sister age 3 would often cry her self to sleep for food she could eat." McBride, "Autobiographical Sketch," 4–5.

When Johnston's army came to Utah and tried to oust the Mormons, my brother Heber, I and also my six week old baby, Fidelia, left Ogden and went to Provo, where I stayed until July [1858]. . . . My husband was left at Ogden on detail, so if the army came our men could burn the houses and everything. Our homes were saved.[35]

Janetta and Jacob's married life was marked by great industry, harmony, and the birth of eleven children in twenty-four years. After their first three children were born, the Ferrin family moved to Huntsville, Utah, where they lived as neighbors to the McKay family. Janetta once told a group of grandchildren, as she introduced them to apostle David O. McKay, that she had bounced him on her knee when he was a baby.[36]

Janetta and her family later moved to a farm in Pleasant View, Utah. One daughter remembered: "This farm was a pleasant place for our large family to grow up. . . . Though every one had to work hard, we were very happy."[37] Janetta, whose industriousness was well-known, described their self-sufficiency:

We raised almost all our living, Beans, Potatoes and cane patches for molasses. Our main source for meat were pigs and sheep. The sheep were raised mainly for the wool which we spun into yarn and made our clothes. We also had an apple orchard. Along with the hard work we had fun going on trips into Ogden Canyon.[38]

In 1881, Janetta once again answered the call of a prophet, this time President John Taylor, to be a pioneer in helping settle the Gila

35. Davis, "Story of Janetta," 11–12.

36. Crockett, "Sketch," 2.

37. Sarah Elizabeth Ferrin Lines, "Life Story of Sarah Elizabeth Ferrin Lines," dictated to daughter Rowena Lines Holladay, Typescript, p. 1, DUP.

38. Ferrin, "My Life with My Husband," 1.

Valley in Arizona. "My husband was not well," she said, "so we decided a warmer climate would benefit his health."[39] Janetta proudly recalled, "We started for Arizona and I drove a team all the way with baby Charlie in my arms."[40]

Janetta had ensured that they were well prepared for the thousand-mile journey, making it more comfortable than her original trek west:

> On the 2nd day of October we started our treck to Az.
> . . . Each morning I mixed yeast bread before we broke
> camp and by night it was ready to bake. We had fresh milk
> for supper. The morning milk was put in a churn and by
> night there was fresh butter. Each wagon had a double bed
> consisting of a mattress supported by a rope strung across
> the wagon. . . . We took lots of dried fruit and in each
> wagon was a sack of applies and a barrel of water. . . . When
> we reached Taylor we were advised to go by way of Prescott
> because the Apaches were on the war path. . . .
>
> We finally reached Pima on Jan. 2, 1882 just 3 mos
> [months] from the day that we left Ut. The town of Pima was
> then 3 years old and had about 25 families who were living
> in cottonwood log shacks, with mud roofs and dirt floors. . . .
> Jacob soon found us an empty house built by standing cot-
> tonwood logs on end and with the usual mud roof and mud
> floor. It was quite luxurious because it was divided into 2
> rooms and we spread our tent on the floor for carpet.

The family enjoyed a time of peace in their new home in Pima, but it was not to last.

---

39. Ferrin, "My Life with My Husband," 1.

40. Davis, "Story of Janetta," 12. Charles Ether Ferrin, Janetta's youngest child, was only six months old.

Jacob earned our living by hauling freight from Wilcox to Globe. We liked Pima and the nice warm climate. Jacobs health was better and it seemed that we were going to be happy here, but our happiness was short-lived. 6 months after we had settled there, my husband was killed by the Apache Indians.[41]

Janetta wrote nothing else of this tragic loss that left her "stricken with sorrow."[42] Her granddaughter provides the tragic details of Jacob's murder:

The freighters came through San Carlos [Indian Reservation] and stopped for their evening meal. The Indians came. . . . Jacob could speak the Indian language and he thought if he could talk to them they would leave the horses. When he started toward the wagons, the other men tried to get him to not go. An Indian shot him, then they took the horses and left. . . . This happened on the 19th of July, 1882. The men brought the sad news back to his wife [Janetta] and family.[43]

At the age of forty-three, Janetta was left a widow with eight children still in her care.[44] The men of the town helped her sons build a one-room adobe house in which they lived for many years.[45] She relied on her skills as an "excellent seamstress" to help earn a

---

41. Ferrin, "My Life with My Husband," 1–2.

42. Davis, "Story of Janetta," 11.

43. Crockett, "Sketch," 3.

44. Janetta records that when they moved to Arizona, "We had 8 of our 11 children with us. We left 3 behind who were married." Ferrin, "My Life with My Husband," 1. Janetta visited Utah several times during the rest of her life to see the three children there and to do temple work.

45. Smith, "History of Janetta," 2–3.

living; the children all found work as soon as they were old enough, and ultimately "the family did very well."[46]

A neighbor remembered: "The Ferrin family were considered honest and of the best of families. Everyone had the greatest respect for them. Sister [Janetta] Ferrin . . . was a faithful Church worker, and she had a talent for leadership and was outstanding in music."[47] Janetta's granddaughter left a further witness of her character:

> Janetta Ann was a good manager and a good house keeper and always had something in the house to eat. . . . She was a life long member of the Latter Day Saints Church. She was a Relief Society Teacher for 49 years, and Primary President about that long. She was a very good singer and belonged to the Choir for about 30 years. One of her virtues was to say nothing bad about anyone.[48]

Janetta indeed "went through all kinds of trials and hardships of pioneer life on the frontier," but she never complained nor wavered in her devotion to the gospel. She raised all of her children to be faithful Latter-day Saints.[49] Many thousands of her descendants today enjoy the blessings of the gospel because of her courage and continue to honor her legacy of steadfast faith: "She found joy in the journey, faith along the way. She saw hope on the horizon, never knew the price she'd pay. . . . Because of her, we're standing here today."[50]

---

46. Davis, "Story of Janetta," 11; see also Lines, "Life Story of Sarah Lines," 3.

47. James Allred Duke, "The Ferrin Family," Typescript, p. 2, private possession.

48. Crockett, "Sketch," 4.

49. Davis, "Story of Janetta," 11. At the time of her death, Janetta had eight surviving children, eighty-five grandchildren, 150 great-grandchildren, and nine great-great-grandchildren.

50. Lyrics by great-great-granddaughter Julia Elizabeth Jenkins Ryan; dedicated to Janetta Ann McBride Ferrin. Sheet music for Ryan/Martin, *Joy in the Journey*, copyright 2006, available by request at inspirationalreserve@gmail.com.

Chapter 6

"The Lord Has Greatly Blessed Us"

Lucy Hannah White Flake (1842–1900)
David F. Boone

Biographical Sketch

Lucy Hannah White was born in Walnut Grove, Knox County, Illinois, on August 23, 1842, to Samuel Dennis and Mary Hannah Burton White. Before Lucy's birth, her family, including relatives on both sides, "embraced the gospell of Jesus Christ of Latterday saints" in 1837 and later settled in Nauvoo.[1]

Although the exact date of their departure from Nauvoo was not recorded, Lucy remembered some of the privations of the Utah pioneer trek during the summer of 1850 but concluded, "we had a very

---

1. Lucy H. Flake, Journals, 1894–1899, 3 vols., Holograph, vol. 1, p. 1, L. Tom Perry Special Collections, Harold B. Lee Library, Brigham Young University, Provo, Utah, hereafter cited as BYU Special Collections. Beginning in 1894, Lucy kept a daily record, eventually filling three large volumes, the first of which also includes an autobiography. An annotated typescript by Chad J. Flake and Hyrum F. Boone, 1973, is available at BYU Special Collections and the Church History Library, The Church of Jesus Christ of Latter-day Saints, Salt Lake City, Utah.

good trip." Eight years old at the time, she recalled, "We eat [ate] our last provisions in the morning and got in some time in the day." The Salt Lake Valley "looked butifull with its nice stacks of Wheat and Hay corn and vegetables."[2]

The White family settled nearly thirty miles south of Salt Lake City in Lehi. This was the first of many moves that continued throughout the remainder of Lucy's life. From Lehi, she moved with her family to the new community of Cedar City and then to Beaver, all in Utah. In 1877 her family was called to colonize Arizona, living first in settlements along the Little Colorado River and then in Snowflake, where she and her husband lived out their remaining years.

Lucy began one diary entry by listing her morning chores, which were no doubt representative of the work of other women living in territorial settlements: "Get up turn out my chickens draw a pail of watter take it over to Brother Whipples chickens let them out then draw watter watter hot beds make a fire put potatoes to cook then brush and sweep half inch of dust off floor and every thing feed three litters of chickens them mix bisquits get breakfast milk besides work in the house and this morning had to go half mile after calves." Then followed a philosophical perspective: "this is the way of life on the farm."[3]

Lucy was an advocate of the rights of women as citizens. She recorded: "There is much to be said of womens rights I don't beleave in equal rights I would like the Franchise [vote] but feel willing for the men to kill the snakes, build the bridges and smoothe down the

---

2. Flake, Journals, 1:1–2. Lucy and her family traveled with the Aaron Johnson Company, departing Kanesville, Iowa, on June 8, 1850, and arriving in the Salt Lake Valley on September 12, 1850. "Aaron Johnson Company (1850)," Mormon Pioneer Overland Travel Database, 1847–68, The Church of Jesus Christ of Latter-day Saints, accessed June 21, 2012, http://mormontrail.lds.org.

3. Flake, Journals, 2:71, May 16, 1896.

high places and hold the offices. I would like to see womens rights respected and held sacrid at all times and in all places."[4]

Lucy bore thirteen children—nine boys and four girls.[5] Eight lived to adulthood. Her greatest emphasis throughout her life was always her husband and children. Less than sixty years after her death, her posterity exceeded seven thousand souls.

Lucy served in the Church as a teacher to children, youth, and women, and presided in her ward and stake Primary and Relief Society auxiliaries.[6] She took great solace in an unusual pronouncement made to her by Eliza R. Snow: "You never shall get old."[7] At the time of her death on January 27, 1900, she was fifty-seven years of age.

LIFE EXPERIENCES

As was true of many women on the western frontier, Lucy Hannah White Flake had not received much formal schooling. "My Mother was a schoolteacher before she was Married," her daughter Lucy wrote. "She taught me my letters out of the Bible as [we] had no school book."[8] Nevertheless, she did not allow her lack of schooling to deter her from writing voluminously.

Lucy Hannah recorded her earliest memories: "My Mother took me to see the Profet Joseph after he was Murdered," and later, "My

---

4. Flake, Journals, 2:n.p., August 15, 1895.

5. James Madison Flake (1859–1946), William Melvin Flake (1861–1861), Charles Love Flake (1862–1892), Samuel Orson Flake (1864–1864), Mary Agnes Flake Turley (1866–1909), Osmer Dennis Flake (1868–1958), Lucy Jane Flake Wood (1870–1952), Wilford Jordan Flake (1872–1872), George Burton Flake (1875–1878), Roberta Flake Clayton (1877–1981), Joel White Flake (1880–1977), John Taylor Flake (1882–1973), and Malissa Flake (1886–1886).

6. Mary H. Larson, "Obituary," Holograph, in "Lucy Hannah White Flake," Mormon Biographical Sketches Collection, Church History Library, The Church of Jesus Christ of Latter-day Saints, Salt Lake City, Utah.

7. Flake, Journals, 1:14.

8. Flake, Journals, 1:3.

Father took me by the hand and led me up the stares to the top" of the Nauvoo Temple. "It was butifull."[9]

"My parents were a mong the last to leave Nauvoo," she recalled. Her father, Samuel, "stayed and helped the rest [of the Saints] off." The White family remained in Winter Quarters for three and a half years and in 1850 joined the Aaron Johnson Company en route to the Salt Lake Valley. After their arrival, the Whites moved to Lehi with extended family. Of her first year in Utah, Lucy recalled:

> We raised good crops and the people was doing well or [our] relitives used to come from Salt Lake and visit us and we visited them in turn we felt thankfull we were liveing so near hedquarters. . . . That October my Father came home [from general conference] and told Mother he was called to move South three Hundred miles Mother felt dredful bad for she had been seperated from her people so much and now we were setled so near them she thought it was cruel she had to go a way so far. . . . The 7 November we started to go where we were called Ceder City Iron County. . . . There we had poverty to condtend with again.[10]

Four and a half years after moving to Cedar City, fifteen-year-old Lucy met nineteen-year-old William Jordan Flake,[11] who "was tall and well built; . . . well mannered and chivalrous as became a son of the South."[12] Lucy reminisced:

---

9. Flake, Journals, 1:1. The bodies of Joseph and Hyrum Smith lay in state in Nauvoo on Saturday, June 29, 1844.

10. Flake, Journals, 1:1, 3–4.

11. William was returning to Utah from southern California following the disbanding of the San Bernardino colony. William, eldest of the seven children of James Madison and Agnes Haley Love Flake, was born July 3, 1839, in Anson County, North Carolina.

12. Roberta Flake Clayton, *To the Last Frontier: Autobiography of Lucy Hanna White Flake* (Mesa, AZ: n.p., 1923), 13. This "autobiography" of Lucy Hannah

William Flake remained in Cedar City and we became acquainted in due time he offered his hand in Marage My Parents being Willing we were Married, Dec 30 1858 by Apostal Amasy M Lyman at my Fathers House had a Wedding Apostle Lyman gave us very good council told us how to treat each other. . . . He said we was not set in our way like we would be if we were older he used most all the evening talking and counciling it was very plesant indeed.[13]

Within weeks, the newlywed Flakes moved to Beaver, Utah. Lucy recorded, "We went to Housekeeping . . . we had verry little to keep house with but we were just as happy as could be we loved each other and loved our home and felt truley thankfull. My Parents lived close by and greatley asisted us. . . . we commenced from the bottom to clime up the ladder."[14]

William supported his family largely by freighting, farming, and livestock raising, which gave Lucy additional responsibilities when he was on the road between Salt Lake and California. In 1859, wrote Lucy, "we was bless[ed] with our first born a son James Madison."

Lucy appears, at least early in their marriage, to have been the spiritual leader in their family. "William was not rligous [religious] being brought up in California . . . and haveing no father to teach him." Lucy encouraged family prayer. "This was somewhat of a trial to me but I loved him and prayed for him in secret. I would often pleade with him to pray in the Familey but he would not. . . . He would say he was going to be religous when he got old."[15]

White Flake was written by her daughter and is based on Lucy's journal and experiences. Roberta undoubtedly heard this description from her mother, but there is no indication that Lucy wrote it.

13. Flake, Journals, 1:8.

14. Flake, Journals, 1:8–9.

15. Flake, Journals, 1:9.

Perhaps as a compromise, just before a long freighting trip, he finally "promised he would [pray with her] if he ever got home again." Three months later, after having returned from the arduous trip, she reminded him of his promise. "He knelt down and praid his first prair I ever herd him pray and I was thankfull and happy."[16] "He kept faith with her," wrote a descendant, "[and] knelt in prayer that night and always afterward when he was home with his family."[17] Lucy was a firm believer in the efficacy of prayer throughout her life and taught and repeatedly modeled the practice in her home and with others.

Her faith was tested. In 1861, Lucy bore her second son, William Melvin. "He seemed a fine helthy child . . . [but two months later] he was called away." Lucy wrote: "I can say his death was the first trial of my faith. It seemed my prairs had alway[s] been answered before but in his sickness it seemed like my prairs did no good but still I kept trying to get my Hevenly Father to here me kept Praying but it seemed he could not here me."[18]

Her petitions, however, were not in vain. After the death of her child, Lucy's yearning to receive temple blessings intensified; she wanted to have her family sealed eternally. During William's long absences "freighting on the western mail line," Lucy felt unsettled:

> I was lonely and had plenty of time to pray as I was anxious for my husbands welfare. Used to pray for the time to come for us to be worthey to go and get our endewments. That fall my Father and Mother was going to Salt Lake to conferance. . . . I wrote to my Husband to meet us in Salt Lake as we were coming to Conferance. He came and we attended all the meetings after Conferance was over Our

16. Flake, Journals, 1:11.

17. Osmer D. Flake, *William J. Flake: Pioneer-Colonizer* (Phoenix, AZ: n.p., 1948), 36.

18. Flake, Journals, 1:9.

Bishop . . . came to my Husband and said Brother William
I want you and your wife to come to the endument House[19]
and have your Enduments he was so surprised he knew not
what to say if the Bishop had told him he wanted him to
go to England he could not [have] felt more surprised he
tried to get excused said he did not think himself worthy
but the Bishop would not let him off. . . . That night I was
so thankfull [I] hardley slept.

On October 9, 1861, Lucy rejoiced, "we recieved that great
blessing and was Seled for time and all Eternity."[20]

A third son, Charles Love, was born in 1862, at a time when
their temporal and spiritual fortunes were improving. William
was able to stay home for longer periods. He acquired additional
land, and his family became more comfortable. Two years later on
October 27, 1864, a fourth son, Samuel Orson, was born. Lucy recorded, "We was onely permited to keep this Precious tresure a short
time as he Died 21 of December. My faith was not so much shaken
this time but felt my troubles was more then almost any one else."[21]

Lucy and her husband both believed plural marriage was of
God, and in the fall of 1868 William "concluded to take another
wife." Lucy explained: "I was quite willing We all went to conferance in October and the 9th of Oct Prudence kartchner was sealed
to him. . . . Sister E R Snow asked me was I willing [I] said yes she
asked do you think you can live in that principal I said am quite
willing to try [as] my Mother and sister live in it and I think [I] can
do as much as them and besides I wanted my Husband to go into

19. Before temples were completed in Utah, other buildings were dedicated for
the administration of temple ordinances. In Salt Lake City one such building was
the Endowment House, which was in operation from 1855 to 1889. LaMar C.
Berrett, "Endowment Houses," *Encyclopedia of Mormonism,* ed. Daniel H. Ludlow,
4 vols. (New York: Macmillan, 1992), 2:456.

20. Flake, Journals, 1:9–10.

21. Flake, Journals, 1:12.

that principal before I was old because I think it right." Throughout the day as their paths crossed, Eliza Snow pronounced several blessings upon Lucy. Among others, Lucy remembered, "she said my reward would be great because I was willing and she said Sister you never shall get old."[22]

Plural marriage seems not to have become a divisive factor in Lucy's marriage. There is no evidence from her journals or from descendants of either woman that suggests the kind of friction that sometimes plagued such relationships.

A second life-changing experience for Lucy was a monumental move from their home in southern Utah to the Latter-day Saint communities in the Arizona Territory. In April 1877 the "St. George Temple was to be Dedicated . . . [and general] Conferance was going to be held" in that city. "William took Prudence and went," Lucy wrote. "I could not go, my little George was quite poorly and some one had to stay at home so there was no chance for me to go. . . . At that Conferance William was called to go to Arizona in the fall. They gave us six months to get redy to go. . . . It was cruel it seemed to me."[23] President Brigham Young instructed William: "Sell all that you have, that you can't take with you. Take your family and go there [Arizona] to settle the Saints. Leave nothing to come back to."[24] "[William] felt dredfull bad," recalled Lucy, "but we was called and there was no other way."[25]

Preparations for their departure included obtaining and outfitting a wagon for each of the wives. "Well we got ready for our trip as fast as we could we sold our farm," Lucy recorded. "The

---

22. Flake, Journals, 1:14.
23. Flake, Journals, 1:18–19.
24. Flake, *William J. Flake,* 56.
25. Flake, Journals, 1:19.

Winter was dredfull cold. . . . Our two oldest Daughters took the diptheria when we had been on the road a bout two weeks they had it dredfull bad and we never had seen a case of it before we did the best we could and the Lord herd our prairs and spared thir lives."[26] The family arrived at Ballenger's Camp,[27] where they lived for a short time, and later moved on to the pioneer settlement of Sunset.

In January 1878 they moved yet again to establish the short-lived community of Taylor on the Little Colorado River.[28] Conditions in Taylor were primitive at best, and the harsh environment bred illness. The river water from the Little Colorado was so muddy that if left in a barrel overnight would yield only six inches of usable culinary water in the morning.[29]

"Our wagons was our home," Lucy observed. Her youngest child, George, grew ill. "I did all I could with medicen and also with faith," Lucy wrote.

My prairs did not seem to be herd but several times each day I went a way from my wagon in secret and prayed. . . .

---

26. Flake, Journals, 1:19–20.

27. Ballenger's Camp was one of the earliest Latter-day Saint communities in northeastern Arizona and was colonized by a group led by Jesse O. Ballenger in March 1876. It was initially a United Order community characterized by a shared "long table" at which the group ate together. The settlement was later called Brigham City. Will C. Barnes, *Arizona Place Names* (Tucson: University of Arizona Press, 1988), 36.

28. Taylor, Arizona, was located on the south side of the Little Colorado River between present-day Winslow and Joseph City (formerly called St. Joseph). It was "made by eight Mormon families from Beaver, Utah, under John Karchner [Kartchner]. They located here in January, 1878. . . . They put in several dams on the river which soon went out. They gave it up at loss of fifth dam and in July, 1878, moved to Snowflake settlement." This community should not be confused with the current-day Taylor, formerly known as Bagley, which is located on Silver Creek, south of Snowflake. Barnes, *Arizona Place Names,* 438.

29. Roberta Flake Clayton, "Roberta Flake Clayton Papers," 1923, Hayden Library, Arizona State University, Tempe, Arizona.

On the morning of July 6th [18]78 I was so deep in sorrow it seemed I could not bare it any longer. I went out in some brush out of site and asked my Father in Heven to take him home for I could not bare it any longer my burden was hevier then I could bare that prair was simple but from my hart. I wint to him he breathed afew times and passed a way so sweetley.[30]

William searched for more suitable land for a settlement and found a site nestled in a little valley called Silver Creek. The water alone posed a significant contrast to what they had experienced in Taylor. "William drew out of the Order and started on the 19 of July to move to a place called Si[l]ver Creek," Lucy recalled. "It was a butiful place."[31] William had been discouraged from purchasing the site for what he considered an exorbitant price. Lucy, on the other hand, was eager to live in a more hospitable place than Taylor and encouraged him to buy the land. "William," she is remembered as saying, "if the place you have found is what you want, I'll do anything in my power to help us purchase the place and make a home for our people there."[32] Another source quotes her as saying, "I will do the man's washing and mending and cooking for him to help pay," thereby showing her willingness to help pay the bill.[33] She could not remain as she was.

The Flakes purchased the property,[34] and upon their arrival with other Taylor residents on July 21, 1878, Lucy remembered, "we womenfolk climbed out [of the wagon] and kneeling down on the

---

30. Flake, Journals, 1:22.

31. Flake, Journals, 1:22–23.

32. Irene S. Flake and Gerda H. Flake, *Descendants of William Jordan Flake,* n.p., 1985, sec. 1, no. 17.

33. Clayton, *To the Last Frontier,* 67.

34. The Flakes were the original purchasers of the property. The land was eventually divided and sold to others at the same price the Flakes had paid for it. Clayton, *To the Last Frontier,* 67.

mossy banks bathed our faces and drank to our hearts' content of the first clear water we had seen in months. . . . This beautiful valley was a bit of Heaven reserved for us as a reward for all we had suffered. . . . I poured out my gratitude" in prayer.[35] Lucy confided to her journal, "We have had meny trials and sorrows but the Lord has greatley blessed us."[36]

William and Lucy established a townsite that soon became populated by many of the former residents of Taylor. They renamed the settlement Snowflake in honor of its founder, William Jordan Flake, and apostle Erastus Snow. Snowflake became the Flakes' permanent home for as long as they lived, and many of their descendants still live there.[37]

As idyllic as Snowflake became for Lucy and her family, it also was a place of tragedy, heartbreak, and trials, which came as part of frontier life and raising a family. One of Lucy's greatest sorrows was the death of her son Charles in 1892. He was then thirty years old and serving as the justice of the peace in Snowflake. An outlaw accused of robbing a bank in New Mexico was also believed to be responsible for seven other deaths. When Charles and his brother James confronted him, a shootout ensued, and both the outlaw and Charles were killed. Lucy wrote:

> It is no use to try to tell of our sorrow how our harts did ache no one but our Hevenly Father will ever know we could not eat or sleep poor James would stand by his

---

35. Clayton, *To the Last Frontier,* 68–69.

36. Flake, Journals, 2:28, June 16, 1895.

37. In addition to Snowflake, William was responsible for establishing at least a half-dozen other Latter-day Saint communities in northeastern Arizona, including Showlow, Concho, Springerville, and Nutrioso. One historian stated that William "was the main stay in the settling of every town in Navajo and Apache County [AZ] except Alpine." James H. McClintock, *Mormon Settlement in Arizona: A Record of Peaceful Conquest of the Desert* (Phoenix, AZ: n.p., 1921), 296; Flake, *William J. Flake,* 88.

Brother and say oh if you [Charles] could have lived and me been taken. . . . It almost killed him.[38]

Lucy was also adversely affected. Each year on the anniversary of Charles's death and of his birth, Lucy's grief returned, and she mourned all over again. She was consoled, however, by her subsequent patriarchal blessing in which she was promised, "The labors of thy martyerd son will add to thy glory a thousand fold."[39] Several months after Charles's death, William, Lucy, and other family members went to Salt Lake City to attend the April 1893 general conference and the dedicatory services for the newly completed Salt Lake Temple. It was a life-changing, joy-filled opportunity, despite the arduous travel required. "We had a very cold hard trip," Lucy recorded. "It snowed and blowed and was very bad. We got in Bever . . . found our People all well and looking for us. We stayed three days changed our clothes and washed and ironed and mended and visited." The journey, which usually took six weeks or more, took about half that since, for the first time in their lives, they "took the cares [railroad cars]" from southern Utah to Salt Lake City.

In Salt Lake, Lucy "met meny Friend I had not seen si[n]ce I was a girl." They attended general conference, and she wrote, "There was so meny [people] they held meeting in the assembley Hall [on Temple Square]. . . . It is grand after being absent from Salt Lake so meny years to go to that Grand Tabernical and here that great Organ it brings tears of joy to my eyes." On April 6, 1893, Lucy "had a butifull bath put clean clothes on preparitory to go to the Temple" for its dedication. It "comenced to rain, trees were blown down in great numbers," and then it "comenced to snow just as hard as it could" while Lucy and her family waited to get inside the temple. "It had been predicted the Devil would howel and shure enough he did," wrote Lucy. Despite the chaos out-of-doors, Lucy's experience

---

38. Flake, Journals, 1:42.

39. Flake, Journals, 1:53.

at the temple dedication was "beond discription [and] butifull in every part."[40]

Two days later on Saturday, April 8, Lucy, William, and their son James "went in the great New Temple to do some work."[41] Because William and Lucy had been sealed in the Endowment House after the births of their two oldest sons, James and William Melvin were not yet sealed to their parents. Lucy recorded: "My Husband, James and myself dressed in Temple clothes. James and his next Brother [William Melvin] was adopted [sealed] to us President Joseph F. Smyth oficiating." Following the sealing, President Smith said to James, "Your names will go down on the great record as the first work in this new Temple." And then to William, "Isent [isn't] that nice Brother Flake you names Will go on the record as the first work done in this Temple that is a great credit to you."[42]

After the ordinances, "Brother J F smith took us in several different rooms showed us a round and explained many things to us." Amidst these joys and the pleasures of visiting friends and relatives in Salt Lake, Lucy had one grief: "Every one had to talk of Charles [death] wich kept the sorrow fresh in our harts all the time but there never was a sweet with out a bitter."[43] During the tour of the temple, apostle Francis M. Lyman put his arms around Lucy and in an effort to console her explained how impossible it was for some of the blessings Charles had been promised in his patriarchal blessing to have been fulfilled in this life. Elder Lyman then noted that "he had been

40. Flake, Journals, 1:46–48.

41. Flake, Journals, 1:48.

42. Flake, Journals, 1:48; "Sealings for the Dead: Children to Parents," Book A, 1893–1895, Salt Lake Temple Records, Special Collections, Family History Library, The Church of Jesus Christ of Latter-day Saints, Salt Lake City, Utah. The ordinances performed that day were the more remarkable because the opportunity to receive them was unexpected, and it came while additional dedicatory sessions were continuing. According to Salt Lake Temple records, the next temple ordinances were not performed until May 24, 1893.

43. Flake, Journals, 1:48–49.

taken in his early manhood and was busy on the other side carrying out the work he was promised he would do by the patriarch."[44]

When Lucy and her family returned to Snowflake, the uncertainties of life on the frontier resumed. Through her own tragedies and concerns, she empathized with the misfortunes of others and was available to assist them in their adversity. It seemed it was a part of her nature to assist others in need, but her availability was often made possible by older children who could carry on at home when emergencies called her to service elsewhere. Lois Hunt was one of her closest and dearest friends. Lucy and Lois had been acquainted since the days when they both lived in Beaver. Later, they were reunited in Arizona to continue their earlier association.

One morning Lois "was found almost burnt to death," Lucy mourned. "She was in the house a lone and was sweeping the floor . . . and fell in the fire when one of he[r] little daughters ran in the house her [Lois's] clothes was most all burnt off. This was the most deploriable sight I ever witnessed in my life."[45] Lois lived nearly six hours after the accident. Her husband was gone from home at the time because government agents were raiding Latter-day settlements, looking for men who had married plural wives. "Most all the sisters came [to assist Lois]," wrote Lucy, "the sisters stayed right with her doing all they could. . . . We formed a surkle [circle] around her bed and prayed." Lois remained conscious until the end, asking that the sisters not pray for her to live if living meant she would be a cripple. "It was hart rendering [for] such a good woman to have to suffer such a death. . . . The Lord was kind in releaseing her."[46]

Lois's death caused Lucy significant reflection and loneliness in the months following. Her closest confidante after Lois's death was Mary Jane West, with whom she served in the Relief Society, but

44. Roberta Flake Clayton, *Pioneer Women of Arizona* (Mesa, AZ: n.p., n.d.), 143.

45. Flake, Journals, 1:30.

46. Flake, Journals, 1:30–31.

in time Mary Jane's family moved to Utah, leaving Lucy without a close friend once more.

The value of Lucy's legacy is not so much in what happened to her but in what she did with it: in the midst of intense trial, she endured. She prayed through her day-to-day struggles and was able to find "meny times of rejoiceing."[47] And she recorded her daily experiences so that subsequent generations could share them and understand her better through them.

Lucy Hannah White Flake's life extended until Saturday, January 27, 1900.[48] Her eulogy said: "We deeply deplore her loss and . . . pray that we may emulate her honest, upright course in life, that our reward may be as sure as we feel dear Sister Lucy Flake's will be."[49]

47. Flake, Journals, 1:55.

48. "Snowflake City Cemetery: December 13, 1878–April 30, 1997" (unpublished manuscript, ca. 1997), s.v. "Lucy Hannah White Flake," 3. The cause of Lucy's death was appendicitis. Larson, "Obituary."

49. Larson, "Obituary."

Chapter 7

"I Will Put My Trust in Him"

Mary Jane Dilworth Hammond (1831–1877)

Alisha Erin Hillam

Biographical Sketch

Mary Jane Dilworth was an early Latter-day Saint convert, teacher, and missionary whose experiences crossing the plains as a pioneer were preparation for the rich and challenging situations in which she found herself afterward. She was born in Uwchlan, Chester County, Pennsylvania, on July 29, 1831, to Caleb and Eliza Wollerton Dilworth. In 1845, at the age of fourteen, she was baptized into The Church of Jesus Christ of Latter-day Saints, and she and her family soon joined the Saints in Nauvoo and then in Winter Quarters. At age fifteen, Mary Jane joined one of the first wagon trains to reach the Salt Lake Valley.[1]

---

1. Mary Jane belonged to the Jedediah M. Grant–Willard Snow Company and arrived in the Salt Lake Valley on October 4, 1847, less than ten weeks after the first wagon train arrived. "Jedediah M. Grant–Willard Snow Company (1847)," Mormon Overland Travel Database, 1847–68, The Church of Jesus Christ of Latter-day Saints, accessed April 19, 2012, http://mormontrail.lds.org.

Under the direction of Brigham Young, who had learned of Mary Jane's efforts at teaching children as they traveled west, Mary Jane began teaching school in the Old Fort in the winter of 1847–1848, making her one of the first schoolteachers in Utah history. A year later, on November 11, 1848, she married Francis Asbury Hammond. Francis was a sailor by trade who had been severely injured in an accident near the Sandwich (Hawaiian) Islands. After his recovery, Francis sailed to California, where he was introduced to the gospel of Jesus Christ, was baptized, and, less than a year later, joined the Saints in the Salt Lake Valley. There he soon met and married Mary Jane.

In 1851, the Hammonds' lives drastically changed with a mission call issued to Francis—back to the Sandwich Islands. Like only a few other missionaries, Francis took his wife with him. Mary Jane thus joined a small but strong and faithful number of Latter-day Saint women who journeyed with their missionary husbands. At this time, their first child was six months old.

For the next six years, Francis preached the gospel to the island natives while Mary Jane supported the family by teaching school and doing needlework. She also helped the Church in various capacities and bore three more children. Despite her exotic surroundings, Mary Jane's struggles were not so different from those that women face today, and the example of her faith resonates all the more strongly for these similarities, even as one admires her courage and determination to serve the Lord in her unusual and difficult situations.

The Hammonds returned to Utah Territory in 1857. The next eight years brought more children (making a total of twelve),[2] various moves in the Ogden area, and a summer mission to the

---

2. Francis Asbury Hammond (1850–1876), Samuel Smith Hammond (1853–1916), Fletcher Bartlett Hammond (1855–1919), Mary Moiselle Hammond Halls (1857–1934), George Albert Hammond (1857–1879), William Edmund Hammond (1861–1879), Lizzie Fontella Hammond (1863–1866), Eliza Dilworth Hammond Peterson (1866–1888), Joseph Heber Hammond (1869–1952), Luella

Sandwich Islands for Francis in 1865. When he returned, the family settled in Huntsville, Utah, where Francis was called to be bishop. Mary Jane served as the Relief Society president there until her death on June 6, 1877, at the age of forty-five.[3]

Life Experiences

The following excerpts are from a diary Mary Jane began in 1853, two years after arriving in the Sandwich Islands and on the day her second child was born. At this time, the Hammonds were well established in their island life. Mary Jane worked to support her family financially by teaching school and was very busy fulfilling her additional responsibilities. She discusses the trials of teaching unruly students, caring for her children, maintaining a home and a school after giving birth, caring for the sick, struggling to feel adequate in Church assignments, and interacting with semipermanent guests. This all takes place against the backdrop of a woman desperately homesick for her family and her often-absent missionary husband, their struggle to earn enough money on which to survive, and the difficulties of living in a land that was foreign to them. Despite these challenges, however, Mary Jane's writings are laced with statements of faith in the Lord and gratitude for all He had given her and her family.

> Tues. 15th of April 1[8]53 This day suffering with child birth. 1/4 before 6.o.c. [o'clock] pm was delivered of a fine son[4] weighing 9 lbs all the assistance was two native women

---

Adelaide Hammond (1871–1922), Maybell Ophelia Hammond Fielding Thomas (1872–1938), and Amelia May Hammond Allred (1877–1910).

3. Orson F. Whitney, "Mary Jane Dilworth Hammond," *History of Utah*, 4 vols. (Salt Lake City, UT: George Q. Cannon & Sons, 1904), 4:151–53, 326; "In Memory of Utah's First School Teacher," *Relief Society Magazine* 8, no. 10 (October 1921): 586–87.

4. Samuel Smith Hammond, the second child of Mary Jane and Francis, often referred to as S. S. or Samuel S.

but the lord was merciful un to me and he shall have the glory. So ends this eventful day.

~~Whens.~~ Sat 16th very comfortable the babe is quite well Mr Hammond teaching school. Set up and put up my hair no milk for the boy to day.

~~Thurs.~~ Sun 17th very comfortable. Mr Hammond imployed in tending to the house affairs as we have no one to help us. no servants. Mr Hawkin, Br Woodbury is here all gone to meeting. So end the day.

Mond 18th Mr H. Commenced school. The baby grows finely his left foot is little crooked. Set up to day took a new schoolar.

Tues 19th [18]53 Set up all day but quite weak. The boy is well he sucks like a old fellow.

When[esday] 20th [18]53 I commenced school to day, quit[e] weak but Mr Hammond has anought [enough] to do besides teach school quite a bad cole [cold] baby sleeps good. . . .

~~Fhad~~[riday], April 22 beautiful morning teaching school. I feel to thank my heavenly Father day by day for his kindness unto us Mr H. blessed our little babe to day, being eight day old.[5] F A jun[6] has a bad cold. . . .

Fri 29th the children is all well little babe is well. We have his little foot bound with little boards and I think it will become straight

Sat April 30th all well, teaching school, children learn fast,

---

5. Howard, Autobiography, 9.

6. Francis Asbury Hammond Jr., the eldest child of Mary Jane and Francis, was often referred to as F. A. Jun. or Frankey.

little Tommey is a very good boy. I have to work pretty hard sewing and tending to my house affairs.

Sun May 1, 1[8]53 all alone with the children. Mr Hammond at meeting. Quite lonely think a great deal of home. . . .

Sund. Nov. 6th [18]53 very pleasent wether all s[t]ill and quiet all gone to meeting. I have a very bad head ache. I should like to be at home in the mountains.

Mond 7th [18]53 . . . Sis [Jane] Lewis is going to live with us for sometime for she has no home of her own. I have a large family to do for and is very hard for me but I trust in the Lord for help.

Tue. Nov 8th [18]53 still keeping my school. Bro Tanner, Woodbury, [and] Green all here. Mr Hammond shoemaking. I do not like to see him working for that is not his mission. When he is off preaching then I feel the best. . . .

Mond Nov 14 [18]53 commenced my school with 14 schoolars. The children learn quite fast I love to teach them when I have no small babes to tend to. . . . Commenced a pair of garment[s] for Mr. Hammond. . . .

Wed Nov. 16 [18]53. Sister Lewis is still with us as she is not very well expects to stop with us for sometime. S S. is not well. Very cross. He is cutting his 2 upper teeth. . . . Still keeping school I am not very well. . . .

Fri Nov. 18th all well with the exception of our cold. Mr. Hd is shoemaking I do not like to have him working at his trade for he was not sent for that buisness but to preach the everlasting gospel to this fallen nation—something more important than shoemaking for my school will keep us, and buy our plase [place]. . . .

Tues Nov 22 [18]53 . . . The brethren [in Kawai] have had hard times they have ~~had~~ meen [been] in confinement for several day[s]. I have been washing this morning. S.S. is well he is commenceing to stand up by chairs, creeps all over the floor. Good deal of trouble. F A jun. is well his cold is better. . . .

Sun. Nov 27 [18]53 very rainy and bad wether there was a gentleman here this morning wanting me to take a little girl about 1½ years old to keep as my own. I do not know wether I can take her or not for I have a great deal to do to teach school and tend to my children, cook and wash, iron, sew for them all. I know it is a great undertaking but the Lord blesses us every day and I will put my trust in him to give me health and strength and any thing to do good I am willing to [go] forward on his cause. . . .

Frid ~~Nov 31~~ D[ecember] 2 [18]53 this day imployed in making a pare of pants for Tommey and teaching school. About 1. o. clock Bro N. Tanner arrived here from *Molokai* he is not well bad cold—it is the changing of the wether and all of us has bad colds. Sis Lewis is getting fat but she will not think so. S. S. is growing finely he is well with the exception of a bad cold. F. A. jun. is well better than he was. . . .

Sat Dec[ember] 3 received a letter from Bro R A Allred he says that Sis Gaston is ready to come in to live with us whenever Mr H. goes after her. I am very glad for I need some help very much for my school takes up all my time. If she will help me I shall feel first rate for I do not have much help. . . .

Sun. Dec 4 [18]53 this being sunday alters the scene for week day—they are all about alike. Mr H atended meeting this fore noon while I washing up my boys and my self

after past 2. O Clock held meeting here about 30 in all Bro.
Tanner preached on the first principals preach[ed] well.
Mr H. spoke after wards. Spoke good. They pade [paid]
good attention. I had to be chorester and that goes very
hard. If I could it would alter the case but I cannot so it
makes it still worse. Little S. S. was some woresome [worri-
some] but F. A. was very good sat still. . . .

Teus Dece 8 [18]53 This day we took Antony Lakes
Daughter Lucy Ann to take care of by the year she is one
year and a half old. Little F. A. is quite sick with a fever and
a cold.

Wed. 9 [18]53 the little girl Lucy seem[s] very quiet she
has a bad cold and bowel complaint. There was a native girl
came to help me for I have quite a good deal to do. 9 in
famiely [family] to do for, 4 is children. . . .

Wed[nesday, December 21] geting tolerable well. Mr H. is
shoemaking and I am teaching school so we are like paul the
prophet when he was on a mission he hired himself a house
for 2 years. I think he must of worked hard like us. . . .

Sun Jan[uary] the 8 [1854] Sunday arose clear wether. Bros
have all gone to meeting S. S. had in the morning a severe
attacked of ear ache I walked the house with him for a about
one hour. M H administered to him and a few minutes he
was better. Faith is the grand moving cause. Without faith
what would we be like? . . .

Tues Jan 10th [18]54 not so many schalars to day. The children love to come to school, Sis Lewis is making a shirt for
Mr Hammond. I have had my feelings hurt a great many
times and so this evning we had some words but it was for
the best. We found each other out better than we ever did
before when there was a understanding it was all right. She
is a very difficult woman to get along with. It would pushe

the best of women.[7] Cleaned house to day and very tired so ends this day.

Tues. J[anuary] 31. [18]54. this is the last day of the month. Paulo brought me some talou kaai [and] gave me some poi. I feel thankful for it for our purse is low and food is high and it is hard times for us but the Lord is kind and remembers us with kindness and praise be unto him.

Mond Feb 27th [18]54 this day ingaged in washing and cleaning bedbugs just discovered that we had any. They came from Sister Lewis things for she was very much troubled with them so that is the way I came with them. I am very sorry but with carefull observing and scallding I think we will get read [rid] of them. . . .

Sat April 22th [18]54 School but half a day. I had to give up to day and lay down although it was against my will. I am getting quite thin I think if Mother was to see me she would hardly know me for I am so old looking and poor. . . .

Mond. April th24 /54 Taken quite sick not able to write up my journal so I will write my feelings as far as I can remember. I have been sick have had many a dull feeling. I never was so home sick since I left home. My faith seem seemed to leave me. I had a very bad cough and I felt somewhat frightened, when Mr Hammond would administer to me I would feel quite well for a short time then the evil spirits would tell me I would have to lay my body here and that I best have a doctor for I could not obtain faith enough to be healed. So axcidently there was a doctor came to see Mr Hammond on buisiness. The judge came with him so the judge spok[e] as it would be good for the doctor to examine me so he

7. Jane Lewis finally left Mary Jane's home on January 16, 1854, to join her husband, Philip B. Lewis, in Honolulu.

done so and pernounced me quite bad much worse then I thought I was. My liver affected and other complaints. In stead of feeling worse thinking I surely would die I finely [finally] thought the doctor did not know any thing although he was counted a skillful doctor but I was disgusted and feeling ashamed of my little faith. I wanted no more of him and thought I would trust in my God that made [me]. If he created me he surely can heal me and from that time I commen[ce]d to get better and felt to trust in my heave[n]ly Father and every day I grew better. . . .

Sund June 6th [4th] [18]54 This being a fine morning I accompanyed Mr H to Native meeting. I had to be Chorister (quite a cross) quite a congregation. Dismissed at past 10 at 2. o:clock I whent with Mr H. to English meeting. I to be chorister. 19 in number. Paid good attention Mr H. preached from Acts on setting up the kingdom of god. A good meeting I enjoyed my self. . . .

Sat July 15 The Bros Allreds arrived here on their way to conference we are all well I dismissed my school to day for 3 weeks or untill I returned from *Honolulu.*

Mond July 17th [18]54 about day light, Mr Hammond was called up to go and baptise a man by the name of *John Evens.* Imployed in getting ready for our voyage to Honolulu. About 5 o clock we left home. Left Samuel S. with Sis Gaston, and the Bro Allreds, Mr Hammond, Francis A jun, and my self [left]. I felt very sory to leave Samuel S but I thought it was for the best so we had prayers and Father blessed Samuel S and bid them good bye. . . .

Thurs. July the 27 [18]54 conference closed at twelve o clock in the after noon we had a excellent meeting every one spok[e]. B Woodbury spoke in toungs Mr. Hammond interpreted. It was good, a cheering to our souls on these

Lands. . . . I neve[r] felt so full in all my live [life]. I hardly could suppress my feeling knowing that it was the Last time that I would here [hear] the sounds of the first Elders voices on these Lands. It made me feel joyful and sad but I injoyed my self very well so much that I would not of mist [missed] it for a good deal.

in the evning we . . . had a blessing meeting. I never heard such blessing[s] pronounced apon [upon] anyone as was then. When they called me to have me blessed I thought there was not much for me for I had not done much but Mr Hammond was mouth [and] he pourd out as good [a] blessing as I evey [ever] heard. When he was done then Bro Karren blessed me seemingly [as] if his heart was full of blessings for me. When he was done Bro George blessed me. Bros prop[he]sied to me that I would be a mighty woman in Zion that there would be none might[i]er than I that I should have a mighty posterity and many other good bless-ing which I just forgoten. I feel thankful that I have had the priveledge of having such blessing pronounced upon me and that the Elders have blessed me. May I eve[r] be blessed by them and Lord still may bless me for ever that I may live as a woman of god praising him and giving him the glory in all thing[s] that I may prove faithful that I may be crowned as Sarah of old that it may said of me "well done good and faithful handmaiden." . . .

I never shall forget the parting of our brethren. I felt sad to part with them I felt almost bad as I did when I left home. They where good men and done a good work on these Lands they all was loved. It seemed somewhat Lonesome after they whent but we felt glad to see them start for there homes. . . .

I have been gone 3 weeks. We landed at Lahaina next day at noon. . . . O how glad I was when I reached my little pleasant home and found them all well. I felt to praise my heavenly father for his kindness to me for preserving us ove[r] the mighty deep and brought us to see our little family in health and strength. . . .

Mond Oct th[e] 2 [18]54 up by dailight this morning baking some cakes for Mr H for he is going to *Lanai*. . . . We bid him good morning and off he went. how lonesome it is when he is absent for when he is at home all is right. He is all I have to comfort me in a foreign land and amongst strangers but when he is gone all is drearyness but I try to be as contented as I can be for I know we did not come here to live together but we must bear well all trials let [them] be what they may. . . .

Wed Oct 4th [18]54 Heard from home very cheering news. A letter from *P[arley] P. P[ratt]*. He says that Bros Lewis, and Hammons need not be in any hurry in returning home but be goverend by the spirit and let that dictate & that was very hard but I reconcile my self in thinking that I am on the Lord[’s] erand and let his will be done but I cryed quite a good deal for I desire to see my Dear Old Mother once [more] but I must be patient and indure to the end. We received a letter from Rebecca, Lavina, Ann & Maria,[8] and o comforting they were especialy at that time for I was just thinking of home pretty strong and they were so cheering and comforting to us that I feel quite in good spirits. . . .

Thurs Oct 5th [18]54 All well to day in school. About 8. o clock in the evening arived the new Brethren from the [Salt Lake] valley. 6 of them came from Oahu. . . . little Josep[h] [F.] Sm[ith][9] is going to stop here. . . .

8. These women and Martha were Mary Jane’s sisters.

9. Joseph F. Smith served as a missionary in the Sandwich Islands from 1854 until 1857. He was fifteen at the beginning of his mission, hence Mary Jane’s references to him as “little Joseph.” He became an apostle in July 1866, a member of

Sund Oct. 8th [18]54 This is sunday morning there was no Early morning meeting. about 10. oclock there was 6 gather[ed] to meeting. Bro Joseph and myself whent [went] in had a little meeting and then dismissed. They were very anxious to have Bro Joseph speak they thought surely he could speak the language. They seem to have a great deal of love for him. All well. Samuel S. beats any thing I ever saw for his fun he climbs every were that he can get and up to all monkey shines. Frankey the same. . . .

Sund. Nov. 15th Thes[e] few weeks I have been ingaged in sewing, teaching school and tending to my domestics affairs and they are many. . . . For these week[s] Mr Hammond has been gone to and fro. He has no stop[p]ing place any more as it were, here and there. . . . Mr Hammond is over to *Lanai.* Mr Hammond has got a Native woman and man to come to live with us which makes 10, in famiely and there is not one of them that I can depend upon. The young woman that is living with us is nothing but an expense she has nothing but to depend on us for clothing and every thing else. I am geting very tired of it and all depend on my school for every thing. I feel like stoping it and then perhaps our famiely will stop. O when will the time come when we can return home and join our friends? I feel old. And a great deal is resting on me. . . .

Sund. Nov. the 15 [18]54 I have been so ingaged that I really have not had time to keep up my journal as I should have done. My labors have been as here to fore every day, just the same. . . . When will the time come for us to leave these *Islands?* O I must be patient and wait and be a wise woman and not get in such a hurry but wait for the *Lords*

---

the Quorum of the Twelve in October 1867, and president of The Church of Jesus Christ of Latter-day Saints in 1901.

time. Mr. Hammond is on the other side of the mountain about 25 or 30, miles from here. . . . I must be contented with my lot and tend to my concerns. . . .

Tues. Nov the 20th [18]54 Early this morning Mr Hammond returned home he is quite well. . . . Mr Hammond was on a tour round the Island and I felt very lonesome not a friend to assist me or comfort me but all I had was he that rules all things and he blessed me and the children. Mr Hammond has been gone a great deal since last July and I have felt his lose [loss] very much. . . . Bro. P[arley] P. P[ratt] has writen to us very often the last letters say we can return home as soon as we can find the means and I Pray that we me [may] obtain the means and return home to the mountains. I hope by next July or next spring we may be able to return. . . . I have to indure much but I hope I may indure to the end and be found faithful in well doing.[10]

It would be three more years before Mary Jane returned to Utah Territory, where she eventually settled in Huntsville. There she served as Relief Society president for more than a decade until her death on June 6, 1877, at the age of forty-five.

Mary Jane's experiences in the Sandwich Islands are inspiring. She was a normal woman who clung to her faith through the trials she faced. Her faith is encouraging, often because so many of her trials span place and time. They are the same ones that women continue to face today: difficult callings, illness, the challenges of young motherhood, financial struggles, working to support a family, dealing with difficult guests, feeling overwhelmed, and being far from

---

10. Mary Jane Dilworth Hammond, Missionary Diary, 1853–1855, Holograph, vol. 1, pp. 1–3, 22–26, 28, 31, 34, 39, 47–49, 54–57, 63–68, Francis A. Hammond Collection, L. Tom Perry Special Collections, Harold B. Lee Library, Brigham Young University, Provo, Utah.

loved places and people—in addition to the complications of living in a foreign country. Throughout these difficulties, Mary Jane's faith stands firm. She credits the Lord with her family's care and successes, no matter what trials she endures. Her example remains relevant for women today who, like Mary Jane, hope to "endure to the end and be found faithful in well doing."

Chapter 8

"I Had Made God My Friend"

ELIZABETH ANDERSON HOWARD (1823–1893)

Steven L. Staker

BIOGRAPHICAL SKETCH

Elizabeth Anderson was born on July 12, 1823, at Carlow, County Carlow, Ireland, to Robert and Lucretia Ward Anderson.[1] Her father was a successful tallow chandler (candle maker) who dabbled in politics and published several long poems expressing his philosophies. Although Presbyterian, both Robert and Lucretia had roots in Ireland's Quaker community, the Society of Friends. Elizabeth was the oldest of four children: she had one brother and two sisters. On June 9, 1841, Elizabeth married William Howard (1815–1890) at Carlow, and she eventually had ten children, whom she called "my treasures."[2] After joining The Church of Jesus Christ of

---

1. "Elizabeth Howard," in Andrew Jenson, *Latter-day Saint Biographical Encyclopedia,* 4 vols. (Salt Lake City, UT: Andrew Jenson History Company, 1901–36), 4:187; "Death of Elizabeth Howard," *Deseret News [Weekly],* March 18, 1893.

2. Elizabeth Howard, June 13, 1868, Diaries and Account Books, 1868–1893, Photocopy of holograph, Elizabeth A. Howard Collection, L. Tom Perry Special

Latter-day Saints in 1851, the Howards emigrated to Utah and lived initially in the Salt Lake Thirteenth Ward. Later, they moved to Big Cottonwood and flourished economically.

Elizabeth associated with other leading Latter-day Saint women in Utah and traveled with them throughout the West to visit Relief Societies.[3] An advocate of women's causes, she served in ward and stake Relief Society presidencies, as a counselor to Mary Isabella Horne in the Senior and Junior Cooperative Retrenchment Association, on the board of directors of the women's Deseret Hospital, and as president of the Salt Lake County Woman Suffrage Association, and she participated in politics.[4] Elizabeth's friend Eliza R. Snow dedicated a poem to Elizabeth that included this tribute: "As a very dear Sister I've valued your worth, / Since our first-born acquaintance on this nether earth."[5]

In 1868 Elizabeth and her husband, William, were called to serve a mission to England. After they returned to Utah in 1869, William married a plural wife, Maria Lucretia Mulhall (1849–1889), on September 27, 1869, in the Salt Lake Endowment House. He became disaffected from the Church and divorced Elizabeth in

---

Collections, Harold B. Lee Library, Brigham Young University, Provo, Utah, hereafter cited as BYU Special Collections. Elizabeth and William's children were Catherine Alice (1843–1928), Lucretia Hannah (1845–1909), William Jr. (1847–1914), Robert Anderson (1848–1849), Elizabeth Bennett (1850–1870), Lucas Babington (1851–1914), Mary Webster (1853–1923), Thomas Anderson (1854–1944), Lockhart Anderson (1856–1894), and Erin John Anderson (1858–1933).

3. For an example of Elizabeth's travels, see "Home Affairs," *Woman's Exponent* 4, no. 3 (July 1, 1875): 21.

4. Kenneth W. Godfrey, Audrey M. Godfrey, and Jill Mulvay Derr, *Women's Voices: An Untold History of the Latter-day Saints, 1830–1900* (Salt Lake City, UT: Deseret Book, 1982), 18. Elizabeth served as president of the Salt Lake County Woman Suffrage Association from October 1891 to October 1892. "Death of Elizabeth Howard."

5. Eliza R. Snow, "Inscribed to Sister Howard," in *Eliza R. Snow: The Complete Poetry,* ed. Jill Mulvay Derr and Karen Lynn Davidson (Provo, UT: Brigham Young University Press; Salt Lake City: University of Utah Press, 2009), 670–72.

1880,[6] possibly to avoid prosecution for bigamy, and stayed with his younger wife. Elizabeth remained faithful in the Church. In 1892 she became a member of the Relief Society general board, and while attending a women's conference in Grantsville, Utah, she was suddenly taken ill, dying there on March 12, 1893.

LIFE EXPERIENCES

After Elizabeth Anderson Howard's death, Emmeline B. Wells wrote the following tribute that gives insight into Elizabeth's life and describes her personality and strengths:

> Among those women of the past whom I dearly loved, I count one among the dearest, Elizabeth Howard, we called her our representative Irish woman, and she was fond of the title; for she dearly loved her country.
>
> In her person she was a magnificent specimen of womanhood. She had been carefully educated, and her opportunities for culture had been excellent. Her father was a man of broad and advanced views, and she had learned much of public matters concerning Ireland by listening to the conversation of Irish gentlemen who visited her father's house. This had been helpful in broadening her own mind and her views of life and its affairs. Moreover, she was so amiable and tactful in presenting her side of the question, that she made friends of those who held entirely adverse opinions.
>
> The younger people were very fond of her society, she was vivacious, witty, winning and attractive. . . . Sister Howard was a gifted speaker, had a full, round-toned voice, and was never at a loss for words to express her sentiments.
>
> Elizabeth Howard was one of the few women in the

---

6. Salt Lake County Probate Court Divorce Records, 1877–1885, Book D, pp. 463–64, Family History Library, The Church of Jesus Christ of Latter-day Saints, Salt Lake City, Utah, hereafter cited as Family History Library.

early days who dressed well, who had rich clothing and handsome jewelry, yet she carried herself in such a becoming manner, that one never felt embarrassed because she was better dressed; she was generous in giving to her friends and to the needy; it seemed to be a part of her nature. . . . In those days when so few people could entertain sumptuously, the Howard home on Cottonwood, was a resort for the young folks who wanted to have a good time. . . . Those who could drive out enjoyed the open-hearted hospitality of the Howards, and those of us who loved rare china, cut glass and silverware and fine Irish table linen, of which there was a scarcity in those days, were sure to be favored with a sight of these luxuries on occasions when Sister Howard entertained her special friends. . . . Her faith in the Gospel was firm and steadfast, and she loved to labor for the cause of truth, and the advancement and onward progress of women's work in the Church.

Sister Howard was one of the foremost champions of equal suffrage and participation of women in the affairs of education and government.[7] She was a fine missionary, never cared for [about] the hardships of journeyings, when jolting over rough roads in lumber wagons, she was a most delightful companion; she had always been, and was during her life a great reader, and her mind was stored with useful knowledge, history, poetry and fiction, and her Irish wit was helpful in keeping up one's spirits when everything went wrong. . . .

. . . Notwithstanding her light-heartedness and buoyancy of spirit which carried her easier over every rough place

---

7. See Steven L. Staker, "Family, Feminism, and Freud: Mothers and Sons at Utah's Constitutional Convention" (Paper presented at the Annual Meeting of the Mormon History Association, Snowbird, UT, 1996), pp. 4–5, Church History Library, The Church of Jesus Christ of Latter-day Saints, Salt Lake City, Utah, hereafter cited as Church History Library.

in life, yet deep down in her soul was the undying love of the truth, for which she left her native land and kindred, and for which she was ready to make any sacrifice required. Such women are a joy along the pathway of other people's lives; they help to lighten the load of care that is a part of all our lives here in this mortal existence.[8]

Preparation to Hear the Gospel

Elizabeth's father was a Presbyterian elder, and during Elizabeth's teenage years their congregation was led by the Reverend Warrand Carlile. Elizabeth was also greatly influenced by the philosophy of the Society of Friends. She described the circumstances of her religious upbringing that predisposed her to accept the restored gospel:

> I was educated strictly moral and religious. I was never allowed to shirk from my prayers, night and morning. My mother generally read family prayers with her children in her own room. The servants being Roman Catholics of course would not come, but when we had Protestants they always attended. I never remember my Father being present at these readings. I never asked why. I used to think he looked on this Custom of my mothers as a little too religious. I only thought so. I never heard him hint any thing of the Kind, but I many a time heard him remark, when in conversation with ministers of the different denominations he was acquainted with "That the Religion Jesus taught would be restored again." I looked on him as a model of perfection, I also considered him a Prophet for I well rec[o]llect hearing him read for his friends, paragraphs out of what he called "My Prophecy." . . . [He] very much rejoiced at his predictions being accomplished.

---

8. Emmeline B. Wells, "L.D.S. Women of the Past: Personal Impressions," *Woman's Exponent* 3, no. 9 (May 1, 1908): 65–66.

[He] never was considered very religiously inclined, neither was I. I had sence enough to see for myself that there
was something wanted that none of the Sects that I was
acquainted with [(]and that was five or six,) corresponded
with the teachings of Jesus and His Apostles. Therefore I
felt inclined to *wait* for the time my father used to speak of
would come. Tho young when thinking of the "Hereafter" I
had the idea that something would transpire to bring to pass
what so many of the old Prophets wrote and prophecyed
about. I recollect that our revered Minister "Rev. Warrand
Carlisle" used to pray every Sunday for "the gathering of
the Jews to Jerusalem." I fully beleived such time would
come. Mr. Carlisle and my Father had full faith in a literal
Millennium, not a spiritual one, as many of the sectarian
ministers of this present time try to persuade themselves
and their votaries to beleive in. I looked forward to all these
things being literally fulfilled. . . .

I am amused now when I look back to the time I went
with my dear mother to the Methodist "Watch Night." Just
before the old clock struck twelve there was a profound si-
lence, after that, what crying and sobbing. I tryed to cry too
(least they might think I was a hardened Sinner) just to keep
them Company, but I certainly did not know what we all
cryed for.[9]

Elizabeth was only seventeen years of age when her mother died.
Shortly before her eighteenth birthday, Elizabeth married William
Howard. William owned a wire working factory in Belfast and had
once studied to become a Methodist minister. She moved with him
to Belfast and joined his church. But this did not satisfy her search
for truth, and she recorded that "there was a want in my heart I

9. Elizabeth Howard, Autobiography, Photocopy of holograph, pp. 3–5,
Elizabeth A. Howard Collection, BYU Special Collections.

could not account for. I felt looking forward to something. I had still the feeling to '*wait.*'"[10]

Elizabeth gave birth to two daughters and then two sons during the 1840s. While William continued with his business, he became involved with the Orangemen who opposed the Catholics in Ireland. During the decade of the Irish potato disaster, William joined a lodge and was elected master. Elizabeth did not approve of this group and recorded that their tactics "disgusted me."[11]

The Howards were not severely affected by the potato famine that began in 1845–46, and Belfast was generally still thriving as a business and commercial center. Elizabeth's record tells of one Orange Day[12] in Belfast: "I think it was the 12th of July 1848, that my husband gave a dinner to the members of his 'Lodge,' their wives, sisters, &c, &cc. when about three hundred persons sat down to partake of the 'fat of the Land.'" His next birthday, the Lodge presented him with a very fine Bible.[13]

Shortly afterwards, a cholera epidemic in Belfast affected the Howard family directly. To Elizabeth it must have seemed as though biblical plagues were wreaking havoc in her beloved native land in preparation for the final judgment. The first peak of this epidemic occurred in March 1849.[14] Its cause was primarily the stagnation of untreated sewage in the city streets and its subsequent release into the water supply.[15] Although the disease struck hardest among the

---

10. Howard, Autobiography, 6.

11. Howard, Autobiography, 6.

12. Orange Day is the annual celebration of the victory in July 1690 of the Protestant William, Prince of Orange, over the Catholic king of England, James II, at a battle in Ireland's Boyne River valley. It represents the triumph of Protestantism over Catholicism in Britain, and its celebration continues to ignite passionate feelings in the Republic of Ireland, where most of the people are Catholic.

13. Howard, Autobiography, 7.

14. Jonathan Bardon, *Belfast: An Illustrated History* (Dundonald, Northern Ireland: Blackstaff Press, 1983), 101.

15. Christine Kinealy and Gerard MacAtasney, *The Hidden Famine: Poverty,*

poor, nobody was exempt. Elizabeth's infant son, Robert Anderson Howard, contracted cholera in the month of April. Death usually came within twenty-four hours after symptoms first appeared. Ten-month-old Robert Howard did not suffer long and died April 13, 1849. Compounding her pain, Elizabeth's own "very dearly beloved Father" passed away just two weeks later. These "two great griefs" had a profound effect on Elizabeth and played an important role in preparing her to receive the message of the Restoration.[16]

Elizabeth described her religious development in Belfast and how it prepared her for the gospel:

> I had good help in taking care of my family, which gave me time to read a good deal, a taste for which I was encouraged in by my husband, one of our Preachers, Rev. W. Vance, and our family Phycisian, Doctor T. K. Wheeler, they procuring for me (what I did not get myself) the standard works of the day. We had of course our daily newspapers . . . [which] tended a good deal to prepare my mind to receive something better than anything I was acquainted at that time.
>
> We had many eminent and talented D.D.s[17] visit Belfast, especially to preach Charity Sermons. One I recollect, preaching in "Frederick St. Chapel" was so well learned in College lore, that when coming out of meeting, I over heard one person say to another, "O man! O man! Was'nt that a fine discourse. I hardly understood a word of it." I thought to myself, there were many fine long words used, and grand oratory, but there was actually nothing in it satisfying to a longing soul.

Hunger and Sectarianism in Belfast 1840–50 (London: Pluto Press, 2000), 6, 19–20.

16. Robert Anderson Howard died on April 29, 1849, in Carlow, Ireland. Howard, Autobiography, 7.

17. Doctor's of divinity.

I attended many prayer and revival meetings. At one time the latter were held several nights in succession. A beloved young friend of mine, on the third night, received the forgiveness of her sins, as she stated. She prayed and entreated for some feeling to be given her that she [might] know that she was accepted of God. She received it, she told me. "A sensation as if burning" came in her chest, it was so severe she almost fainted, but she was sure of her full acceptance by her Maker. She was exceedingly anxious I should undergo the same ordeal, by going forward to the "Anxious Seat" but I firmly declined. I never could be persuaded to go there.[18]

Conversion

Elizabeth's conversion was somewhat unusual for her times. Although many Latter-day Saints became convinced of the truth by hearing missionaries preach to large groups on the street or to congregations in public halls and churches, Elizabeth's story is an early example of member missionaries reaching out to their neighbors with friendship, conversation, and missionary literature. In Elizabeth's case her neighbors provided her a copy of Parley P. Pratt's *A Voice of Warning*. This is the story in her words:

> After ten years had passed over [1851], my husband's health became slightly impaired. He was ordered change of air, to go to the sea side for a short time, tho' in the Winter, he went and rented rooms from M^r and Mrs Daniel M. Bell at Ballygrott . . . on the shore of the Belfast Lo[ugh].
>
> The Bells were "Mormons." Having read and heard so much derogatory to them in almost every publication of the Period, I warned my husband [to] beware of them. They were a fearful bad people. I begged of him to be on his

---

18. Howard, Autobiography, 9.

guard, not listen to them, or pay any attention whatever [to] their conversation. While there I went [to] visit him. And of course had quite a desire to see a "Mormon." I expected they should l[ook un]like any thing I had ever seen.

"I went, I saw," and in six months I was "conquered." Mrs Bell was an exceedingly kind good Lady. Mr Bell appeared to me to be a most extraordinary character, he had a most peculiar method of expressing himself, and in general conversation mixing passages and ideas from the Bible quite new to me. I would say to him (sometimes as much for the sake of controversy as any thing else) "that is in your Mormon Bible, not in mine" he would answer, "Madam, it is in King James' translation." Before very long, the warning I gave my husband proved futile in regard to myself. I received with pleasure the Doctrines and principles he offered me. He lent me a book called "The Voice of Warning" such it proved to be too. I took it, my Bible, and all the Commentaries I could procure. I compared them, the Mormon Books said the Bible meant what it said, in regard to law and principle. The Commentators "supposed" that such a one translated so and so, to mean such and such, and another honestly confessed they did not know any thing about it, only they would take what such a one said for granted. It all seemed so unsatisfactory to me . . . that I came to the Conclusion I had found what I had "waited" for. I had lived to see the day that by *Revelation* the principles, manners and Customs that Jesus taught had been again restored. One principle among many I was much impressed with, "Baptism for the Dead." St. Paul touches on it in one of his letters. I was delighted with it. I was satisfied. I knew I had found what my reason, my heart, and soul had long looked for.

The Sprinkling of Infants was another subject I had often thought about. I did not pay much attention to it, some of my own ten children were never christened untill old enough to be dressed very nicely and then [I] gave an invitation to a large company to wittness the imposing ceremony. How much more preferable this religion of Mr Bells, that required Babies to be "Blessed" at eight days old,[19] and given the name they would be Known by for life, then when eight years old to be baptized [and] become members of the Church. After *that* they [are] responsible for their sins, not before. There was something so reasonable and consistent in that doctrine that I received it with joy. I also accepted the doctrine of a Personal God. The one great preposterous "Nothing" the Church of England presents to its votaries as a thing to be worshiped, I could not comprehend. I never tried. But they declare "it" to be "incomprehensible," I forgot that, The True and Living God the maker of Heavens, and the Earth, the Father of my immortal Spirit. I gloried in such a Personage and also in His Only Begotten Son, my Saviour.

Principles like these I was quite prepared to receive and could readily comprehend them. I also knew that only

---

19. An 1830 revelation required parents to bring their children "unto the elders before the church" to have them blessed. Robin Scott Jensen, Robert J. Woodford, and Steven C. Harper, eds., *Manuscript Revelation Books,* facsimile edition, first volume of the Revelations and Translations series of *The Joseph Smith Papers,* edited by Dean C. Jessee, Ronald K. Esplin, and Richard Lyman Bushman (Salt Lake City: Church Historian's Press, 2009), 83 (D&C 20:70). The typical modern practice is to bless children in a fast and testimony meeting within a few weeks of their birth. Lowell Bangerter, "Blessing of Children," in *Encyclopedia of Mormonism,* ed. Daniel H. Ludlow, 4 vols. (New York: Macmillan, 1992), 1:268. Joseph F. Smith captured an earlier practice when he wrote: "However, a father holding the higher Priesthood, may desire to bless and name his child at home, perhaps at an earlier date than would be convenient or possible for mother and babe to attend a fast meeting in the ward. Many elders desire to perform this ordinance within the circle of their own families on or about the eighth day of the child's life." *Gospel Doctrine* (Salt Lake City, UT: Deseret Book, 1970), 291.

through and by the Power of God could they be known to man, and the more I investigated the principles taught by the Latter Day Saints, the more I was satisfied that what I had long been looking for had indeed come, and in the month of August 1851, I was baptized by Mr Bell, and from that time commenced leading a new life, realizing as I did, that my sins were forgiven through obedience to the requirements of the Gospel. I felt I had a sure foundation on which to build my hopes of gaining Eternal life and felt willing to forget every thing of a worldly nature to attain it. I felt assured I had found the Truth & I was desirous my friends & Relations should also come to a knowledge of it. For this purpose, I took every opportunity of presenting to them the principles I had embraced by my books & by correspondance, but I faild to make any impression upon them. They were so wraped up in the Theories & Traditions of their Forefathers to accept or even investigate the glorious Truths, which had been once more revealed to mankind, but this did not influence me from following on in the path I had commenced to travel. I felt the Assurance day by day that God my Heavenly Father had accepted of my obedience, and I was quite satisfied that all would work out together for good & though my friends turned their backs upon me, I had the satisfaction of Knowing that indeed I had made God my friend.[20]

When Elizabeth was baptized, William had already been a member for two months. He was baptized on June 21, 1851, by Elder Gilbert Clements, who was laboring at the time as a missionary in Belfast.[21] One of the first consequences of the Howards' conversion

20. Howard, Autobiography, 9–13.

21. Missionary Book A, The Church of Jesus Christ of Latter-day Saints, 11, #426, Family History Library.

came when William determined that he should sever his relationship with the Orangemen. Elizabeth said he could not reconcile
"his religion and any thing antagonistic to 'Peace and good Will.'"
She happily approved this decision because of her opposition to the
Orangemen tactics. William sent his resignation to the lodge, but
they "indignantly refused" to accept it so that they could have "the
pleasure and satisfaction of expelling him." They said, according
to Elizabeth, "[we] might as well have a Roman Catholic Priest for
'Master' as a 'Mormon.'"[22]

Emigration

Elizabeth wrote that one principle taught by the Latter-day
Saints caused her "sincere sorrow": the concept of gathering to
America. She described the idea of her departure from her "beloved
native Land . . . and all that seemed near & dear" as a "great trial."
She struggled with the idea for two days, praying earnestly to receive
a testimony that it was "a Command from God." Her quest for con-
firmation was successful, and she "felt perfectly resigned to endure
the annoyances & privations Incident to such a long journey." Her
family "commenced making preparations" to emigrate, and William
"dispose[d] of his bussiness and property" before leaving.[23]

In February 1853 they left for Liverpool, England, and then for
Philadelphia in the United States. The Howards traveled with the
Bells, who had introduced them to the Church. When they departed
from England, there were six Howard children, ranging in age
from nine years to six weeks old. The immigrants journeyed overland from Philadelphia to St. Louis, where they stayed for several
months, and then traveled on to Council Bluffs, Iowa, for the trek
west. Just as they were leaving Council Bluffs, Elizabeth was thrown

----

22. Howard, Autobiography, 7
23. Howard, Autobiography, 14.

from a horse-drawn carriage. Despite this accident, they arrived in Utah "safe and well" in September.[24]

Mission to the British Isles

Almost fifteen years later, Elizabeth left her seven unmarried children in the care of her trusted friend Hannah Tapfield King and accompanied her husband on a mission to the British Isles. Eliza R. Snow promised that her children would be safe until her return, and Elizabeth placed great faith in this promise.[25] About her mission experience Elizabeth wrote:

> In 1868 I went with my husband on a mission to England; had a pleasant, interesting time, and astonished many who thought "no good thing could come out of Utah." While there I was the subject of no little curious questioning, and therefore had many opportunities of explaining the principles of the gospel. There was one principle I gloried in telling them about—the principle of plural marriage; and I spared no pains in speaking of the refining, exalting influence that was carried with the doctrine, wherever entered into in a proper manner.[26]

The Howards visited family members and acquaintances during their mission. Elizabeth told of her conversion and bore her testimony of the gospel in England, Ireland, Scotland, and the Isle of Man. She and her husband returned to Utah in 1869. The Howards had left Utah in a wagon, but on their return they rode from New York to Salt Lake City on the newly completed railroad.

Commenting on Elizabeth's mission, Augusta Joyce Crocheron

---

24. Edward W. Tullidge, *The Women of Mormondom* (New York: Tullidge & Crandall, 1877), 462.

25. Howard, June 14, 1868, Diaries.

26. Tullidge, *Women of Mormondom* 462–63.

observed: "Divines and others found Mrs. Howard quite ready and able to meet and answer them on every point. I[n] fact her part of the mission has often been referred to as something exceptionally creditable and important. It was at a time, too, when woman had scarcely been heard to speak upon our faith, outside the home circle."[27]

As Elizabeth visited Latter-day Saint women, she had occasion to relate her own conversion story and the circumstances surrounding it in many gatherings.[28] Her unexpected death on March 12, 1893, occurring while she visited women of the Church, seemed a fitting end for Elizabeth, who had consecrated herself to the gospel. At her funeral, her descendants were exhorted to "emulate her noble example and never swerve from the path which she had trod." Her testimony was an expression of her faith and an important part of the legacy she left to her children and the women of the Church.[29]

27. Augusta Joyce Crocheron, *Representative Women of Deseret: A Book of Biographical Sketches to Accompany the Picture Bearing the Same Title* (Salt Lake City, UT: J.C. Graham & Co., 1884), 47.

28. Records of Elizabeth's speeches are found throughout the issues of the *Woman's Exponent* and include "F. R. Society Reports," *Woman's Exponent* 12, no. 20 (March 1, 1873): 147; "Expression of Sorrow," *Woman's Exponent* 21, no. 18 (March 15, 1893): 144.

29. "Elizabeth Howard," 141.

Chapter 9

"THE LORD'S BLESSING WAS WITH US"

JANE ELIZABETH MANNING JAMES (1822–1908)
Margaret Blair Young

BIOGRAPHICAL SKETCH

Born on September 22, 1822, in Wilton, Fairfield County, Connecticut—the daughter of former slaves Isaac and Fillis Manning—Jane Elizabeth Manning was baptized in 1842 into The Church of Jesus Christ of Latter-day Saints, which brought her great reproach. This was the beginning of many trials for Jane as a convert of African descent. Denied passage on the ship that was to transport her family from Buffalo, New York, the Mannings (including Jane, her mother, several siblings, and two in-laws) braved the elements to walk the entire distance to Nauvoo, Illinois. Once they arrived, they encountered much "rebuff" in the city that Jane described as "our destined haven of rest." The rebuff ended, however, as soon as they found the home of Joseph and Emma Smith. There, they were welcomed warmly. Joseph told them they were "among friends." Eventually, Jane became a household servant to the Smiths and was even invited to be adopted to them as their child, an invitation she declined.[1]

After the deaths of Joseph and Hyrum Smith, all the Mannings but Jane remained either in Illinois or Iowa. Jane married Isaac James, and the two of them migrated with the Saints to the Salt Lake Valley with Jane's son, Sylvester, born before Jane's conversion to the Church. Jane gave birth to another son, Silas, during the journey and a daughter, Mary Ann, soon after their arrival.

Conditions were harsh as the pioneers sought to build a settlement, and food was often scarce. Though Jane had little to feed her own family, she nonetheless shared half her flour with a white pioneer, Eliza Partridge Lyman, at a time when the Lyman family was near starvation.[2]

Over the next two decades, part of which time the rest of the nation was embroiled in the Civil War, Jane worked as a laundress and soap maker in Utah, and her husband was employed as a coachman for Brigham Young. But the marriage of Jane and Isaac James did not survive; the couple divorced in 1870. As a single parent, Jane grew poorer, and she moved to a smaller home. Over the next fifteen years, she faced her greatest trials as she lost three of her eight children and seven grandchildren.

On Christmas day 1884, Jane went to President John Taylor's home, eager to ask if she might enter the temple. The response was a recommend for Jane to do baptisms for her deceased relatives. She performed many of these proxy baptisms, but she did not stop petitioning for her endowment, though her request was consistently denied.

---

1. Jane Manning James Autobiography, 1893 [ca. 1902], dictated to Elizabeth J. D. Roundy, Holograph, pp. 17, 20, Church History Library, The Church of Jesus Christ of Latter-day Saints, Salt Lake City, Utah, hereafter cited as Church History Library.

2. Eliza Maria Partridge Lyman journal, April 25, 1849, Holograph, L. Tom Perry Special Collections, Harold B. Lee Library, Brigham Young University, Provo, Utah; reprinted in Kate B. Carter, *Treasures of Pioneer History*, 6 vols. (Salt Lake City, UT: Daughters of Utah Pioneers), 2:213–85.

The final years of Jane's life brought two important men back to her: her former husband, who arrived ill and in need of care—which Jane gave him, even hosting his funeral at her home—and Isaac Lewis Manning, her brother. The two siblings, now aged, occupied designated seats in the front of the Salt Lake Tabernacle during services there.

When Jane died on April 16, 1908, the *Deseret News* reported: "Jane Manning James, an aged colored woman familiarly known as 'Aunt Jane,' passed away about noon today. . . . Few persons were more noted for faith and faithfulness than was Jane Manning James, and though of the humble of earth she numbered friends and acquaintances by the hundreds."[3]

LIFE EXPERIENCES

In her life story, Jane Manning James said she tried to set a good example "in my feeble way."[4] There was nothing feeble about her, though. She was a paradigm of faith and faithfulness in the face of sometimes unthinkable opposition.

Jane's entrance into Latter-day Saint history begins like many other conversion stories: seeking for a new religion and not being content with what she found heretofore. She describes her faith journey in her life history, as dictated to Elizabeth J. D. Roundy. The short autobiography is distinctive in its structure. Jane reports a trial or a struggle but immediately follows up with praise for God, who, she is certain, has helped her get through it. She viewed everything through a lens of faith. In the passage that follows, she describes her conversion to the Church:

> When about fourteen years old I joined the Presbyterian Church. Yet I did not feel satisfied it seemed to me there was something more that I was looking for. I had belonged

---

3. "Death of Jane Manning James," *Deseret News,* April 16, 1908.

4. James, Autobiography, 22.

to the [Presbyterian] Church about eighteen months when an Elder of the church of Jesus Christ of Latter-day Saints [who] was travelling through our country preached there. The pastor of the Presbyterian Church forbid me going to hear them as he had heard I had expressed a desire to hear them, but nevertheless I went on a sunday and was fully convinced that it was the true Gospel he presented and I must embrace it.

The following Sunday I was baptized and confirmed a member of the Church of Jesus Christ of Latter-day Saints.[5]

Her new status as a Latter-day Saint resulted in her abrupt ex-communication from her earlier church,[6] but by the time she was dismissed, Jane and her family had already left for Nauvoo, a journey that proved far more arduous than any of them had imagined. Jane gives the details of the trip and then glories in the divine help that attended them:

One year after I was baptized I started for Nauvoo with my mother Phillis Eliza Manning[7] my brothers Isaac,

<hr />

5. James, Autobiography, 15.

6. The records of the New Canaan Congregational Church (indistinguishable from the Presbyterian at that time) tell us that Jane was baptized on February 14, 1841, and then excommunicated on February 22, 1844, after her departure for Nauvoo. The record states: "The case of Jane E. Manning was further considered, and the church adopted the following preamble and resolution: Whereas Jane E. Manning has without our approbation or consent wholly withdrawn and separated herself from the fellowship of this church and has since gone to a distant part of the country (Nauvoo?, Illinois) and thus placed herself beyond the reach of this church to labor farther with her; therefore *Resolved* that we withdraw our watch and care over her, and consider her as no longer a member of this church." New Canaan Congregational Record Book, Typescript, pp. 27, 45–46, Rev. Theophilus Smith Collection, New Canaan Historical Society Library, New Canaan, Connecticut.

7. Jane's mother was known as Ph[y]llis [Fillis] Abbott during slave years and changed her name to Eliza Mead after slavery was abolished in Connecticut in 1848. Records of Jane's life, including her patriarchal blessings, usually have her

Lewis[8] and Peter,[9] my Sisters Sarah Stebbings,[10] and Angeline Manning. My brother in Law Anthony Stebbings, Lucinda Manning[11] a sister in law. . . . We started from Wilton Conn[ecticut], and travelled by Canal to Buffalo NY. We were to go to Columbus Ohio before our fares were to be collected, but they insisted on having the money at Buffalo and would not take us farther. So we left the boat, and started on foot to travel a distance of over eight hundred miles.

We walked until our shoes were worn out, and our feet became sore and cracked open and bled until you could see the whole print of our feet with blood on the ground. We stopped and united in prayer to the Lord, we asked God the Eternal Father to heal our feet and our prayers were answered and our feet were healed forthwith.[12]

As they continued their journey to Nauvoo, additional incidents occurred, including an escape from arrest because the Mannings

---

mother listed as "Fillis" (with alternate spellings), which is stricken out and replaced by "Eliza." Eliza Mead, also known as Fillis Abbott, married Cato Treadwell, a veteran of the Revolutionary War, after her first husband died. Connell O'Donovan, personal communication to Margaret Young, July 20, 2009; Henry J. Wolfinger, "A Test of Faith: Jane Elizabeth James and the Origins of the Utah Black Community," in *Social Accommodation in Utah*, ed. Clark Knowlton (Salt Lake City: University of Utah American West Center Occasional Papers, 1975), 128.

8. Isaac Lewis Manning, with his second wife, Rachel, joined the Reorganized Church of Jesus Christ of Latter Day Saints, but after the deaths of his wife and son, he went to Salt Lake City to live the remainder of his years with his sister, Jane. O'Donovan, personal communication.

9. Peter Manning was Jane's youngest brother.

10. Sarah Stebbins was married to Anthony Stebbins, to whom Joseph Smith gave a horse for the purpose of purchasing a "dear child" from slavery. Hyrum L. Andrus, *Joseph Smith: The Man and the Seer* (Salt Lake City, UT: Deseret Book, 1960), 33.

11. Lucinda Manning was the first wife of Isaac Lewis Manning.

12. James, Autobiography, 15–16.

possessed no papers identifying them as free, and challenges due to the weather and terrain. Jane concluded her report by again praising God for abiding with them:

> When we arrived at Peoria Illinois the authorities threatened to put us in jail to get our free papers. We didnt know at first what he meant for we had never been slaves, but he concluded to let us go, so we travelled on until we came to a river and as there was no bridge we walked right into the stream, when we got to the middle the water was up to our necks but we got safely across, and then it became so dark we could hardly see our hands before us, but we could see a light in the distance, so we went toward it and found it was an old Log Cabin. Here we spent the night; next day we walked for a considerable distance and staid that night in a forest, out in the open air. The frost fell on us so heavy that it was like a light fall of snow. We rose early and started on our way walking through that frost with our bare feet, until the sun rose and melted it away. But we went on our way rejoicing, singing hymns and thanking God for his infinite goodness and mercy to us, in blessing us as he had, protecting us from all harm, answering our prayers and healing our feet.[13]

Near Nauvoo, Jane and her family met a Latter-day Saint family with an ill child. Jane reported, "At La harpe we came to a place where there was a very sick child. We administered to it, and the child was healed. I found after [that] the elders had before this given it up as they did not think it could live."[14]

Having seen what they interpreted as God's mercy, the Mannings made their way to the Saints' dwelling place, arriving

---

13. James, Autobiography, 16.

14. James, Autobiography, 17.

in Nauvoo in mid to late November 1843.[15] Unfortunately, in this time of widespread prejudice against blacks and only seven years before the nation's legislature would enact the brutal Fugitive Slave Act of 1850, the family was met with "all kinds of hardship, trial, and rebuff."[16] Once again, though, Jane concluded with implicit praise to God as she described Emma Smith welcoming them into the Mansion House and Joseph blessing them:

> Sister Emma was standing in the door, and she kindly said come in, come in!
>
> Brother Joseph said to some white Sisters that was present, Sisters I want you to occupy this room this evening with some brothers and sisters that have just arrived. Brother Joseph placed the chairs around the room then he went and brought Sister Emma and Dr. [John Milton] Bernhisel[17] and introduced them to us, brother Joseph took a chair and sat down by me, and said, you have been the head of this little band, havent you? I answered Yes sir! he then said God bless

15. We can estimate the date of the arrival of the Manning family through at least one document, provided by Wolfinger in "A Test of Faith," 171n93: "The following notice from the *Nauvoo Neighbor* of December 6, 1843 is pertinent: 'About six weeks ago a company of saints arrived . . . escorted by Elder Wandal [Charles Wesley Wandell] who had in his charge a trunk belonging to Jane Elizabeth Manning:—Sister Manning was not here then but has since arrived and can obtain no intelligence of her trunk.'" We know, then, that Jane and her family arrived after late October, when the Wandell group apparently reached Nauvoo, and before December 6. A mid to late November arrival for the Mannings seems a reasonable assumption.

16. James, Autobiography, 17.

17. John Milton Bernhisel (1799–1881) served as Joseph Smith's personal physician. He later became the first delegate of Utah Territory to the U.S. House of Representatives. "John Milton Bernhisel," in Andrew Jenson, *Latter-day Saint Biographical Encyclopedia,* 4 vols. (Salt Lake City, UT: Andrew Jenson History Company, 1901–1936), 1:723–24.

you! Now I would like you to relate your experience in your travels.

I related to them all [my experience]. . . . Brother Joseph slapped Dr. Bernhisel on the knee and said, What do you think of that Dr, isn't that faith? The Dr said, Well I rather think it is, if it had have been me I fear I should have backed out and returned to my home! [Joseph Smith] then said God bless you, you are among friends, now and you will be protected. They sat and talked to us awhile, gave us words of encouragement and good counsel. We all stayed there [in the Mansion House] one week.[18]

Jane's description of her first interaction with Joseph Smith became a touchstone for what she told young women sixty-two years later when they interviewed her, elaborating further than she did in her dictated life story:

Yes, indeed, I guess I did know the Prophet Joseph. That lovely hand! He used to put it out to me. Never passed me without shaking hands with me wherever he was. Oh, he was the finest man I ever saw on earth. I did not get much of a chance to talk with him. He'd always smile, always just like he did to his children. . . . I knew it was Brother Joseph because I had seen him in a dream. . . . We had come afoot, a thousand miles. We lay in bushes, and in barns and outdoors. . . . I could not tell you, but I wanted to go to Brother Joseph.

I did not talk much to him, but every time he saw me he would say, "God bless you," and pat me on the shoulder. . . . After I saw him plain, I was certain he was a prophet because I knew it. . . . Did not have to tell me because I knew

---

18. James, Autobiography, 17.

him. I knew him when I saw him back in old Connecticut
in a vision, saw him plain and knew he was a prophet.[19]

At the Mansion House, Jane was treated well. She reported further experiences confirming her sense that she was not only "among
friends" but in a religion that would reward her faith with spiritual
gifts and unique invitations, such as the one she received from Lucy
Mack Smith, Joseph's mother:

> On the morning that my folks all left to go to work, I
> looked at myself, clothed in the only two pieces I possessed.
> I sat down and wept. Brother Joseph came into the room
> as usual and said, Good morning. Why—not crying? [I an-
> swered,] Yes sir. The folks have all gone and got themselves
> homes, and I have got none. He said yes you have, you have
> a home right here if you want it, you mustn't cry, we dry
> up all tears here. I said I have lost my trunk and all my
> clothes. . . . Brother Joseph said dont cry you shall have your
> trunk and clothes again.
> Brother Joseph went out and brought Sister Emma
> in and said Sister Emma here is a girl that says she has no
> home, havent you a home for her? "Why yes if she wants
> one." He said she does and then he left us. . . .
> The next morning she brought the clothes down in the
> base ment to wash. Among the clothes, I found brother
> Josephs [temple] Robes. I looked at them and wondered. I
> had never seen any before, and I pondered over them and
> thought about them so earnestly that the spirit made mani-
> fest to me that they pertained to the new name that is given
> the saints that the world knows not of. I didnt know when I
> washed them or when I put them out to dry. . . .

---

19. Jane James, "Joseph Smith, the Prophet," *Young Woman's Journal* 16, no. 12
(December 1905): 551–53.

I had to pass through Mother Smiths room to get to mine. She would often stop me and talk to me, she told me all Brother Josephs troubles, and what he had suffered in publishing the Book of Mormon. One morning I met Brother Joseph coming out of his mothers room. He said good morning and shook hands with me. I went in to his mothers room she said good morning bring me that bundle from my bureau and sit down here. I did as she told me. She placed the bundle in my hands and said, handle this and then put [it] in the top drawer of my bureau and lock it up. After I had done it she said sit down. Do you remember that I told you about the Urim and Thumim when I told you about the book of Mormon? I answered yes mam. She then told me I had just handled it, you are not permitted to see it, but you have been permitted to handle it. You will live long after I am dead and gone and you can tell the Latter-day Saints, that you was permitted to handle the Urim and Thumim.[20]

Jane's days with the Smiths were limited, however, and she moved to nearby Burlington when the Mansion House was "broke up."[21] Shortly thereafter, Joseph Smith was assassinated in Carthage Jail. In her 1905 interview, Jane recalled the grief of that day:

When he was killed, I liked to a died myself, if it had not been for the teachers, I felt so bad. I could have died, just laid down and died; and I was sick abed, and the teachers told me, "You don't want to die because he did. He died for us, and now we all want to live and do all the good we

---

20. James, Autobiography, 18–20.

21. James, Autobiography, 20. Joseph Smith and his family had lived in the Mansion House only a few months when Joseph leased it to Ebenezer Robinson. Richard Lyman Bushman, *Joseph Smith: Rough Stone Rolling* (New York: Alfred A. Knopf, 2005), 503.

can." Things came to pass what he prophesied about the colored race being freed.[22]

Apparently, Joseph Smith had also told Jane that her son would serve a mission; she continued to hope it would yet happen, even years after her son Sylvester was grown. Lydia Alder reported in 1893 that Jane "hoped light would yet reach her people and prayed that her son might be faithful and go to them, as the Prophet Joseph had predicted."[23]

As Jane described the next steps in her life—her marriage to Isaac James and their journey to the Rocky Mountains—she again concluded by giving glory to God:

> I went to live in the family of Brother Brigham Young; I stayed there until he was ready to emigrate to this [Salt Lake] valley. While I was at Bro. Brighams I married Isaac James. . . . In the spring of 1846 I left Nauvoo to come to this great and glorious Valley. We travelled as far as winter quarters [and] there we stayed until spring. At Keg Creek my son Silas was born. In the spring of 1847 we started again on our way to this valley. We arrived here on the 22nd day of September 1847 without any serious mishaps,[24] the Lords blessing was with us and protected us all the way.[25]

22. James, "Joseph Smith, the Prophet," 553.

23. "Ladies' Semi-Monthly Meeting," *Woman's Exponent* 22, no. 11 (December 1, 1893): 66.

24. Jane and her family traveled in the Daniel Spencer–Ira Eldredge Company. They began their journey on June 17, 1847. "Daniel Spencer/Ira Eldredge Company (1847)," Mormon Pioneer Overland Travel Database, 1847–68, The Church of Jesus Christ of Latter-day Saints, accessed April 20, 2012, http://mormontrail.lds.org.

25. James, Autobiography, 20.

In Jane's details about life in Utah, she listed even more challenges and once more rejoiced that God had supported her through them:

> My husband Isaac James worked for Brother Brigham, and we got along splendid accumulating Horses, cows, oxen, sheep, and chickens in abundance. I spun all the cloth for my family clothing for a year or two, and we were in a prosperous condition, until the grasshoppers and crickets came along carrying destruction wherever they went, laying our crops to the ground, strip[p]ing the trees of all their leaves and fruit, bringing poverty and desolation throughout this beautiful valley. It was not then as it is now. There were no trains running bringing fruits and vegetables from California or any other place. All our importing and exporting was done by the slow process of ox teams.
>
> Oh how I suffered of cold and hunger and the keenest of all was to hear my little ones crying for bread, and I had none to give them; but in all the Lord was with us and gave us grace and faith to stand it all.[26]

In 1870, Isaac James and Jane divorced, and Isaac left Utah for parts unknown. Jane had a brief two-year marriage with a former slave, Frank Perkins, but soon resumed life as a single parent and grandparent. Then, after a twenty-year absence, Isaac, now very ill, returned to Utah. Though the two did not remarry, Jane cared for her former husband in his sickness, and his funeral was held at her home. She does not acknowledge the divorce in her history, but she does talk about Isaac and the loss of all her children but two, yet again she gives praise to God: "I am a widow, my husband Isaac James died in November 1891.[27] I have seen my husband and all

---

26. James, Autobiography, 21.

27. James died on November 19, 1891, at age seventy-three. "Isaac James,"

of my children but two, Laid away in the silent tomb. But the Lord protects me and takes good care of me, in my helpless condition."[28]

Jane was ultimately bolstered by the relocation of her brother, Isaac Lewis Manning, to Utah in the early 1890s.[29] Though he had joined the Reorganized Church in Iowa, he was soon rebaptized in Utah and became his sister's constant companion, which she mentions gratefully in her life story: "I live in my little home with my brother Isaac, who is good to me. We are the last two of my mothers family."[30]

Jane's history might seem typical of other pioneers' in some ways, but because of her African lineage, she was not allowed some of the privileges that white Latter-day Saints had, the most significant being receiving temple ordinances. Some of Jane's most poignant words are in letters she dictated and either mailed or hand carried to Church leaders. In these letters, Jane boldly petitioned to receive the endowment. Though she understood that policy at the time would deny her entrance to the temple because of her race,[31] she showed remarkable theological sophistication as she reminded her letters' recipients of the Abrahamic covenant.

Her first letter, dated December 27, 1884, was directed to Church president John Taylor. It read in part:

Dear Brother

I cauled at your house last thursday to have conversation with you concerning my future salvation. I did not explain

---

Utah, Salt Lake County Death Records, 1908–1949, FamilySearch, The Church of Jesus Christ of Latter-day Saints, accessed April 20, 2012, http://familysearch.org.

28. James, Autobiography, 22.

29. Wolfinger, "Test of Faith," 139.

30. James, Autobiography, 22.

31. The policy was changed with the 1978 revelation on priesthood received by Church president Spencer W. Kimball. Edward L. Kimball, "Spencer W. Kimball and the Revelation on Priesthood," BYU Studies 47, no. 2 (2008): 4–78.

my feelings or wishes to you. I realize my race & color & cant expect my Endowments as others who are white. My race was handed down through the flood & God promised Abraham that in his seed all the nations of the earth should be blest & as this is the fullness of all dispensations is there no blessing for me?[32]

She subsequently implored not only President Taylor but also President Wilford Woodruff and Relief Society general president Zina D. H. Young for the privilege of entering the temple. After she received a recommend to do baptisms for the dead, she wrote a moving letter to the man who would preside over the Church at the time of her death, Joseph F. Smith, requesting more than she had been given. To him she wrote on February 7, 1890:

Dear Brother

Please excuse me taking the Liberty of Writing to you—but be a Brother—I am anxious for My Welfare for the future . . .—and has i hope to be one, Bye and Bye, bearing the same name as yourself—I was requested to write to you—Hoping you will please show kindness to me. . . .

. . . Can i obtain Endowments for my Dead? Also, I had the privilige of being babtised for My Dead, in October Last. . . . Can i also be adopted in Brother Joseph Smiths the prophet['s] family, I think you are somewhat Acquainted with me—I Lived in the prophets family With Emma and others, about a year—and Emma Said Joseph told her to tell me—I could be adopted In their family, she asked me if i should Like to. I Did not understand the Law of adoption then—but Understanding it now. Can that be Accomplished and When—

---

32. Jane E. James to John Taylor, December 27, 1884, quoted in Wolfinger, "Test of Faith," 148. Original located in the John Taylor Collection, Church History Library.

> I have heard you attend to the prophets Business in those matters—And so have Written to you for information.[33]

Jane was not allowed to receive her endowment and was eventually sealed to Joseph Smith as a servant, not as a child. Nonetheless, she referred to her temple experiences with reverence and hope:

> I have lived right here in Salt Lake City for fifty two years, and I have had the privelege of going into the Temple and being baptized for some of my dead.
>
> I am now over eighty years old and I am nearly blind which is a great trial to me. It is the greatest trial I have ever been called upon to bear, but I hope my eysight will be spared to me poor as it is, that I may be able to go to meeting, and to the temple to do more work for my dead.[34]

On April 16, 1908, Jane Elizabeth Manning James passed away. As she had requested, her life story was read at her funeral, which was attended by many Church leaders, including President Joseph F. Smith. Jane's story concludes with her testimony:

> And I want to say right here, that my faith in the gospel of Jesus Christ as taught by the Church of Jesus Christ of Latter-day Saints, is as strong today, nay, it is if possible stronger than it was the day I was first baptized. I pay my

33. Jane E. James to Joseph F. Smith, February 7, 1890, quoted in Wolfinger, "Test of Faith," 149. Original located in Joseph F. Smith Papers, Church History Library.

34. James, Autobiography, 22. For information about Jane's sealing to Joseph Smith, see Salt Lake Temple, Adoptions and Sealings: living and dead, 1893–1961, Book A, May 18, 1894, p.26; Devery S. Anderson, ed, *The Development of LDS Temple Worship, 1846–2000: A Documentary History* (Salt Lake City, UT: Signature Books, 2011), 97–98; Newell G. Bringhurst, "The 'Missouri Thesis' Revisited: Early Mormonism, Slavery, and the Status of Black People," in *Black and Mormon,* ed. Newell G. Bringhurst and Darron T. Smith (Champaign: University of Illinois Press, 2006), 23–24.

tithes and offerings, keep the word of wisdom, I go to bed early and rise early, I try in my feeble way to set a good example to all.[35]

Though she herself would not recognize it, Jane's example has nothing feeble in it. It serves as one of the strongest and most thoroughly proved of any in Latter-day Saint history.

---

35. James, Autobiography, 22.

Chapter 10

"Strength According to My Day"

Ann Prior Jarvis (1829–1913)

Amy Tanner Thiriot

Biographical Sketch

Ann Prior was born December 30, 1829, to William and Catherine McEwan Prior.[1] Ann was a middle-class London schoolgirl until her father's shop burned and he died, leaving her family in poverty. Ann persuaded her widowed mother to allow her to stop school at age eleven so she could work as a seamstress. Five years later, Ann married sailor George Jarvis, and they began their family, living on board ship for several years.

When George heard the missionaries of The Church of Jesus Christ of Latter-day Saints preaching in London, he went home and told his wife about their message. Ann immediately responded, "George, it is true!" Their baptism began a voyage of faith that took

---

1. Church of England, St. George Parish (Middlesex), Parish registers, 1754–1906, London Metropolitan Archives, London. William and Catherine McEwan Prior had three children: Margaret, born in 1823; a child who died at birth; and Ann.

Ann and George around the world to start life over again as some of the first settlers of St. George, Utah, where they spent the rest of their lives, dying four days apart in 1913.

Their journey to Utah took many years due to poverty and illness. To earn money to emigrate, George signed on as a sailor on a voyage to China, and Ann scrimped and saved and took in washing in London. After sailing around the world and back, George returned with enough money that he and Ann could afford to leave for America in 1857 with their five small children.

They could afford to go only as far as Boston, and they spent three difficult years there. Two daughters were born in Massachusetts, but the younger of the two died from cholera. In early 1860, Ann's health was very precarious. President George Q. Cannon told her that she might die on the plains but she would certainly die if she remained in Boston, and he arranged to help the family to reach Utah.

The Jarvis family walked most of the way from Florence, Nebraska, to Utah Territory. Six weeks after they arrived in the Salt Lake Valley, Ann gave birth to her eighth child.

George and Ann had just started to establish themselves in the Salt Lake Valley when Brigham Young called for volunteers to grow cotton in southern Utah Territory ("Dixie"). George Jarvis volunteered for the settlement: "So for Dixeys land we started."[2]

The Jarvis family helped build the St. George Temple and Tabernacle and were instrumental in developing irrigation systems. They were involved in early efforts to introduce agriculture to the area, including grape production.

Three more children were born to Ann and George, making a total of eleven. The youngest, Thomas William, was killed by lightning on the steps of the St. George Tabernacle.

---

2. Ann Prior Jarvis, "Short Sketch of the Life of Anne Prior Jarvis," 1890, Microfilm of Holograph, p. 32, Church History Library, The Church of Jesus Christ of Latter-day Saints, Salt Lake City, Utah.

Ann and George Jarvis had ninety-nine grandchildren and today have a large posterity.

LIFE EXPERIENCES

Ann Prior Jarvis kept a journal from 1884 to 1899 and left for her descendants several autobiographies in which she emphasized faith in the gospel and the leaders of the Church, the principles of hard work and education, and the importance of family relationships. The following account is from two of her autobiographies:

> I was born in the year 1830 [1829] in St. George Middlesex London England. . . . Before I was eight years of age I was fatherless. . . .
>
> My mother was compeled to work very hard to support us and pay my schools bills She was a noble woman and when Ill through working to hard would plead with the Lord to spare her life to raise me. . . . When I was about ten years old I would beg of mother to let me go to work for my living. After I was Eleven years I worked at making shirts, would earn about fifty cents a week I was very pleased when I brought my wages home. In a few months she apprenticed me to dress making. . . . My beaus would be waiting for me when I left of an evening and I would take a walk every evening. What history is complete of a girls life with out beaus. . . .
>
> In my happy days I met my fate. I was sent for to Phillys [Jarvis] Robinson. I had worked with her. It was sunday I went and saw her brother [George Jarvis]. My mother asked what I was sent for. I replied to be shown my future husband. . . . We got married so ends the love affairs. . . . I went to my work as usual for five months my mother was in the hospital; my husband was at Woolwich [Dockyard, England]. I lived in my mothers cottage. When she came home I went on board the ship with my husband.

When I was seventeen years and a half old my eldest
son was born at my mothers residence June 16 1847 he was
named George Fred[e]rick. My eldest daughter was born
Oct 27 1848 at the same place, Ann Cath[e]rine. When she
was two weeks old her father heard the Gospel. My husband told me what he had heard the strange news that an
Angel had appeared to Joseph Smith. I listened and then
said George it is true. I believed every word of It And were
baptized in the river Thames on Christmas night 1848. We
were living on board of one of Her Magesty Ships at the
time. . . . I believe we were as honest in going into the water
that night and beleived with all our hearts And the Lord
was well pleased with us. We did not obey the commandments of God to pleas our friends or relations our only mo-
tive was to do right for we had no friends or relatives in the
Church. . . .

The President wanted Br Jarvis to be useful so he
left the Royal Navy and Joined the Poplar Branch of the
Church. . . . I moved to Garden place and lived on land
[illegible] or as the sailors would say on shore. My husband
was ordained a teacher and then a priest. He was a very energetic man would work hard during the week, distribute
tracts in the evenings. On Sundays we would go a distance
to try to raise a nother branch. I would go with him to start
the singing. . . .

His wages were very small, scarcely enough to enable
us to obtain the necessaries of life. . . . We were obliged to
cease using sugar and we would do with bread and water for
months. I felt rather Ill at times as I was always dainty. . . .

My eldest daughter had a very bad fever we had her administered to by the Elders. She was getting worse . . . so I
prayed to the Lord to let me know what I was to do. I told
him I kept the word of wisdom and I had her blest by the
Elders and I wanted to know in a dream what to do. I had a

dream that night that I must fast so I fasted and then called a poor brother in to administer to her and then I frightened the doctor so he never came again. He came in the parlour as usual and he spoke very low and said she is gone then? I said yes Sir she is gone into the kitchen. He went with me to the kitchen. I know the change was so great he was frightened. It was a miracle certainly. . . . I give God the glory to this day for I know He answers prayers. . . .

Soon after that time my mother had a dream about me she thought my husband went to her and told [her] we were going to the [Salt Lake] valley. Oh she said I never can say good bye to my darling child the dream troubled her so much. . . . Father [Br Jarvis] would say have you told your mother . . . he thought it was wrong not to tell her so he went to her one day and when he told her she fell on her chair and said I can never say good bye and what else she said he never would tell me. In dark hour of trial she has been with me in my dreams to comfort me. . . . To think I shall see her again when I lay my body down It allmost make [me] want to go. I shall never have a friend quite so true to me under all circumstances. Peace to her memory. . . . When we parted she said it was worse than death Oh the agony of mind when we part from those we love. Knowing I was obeying Gods command comforted me, and I never realized how my poor mother felt, untill I had my children leave. . . .

With our economy we could not get means with which to emigrate and my husband counsel of the president was advised to take a voyage to try and get means. . . . Parting again my husband started for China. While absent on this voyage I washed for three families and lived frugally and by so doing did not owe what he earned. . . .

When Br Jarvis went away the chief engineer said he would have him stay with him on the steamboat that was to run from Shan[ghai] to Hong Cong and he thought he would get enough money to emigrate us. . . .

As soon as he reached his destination the chief enginee[r] discharged him and kept another man on. Br Jarvis wanted to know if he did not please him. He said yes George but you are a married man I think you had better go back to Eng[land]. B Jarvis was vexed as he knew he would not have enough money to Emigrate so he tried to get on other steamboats. . . . Everything was against his wishes to stay in China so he went on top of a mountain to ask the Lord what to do. The impression was go home so he started for Eng[land] and the first port they stoped at they heard of the massacre of the Urirepeans [European] Sailers. The last Chinese war had begun with Eng[land].[3] Had he stayed there he might have been one of the slain but the Lord had worked on the heart of a man that was fond of him . . . and against the wishes of all he had to come home. When he returned we had barely enoug money to pay our passage to Boston. . . . [4]

The servants of God Orson Pratt and other promised us a prosperous voyage and we realized they spoke by the spirit of God. Plenty of singing on board. . . . They had paid the passage of a brother to cook for the Saints but he was Sea sick. There was Eight hundred saints. They found out that father was a seafaring man and wished him to cook for

---

3. Ann was referring to the 1856 massacre of the crew on the steamer *Thistle* and the Second Opium War. W. Travis Hanes III and Frank Sanello, *The Opium Wars: The Addiction of One Empire and the Corruption of Another* (Naperville, IL: Sourcebooks, 2002).

4. The Jarvises traveled on the *George Washington,* a ship chartered for Latter-day Saint emigrants. It departed from Liverpool on March 28, 1857, and arrived in Boston on April 20, 1857. "George Washington," Mormon Migration Index, Brigham Young University, accessed February 29, 2012, http://lib.byu.edu /mormonmigration/index.php.

them. I thought I should have quite a treat and a pleasure trip with my husband. I do not think I exchanged a doxen [dozen] words on the voyage. He cooked for the eight hundred with one assistant [William Lawrence Hutchings]. . . .

[Once in Boston] my husband went to get lodgeing for us no one was very willing to have a family of seven off a Ship but Father declared we had no fever was healthy. The saints had all landed and had gone on to the Valley or to different places but one sister, an old maid and a very croos [cross] one at that, she told me she had no place to go. . . .

I told [Br Jarvis] when he came back we could not leave her there alone. He said he had rented a room one doll[ar] 75 a week so we went to our new home. It was a large room close to the water. . . . This sister went out to get a situation and the first thing I done was to cry. I felt a stranger in a strange land. . . . My husband bought a second hand stove. I had never seen one before. We did not want it very bad for we could not get any to eat. He could not get work. . . .

Br Jarvis got work at a d[ol]lar a day wheeling coals in large wheelbarreys and the Irish men would try to run him off. We could only afford bread. . . . Father would walk seven miles in and out made fourteen miles a day and the men did not want a english man to work so he had to leave there. My Maggie was born in that house in Boston City. . . . I used to do the work for my family but was very sick with fever. I had no nurse for my baby. George [Frederick] would do the work. Father would give the baby some food twice a day. I[t] was four months I could not raise my hand to my head they thought I should die. I should have like[d] to but for my children. . . . I had prayed to the Lord to know if I had to leave my children motherless in a foreign land. I had been told in a dream I should go to Zion. . . .

My health was very poor although I had swolen to such a size I had no dress I could wear. Br George Q Cannon came to administer to me and persuaded father to try to get to florence or winter quarters. He said I of course might die if I went but it was my only chance. . . .

I awoke one night withe the touch of the cholera and then my baby girl Frances Elizbeth took it. I felt certain she would die. I carried her to our President for him to administer to her. . . . he said what did you bring her to me for? I replied because her father is away but She will die. She was dead before the week was out. . . .

I sold the stove, bed and give my furniture a way and with three hundred pounds Draught [load] we started for florence [Nebraska]. When we got there father was employed by President [George Q.] Cannon to make tents & waggon Covers. Father wanted to get a hand cart and hurry to the valley Br Cannon said I should come comfortable with his waggon. Some nights when we went to bed in a large building we would be afloat in the night as there was no protection from rain. We done very well. . . . Br. Cannon had a team lightly loaded so the two familes could come with it.[5]

The Oxen and Wagons had been sent several days from Florence a few miles on where there was feed for the cattle. One day we were told to follow. We caried our cooking utensils and marched along. It was a warm day and I would have liked to lie down for my head ached. When we arrived at the Wagon we were destined to walk by and hang our cooking utensils underneath I had not seen Br [William H.]

5. The Jarvises and the William and Margaret Hunt family shared one of George Q. Cannon's wagons. They traveled with the Jesse Murphy Company and departed from Florence, Nebraska, on June 19, 1860, arriving in the Salt Lake Valley on August 30, 1860. "Jesse Murphy Company (1860)," Mormon Pioneer Overland Travel Database, 1847–68, The Church of Jesus Christ of Latter-day Saints, accessed February 29, 2012, http://mormontrail.lds.org.

and sister [Margaret Stout Vanderhoof] Hunt.[6] I saw her now dressed in bloomer costume she was busy Cooking for the journey. . . .

I began to learn a few things. They were very unkind to us. If we put our baby at the back end of the wagon they would close it. Some of my children never rode a minute on that journey. My boy of five has walked eighteen miles without resting he was the only one that rode in the wagon and they would beat him so he did not want to ride. . . . I think it was a hard journey. . . . [Br Jarvis] had to stand guard for others because they refused and the Captain of the Guard would ask him. I beleive we had the good feelings of the whole camp, and did not murmer. . . .

I suffered with Kidney complaint so bad once I stoped behind the camp and said to a young servant girl we called Mary I was going to rest If the Indians did get me. We both lied down and was asleep in a few minetues. My little girl about seven years of age woke us by saying the Indians are coming they were nearer to the [wagon] train than we were they seemed to cross the trail but we ran to get to the waggons that we could see in the distance like a speck. We found it was our brethren that had been out shooting. It taught us a lesson, we found we did care and we did not want the Indians to have us. . . .

When I saw the valley where Gods people where I felt I could endure a great deal more for the same privilege. I felt thankful to be able to see Brigham Young the Lion of the Lord. The Lord did bless us. Br and Sister [Thomas and

---

6. "William H. and Margaret Hunt," Mormon Pioneer Overland Travel Database, 1847–68, The Church of Jesus Christ of Latter-day Saints, accessed October 30, 2011, http://lds.org/churchhistory/library/pioneerdetails/1,15791,4018 -1-23253,00.html.

Matilda Jinkerson] Stolworthy took us home.[7] We had been
kind to them in Eng[l]and and they was grateful and gave
shelter. My husband went to work for Brigham and he paid
him flour and beef in advance. . . .

My Boy Heber was born . . . less than six weeks after I
arrived in Salt Lake City is it not written that the women
spoken of in the Book of Mormon suffered while traveling?
I think I suffered on that Journey something like them. . . . [8]

My husband went to work and up to this year we have
worked hard for all we have had. I feel thankful for this. . . .
Father worked in the Paper Mill by day and cultivated a
piece of land at night he raised a good crop. . . .

At the October Conference 1861 Brigham [Young]
called for volunteers to Dixie. My husband was one of the
volunteers he had no waggon and he had always said he
would never travel again with out a team. I felt grieved I had
sufferd on the plains to come to head quarters we was doing
well and I thought we had to go through poverty and privations witch we would get no credit, we would bring them
upon ourselves. . . .

When Br Jarvis was determined to come I advised him
to buy an old waggon that a brother did not think was safe
to start from Nauvo with but Brigham told him to start
with it and he came with it all right so Br Jarvis when he
bought it he went to Brigham to buy a yoke of steers but the
President said you will want steady cattle for that journey
and the President B Y was oweing him enough to get a good
yoke of Cattle so for Dixeys land we started. . . . We walked
most of the way and I and my Children would move the

7. "Henry Thomas Stolworthy," The Hendrik and Everdina Winkel Family
Web Page, http://www.winkel.org/black/histories/henstol.pdf, accessed October
30, 2011.

8. See 1 Nephi 17:2.

rocks and make it better for the wagon. When we arrived here on the 5 Dec 1861 . . . it was not a promised land to us. The 25 Christmas day we had bran for our dinner.

I did not have a stove to cook with and It rained forty days and nights. . . . By all working we never had a hundred dollars surplus but I have seen my children cry and I have seen the silent tears roll down their Cheeks.

I was about thirty one years old had eight children. One was in East Boston the seven was alive and hearty hungry children. My husband was strong did not know his own strenth was willing to work plenty of work. . . . We sold the splendid Cattle for a few hundred of flour. Mortgaged our land after it was cultivated for one hundred seventy five pounds of flour. I expect we would sell ourselves for flour if any one would buy us. . . .

I had a daughter born on March twenty first 1863. I cut up some of the tent for her—well I wont say what for.[9]

I have three Children born in St George. My sons helped to build the Tabernacle—one plastered, one carried the hod.[10] I would look and see him at the top. My husband worked on the Temple three years half and was among the first to get the greatest blessings the Lord has to bestow on us. . . .

My youngest darling child . . . was going to Martha Snow['s] school kept in the tabernacle. He was killed by lightning on the top of the steps. I tried to be cheerful and tried to comfort my family. I knew it was wrong to be self-ish even in grief and althou I kissed the rod and thought the Lord wanted to chastise me yet I know the Lord did comfort me and ruled it for my good. I had a dream before

9. Jarvis, "Short Sketch," 1–7, 9–12, 14–17, 19–20, 23–29, 31–33.

10. A hod is a three-sided box on a long pole handle used to transport bricks, mortar, and other building materials.

he died that I lost him in a crowd and I knew I could never find him. Two little boys came to me and tried to comfort me. I told them they were dear Boys but that they were not my Willie. he was very kind to me two nights before he was killed he jumped up out of bed when I was groaning with the pain of my chest. He laid his hands on me and prayed in the name of Jesus. . . . He was an active quick inteligent child. Br [Erastus] Snow gave me great comfort when he returned from the City he spoke about the accident in his fatherly manner. . . .

In my Patriarchal blessing it says that I should lay hands on my sick children in the name of Jesus. I have never employed a doctor only twice in my life for my children. . . . We can live so we will have the whisperings of the good spirit all the time. I know that every trial and affliction will tend to purify us. . . . This body is getting diseased and I feel very useless, and I know this body must die but I am thankful for the teaching of this church has takeing the fear of death away. . . .

If this church was in error like the others churches and had no authority, even then I should be glad I had joined it for the peace it has given me in this life but there would be no power to bless if the church was not owned and directed by God himself. . . . When my husband told me that the angel had come [to Joseph Smith] and there was apostels in the church it charmed me. I believed it. . . . I had opposition on every side but the good spirit would wake me up in the night and whisper if to day thou wilt hear my voice harden not your heart. . . .

I shall never forget the feeling I had the first time I went to meeting to be confirmed a member. They sung Come All Ye the Sons of Zion and let us praise the Lord. I have never heard it sung since with out thinking of the feeling I had when I first heard it. . . . I go some times to the Temple to help to clean it. I have been for my dead relatives but I have only been for a few not knowing many and at present no way of finding out my ancestors record. . . .

I am having a very good time now I have a quiet life what old age requires. I feel thankful for the blessings I enjoy. How long I can enjoy life as I do at the present I know not or what trials I may be called to pass throu[gh] I know not but if the Lord will bless me with his Holy Spirit I know I shall have strenth according to my day.[11]

11. Journal of Ann Prior Jarvis, Book C, 1884–1885, Digital scan of holograph, pp. 13–16, 20, George and Ann Prior Jarvis Family Web Site, accessed February 29, 2012, http://www.george-and-ann-prior-jarvis.org.

Chapter 11

"UNITED IN ALL THINGS"

JANE CADWALADER BROWN JOHNSON (1832–1908)

Patricia Lemmon Spilsbury

BIOGRAPHICAL SKETCH

Jane Cadwalader Brown, born June 5, 1832 in Damascus, Columbiana, Ohio, was the second daughter of Dr. Abia William and Abby Cadwalader Brown.[1] Her parents were Quakers and raised their children in that faith. The family moved from eastern Ohio to Nauvoo, Illinois, in early 1848, hoping to take advantage of lower land prices. Jane's father died unexpectedly in August, leaving the family in precarious financial circumstances. Within six months, at age sixteen, Jane married William Derby Johnson, eight years her senior.[2] Two years later, on September 10, 1850, she was baptized into his faith, The Church of Jesus Christ of Latter-day Saints.

---

1. The spelling of Abby Cadwalader's surname is based on her marriage record. Monthly Meeting Records, 1808–1931, Society of Friends, Damascus, Columbiana, Ohio, Microfilm of holograph, p. 19, Family History Library, The Church of Jesus Christ of Latter-day Saints, Salt Lake City, Utah.

2. William Derby Johnson (1824–1896) was the fourteenth of sixteen children

The couple followed the Saints west, stopping for a time in Council Bluffs, Iowa, and Winter Quarters, Nebraska. William worked in his brother's store, which helped supply those who were embarking on the westward exodus. The Johnson family made the trek to the Salt Lake Valley and arrived in September 1861, traveling with the Sixtus Ellis Johnson Company.[3] They settled next to William's older brothers in the Fifteenth Ward in Salt Lake City. On May 10, 1862, Jane and William were sealed in the Endowment House.[4] In 1871, at the suggestion of Brigham Young, four Johnson brothers, including William, moved south and established the small settlement of Johnson, twelve miles east of Kanab, where William and Jane kept a store. They lived in Johnson until 1890. After much consideration and a trip south in 1888, they followed their children to the Mormon colonies in Mexico, where they lived for the rest of their lives. William died in 1896, and Jane in 1908.

LIFE EXPERIENCES

Jane Cadwalader Brown Johnson's surviving personal writings are few. They include only one extant journal, covering the years 1880 through 1882, and several articles printed in the *Woman's Exponent*. They are enough, however, to illustrate her life and to

---

born to Ezekiel and Julia Hills Johnson. His mother and older siblings joined the Church between 1831 and 1832, but his father did not. Because of family discord, William was not baptized until 1836 at age twelve, three years after his family moved to Kirtland, Ohio. Kerri Robinson and Marcie Gallacher, "'The Joy and the Song': Julia Hills Johnson," in *Women of Faith in the Latter Days, Volume 1, 1775–1820*, ed. Richard E. Turley Jr. and Brittany A. Chapman (Salt Lake City, UT: Deseret Book, 2011), 101–14.

3. Sixtus Ellis Johnson, son of Joel Hills Johnson, was William's cousin and six years his senior. "Sixtus E. Johnson Company (1861)," Mormon Pioneer Overland Travel Database, 1847–68, The Church of Jesus Christ of Latter-day Saints, accessed May 23, 2012, http://mormontrail.lds.org.

4. "Jane Cadwalder [sic] Brown," Endowment House Records, Book D, 63, entry no. 4726, Family History Library, The Church of Jesus Christ of Latter-day Saints, Salt Lake City, Utah, hereafter cited as Family History Library.

demonstrate the support she provided to her husband, family, community, and Church congregations. They also affirm that Jane's view of the world was not confined to her dooryard. She was aware of contemporary issues facing her state and nation and responded to them.

To provide for their family, Jane and her husband, William Derby Johnson, maintained a store adjacent to their home and, next to the store, a shop where William made trunks, chairs, household furniture, and harnesses, as well as natural medicines.[5] Jane contributed to the merchandise in the store through cooking, baking, and preserving food, sewing clothing and other items, papering trunks, and painting chairs. In Johnson, Utah, they also kept an inn for travelers.

Jane was the mother of twelve children, nine of whom lived into adulthood.[6] Her household was a busy one, and on top of teaching and caring for her children and grandchildren and running the store and inn when her husband was away, she also taught young women from the community in her home, helping them prepare for their future roles and, at the same time, benefiting from their help. Several of her journal entries illustrate life in the Johnson home in the early 1880s:

> Nov 6 [1880] saturday it is nearly a week since I have had time to write with work and buisness I was to tired. Tuesday the 2d was election day all voted in this plase for delegate to

5. Elmer Wood Johnson, "Life of Elmer Wood Johnson," *Johnson Bulletin* 18, no. 2 (September 1971): 24.

6. Jane and William had twelve children: William "Willie" Derby Johnson Jr. (1850–1923), Elmer Wood Johnson (1854–1936), Jennie Ann Johnson Laws (1856–1925), Julia Abby Johnson Pulsipher (1858–1919), Esther "Ettie" Almera Johnson Cram (1860–1919), Nancy Maria Johnson (1863–1863), Abia Ezekiel Johnson (1865–1932), Byron Elwood Johnson (1867–1904), Joseph "Josey" Hills Johnson (1869–1927), Carlos Smith Johnson (1871–1872), Hannah Zelnora "Zellie" Johnson Richins (1872–1920), and Lodemia Viola Johnson (1876–1877).

congress George Q Cannon Wendsday Bro. Wm.[7] come[n]
ced to move to Kanab he has taken two loads, now come
for the family. Dillie[8] wash for Jennie.[9] A letter from pah he
was at hills dale—all well. Thursday dillie came and Ironed.
I am so busy in the store I do not get much time for any
thing. Fryday bought 3000. 700 lbs barly an[d] wheat paid
2½ cash and store pay. I was up untill eleven oclock. To day
I have been very busy I cleaned my bed room and fixed it up
not much custom. Weath[er] fine. boys got the fence done
at last. I feel well satisfied with my weeks labor. . . .

Nov 13 saturday It is Just a week since I have had time to
write in my Journal. Sunday the sixth [7th] was cold and
disagreable. Sundy school and meeting not many out. I had
to lead the sin[g]ing so it was done in prime order. I was
very lone some all gone but Abia, Zellie, Wm and family,
Byron, Charly Navj[ajo] gone to Kanab. Monday 8. cold
wind I tried to quilt up stairs, could not, brought it down.
Byron an Charly came. Ettie came with him. did not do
much on the quilt, Tuesday 9 Dillie came to wash. We fin-
ishd the quilt. 10 [Wednesday] rec[ei]ved a card and a letter

7. Jane had many Williams in her family. She differentiates between them in
her journal in several ways. In this instance, Jane is referring to her brother, Abia
William Brown Jr. She usually refers to him as "Bro Wm." "Pah" always refers to
her husband, William Derby Johnson, unless she is relating something he did in
an official capacity, such as speaking at Church or serving in the Sunday School,
when she refers to him as "W. D. Johnson" or "William D. Johnson." "Willie" usually refers to her son William Derby Johnson Jr. or her grandson William Derby
Johnson III, though the latter is often referred to as "Willie the third."

8. Adelia "Dillie" Lucille Buchanan (1865–1935), daughter of German and
Barbara E. Buchanan, lived with the Johnsons for some time. On October 26,
1880, Dillie returned to her parents' home to live, but she continued to help in
Jane's household.

9. When the journal was written, Abia, Byron, Josey, and Zellie were living at
home with their parents.

from pah. Thursay 11 Ettie went to see Jennie. I was very busy all day. Willie and Bro Nuttal came also Tom Miles and Charly Pulsipher an Ida P[10] with grain 3,000 lbs and over.

Nov 12 Fryday [I] was up at five oclock to get breakfast for Wm Bro Nuttal so much to do such a crowd and store to attend to I was nearly wore out to day. The 13 [I] was a going to do lots of work but could not had to be in store most of the day. The Pulsipher crowd left this morning Dillie came to help me. got a letter from pah at the city. Josy stoped at spring Lake.[11] Tis evening the days work is done and I am so weary. Children are washing for bed. Etties baby has quite a cold she is doctoring it. I wonder if it will be a week again before I write in my journal very cold to day.

Nov 15 Monday weath[er] moderated some. Many emegrants passing all the time I have been very busy tending store and trying to sew. Got a bad cold feel miserabl. Send for petersons Magazine[12] an wrote to pah and Josey. Reli[e]f soci[e]ty three members present we sewd rags. . . .

Nov 19 Fryday Weathr some what moderated, yestrday very cold. Bro Frost[13] came with his Mother she is 70 years old. She came all the way from England this fall to see her son

10. Ida P is probably Mary Ida Pulsipher (1867–1943), a daughter of Charles Pulsipher and Sariah Eliza Robbins.

11. Spring Lake was the residence of Jane's brother-in-law Benjamin Franklin Johnson.

12. *Peterson's Magazine* was the most widely read women's fashion and literature magazine in the 1880s. It was published between 1842 and 1898. Mary M. Cronin, "Peterson's Magazine," in *Women's Periodicals in the United States: Consumer Magazines,* ed. Kathleen L. Endres and Therese L. Lueck (Westport, CT: Greenwood Press, 1995), 270–74.

13. Allen Lewis Frost (1838–1901), probably an acquaintance from Kanab, and his mother, Harriet Druce Frost (1811–1882). Harriet died in Kanab.

in her old age. We are all well and feel blessed peace reigns in our habatation. Ettie and baby are still here We done our ironing and many other little jobs besides. Nothing of note has happened to day. . . .

July 9 [1881] saturday quite windy Ellen[14] is about sick. I arose at half past four oclock, dress, washed, cleaned my teeth and prepared breakfast. We had fried goat meet and gravy pancakes Jack Indian and pappoos[15] had bread and peaches for their breakfast. The next thing was to put away the vi[c]tualse, churn, work our butter, feed the chickens, put apples on to cook and beans, sweep the dining room and dust of[f], clean the lamps an fill them, make up the bread and bake it, fix the cheese and make sweet cakes, get dinner. That over, now up stairs to make beds and dust of[f] in seting room, straiten around also bed room, do some mending, 4 ocllock Primary meeting—several of the children absent. We went through our exercises well. Some of the children brought some Indians relic. We are getting up a curosity box I spoke at quite a length about old ruins an a fallen people and cities that have been distroyed on acount of their wick[ed]ness. Dismised got supper tended to my plants, set some out trimed some up. Supper over read about the assanation of President Garfield and some other subjects. So ends saturdy night.[16]

---

14. Ellen Glover was a young English immigrant who boarded in the Johnson home, helping with the many tasks required to run the store, inn, and family.

15. Jack Indian's relationship to the Johnson family is unknown. He could have been hired help or, because Jane and her husband ran an inn, he could have been one of many who stopped by for food or shelter on their journey.

16. Jane Cadwalader Brown Johnson, Journal, Microfilm of holograph, pp. 16–17, 55–56, Church History Library. The holograph is located at the Pioneer Memorial Museum, International Society Daughters of Utah Pioneers, Salt Lake City, Utah.

The Word of Wisdom

In the midst of this busy-ness, Jane was making a conscious effort to conform her personal life to the teachings of the gospel. Her son William recorded his struggle to keep the Word of Wisdom and the promises he made to his mother to improve.[17] As she watched the struggles of her children and others in her community and listened to counsel from Church leaders, Jane committed to adhere more completely to the Word of Wisdom:

> Aug 29 [1880] sunday . . . all went to Sunday school. . . .
> Bishop Willie Johnson spoke concerning our duty to our selves and our god and that we were to[o] negle[ge]nt with out thinking and should wake up and stir about our selves and keep our lamps trimed. . . . I left off drinking tea to day
>
> Aug 30 1880 . . . I am trying to finish my dress but feel so shiftless. I have not had any tea since yesteday. I am trying to leave off such habbitts.[18]

Two and a half weeks later, she reported on her progress:

> Sept 15 1880 Wendsday . . . Three weeks has passed and I have not tasted tea nor do I care for it. It was no hard ship at all to quit.[19]

The *Woman's Exponent* printed a letter from Jane, a portion of which she devoted to the importance of keeping the Word of Wisdom:

> I comment on . . . "The Word of Wisdom," the neglect of which is increasing very fast among our young people.

---

17. William Derby Johnson Jr., January 1869, "Diary Excerpts, 1850–1894," Typescript, p. 3, private possession.

18. Johnson, Journal, 5–6.

19. Johnson, Journal, 8.

How are we to prevent it? Fathers and mothers, let hot drinks alone, and set a good example yourselves, or I believe our Heavenly Father's Spirit will be grieved; for He will not always bear with his children.[20] Let us put them from us as a thing to be shunned and despised, especially by our young people, who have always been taught that they were not good for the body.[21]

Women's Political Progress

Jane was attentive to local and national politics—in Johnson, her home was the polling place—and she followed women's political progress with great interest. Jane wrote to the *Woman's Exponent:*

> Truly this is an age of progression. The ladies' speeches are good, and I hope they will succeed in their efforts to obtain the suffrage. Let woman stand up for her own rights *in wisdom,* and help to make man better, that both sexes may become equal in intelligence and influence and assist each other in doing right, and fulfill the mission they were placed here to work out, which would exalt them to a higher sphere and greater honor in the future.[22]

On February 14, 1870, Utah women received the right to vote, and Jane was alarmed by intimations that they could be

---

20. See Ether 2:15.

21. J. C. Johnson, letter to the editor, July [August?] 29, 1880, in "Correspondence," *Woman's Exponent* 9, no. 8 (September 15, 1880): 63. The letter as it appears in the *Exponent* is dated July 29. It appears that date is an error. If, in fact, the letter were dated August 29, it would directly coincide with her journal entry of that date.

22. Jane wrote in response to a *Woman's Exponent* article summarizing the proceedings of the National Woman Suffrage Association convention held in May 1880 in Indianapolis, Indiana. "Woman's Convention," *Woman's Exponent* 9, no. 4 (July 15, 1880): 31; Johnson, "Correspondence," 63.

disenfranchised due to federal and local political tension. She noted in her journal:

Oct 10 [1880] . . . I wrote to [Woman's] Exponent. Fixed my 'scrap' Book see a piece in the [Deseret] News trying to disenfrainc[h]ise Women.[23] The Liberal [political party][24] say they are not legal voters as they are not tax payers. The women are very indignant about it.[25]

Less than three weeks later, her letter appeared in the *Woman's Exponent*. She argued:

Are women not tax payers? In looking over the "News" of the 29th Sept., my eye rested on disfranchisement of Women; . . . *not tax payers?* Ah! I think we are very heavy tax payers. Does not every wife own property . . . with her husband? I think so. Does not her labor help to make that property? Does she not stand by her husband as a help, and rear the boys to work out the *poll tax?* Yes *we do,* and often our lot is hard and tedious, are we not always ready to advise and counsel for the best, and willing to suffer with our husbands, sons, fathers? Yes we are, and lend a helping hand when needed. Have these would be "liberal" men a mother a wife a sister? It would seem not; or do they think Mormon women so weak-minded that we will not try to defend ourselves? We ask for the justice and freedom that belong to

23. "'A Privileged Class of Voters,'" *Deseret News [Weekly]*, September 29, 1880.

24. The Liberal political party was formed in 1870 to oppose the Church's marriage practices, economic policies, and political influence. The Saints responded by creating the People's party. James B. Allen and Glen M. Leonard, *The Story of the Latter-day Saints,* 2d ed. (Salt Lake City, UT: Deseret Book, 1992), 351.

25. Johnson, Journal, 14.

American citizens, and wish to vote for men of integrity and those that will stand by the constitution of our country.[26]

Several months later, a controversy erupted over the seating of Utah's delegate to the U.S. Congress, George Q. Cannon, who was declared ineligible for the position.[27] Jane commented on that issue, as well as the proposed Edmunds Anti-Polygamy Act[28]:

Jan 23 [1881] sunday . . . I spent the evening reading the News and [Salt Lake] heareld which was fil[l]ed with clippings from other papers of the meannes of our new governer Eli Murry in trying to have our delagate to congress removed from his seat and a gentile put in his plase. Bro George Q Cannon [is] the choise of the people and received a majority of votes I cannot express my indignation in words. . . .

26. Jane C. Johnson, "Women Are Tax Payers," *Woman's Exponent* 9, no. 11 (November 1, 1880): 88.

27. George Q. Cannon, first counselor in the First Presidency, was overwhelmingly reelected to a fifth term as Utah's delegate to Congress. Nonetheless, Utah's governor, Eli H. Murray, reasoned that Cannon's foreign birth and practice of plural marriage barred him from office, and Murray certified Liberal party candidate, Allen G. Campbell, as the rightful representative. Even anti-Mormons denounced Murray's misuse of power, and Cannon was seated. After the passage of the 1882 Edmunds Act, polygamists were banned from holding political office and Cannon lost his seat. The House, however, did not vote to seat Campbell, and the office remained vacant for the rest of the term. Davis Bitton, *George Q. Cannon: A Biography* (Salt Lake City, UT: Deseret Book, 1999), 239–58.

28. The Edmunds Anti-Polygamy Act of 1882 made bigamous cohabitation a misdemeanor. As a result, approximately 1,300 polygamous men were imprisoned. Women were seen as victims of the marriage system and were not tried in court, although they were called upon to testify against their husbands. Polygamists also lost their right to vote and were deemed ineligible to hold public office. Utah Commission, *The Edmunds Act, Reports of the Commission, Rules, Regulations and Decisions* (Salt Lake City, UT: Tribune Printing and Publishing, 1883), 3–5; Ray Jay Davis, "Antipolygamy Legislation," in *Encyclopedia of Mormonism,* ed. Daniel H. Ludlow, 4 vols. (New York: Macmillan, 1992), 1:52–53.

Feb 12 [1882] sunday clear and pleasant a snow storm yest[d]ay. Byron came up with the mail. . . . Reading the contested Cannon and Camble case, also a prosephy of Garfield death[29] by a strange poor man in Cleaveland. That is exciting—the wonder of the present time. . . .

Feb 26 . . . Wm Laws read the Edmun[d] bill. . . . It rather aroused the feelings of some of the polygamist boys as it would naturaly as it makes them all illigetimate children and prevents any polygamist from voting or holdin an office of any kind It is hoped that it will not be permited to pass. . . .

April 23 Sund[a]y . . . All went to sundy school, also meeting. Bro Pulsipher was the speaker he touched on many good subjects also the noted Edmund bill [and] the great necesity of us living our religion and being united in all things. Told of several incidents of the whispering of the holy spirit and its manifestations which was very cheering. They went to Jennie's to spend the evening. I took a ramble with Zellie and pah to see his bee apira [apiary]. It is nice such a pleasant view of the country.[30]

Jane was called as Relief Society president in Johnson in 1878 and as Primary president in 1881, positions she took very seriously. Eliza R. Snow, Zina D. H. Young, and Minerva Snow visited nearby Kanab in February 1881, and Jane recorded her experiences with them:

Feb 11 Fryday pleasant a[nd] fine a card from Willie [in Kanab] wishing pah and me to come down to a picnic to

29. Four months after his inauguration, United States President James A. Garfield was shot by Charles Guiteau, a disgruntled lawyer whose application to become the United States ambassador to France had been denied. Garfield died ten weeks later on September 19, 1881.

30. Johnson, Journal, 29, 86–87, 95.

night. The sisters E R snow, Z D Young, M snow are there now we conclude to go hurry off 2 oclock started. Ann Marsh goes with us. Arive thare at six. Meet the sisters they are glad to see me we have a good chat over old times. Off to the picnic. House crowded with songs and rec[i]tation, reading a[nd] speaking. The evning is pased pleasant[l]y away. We go to sister stewarts to stay all night. . . .

Feb 13 sunday Went to Etties to breakfast. 12 oclock went to Bro Buntings to dinne[r]. The sisters were theare now off to meeting. After meeting go to Willies [to] get supper. Back to meeting. The sisters are to have one. Sisters snow young an snow gave us some good instructions Sister E R Snow spoke in toungs sister Zina interpreted what she said. She blessed this place and the sisters and the Presidents of the societys and gave us all most excelent promises if we would strive to be faithfull. They organ[i]sed a silk Association for this stake.[31] They chose me as President, sister Bunting and Perces Spence as councillers, Jennie secatry, sister stewart treasure[r]. Meeting out. Pah, my self, Ettie Victor Janey Julia all went to Bro William Browns and spent the evening [then] back to Sister stewarts at 10 oclock. . . .

---

31. Brigham Young encouraged women to establish home industries to create a self-sustaining economy and supplement their families' income. He considered "locally produced silk as a practical textile and as a light industry that could be maintained at home by women and children." Although the task was rarely lucrative, women persisted in it from leaf to fabric, spinning thread from silkworm cocoons. As counselor in the general Relief Society presidency, Zina D. H. Young headed the movement and endeavored to organize a chapter of the Deseret Silk Association in every stake Relief Society. Elizabeth H. Hall, "Silk Culture," in *Encyclopedia of Mormonism,* ed. Daniel H. Ludlow, 4 vols. (New York: Macmillan, 1992), 3:1314–315; Eliza R. Snow, "Talk Number One: To Every Branch of the Relief Society in Zion," *Woman's Exponent* 3, no. 21 (April 1, 1875): 164–65; Chris Rigby Arrington, "The Finest of Fabrics: Mormon Women and the Silk Industry in Early Utah," *Utah Historical Quarterly* 46, no. 4 (Fall 1978): 376–96.

22 Feb tuesday . . . Eleven oclock Sisters E R Snow Z D Young Minerva Snow Bro Hoyt arived, had dinner. They held meeting with the Relief Society also the Brethren were invited to come. They spoke word of encouragement and cheered us up and told us what we might do and how to obtain the spirit of god and how to keep it. Sister Minervia snow spoke in toungs Sister Z D Young interpeted what she said. She blessed this plase and the children she said they would grow mighty and strong she blessed me and gave me many promises if I was onely faithfull and blessed the relief society. Said they would grow in Knollage and the spirit of the Lord would dwell with us. Spoke about the R S raising silk. They knew we could make mony easyer by raising silk than any other way. Meeting out past 4 oclock gave out meeting at seven oc. Willie has got back from the Pahreah. A full house. Several spoke, there object to cheer us up and [e]ncourage us to attend more closely to our spiritual affairs and feed the soul. Past 12 oclock just going to bed.

23 Feb Wendsday up and a doing, getting ready for meeting. The sisters are going to organise a primary asociation. To meet at 10 oclock. A genral turn out. After talking to them a while and asking them many questions they sang and sister Minerva Snow gave the opening prayer and then they proceeded to organise. . . . The children sang and was dismissed all feeling well paid for their good attention. Having dinner over, they left for home leaving a heavenly spirit behind them never to be forgotten by old and young. May the Lord ever continue to bless them through the remainder of their life.[32]

---

32. Johnson, Journal, 31–32, 34–35.

Husband and Wife

Amidst Jane's full life of family, social, Church, and work responsibilities, she relished the opportunity to spend time quietly with William. She wrote:

Jan 17 [1881] Monday . . . A dance at Bro Maces all have gone but pah Zellie and me. We are having a cosy evning to our selves whic[h] seemes very pleasant to be alone ocasionaly.[33]

Jane's relationship with her husband reflected her philosophy of the equality between men and women—a natural outgrowth of her egalitarian Quaker upbringing, augmented by the teachings of the Church. Though nearly all members of her primary and extended family had entered into plural marriages, Jane and William had not.

According to William's older brother, Joseph Ellis Johnson, when Jane and William were married on November 9, 1848, in Nauvoo, Jane "would not stand at the altar until she had exacted a pledge from [William] that he would not take another. This pledge he kept."[34] Joseph described Jane as "a strong minded lass who never gave William permission to take another [wife]."[35] (Joseph added, in retrospect, that William might not have wanted to enter plural marriage.) But as Jane and William matured in their relationship, their views changed.

One reason for this change was the situation of Mary Atherton Glover, who was the mother of Ellen Glover, a young English immigrant who served as live-in help for the Johnson family in the early

---

33. Johnson, Journal, 28.

34. Rufus David Johnson, *J. E. J. Trail to Sundown: Cassadaga to Casa Grande, 1817–1882: The Story of a Pioneer, Joseph Ellis Johnson* (Salt Lake City, UT: Deseret News Press, 1961), 84. It is unknown whether Jane made this statement at the time of their marriage in 1848 or at their sealing in 1862.

35. Johnson, *J. E. J. Trail to Sundown*, 312.

1880s. Ellen had migrated to Zion in 1880 with her friend, Ann Marsh. In 1881, William and others provided funding for the rest of the Glover family—Ellen's parents, Mary and James, and two sisters—to travel to Zion. In 1883, a little over a year after their arrival in Johnson, James died. With no means of support, Mary moved in with Jane and William to earn her living, helping with the many chores and activities in that busy household.

Mary had sacrificed much for the gospel. At the time of her husband's death, they had not yet received the blessings of the temple; her family was not sealed. This surely was a concern for Mary, and one can surmise that as Mary and Jane became better acquainted, it became a concern for Jane.

Echoing Joseph Smith, Orson Pratt taught in 1852 that any marriage not sealed for time and eternity ended at death.[36] During the nineteenth century, the doctrine was at times interpreted to mean that a sealing must be performed during one's life on earth.[37] That meant that because James and Mary had not been sealed in life, their marriage had ended with his death, and Mary's children, seven of whom had already died, would not be with her in the hereafter.

Another reason Jane's and William's attitudes changed was that men in local leadership positions were increasingly urged by general authorities to enter into plural marriage. As antipolygamy laws began to be aggressively enforced, some Church leaders preached plural marriage more adamantly. In an 1882 assembly of the First Presidency, the Twelve Apostles, and stake presidents, John Taylor stated, "A man obeying a lower law is not qualified to preside over those who keep a higher law," directly referencing plural marriage.[38] The issue intensified even more when George Q. Cannon, first counselor in the First Presidency, visited the St. George area in 1884.

---

36. "Celestial Marriage," *Journal of Discourses,* 26 vols. (Liverpool: F. D. Richards, 1855), 1:64–65; D&C 131:1–4; 132:15–16, 19.

37. Daynes, *More Wives Than One,* 4.

38. Daynes, *More Wives Than One,* 72.

He said he "did not feel like holding up his hand to sustain anyone as a presiding officer over any portion of the people who had not entered into the Patriarchial order of Marriage."[39] William was then bishop of the Johnson Ward.

In addition to these reasons, Jane felt concern for William and a desire to help him progress to his full potential, a sentiment she had expressed in an earlier letter to the *Exponent*.[40] Annie Clark Tanner summarized the understanding of some contemporary Latter-day Saints' attitudes about plural marriage when she said: "The principle of Celestial Marriage was considered the capstone of Mormon religion. Only by practicing it could the highest exaltation in the Celestial Kingdom of God be obtained. . . . The tremendous efforts and sacrifices of the Mormon people can be understood only if one keeps in mind this basic otherworld philosophy."[41]

There was at least a partial solution to Mary Glover's dilemma, but it required Jane's change of heart. In January 1884, Jane, Mary, and William traveled from Johnson to the St. George Temple, where on January 16 William and Mary Atherton Glover were sealed to each other.[42] All three of them—William, Jane, and Mary—were in

39. Charles Lowell Walker, *Diary of Charles Lowell Walker*, ed. A. Karl Larson and Katharine Miles Larson, 2 vols. (Logan: Utah State University Press, 1980), 2:629.

40. Johnson, "Woman's Convention," 31.

41. Annie Clark Tanner, *A Mormon Mother: An Autobiography* (Salt Lake City: Tanner Trust Fund, University of Utah Library, 1969), 1–2. In 1912, Charles W. Penrose of the First Presidency responded to the question, "Is plural or celestial marriage essential to a fulness of glory in the world to come?" He answered, "Celestial marriage is essential to a fulness of glory in the world to come, as explained in the revelation concerning it; but it is not stated that plural marriage is thus essential." "Peculiar Questions Briefly Answered," *Improvement Era* 15 (September 1912): 1042.

42. The sealing of Mary and William was cancelled in 1921, and Mary and James Glover were sealed. Sealing of Living Couples, 1877–1956, Church of Jesus Christ of Latter-day Saints, St. George Temple, Microfilm, p. 106, Family History Library.

the temple. Given William's earlier pledge not to take another wife without her permission, Jane had evidently given permission and observed the sealing that day. Jane's view of marriage and the reflection of her life with William in her journal show that their marriage was an equal relationship and that they supported each other. It required an intense journey of faith for her, not only for the sealing to occur but also for all three of them to live together in the same household. That she made such a journey is a demonstration of her great love for her husband as well as her compassion, empathy, and love for the Glover family.

That love and mutual respect were reflected in the autobiography of Mary's daughter, Mary Glover Johnson, wife of William's nephew Joseph Johnson. She said that in 1884 her mother "finally married" William Johnson, and she referred to him and Jane as "Uncle William and Aunt Jane."[43] Whatever the role each played, they appeared to be at peace with the decision.

One is reminded of Jane's declaration made in the *Woman's Exponent* in 1880:

> Let woman stand up for her own rights *in wisdom,* and help to make man better, that both sexes may become equal in intelligence and influence and assist each other in doing right, and fulfill the mission they were placed here to work out, which would exalt them to a higher sphere and greater honor in the future.[44]

Jane's deep and abiding belief in marriage as an equal partnership surely was a factor in her decision. Also, a comment from an earlier journal entry—"my heavenly father helped me out as he always

---

43. Robert Edward Laws and Mary Glover Johnson, "Life History of Mary Glover Johnson, 1869–1950," Typescript, p. 4, in Robert Edward Laws, Journal, 1912–1913, Typescript, Church History Library.

44. Johnson, "Correspondence," 63.

does when I am faithfull"[45]—demonstrates her great faith and trust in God.

The passage of the Edmunds-Tucker Act in 1887 disincorporated the Church and intensified prosecution of polygamists, making it nearly impossible to live peacefully in plural marriage. Jane watched most of her children, all but one of whom practiced polygamy, move south to Mexico to escape antipolygamy prosecution. After many requests from them, Jane and William decided to move to Mexico themselves. Mary stayed in Johnson for the same reason that William and Jane decided to move south to Mexico—her children were there.

In the fall of 1890, Jane and William traveled to their final home in Colonía Diaz, Chihuahua, Mexico, where they were surrounded once again by family. Jane's life there was surely as full of her children and grandchildren as it had been in Johnson. William died in Colonía Diaz in 1896, and Jane followed him twelve years later, in 1908.

Jane's journal ends much as it began, telling of her children and the people who filled her life. One of the last entries reflects the common feeling that one's own life may not be particularly noteworthy:

> Aug 17 [1882] Thusday Elme[r]s folks gone home. . . . Now thare is just Julia and children and Elmer left. I am about used up. . . . Will Laws about sick Jennie is better Byron is painting the porch Elmer is fixing to haul hay, now this book is filled I wonder if it will be Interesting to a[n]y one when I am gone.

The preservation of Jane's single journal permits a glimpse of the life of this valiant woman of faith—faith that grew with experience and solidified as she leaned on the Lord for his constant support.

---

45. Johnson, Journal, April 3, 1881, 40–41.

Chapter 12

"The Lord Alone Knows How Deep the Sorrow Has Been in My Heart"

MARY MINERVA DART JUDD (1838–1909)

Todd M. Compton

BIOGRAPHICAL SKETCH

Mary Minerva Dart was born on March 31, 1838, in Groton, Tompkins County, New York, to John Dart, a blacksmith and storekeeper, and Lucy Ann Roberts Dart. Mary was the fourth child of nine. When she was still a young girl, the family moved to Bridgeport, Fairfield County, in southwest Connecticut.

The Darts were introduced to The Church of Jesus Christ of Latter-day Saints in 1848 and decided to gather with the Saints even before receiving baptism.[1] Eleven-year-old Mary, with her family, started the long trip west in April 1849 and crossed the plains to

---

1. According to a family history, John and Lucy were baptized in July 1850; however, another part of the history states that John had not yet been baptized when he lived in Parowan, Utah. In any event, he had conflicts with the Church in Parowan and left Utah for California in 1853. He died in 1876 in Kansas. Delna Swapp Powell, "John Dart of Stratford, Fairfield, Connecticut," Typescript, 2005, private possession.

167

Utah with the Warren Foote Company in June 1850.[2] This was a bad cholera year on the overland trails, which led to tragedy for the Darts. In her autobiography, Mary wrote that before she reached Fort Laramie, "My Mother and sister Hariet and brother George died in one week with that plague the Colery and we buried them on the planes wraped in a quilt with out any coffins."[3]

The Darts had not been in Utah long when John volunteered to join the Iron Mission in southern Utah.[4] They "landid in Parowan May 12 1851," Mary wrote.[5] She would spend the rest of her life in southern Utah and Nevada.

In Parowan, Mary made the acquaintance of twenty-five-year-old Mormon Battalion veteran Zadok Knapp Judd, a farmer. On November 14, 1852, when Mary was only fourteen, they were married. They eventually became the parents of fourteen children and adopted three Indian children.[6] Their first two children, Lucinda

---

2. They arrived in Salt Lake City in September 1850. "Warren Foote Company (1850)," Mormon Pioneer Overland Travel Database, 1847–68, The Church of Jesus Christ of Latter-day Saints, accessed May 29, 2012, http://mormontrail .lds.org.

3. Mary Minerva Dart Judd, Autobiography, 1879–1926, Holograph, p. 10a, Huntington Library, San Marino, California. The holograph contains two different versions of Mary's autobiography. Because only every other page is numbered, facing pages will be labeled as 1a and 1b, 2a and 2b, and so on. See also Zadok Knapp Judd Jr., "Autobiography," Typescript, in Esther Brown Judd, *The Descendants of Thomas Judd,* 1953, Huntington Library, San Marino, California; Derrel Wesley Judd, "Zadok Knapp Judd: Soldier, Colonizer, Missionary to the Lamanites" (master's thesis, Brigham Young University, 1968).

4. Created in 1850, the Iron Mission was established for "exploring, surveying, settling, and farming as well as manufacturing iron" from iron deposits in southern Utah. The ironworks was ultimately unsuccessful, but settlements in the Iron Mission remained. Morris A. Shirts and Kathryn H. Shirts, *A Trial Furnace: Southern Utah's Iron Mission* (Provo, UT: Brigham Young University Press, 2001), xx.

5. Judd, Autobiography, 10b.

6. The children of Mary and Zadok were Lucinda Abigail Judd Oliphant

Abigail and Zadok Knapp Jr., were born in 1853 and 1855. In addition, the Judds adopted an Indian boy whom they named Lamoni.

Zadok's sister Rachel and her husband, Jacob Hamblin, a lifelong missionary to the Indians, convinced Zadok and Mary to join them in the year-old settlement of Santa Clara. This town was situated on the Santa Clara River southwest of Parowan, over the Rim of the Basin. Mary and her children arrived in March 1856, moving into a new fort that Zadok had been helping to build. The few whites in Santa Clara were surrounded by Paiutes, and Zadok and Mary became part of the Southern Indian Mission.

Four children were born to Mary and Zadok in Santa Clara, three of whom died before the age of five. In addition, they adopted two more Indian children, Matilda (died at age three) and Nellie.

Zadok was called to be a bishop in Santa Clara in June 1859. Mary was "ordained as midwife" and often tended the sick.[7] She was proud of the part she played in pioneering the cotton mission, for she, Zadok, and other Santa Clara Saints grew the first cotton and created the first cotton clothing in southern Utah.

In 1865 Mary and Zadok, with a group of old Santa Clara settlers, moved to Eagle Valley, Lincoln County, in what is now Nevada. There the Judds had three children.

When the state of Nevada ruled that Mormon settlements in southern Nevada were not in Utah and demanded back taxes in hard currency, the Judds, with many other Nevada Mormons, moved back to southern Utah. In spring 1871, Mary and Zadok settled in

---

(1853–1929), Lamoni Judd (adopted 1854; died 1865), Zadok Knapp Judd Jr. (1855–1952), Harriet Paulina Judd (1858–1858), Matilda Judd (adopted 1858; died 1861), Lois Sabina Judd (1859–1863), Henry Eli Judd (1861–1949), Nellie Judd (adopted 1862; death date unknown), Ezra Abner Judd (1864–1865), Esther Irene Judd Ford (1866–1946), Asa Walter Judd (1868–1893), Samuel Ami Judd (1870–1960), James Arthur Judd (1873–1873), William Leonard Judd (1874–1875), Mary Gertrude Judd Cottam (1876–1963), Orza Orange Judd (1880–1881), and John Lael Judd (1881–1882).

7. Judd, Autobiography, 12a.

Kanab, Kane County, which Jacob Hamblin had refounded as an Indian farm in 1868. Kanab turned out to be the Judds' final home. They had five more children in this place, though only one of them grew to maturity. The deaths of the last four of her beloved children devastated Mary, leaving her nearly inconsolable.

In Kanab, Zadok built a two-story home and farm and tended orchards, vineyards, and gardens. Many of the Judd children married and put down roots in Kanab. Mary wrote, "Here in my comfortable home I would like to stay, the rest of my days, if my children and grandchildren felt the same and I would like to keep those dear to me close by . . . because all the comfort I can take in this or any other life will be in the company of all my children and grandchildren."[8]

Zadok died on January 28, 1909, in Kanab; Mary died six months later, on August 5.

LIFE EXPERIENCES

Mary Minerva Dart Judd's autobiography vividly describes the struggles of taming new territory and pioneering settlement after settlement. It is haunted by death and loss. Losing children to death was a typical part of the experience of pioneer women; life on the edge of the frontier, far from medical help, often living with substandard food and shelter in the beginning years of a settlement, caused significant health risks, especially for children.[9] As a resident

---

8. Mary Minerva Dart Judd, "Sketch of the Life of Mary Minerva Dart Judd," Typescript, p. 52, private possession.

9. Julie Roy Jeffrey, *Frontier Women: "Civilizing" the West? 1840–1880,* rev. ed. (New York: Hill and Wang, 1998), 89; Louis Fairchild, *The Lonesome Plains: Death and Revival on an American Frontier* (College Station: Texas A&M University Press, 2002), 59–86, esp. 65–66, 75–76; Joan M. Jensen, *Calling This Place Home: Women on the Wisconsin Frontier, 1850–1925* (St. Paul: Minnesota Historical Society Press, 2006), 152; Jessie L. Embry, "Women's Life Cycles: 1850 to 1940," in *Women in Utah History: Paradigm or Paradox?* ed. Patricia Lyn Scott and Linda Thatcher (Logan: Utah State University Press, 2005), 394–415, esp. 405.

of early Parowan, Santa Clara, Eagle Valley, and Kanab, Mary lived on the outer edge of the Mormon frontier for much of her life. After moving to her final home in Kanab, she wrote, wryly, "This lot is the fifty[eth] place my husband has made since our marriage. Good homes that some one is enjoying the fruit of in divers places in Utah."[10]

Mary was proud of her pioneering experiences in southern Utah. When she had lived in Santa Clara only a few days, Church leaders called the Santa Clarans back to Harmony because of an Indian war in northern Utah. "We obeyed orders and made the first wagon trackes that there ever was made south of harmony over the black ridge," she wrote. "We travelled about 75 miles without any wagon track."[11]

In his diary-autobiography, Jacob Hamblin wrote, "We had allways herd that [this route through the mountains] was impasable for wagons [but] we all felt like trying it."[12] Mary wrote:

> We washed our clothes and packed up and started over the mountaines where there had no wagon had ever travelled before and went thrue misqueet [mesquite] flatt where the sity of saint geor[ge] now standes and thrue the sand onto the riovergin [Rio Virgin] and camped that knite and so on the next day with no road Br [Samuel] Knite and [Prime] Colman, thales hascal [Thales Haskell] riding a head to serch out the best track for us to follow. So we travelled on

---

10. Judd, "Sketch," 51.

11. Judd, Autobiography, 11a. It is possible that an exploring company (which included Zadok Judd) had taken wagons over the Black Ridge in 1852, but there was certainly no wagon road. John D. Lee, letter to editor, February 20, 1852, in "Letter from Elder John D. Lee," *Deseret News,* April 3, 1852.

12. Jacob Hamblin, March 1856, Diary and Autobiography, Holograph, p. 68, Jacob Hamblin Papers, 1850–1877, Church History Library, The Church of Jesus Christ of Latter-day Saints, Salt Lake City, Utah, hereafter cited as Church History Library.

untill we came to fort harmony. Here we stoped to fix up as
we had torne our close [clothes] terably travling thrue brush
and rockes with no road of any kinde.[13]

The "black ridge" was a section of the canyon filled by a
black, jagged lava flow that was legendary for its difficulty. Apostle
George A. Smith called it "the most desperate piece of road that I
ever traveled in my life, the whole ground for miles being covered
with stones, volcanic rock, cobble heads . . . and in places, deep
sand."[14] At nearby "Peter's Leap," wagons had to be lowered down a
precipitous gorge with ropes.

According to Jacob, this grueling, trailblazing journey took four
days, and when the group arrived at Fort Harmony, it "surprised
Some of the Brothren."[15] Mary's account is the fullest extant record
of this historic pioneering feat in spring 1856.

Mary was also proud of being part of another first, the beginning of the cotton mission in southern Utah:[16]

The first cotton pach [patch] was planted in Utah santa-
clara in 1855. There was seed enough raised so we could
raise a crop of cotton to spin. In [18]56 we went up to the
city of salt lake that fall and baught a pare of cotton cardes
there and a spining wheel in Parowan and I learned to spin
and card. I spun the first peas of cloth that was made of
cotton raised in the mountaines of Utah and the misionar-
ies raised the seed that stocked all southern Utah and my

---

13. Judd, Autobiography, 21b–22a. More details in Judd, "Sketch," 25–29.

14. "History of the Settling of Southern Utah," October 17, 1861, Holograph,
p. 456, in History of the Church, 1839–[ca. 1882], Church History Library.

15. Hamblin, Diary and Autobiography, 69.

16. See Leonard J. Arrington, "The Mormon Cotton Mission in Southern
Utah," *Pacific Historical Review* 25, no. 3 (August 1956): 221–38.

husband made the jin that took the lint frome the seed[,] maid it off [of] roolers [rollers] of wood with a crank to turn.[17]

Zadok Knapp Judd Jr. wrote, "I remember a suit that mother made which I was very proud of; a waist and pants that were colored. The coloring was had from a bush that was boiled and the cotton dipped in the water then carded and spun and woven."[18] Mary, working with Zadok, made these clothes in their entirety, including fabric and dye.

Raising cotton, ginning it, carding it, and making clothes was extremely laborious. Zadok Jr. remembered that his father "made his own cotton rope of cotton he had raised, the seed taken out by a machine he had made and Mother carded and spun the cotton and together they twisted it into a rope and during all these days of labor and hardship I do not remember one word of complaint. But I do know of their reading and singing and praying, and the association with the neighbors."[19]

For early Mormon women, work was almost a religion,[20] and sewing was a work that was especially beloved. Mary's life writings reflect her great satisfaction with creating and sewing clothes. In her autobiography, mentions of important items she had sewn are interspersed with important family events. The births and deaths of children, as well as general community events, are punctuated by Mary's accomplishments in sewing and weaving. She wrote strictly

---

17. Judd, Autobiography, 11a–11b.

18. Zadock Knapp Judd Jr., "Biography of Zodak [sic] Knapp Judd, Jr. and his wife, Ada Marie Howell Judd," ed. Esther Brown Judd, Typescript, p. 6, Utah State Historical Society, Salt Lake City, Utah.

19. Judd, "Biography," 6.

20. On the work of frontier women, see Glenda Riley, *A Place to Grow: Women in the American West* (Arlington Heights, IL: Harlan Davidson, 1992), 147–96; Todd Compton, "Civilizing the Ragged Edge: The Wives of Jacob Hamblin," *Journal of Mormon History* 33, no. 2 (Summer 2007): 155–98, 173, 181, 195.

chronologically, alternating dates with events that were important to her but not thematically connected:

> Jan 14 [1858] I had a daughter born [Harriet Paulina]. I made a long peas of lincy coth [linsey cloth]. My baby died aged 9 monthes. We baught an indian girl Matilda in March 19. Up to this time I had made severall yardes of cloth. We moved from the fort on to the city lotes and tried to improve them. In the same fall I was ordained as midwife and the president[21] said that I should understand the government and use of all usefull herbes and be blessed in my calling. I took wool on the shares and made Jeanes. This year 1859 I had another Daughter born July 24 Lois Sabina.[22]

Santa Clara gradually became a comfortable town. Mary recounted:

> This Plase santaclara was quite A nise well shaded town with quite nise orchardes and vine yardes as some years before there had been Some of the breatheren sent to california for greap [grape] cuttins and vines so that there was quite a start of greapes in the plase. . . . A Br Samuel Lee and others built mew [new] adobie houses and bishop Z K Judd raised quite a nise crop of corn and cane and quite A quantity of wheet and beans and other vegetabells so the plase seemed in A prosperous condition.[23]

But the old Santa Clara soon came to a stunning end. Mary powerfully records her experience with the cataclysmic flood of January 1862:

---

21. Possibly Church president Brigham Young or possibly Jacob Hamblin, president of the Southern Indian Mission.

22. Judd, Autobiography, 12a.

23. Judd, Autobiography, 27b–28a.

There was A great rain storme. It lasted 3 weekes and then there came a great flood that washed down our town houses and orchardes and vineyardes land and all went down the stream and my husband and Jacob Hamblin came near loosing their lives in the flood. I had the chilles and fever[24] at this time. We were all of us out of house and home atthis [at this] time and in the winter. We saved all we could from the flood and mooved down the crick about 2 miles and co-mensed to setout orchardes and vineyardes fince [fence] city lotes and to build a city again. Here we got a house built and an orchard and vineyard setout.[25]

The township they built is modern Santa Clara. Mary's unique juxtapositional style continues in her account: "Our Daughter Sabina Lois died october 12 1863 aged 4 yeares. I made some flanell for dresses also 4 shaules and bead [bed] ticking."[26]

When Brigham Young sent hundreds of new settlers to St. George and ninety Swiss converts to Santa Clara in late 1861, com-petition for water, combined with flooding, made farming difficult. So in spring 1865, the Judds moved to Nevada: "We made A new home in the nise little valley Eaglevalley where the grass grew green. The people built there homes close to gather [together] that they mite be protectid from the Indians." As in Santa Clara, they lived in a fort at first and later moved onto "city lotes."[27]

Soon after the Judds arrived in Nevada, measles struck their household. They were sharing their house with children of Zadok's brother Hiram and with Maryette Hamblin Young, a daughter of

----

24. Probably malaria.

25. Judd, Autobiography, 12b–13a. More details about the flood are in Mary's autobiography and "Sketch." For background, see Todd Compton, "The Big Washout: The 1862 Flood in Santa Clara," *Utah Historical Quarterly* 77, no. 2 (Spring 2009): 108–25.

26. Judd, Autobiography, 13a.

27. Judd, Autobiography, 33a.

Jacob Hamblin, and her two children. They all came down with measles, and "I had so much care on my handes at this time with sickness and death on every hand," Mary wrote. Lamoni and baby Ezra died.[28]

Indians are an important presence in Mary's autobiography. For example, when she and Zadok crossed the Rim of the Basin, passing from the cold Cedar City area to Dixie in 1855, "then it became as warm as sumer then the indians swarmed around us like bees." Mary and her husband had heard stories of solitary whites being killed by Paiutes south of Harmony, and so they were unnerved. But they sent a note to Jacob Hamblin by a trusted "indian runner" and felt they would be safe.[29] Later, on the Santa Clara River, they came to a hill too steep for their team and wagon. Zadok went ahead to a Paiute village and brought back some men he knew. They unloaded the wagon, carried heavy sacks up the hill, took the wagon to the hill-top, and reloaded it. Zadok Knapp Jr. wrote, "Mother walked and carried me and my little sister walked beside her. Father made camp on top of the hill and cooked a big pot of mush which he served to the Indians and so all were benefitted."[30] Jacob Hamblin met them at noon. This was Mary's introduction to Dixie.

White women on the frontier often felt real tensions when they had frequent dealings with Indians (in fact, Mary tells how Thales Haskell's wife Mariah was shot accidentally by a young Paiute man); white women were nevertheless often generous and sympathetic to Indians.[31] When non-Mormon miners in Nevada attacked local

---

28. Judd, Autobiography, 24a.

29. Judd, Autobiography, 21a.

30. Judd, "Biography," 2.

31. Glenda Riley, *Women and Indians on the Frontier, 1825–1915* (Albuquerque: University of New Mexico, 1984), 205–27. Riley notes that frontier women were often more sympathetic to Indians than to other minorities, such as Mormons). Jeffrey, *Frontier Women*, 72–73; Sandra L. Myers, *Westering Women and the Frontier Experience, 1800–1915* (Albuquerque: University of New Mexico Press, 1982), 37–71, esp. 62; Compton, "Civilizing the Ragged Edge," 174.

Paiutes, Mary wrote, "There was one or more Indians killed. It seamed teribell to see them [the Indians] running for life and the men miners I think going after them with all spead on hors back shooting at every step. Our Indian girl Nellie and boy Lamonie Lamonites felt very bad as I did my self."[32]

All together, Mary and Zadok adopted three Paiute children. While Mary recorded these adoptions in commercial language— "we baught a lamonite boy," "we bought a lamanite girl"[33]—she and Zadok nevertheless raised them as adopted children: "Our girl Nellie went to panacho [Panaca] and washed and spun for the sisters . . . telling them her Mother had learnt her to work as our Indian children had always called us Father and Mother Just the same as our own children."[34] Lamoni and Matilda died young, a common occurrence with adopted native children, as Indians had no inherited resistance to many European sicknesses, but Nellie grew to maturity and married "a young Indian big Jim so called by the people."[35]

In the 1860s, Navajos living in Arizona crossed the Colorado River and raided Mormon herds in southern Utah. Jacob Hamblin was able to negotiate a peace with Navajo leaders in 1870, but this peace was fragile: the Navajos were not a politically unified nation,

32. Judd, Autobiography, 32b. Mormons, Indians, and miners were in southern Nevada at this time. See W. Paul Reeve, *Making Space on the Western Frontier: Mormons, Miners, and Southern Paiutes* (Urbana: University of Illinois Press, 2006).

33. Judd, Autobiography, 10a, 11b. For Mormons adopting Indian children, see Juanita Brooks, "Indian Relations on the Mormon Frontier," *Utah Historical Quarterly* 12 (Jan.–April 1944): 1–48, esp. 4–9, 13–15, 33–35 (the Judd family and their adopted Indian children are mentioned on pp. 13 and 33); Brian Q. Cannon, "Adopted or Indentured, 1850–1870: Native Children in Mormon Households," in *Nearly Everything Imaginable: The Everyday Life of Utah's Mormon Pioneers,* ed. Ronald W. Walker and Doris D. Dant (Provo, UT: Brigham Young University Press, 1999), 341–57; Martha C. Knack, *Boundaries Between: The Southern Paiutes, 1775–1995* (Lincoln: University of Nebraska Press, 2001), 56–57.

34. Judd, Autobiography, 35b–36a.

35. Judd, Autobiography, 35b.

and many of them wanted to keep raiding. Not long after the Judds arrived in Kanab in 1871, when they were still living in a camp, a group of thirty Navajos showed up suddenly at the small town and "seemed very hostile," as Zadok Judd Sr. remembered the incident. They made threatening movements with their bows and arrows and demanded an outrageous supply of provisions. A group of leading Kanab citizens counseled with Jacob Hamblin and asked, "What shall we do?" Zadok wrote:

> [Mary] replied: "Lets give them their breakfast."
>
> Jacob Hamblin remarked; "That's a very sensible idea. Will you feed a few of them?"
>
> "Yes, I can feed four or five."
>
> Jacob Hamblin then went out among the crowd and brought four or five to our camp. My wife made a pot of mush, roasted a few ears of corn and soon gave them breakfast.
>
> While these were breakfasting, Jacob Hamblin went out among the crowd and scattered them around, taking a few to each camp, until all were provided for. This seemed to satisfy them, and after trading a little with us, they went off and left us. Thus a peaceful policy avoided trouble.[36]

So Mary helped to defuse a potentially violent conflict. The once-hostile Navajos became trading partners with the Mormons of Kanab.

In the book that contains Mary's autobiography, one diary entry stands alone. That Mary felt the need to record this event in full diary format shows that it was an overwhelmingly important and deeply moving experience for her. The meeting was, for Mary, an expression of women's "power and authority" in the gospel:

---

36. Zodak [sic] Knapp Judd, "Autobiography," Typescript, pp. 41–42, Utah State Historical Society.

February 2 .18.81. I atended a meeeting of the Relief sosiety
apointid to sowing [sewing] of all Kindes in the afternoon
we wer visited by 2 two of the wives of Joseph Smith the
Prophet who [the wives] took two of my children in there
arms . . . Aunt S[iste]r Zina took my son orange in her arms
and blessed him as a wife of the prophet Joseph. They gave
much good in struction to the young ladies as well as the
old. Sa[id] they [the young ladies] should be mothers to
sones that would be as the brother of Jared was who should
see the Lord fase to fase. Exorted the sisters to faith and
pasience and good workes told them they should administer
to and wash and anoint the sick whenever called upon the
same as the bretheren. They administered to sisters that had
ben afflicted, a long time with fites [fits] Said she should
beas [be as] the woman that tutched [touched] the hem of
the garments of our savior who [was healed]. They had the
[s]piret of the Lord with them to a great degree and blessed
us by all the pow[er and au]thoraty they held to bless in the
name of [the] lord.[37]

These two visitors were Eliza Roxcy Snow Smith Young, general Relief Society president, and Zina Diantha Huntington Smith
Young, her counselor. After the death of Joseph Smith, to whom
both were plural wives, they had both become plural wives of
Brigham Young. Eliza and Zina traveled to Dixie in 1880 and 1881
to visit local Relief Societies and also to work in the St. George
Temple.[38]

In the nineteenth-century Church, women's meetings often included speaking in tongues and administering to the sick.[39] Such

37. Judd, Autobiography, 57a–57b.

38. For this trip to Dixie in 1880 and 1881, see A. Karl Larson and Katharine
Miles Larson, eds., *Diary of Charles Lowell Walker*, 2 vols. (Logan: Utah State
University Press, 1980), 2:510–12, at Nov. 24, 29, 1880.

39. On women and healing in the early Church, see Jonathan A. Stapley and

charismatic meetings were held in Winter Quarters, with Eliza acting as a leader and Zina a participant.[40] Now they were continuing
in Utah, even in far-flung Kanab.

The single most striking element of Mary's autobiography is her
record of the overwhelming grief she felt at the death of her children. As she grappled with this suffering, she called upon her faith
to help her endure:

> My sone James Arther born Jan 30 1873 and died May
> 30 aged 4 monthes. This is the 4th childe we hav Lost. It
> seames as if there was some thing to keep us thought full
> and sober and to keep us prayerfull our mindes constant-
> ley called out to the Lord that we may be prepared to meet
> those that are called away and be worthey to reseive them
> again in that beter Land.[41]

Mary gave some details of the death of William Leonard at the
age of a year and four months:

> My husband was called to go to the herd or dary. My
> baby William Lenard was very sick with the canker [any of
> various oral diseases that cause ulcers] and I wanted to go to
> the dary with my husband but they thaught it best not to go
> so I Stayed at home and took the best care of my babe that
> I could but my baby grew worse and I thaught I would go
> to [the] dary with him where my hunband [husband] was
> to see if it would not help him. They the E[l]ders up there

Kristine Wright, "Female Ritual Healing in Mormonism," *Journal of Mormon
History* 37, no. 1 (Winter 2011): 1–85.

40. Maureen Ursenbach Beecher, *Eliza and Her Sisters* (Salt Lake City, UT:
Aspen Books, 1991), 92–97; Donna Toland Smart, ed., *Mormon Midwife, the
1846–1888 Diaries of Patty Bartlett Sessions* (Logan: Utah State University Press,
1997), entries of January 1, February 4, May 29, and June 1, 1847.

41. Judd, Autobiography, 14a–14b. For more on frontier parents turning to
faith to deal with infant mortality, see Fairchild, *Lonesome Plains,* 81–84.

Administerd to him but death came and we had no power
it seamed but I could not give him up and did not untill
he was buried and then it seamed as thoe I buried my heart
with him. I had buried 4 children before and felt as tho the
Lord gave and the Lord taketh away but this time I thought
he did not want so many of our children. If we onely k[n]ew
how to stay the hand of death. He died in August 1875 and
I have felt as tho I would never feel joyfull any more but
try and say as little as I can and drive it away as much as
posible.[42]

Mary may have added to her autobiography year by year, as
sometimes she speaks in the present tense. "I had A daughter born
June 22 1876 [Mary Gertrude] and time past on. . . . We had another boy born Irza [Orza] Orange and he died aged 8 months. It
seames as tho death is the only visitor and time paseth on."[43] We see
the toll the deaths of her children have taken on Mary: "death is the
only visitor."

Mary's autobiography culminates in a heartbreaking paragraph
that records the death of her last child:

I have had another boy [John Lael]. This is the 14th
child we have had 9 boys & 5 girls and now we must give
this boy up to the monster death and 7 of our 14 teen [four-
teen] are buried beneath the sod and what is earth but A
plase to mourn. But if it would only give us power to be
as Abraham of old to [be] saintes in deed then we mite re-
jois in all our sorrow and death in this life. The Lord alone
knowes how deap the sorrow has been in my heart. No
other one could tell off all I have felt and past thrue in so
much death.[44]

42. Judd, Autobiography, 14b–15a.
43. Judd, Autobiography, 15a–15b.
44. Judd, Autobiography, 15b.

"What is earth but A plase to mourn." "I have felt as tho I would never feel joyfull any more." And when William Leonard died, "it seamed as thoe I buried my heart with him." Nevertheless, she hoped that such trials could help her and her people to be as Abraham of old, to be "saintes" in deed. Mary's last words—"the Lord alone knowes how deap the sorrow"—warn us that as much as we try to empathize with her experience of loss, as human beings we will fail. But the Lord does understand. His supernatural compassion is her only comfort.

Mary lived the last thirty-eight years of her life in Kanab, with many children and grandchildren nearby. After the earlier years of struggle and loss on the frontier, these last decades of her life provided a welcome time of stability until her death in 1909.

Chapter 13

"I HAILED IT WITH JOY"

SUSANAH STONE LLOYD (1830–1920)

David R. Cook

BIOGRAPHICAL SKETCH

Susanah Stone[1] was the only member of her family to journey west in the Willie Handcart Company of 1856. Her faith was tried, and she received miraculous support. Her courageous story is stirring, and in the end she declared, "Although we have suffered many hardships we have never murmured or felt to regret the sacrifice we made."[2]

---

1. The spelling of Susanah's given name varies among records. Her death certificate, Latter-day Saint baptismal record, and an extant signature all indicate that she spelled her name Susanah; therefore, that spelling will be used in this text. "Susanah S. Lloyd," 1920, State of Utah Death Certificate, no. 26; "Susanah Stone," Record of Members Collection, Bristol Branch (England), British Mission, Microfilm of holograph, no. 279, Church History Library, The Church of Jesus Christ of Latter-day Saints, Salt Lake City, Utah, hereafter cited as Church History Library; Susannah Stone Lloyd, Autobiography, 1992, Photocopy of holograph, Church History Library.

2. Susanah Stone Lloyd, "The Sketch of Susanna Stone Lloyd," in Information on Thomas and Susanna Lloyd, ca. 1915, Typescript, p. 3, Church History

Susanah Stone was born on Christmas Eve 1830[3] in Bristol, England. She was the eldest of nine children: four girls and five boys. Her parents, William and Diana Grant Stone, were "honest and up- right people teaching their family that chastity of thought and ac- tion was necessary to a successful life."[4] Her parents espoused differ- ent faiths. Susanah wrote: "Father's people belonged to the Church of England, and Mother's people to the Wesleyans." Susanah had a spiritual nature, attended the Wesleyan Sunday School, read the Bible, and wished to have lived in the days of apostles and proph- ets. When she heard the "everlasting gospel had been restored to the earth," she "hailed it with joy."[5] She was baptized a member of The Church of Jesus Christ of Latter-day Saints at age eighteen on June 15, 1849. Her sister Sarah was baptized a few months later on November 29. Her mother subsequently joined and was baptized December 7, 1849.[6] Susanah often walked many miles to attend Church meetings.

Susanah had the spirit of gathering and, contrary to her parents' wishes, desired to gather with the Saints. She gained employment

---

Library; Susanah Stone Lloyd, "The Sketch of Susanna Stone Lloyd," in Lloyd Family Sketches, ca. 1915, Typescript, Church History Library. Two transcribed versions of Susanah's autobiography are available at the Church History Library.

3. "Susanah Stone," Record of Members Collection; Lloyd, "Sketch," in Information on Thomas and Susanna Lloyd, 1.

4. "Mother of the Lloyd Family," ca. 1912, in James T. Jakeman, *Album: Daughters of the Utah Pioneers and Their Mothers* ([Salt Lake City, UT]: Western Album Publishing, 1916), 182.

5. Lloyd, "Sketch," in Information on Thomas and Susanna Lloyd, 1.

6. Record of Members Collection, Bristol Branch (England), British Mission, Microfilm, no. 279, 382, 384, Church History Library. Records indicate that Susanah's mother chose not to remain in fellowship with the Saints. In 1857, Susanah's sister Sarah Stone sailed to New York, where two years later she mar- ried John Deakin. She and her husband journeyed by oxcart to Utah in 1861 and settled near Susanah's family. Sarah Stone Deakin had no children of her own and helped as a second mother to her sister's large family. "Mother of the Lloyd Family," 182.

with a Mr. Barker, who was generous with her wages, and she saved enough for the journey.[7] In May 1856 Susanah, at age twenty-five, left Liverpool, England, on board the ship *Thornton* bound for New York. The party was directed by Captain James Willie.[8]

The Willie and Martin handcart companies faced more adversity from weather and death than any other Latter-day Saint company during the pioneer migration west.[9] Given the difficult circumstances these pioneers experienced, it is miraculous that the death toll was not higher. The only member of her family in the Willie company, Susanah's support came from friends on the trail. The single women traveled together, pulling their handcarts during the day and sharing two tents at night.

Susanah had suitors both in England and in her traveling company, but she had been advised not to marry before she reached Salt Lake. Her suitor in the company died on the trail. She married Thomas Lloyd shortly after reaching the valley. Thomas was also from England and had migrated the year before. They settled in Farmington, Utah, and later moved to Wellsville, Utah.

In her early womanhood, the blessings of a large posterity had been pronounced upon her head,[10] and she looked forward to the

---

7. George F. Lloyd, "Poem," 1918, Typescript, p. 3, private possession.

8. Susanah was listed on ship passenger lists as Susan Stone. Mormon Migration Index, Harold B. Lee Library, Brigham Young University, accessed June 18, 2012, http://lib.byu.edu/mormonmigration/index.php. In addition to her sister Sarah, two of Susanah's brothers also journeyed to America. William Stone traveled to New York but ultimately settled in Sydney, Australia, in 1877. Charles Stone later settled in Logan, Utah, where he lived for more than twenty years. Susan Rush Packer, *History of the Descendants of William Stone and Mary Ann May* (Kaysville, UT: privately printed, 2003), 1–2.

9. About 15 percent of the Willie company died on the journey, and between 18 and 26 percent of the Martin company died. Andrew D. Olsen, *The Price We Paid: The Extraordinary Story of the Willie and Martin Handcart Pioneers* (Salt Lake City, Ut: Deseret Book, 2006), 84, 401.

10. Lloyd, "Sketch," in Information on Thomas and Susanna Lloyd, 1.

fulfillment of that promise. Susanah became the mother of fourteen children, twelve of whom lived to adulthood.[11] In addition to the service she rendered her family, she served faithfully in the Church. Among other callings, she served as a secretary and teacher for the Relief Society.[12]

After Susanah's husband died in 1894, she moved from Wellsville to Logan, Utah, to live with her children. She died in Logan on January 23, 1920.[13]

LIFE EXPERIENCES

In 1915, five years before her death, Susanah Stone Lloyd prepared an autobiographical sketch that captured the highlights of her life and reflected her indomitable spirit:

> I, Susanna[14] Stone Lloyd, being impressed to make a [s]ketch of my early life, will endeavor to do so. I was born of honest parents, in the town of Bristol, England, December 24, 1830. My father was William Stone, who was a master painter, born in London. My mother, Diana Grant Stone, was born in Glostershire, England. . . . My father's people belonged to the Church of England, Mother's people to the Wesleyans. I attended the Wesleyan Sunday School.

---

11. Her children were Thomas William Lloyd (1857–1946); Joseph Benjamin Lloyd (1858–1926); Jesse Willard Lloyd (1860–1952); Sarah Susannah Lloyd Redford (1861–1916); Daniel David Lloyd (1863–1935); Charles Edward Lloyd (1865–1926); Mary Dian[n]a Lloyd Hendrickson (1866–1950); Brigham Samuel Lloyd (1868–1868); Annie Elizabeth Lloyd Osmond, twin (1869–1961); Heber Lorenzo Lloyd, twin (1869–1869); Ezra Timothy Lloyd (1871–1961); John Ephream Lloyd (1872–1895); Olive Margaret Lloyd Bjorkman (1874–1948); and George Francis Lloyd (1876–1952).

12. "Mother of the Lloyd Family," 182.

13. "Susanah S. Lloyd," Utah Death Certificate; "Funeral Held for Mrs. Lloyd on Tuesday," *Logan Republican,* January 29, 1920.

14. Alternate spelling used at the time of transcription.

I used to read the scriptures and wish that I had lived in the days of Apostles and Prophets, not knowing then that the Everlasting Gospel had been restored to the earth. When I heard it preached I hailed it with joy. I joined the Church of Jesus Christ of Latter Day Saints about the year 1848 [June 15, 1849[15]]. This caused my heart to rejoice. I have seen that the hand of the Lord has been over me for good from my earliest childhood and I know that His Holy Spirit has been my constant guide and companion. I never shall forget the many manifestations of the Lord's goodness and blessings unto me and mine. My parents, relatives and friends did all in their power to keep me from coming to America, but I had the spirit of gathering and the Lord opened up my way and I came to Utah in 1856 with the Hand Cart Company.[16]

Susanah recorded for a group of young women a short, handwritten reminiscence of her experiences as a member of the Willie Handcart Company:

> Being requested By Some of the Officer[s] and members of the young Ladies association to give a Sketch of our travels in crossing the Plains in Early days with handcarts I will indeavor to do So as far as my memory will Serve me—
> My Parents and relatives [blank]. In the year Eighteen hundred and fifty Six President Young advised the young Peopel of the Church in the British Isles to gather to zion. We was young then. Menny of us young Peopel having the Spirit of gathering was willing to make Every Sacrifice to get hear. So we left our houses and all to gather with the Saints that we [illegible] in an earthly sence.
> We Started in May to Cross the great atlantic ocean and

---

15. "Susanah Stone," Record of Members.

16. Lloyd, "Sketch," in Information on Thomas and Susanna Lloyd, 1.

we Came to liverpool the first week in May and we Crossed
the Sea on the Ship Thornton, we landed in new york in
July. We was detained by fogs which threw us later in the
Seasan. It was A Sailing vessel. after arriving in new york
we Stayed at A Place Called Castel Gardens for A few days,
then went up the rivers on Steam Boats up threw the State.
we traveled Some by rail untill we Came to the fronteers
which was Ioway Campground whear our outfits were being
made ready—oxendrawed our ~~Prov~~ Provisions and tents—
and we brought anough Clothing to last us to the end of
our journey if we had not been detained on our hand Carts.
the rest of our Clothing was brought the next of Spring by
the Walker Brothers. I never Shall forget the Day that we
Started from the Camp grounds

Brother James Willy was our Captin Brother Millen
Atwood was his Councilor they were two good fatherly Men
they done all in their power to make ~~it~~ our journey Pleasent
under the Circumstances—Some of our Bretheren from Salt
Lake was on the Campground when we Started with our
hand Carts. they Showed us how to Push and Pull we traveled very Slowly the first few days but After we got more
used to traveling we made better head way. It was very warm
weather the forepart of our journey but it was Plesent morn-
ings and Evenings. A few days after we had traveled we met
A Company of indians with an indian Interpreter telling
us that their had been A Massacree—the parties mentioned
was Coulnal Babbet and his teamsters that were taking A
train of goods to Salt lake. The year we Crossed the Plains
we met Severel indian tribes going East to war as we were
comming West. but nothing daunted us for we new that we
was on the Lords Side and we knew that he could protect
us. we passed the Campgrounds of Severel famlies that was
masacreed the Same Season that was on their way to the
gold fields of California

After we had got quite A distance on our journey we lost as near as I can remember forty head of Cattel or oxen that drawed the provision waggons that delaid us Severel weeks while they was hunting them Some Suposed that they were Stampeded by bufalo others thought that the indians had driven them off. this threw us latter in the Season which brought us to Suffer with the cold as well as throwing our Provisions Short. after we had traveled about Seven hundred miles we Came to Larime Station, where our Captain Bought all the Provisons that Could be bought after we got within an hundred and fifty miles of Salt lake our provisions again became very Scarce but the Lord in A meracilous way opened up our way by inspireing his Servent President Young to Send releif. I remember the Morning when our Captain Started out on horseback and told us that when he See[s] us again it would be with good news. The morning that he Started it became very Cold and it Snowed and the bretheren that had charge of the company Said that we had better Stay untill the Storm was over and for all we were under Sutch trying Circumstances the Lord blessed us with Sutch an out pouring of his holy Spirit that our hearts were filled with Joy and we Sang the Songs of zion.

Soon after the Storm abated we Saw our good old Captain Coming over the Brow of the hill waving his hat and when he Came to us he told us their was A Company of Brethren on their way to meet us Ladened with Provisons Buffelo robes and blankets and teams to take us home to the valley. You Can better Emagin then I can describe the joy & rejoycing that filled the Camp Some of our brethren that Came to meet us was old acquaintences you may guess wha[t] A happy meeting that was

Their was A Company that Started before us they got in in good time before the Cold weather Started and their was one that was a Little behind us.[17] I believe that it was about five hundred in our Company when we started but some Stayed back in the States others died with the hardships of the journey we got into Salt Lake on the fifth of november 1856[18] nine years after the Pioneers

Our journey Emortalized the Lives of those that re-mained faithful.[19]

In her formal life sketch, Susanah continued:

I am thankful that I was counted worthy to be a pi-oneer and a hand cart girl. It prepared me to stand hard times when I got here. I often think of the songs we used to sing to encourage us on our toilsome journey. It was hard to endure, but the Lord gave us strength and courage. Yes, the Lord has multiplied blessings upon my head, and I praise His Holy Name and pray that I may be worthy of the many blessings that are promised to the faithful. After we had traveled about seven hundred miles our provisions being short, our captain bought up all the biscuits and flour that he could get in Laramie. We had to live on short ra-tions and it became very cold. A number of our older people died. Sixteen were buried at one time. Traveling as we were with scant clothing and lack of sufficient food, we suffered greatly from the severe cold and snow. On account of the loss of cattle, it became necessary for each hand cart to take

---

17. Susanah may have been referring to the Edward Bunker Handcart Com-pany, whose members arrived in the Salt Lake Valley on October 2. The handcart company behind hers was the Edward Martin Handcart Company, whose mem-bers arrived in Salt Lake City on November 30.

18. The James G. Willie Handcart Company arrived in Salt Lake City on November 9, 1856. "James G. Willie Company (1856)," Mormon Pioneer Overland Travel Database, 1847–68, The Church of Jesus Christ of Latter-day Saints, accessed September 24, 2012, http://mormontrail.lds.org.

19. Lloyd, Autobiography.

additional load, but each taking a share of the provisions that were left.

We waded thru the cold streams many times but we murmured not for our faith in God and our testimony of His work were supreme. And in the blizzards and falling snow we sat under our hand carts and sang, "Come, come, ye saints, no toil nor labor fear, but with joy wend your way. Though hard to you this journey may appear, grace shall be as your day," etc. Only once did my courage fail. One cold dreary afternoon my feet having been frosted, I felt I could go no further, and withdrew from the little company and sat down to wait the end, being somewhat in a stupor. After a time I was aroused by a voice, which seemed as audible as anything could be, and which spoke to my very soul of the promises and blessings I had received, and which should surely be fulfilled and that I had a mission to perform in Zion. I received strength and was filled with the Spirit of the Lord and arose and traveled on with a light heart.[20] As I reached camp I found a searching party ready to go back to find me, dead or alive. I had no relatives but many dear and devoted friends and we did all we could to aid and encourage each other. My frosted feet gave me considerable trouble for many years but this was forgotten in the contemplation of the many blessings the Gospel has brought to me and mine. A young man [Theophilus Cox[21]] whom I had kept company with in England but would not promise to marry,

---

20. Two of Susanah's sons also wrote about this experience: George Francis related that Susanah heard a voice say, "Awake Susannah, you've only started upon your way." George F. Lloyd, "Poem," 1918, 4. Ezra Timothy related that the voice she heard said, "Susannah, take up your cross and follow the rest of the company. You have a great work to perform in Zion." Ezra Timothy Lloyd, *The Story of My Parents (Thomas Lloyd and Susannah Stone Lloyd)*, 1957, Typescript, p. 1, private possession.

21. Lloyd, "Poem," 4.

as I wanted to be free, died enroute and was buried on the plains with many others.

When we were within about a hundred miles from Salt Lake our captain had a dream that a company was coming from Salt Lake to meet us. . . . When we got near the City, we tried to make ourselves as presentable as we could to meet our friends. I had sold my little looking glass to the Indians for buffalo meat, so I borrowed one and I shall never forget how I looked. Some of my old friends did not know me. We were so weather beaten and tanned. When we got near Salt Lake Valley, President Young with a company of our brethren and sisters came out to meet us, and bade us welcome and when we got into the city we were made very comfortable until we met our friends and relatives. There were many things that would be interesting if I could remember them in their proper order. While we were traveling thru the United States the people tried to discourage us by telling us there was famine in Utah, that the grasshoppers had eaten up everything and that there had been a grasshopper war, etc., but we traveled on, trusting in God.

We raised good crops the next year. I had many chances to marry in England, but we were advised to wait until we got to Zion. Among others, who came to meet their friends, was a handsome young man, Thomas Lloyd, who had immigrated the previous year, 1855, from Wover Hampton [Wolverhampton], England. He had proved his integrity to his newly found faith by renouncing everything offered by a wealthy maiden aunt who had raised him, his parents having died when he was but two years old,[22] and he would have fallen heir to her fortune, but was cut off because he did not renounce Mormonism. He had learned a

22. Thomas's mother died when he was four years old, and his father died when Thomas was six.

trade, however, that of saddle and harness making, which proved a great blessing in the new country. He had settled in Farmington, Davis County, and had already a small cabin which served as home and workshop. We were both favorably impressed at our first meeting, he having received a very satisfactory recommendation from his Bishop and on advice of President Young we were soon married and the fulfillment of the blessings which had been pronounced upon my head in the numerous posterity began to be realized and in the following year our first son, Thomas W. Lloyd was born.

The following year Johnstown's [Johnston's] Army came to Utah and we had to move South under very trying circumstances. After this scare was over we were glad to get back to our homes again. We remained in Farmington until about 1864, when it became necessary for us to procure more land to take care of our growing family. We lived in forts, when Wellsville was first settled, to protect us from the Indians. The grasshoppers and crickets were very troublesome and ate up many of our crops, but we managed with the help of the Lord to take care of our growing, and by this time, numerous family. We were blessed with ten sons and four daughters, all of them are healthy and all members of the faith for which their parents had sacrificed and this is a joy to me in my declining years.

As Cache Valley became more settled the Lord blessed the land for our sakes and although we have suffered many hardships we have never murmured or felt to regret the sacrifice we made.

After my companion died, I sold my home in Wellsville and moved to Logan, where several of my children were living, and I have lived to realize the promises made by the patriarch that my age should be renewed ten years, and that my last days should be my best days.

One of Susanah's daughters concluded the sketch by writing, "Mother Lloyd died January 25th [23] 1920, surrounded by her family and a host of loving friends and relatives."[23]

Susanah Stone Lloyd's story has been recounted by her children and other descendants, as well as by Church leaders and members.[24] Mary Ellen W. Smoot, Relief Society general president from 1997 to 2002, spoke of developing inner strength and used the experience of Susanah Stone Lloyd as an example. Recounting Susanah's story about borrowing a mirror at journey's end and not being able to recognize herself, Sister Smoot commented: "[Susanah] was a different person, both inside and out. Over the course of rocky ridges and extreme hardship came a deep conviction. Her faith had been tried, and her conversion was concrete. She had been refined in ways

---

23. Lloyd, "Sketch," in Information on Thomas and Susanna Lloyd, 1–3.

24. Susanah's youngest child, George Francis, wrote a four-page poem about his mother and presented it to her on Christmas 1918 (cited previously; see nn. 20, 21). Two of Susanah's great-grandchildren, Jeannie Lloyd Goalan and Joseph Lloyd Hatch, prepared a children's book, *Susannah Stone: I Was a Handcart Girl* (n.p.: privately printed, 2009). A painting by Stephen Mark Bartholomew titled *Final Preparations at Rocky Ridge* was published in the October 2008 *Ensign* magazine, and the caption to the painting underscored the story of Susanah. "Pray Always," *Ensign*, October 2008, 40–43. Other published books that include Susanah's story are Andrew D. Olsen, *The Price We Paid: The Extraordinary Story of the Willie and Martin Handcart Pioneers* (Salt Lake City, UT: Deseret Book, 2006); Carol Cornwall Madsen, *Journey to Zion: Voices from the Pioneer Trail* (Salt Lake City, UT: Deseret Book, 1997); and Lynne S. Turner, *Emigrating Journals of the Willie and Martin Handcart Companies and the Hunt and Hodgett Wagon Trains* (Taylorsville, Utah: printed by author, 1996). In the 2011 movie about the Willie and Martin Handcart Companies, *17 Miracles,* directed by T. C. Christensen, Susanah's picture is shown during the credits.

On July 25, 2004, Lloyd Newell, a descendant of Susanah who serves as the voice of the Mormon Tabernacle Choir's *Music and the Spoken Word* program, highlighted her history on a broadcast celebrating Pioneer Day in Utah. He used Susanah's story as an example of faith in God and finding peace in adversity. He said, "What the pioneers came to know, we can know: God slumbers not nor sleeps as He watches over His children [Psalm 121:4]." *Music and the Spoken Word,* broadcast number 3910, July 25, 2004.

that the very best mirror could not reflect. Susanna had prayed for strength and found it—deep within her soul." Sister Smoot went on to encourage Church members to develop "inner strength . . . [and be] converted to the truth, so full of faith, so dependent on God that we are able to meet trials and even be strengthened by them."[25]

In Susanah's writing, she humbly declares that she and the other members of her emigrant company were "almost pioneers" because most of the road they traveled had already been laid out by those who went before them. She expresses concern about receiving the blessing of the faithful, not seeing that, yes, without question, she was a pioneer in her own right. Susanah took courage by faith through difficult times across the plains, and through it all she "traveled on trusting in God," concluding thankfully that she was "counted worthy to be a pioneer and a handcart girl."[26]

---

25. Mary Ellen W. Smoot, "Developing Inner Strength," *Ensign,* May 2002, 13.

26. Lloyd, "Sketch," in Information on Thomas and Susanna Lloyd, 1.

Chapter 14

"HOPE IN THE GOSPEL"

ROSA CLARA FRIEDLANDER LOGIE (1837–1913)
Marjorie Newton

BIOGRAPHICAL SKETCH

Rosa Clara Friedlander was born on the Isle of Guernsey on January 16, 1837, the daughter of Henry and Eliza Sampson Friedlander. Rosa's father died when she was a child, and her widowed mother left the Channel Islands and moved to London before migrating to Australia with her children. On March 11, 1849, Eliza, with Rosa (who turned twelve during the voyage) and eight-year-old James, arrived in Sydney on the *St. Vincent*. Eliza, a competent dressmaker, soon found work in Sydney, and in September 1851 she married recently widowed George Wright Watson. Six months later, George, Eliza, Rosa, and James were all baptized into The Church of Jesus Christ of Latter-day Saints by Elder Charles Wesley Wandell. They became active in the newly organized Sydney Branch.

In May 1853, at the age of sixteen, Rosa married another Latter-day Saint convert, Charles Joseph Gordon Logie. Two years later, Charles and Rosa and their one-year-old daughter sailed for

California with a company of migrating Saints. Just four weeks into the voyage, their vessel, the *Julia Ann,* was wrecked on a reef, and five of the Saints were drowned. After two months on a coral atoll, the survivors, including the Logie family, were rescued, finally reaching California in 1856. After some months in Nevada, the Logies arrived in Utah the following year and eventually settled in American Fork, where Rosa and Charles raised a large family of eleven children. Rosa died there on June 15, 1913, at the age of seventy-six.

Life Experiences

In the 1840s, a voyage by sailing ship from England to the British colony of New South Wales was long and hazardous; however, thousands of emigrants gladly risked the dangers in hope of a better life in Australia. Among these were eleven-year-old Rosa Clara Friedlander, who traveled with her mother, Eliza, and younger brother, James. After just six years in Sydney, Rosa—now aged eighteen and married—faced another long, dangerous journey by sailing ship. This time she sailed from Sydney, New South Wales, to California and then traveled by mule train across the deserts and mountains to the Salt Lake Valley. By the time she was out of her teens, Rosa Clara Friedlander Logie had almost circled the world and along the way had experienced conversion to The Church of Jesus Christ of Latter-day Saints, marriage, the birth of her first child, and shipwreck. Her journey was not only temporal but spiritual.

By the time the Friedlander family arrived in Sydney, the town, which had been founded as a penal settlement in 1788, was a thriving metropolis trying to forget its convict origins. While a few Latter-day Saint immigrants from Britain were striving to spread the restored gospel in the widely scattered British colonies in Australia, it was not until the arrival of the first American missionaries that the work really began to take hold. Elders John Murdock (father of the twins adopted by Joseph and Emma Smith) and Charles W. Wandell arrived in Sydney at the end of October 1851 to officially open the Australasian Mission, just six weeks after Rosa's mother, Eliza, and

George Watson were married. The missionaries baptized a handful of converts before Christmas and organized the Sydney Branch of the Church on January 4, 1852.[1]

Eliza Friedlander Watson was baptized on February 19, 1852; fifteen-year-old Rosa on March 21; her stepfather, George W. Watson, the following day; and eleven-year-old James on March 28.[2] They became active members of the fledgling Sydney Branch, attending Sunday meetings in the Old Assembly Rooms in King Street. During the week, priesthood meetings, choir practice, and cottage meetings[3] were held in the homes of members or the mission president's rooms, and the Watson family participated in these. Several of these meetings were held in their home.

George Watson, who had been ordained a priest soon after his baptism, agreed to move to Melbourne, five hundred miles south, and work as a part-time missionary there while plying his trade as a shoemaker. By July 1852, he had arrived in Melbourne with Eliza and James.[4] Fifteen-year-old Rosa, who did not get along well with her stepfather, was allowed to remain in Sydney under the guardianship of successive mission presidents. She lived at Kissing Point, some miles along the Parramatta River, with a young, newly married Latter-day Saint couple, Robert and Mary Ann Evans. The Sydney

---

1. Marjorie Newton, *Southern Cross Saints: The Mormons in Australia* (Laie, HI: Institute for Polynesian Studies, 1991), 26–29.

2. Manuscript History and Historical Reports, February 1 and March 3, 1852, Australasian Mission, Church History Library, The Church of Jesus Christ of Latter-day Saints, Salt Lake City, Utah, hereafter cited as Church History Library.

3. Cottage meetings were small gatherings where interested persons were taught Latter-day Saint beliefs. Proselyting missionaries typically taught the groups. William E. Berrett, "Cottage Meetings," in *The Gospel Message: Sunday School Lessons for The Church of Jesus Christ of Latter-day Saints* (Salt Lake City, UT: Deseret Sunday School Union, 1944), chap. 22.

4. "Quarterly Conference of the Church of Jesus Christ of Latterday [sic] Saints in Australia," *Millennial Star* 14, no. 42 (December 11, 1852): 663–64.

branch began to grow, numbering sixty-three members in March 1853.[5]

Mary Ann Evans and Rosa Clara Friedlander were good friends, and they enjoyed the activities of the Sydney Branch. Every Sunday, Rosa and her friends walked twelve miles to King Street, Sydney, where they attended the Sunday meetings of the little branch. On Thursday evenings, Rosa attended the weekly "singing meeting" held in a member's home or the mission president's rooms and sang in the choir (led by her friend Mary Ann) on Sundays. She helped distribute tracts and, like most branch members, tried hard to help spread the gospel in Sydney.

Among the new converts was a young man named Charles Joseph Gordon Logie, was born in London in 1829. The Logie family traveled first to Sydney and then to New Zealand, where they were among the earliest British immigrants, arriving about 1840. Charles, the eldest of a large family, went to sea in his late teens.[6] One day Charles, now in his early twenties, found himself on shore leave in Sydney. According to Logie family history, Charles and a group of sailor friends were walking along a Sydney street when they spotted beautiful young Rosa Friedlander on the upstairs balcony of a Latter-day Saint meeting place. Charles reportedly declared, "I'm going to marry that girl," and climbed up the supporting posts and introduced himself to her. Soon he was taught the gospel by Elders James Graham and John S. Eldredge. As Charles attended Mormon meetings, his friendship with Rosa grew. He was baptized in April 1853, and a month later he and Rosa were married.[7]

---

5. "Foreign Intelligence—Australia," *Millennial Star* 15, no. 37 (September 10, 1853): 603.

6. Lee Drew, "They Were Pioneers," Lineagekeeper's Genealogy, accessed April 11, 2012, http://www.famhist.us/genealogy/histories/logiecharlesrosapioneers.php.

7. Laura Clara Logie Timpson, "A Brief History of the Lives of Charles Joseph Gordon Logie & Rosa Clara Friedlander Logie," 1965, Photocopy of typescript, private possession. The exact date of the baptism is not recorded, but the

At that early date, Latter-day Saint elders were not legally authorized to perform a marriage in any Australian colony. Accordingly, twenty-three-year-old Charles and sixteen-year-old Rosa were married at the Scots Church in Pitt Street, Sydney, on May 21, 1853. They were married by a well-known Presbyterian minister, the Reverend James Fullerton, an outspoken opponent of the Mormon missionaries. The new mission president, Augustus A. Farnham, and Mary Ann Gingell, another Latter-day Saint branch member, signed the register as witnesses. Although family records give the date of Rosa and Charles's marriage as May 24, 1853, an entry for that week in President Farnham's journal states, "May 21 Saturday . . . attended the Weding of Bro Logie and Sister Rose Clara Freelander at Parson Fulerton Returned to Bro Gangels and Mareid them over again."[8] Friends from the Sydney Branch then enjoyed a small reception for the young couple in the home of William and Mary Gingell. "Spent the Evening very happily enjoyed good Cake, Wine and fruit all in good Spirits, peace and harmony," wrote President Farnham.[9]

Rosa Logie's life as a young bride was not one of carefree married bliss. Charles did not go to sea again but probably worked as a carpenter, gaining skills that came in useful in later life. Rosa showed outstanding compassion and maturity when it became obvious that

---

missionaries who taught and baptized Charles Logie did not arrive in Australia until the end of March 1853.

8. Though the marriage register of the Scots Church omits the actual day, the previous marriage entry is dated May 19, and the following entry is dated May 23. A perpetual calendar shows that the Saturday between these dates was May 21, confirming the date recorded by President Farnham. State Records of New South Wales, Early Church Records, 1853, vol. 81, no. 534, Marriages at the Scots (Presbyterian) Church, Pitt Street, Sydney.

9. Augustus A. Farnham, Journals, 1852–1856, May 21, 1853, vol. 1, Holograph, Church History Library. Observance of the Word of Wisdom "was sporadic from the late 1830s until the early years of the twentieth century. . . . No binding Church policy was articulated during this time." Joseph Lynn Lyon, "Word of Wisdom," in *Encyclopedia of Mormonism*, ed. Daniel H. Ludlow, 4 vols. (New York: Macmillan, 1992), 4:1584–85.

American missionary John Hyde was dying of cancer. Elder Hyde was admitted to the Sydney Benevolent Asylum, a charitable hospital for the destitute. Conditions there were not ideal, and Rosa Logie, aged sixteen and only three months married, offered to care for him. On Saturday, August 20, President Farnham hired a carriage and conveyed the desperately ill Elder Hyde from the hospital to the Logie home. Here Rosa nursed him until he died the following Friday, August 26, with his mission president at his bedside. After engaging an undertaker and organizing Elder Hyde's funeral, President Farnham touchingly recorded in his journal that he returned to the Logie home and helped Sister Logie in "puting the house to rights."[10]

Only weeks later, Rosa must have realized that she was pregnant. A little daughter was born to the young couple on June 27 the following year, 1854. They named her Annie Augusta, the latter name a tribute to mission president Augustus A. Farnham. Rosa and Charles rejoiced in their first child, and Rosa would have found life as a young mother busy and fulfilling. Charles also was busy and faithful in his priesthood duties and was ordained an elder on October 3, 1853.[11]

The Saints in Sydney, like converts in Europe, longed to gather with the Latter-day Saints in Zion. Three companies of Saints baptized in the Australian colonies had already sailed for California by the middle of 1855. Charles and Rosa Logie planned to travel with the next company, which was to sail from Sydney on the barque *Julia Ann*. The vessel was relatively new and had already taken one company of Latter-day Saints from New South Wales to California. Charles Logie, an experienced sailor, was taken on as a crew member to work for his passage, and somehow Charles and Rosa found enough money to pay Rosa's fare. They sailed through the heads of

10. Farnham, Journal, August 27, 1853.

11. Manuscript History and Historical Reports, October 3, 1853, Australasian Mission, Church History Library.

Port Jackson (Sydney Harbour) on Friday, September 7, 1855, with Latter-day Saints being half of the "fifty-six souls on board."[12]

As was customary, the gathering Saints were well organized. Convert John Penfold, who had previously served as president of the Clarence Town Branch and the Hunter River Conference north of Sydney, was set apart as company president. Counting returning missionaries James Graham and John S. Eldredge, there were twenty-eight Latter-day Saints on board.[13]

There were no premonitions of disaster, and life on board proceeded smoothly and harmoniously. About 8:30 P.M. on the evening of Wednesday, October 3, 1855, just one month after sailing from Sydney, the *Julia Ann* struck a reef near the atoll known as the Scilly Isles, named by an eighteenth-century navigator for a perceived similarity to the Scilly Isles off Cornwall, England.[14] No one was at fault. The navigation chart the captain was using was inaccurate, but at this date there were no accurate charts of the Scilly Isles, 340 miles west of Tahiti. Investigations later found that although the captain's calculations were correct, the chart was wrong, and the vessel was actually sixty to ninety miles off course.[15]

When the *Julia Ann* violently struck the reef, Rosa was putting her baby to bed in the cabin in the company of Andrew and Elizabeth Anderson and Eliza Harris, who were also putting their

---

12. "Capt. Pond's Narrative of the Wreck," Benjamin F. Pond to James O. Pond, February 9, 1856, in Benjamin Franklin Pond, *Narrative of the Wreck of the Barque "Julia Ann"* (New York: Francis & Loutrel, 1858); Benjamin Franklin Pond, Autobiography, 1895, Microform, Library of Congress. Typescript of applicable portion available as "Wreck of the *Julia Ann*," Mormon Migration Database, Brigham Young University, accessed April 11, 2012, http://lib.byu.edu/mormon-migration/voyage.php?id=204#account767.

13. "A Compilation of General Voyage Notes," September 7, 1855, in "Julia Ann," Mormon Migration Database, Brigham Young University, accessed April 11, 2012, http://lib.byu.edu/mormonmigration/voyage.php?id=204#account767.

14. Known today as Manuae Atoll.

15. Pond, Autobiography.

children to bed. Several other Saints were sitting on top of the midship house singing hymns.[16] It quickly became obvious that the tilting vessel was taking water and was badly damaged. Huge waves broke over the ship, which shuddered with each impact so the passengers found it almost impossible to stand. At first all was confusion and terror in the tropical darkness, but one of the sailors, an expert swimmer, managed to reach the reef and secure a rope. Back on board, the captain fashioned a sling, and one of the crew prepared to take the women and children one by one off the sinking ship.

The women were badly frightened, not knowing what awaited them. Young Rosa Clara Logie bravely volunteered to go first. She helped tie baby Annie securely to Charles's back in a brown woolen shawl and readied herself to be taken to the reef.[17] Suddenly a giant wave smashed onto the stricken vessel, and Rosa watched in horror as her husband and baby were swept overboard. Despite having been a sailor for several years, Charles did not know how to swim; however, a brave seaman dived into the pounding surf and grasped Charles by the hair, and soon he and baby Annie were relatively safe again on board. Rosa courageously climbed onto the lap of a sailor seated in the sling and held on tightly while they were hauled through the crashing waves to the reef by the sailors already there.[18] Once there she had to climb down so the sailor could return for the other women and children. As more passengers arrived, they were left standing in the darkness on the sharp coral reef, waist deep in water as the surf broke relentlessly over them.[19]

Back on the vessel, Andrew Anderson and young Peter Penfold tried their utmost to save the women and younger children still

16. Peter Penfold to Charles Penfold, February 17, 1856, in *Zion's Watchman* 2, no. 5 (May 24, 1856): 75–77.

17. John McCarthy to [George Q.] Cannon, April 25, 1856, in "Editor of the Standard," *Deseret News [Weekly]*, July 2, 1856.

18. Pond, "Narrative of the Wreck," 115.

19. Timpson, "Brief History," 2.

trapped below deck in the cabin. Some of the women and older children successfully reached the poop deck. Peter then passed two small children up from the cabin to Brother Anderson on the deck. As Brother Anderson grasped them, he watched helplessly as his own ten-year-old daughter, Marian, and nine-year-old Mary Humphreys were washed off the poop deck and drowned. As the ship broke in two, two Latter-day Saint women, Eliza Harris and Martha Humphreys (mother of nine-year-old Mary), together with Eliza's six-week-old baby boy, were drowned in the flooded cabin. The heavier half of the vessel, weighed down by its cargo of coal, sank immediately, but the lighter section of the vessel—with some of the migrating Saints still clinging to it—was washed high onto the reef, or more lives would have been lost.

Thus by midnight, the rest of the ship's company had arrived safely on the reef either by rope or on the washed-up wreckage. For the stranded survivors—bruised from being tossed around when the ship struck the reef and bleeding from cuts caused by the sharp coral—the night dragged interminably. There was no moon, and they were in utter darkness. The ship's mast lay horizontal in the nearby waves. While some of the shipwrecked passengers and crew stood on the reef, others sat on the broken mast, all of them waist-deep in salt water and without food or drinking water. All they could hear was the ghostly tolling of the ship's bell as the wreckage shifted, and the heartbroken sobbing of Elizabeth Anderson as she mourned her lost daughter.[20]

At last daylight revealed a small islet a few miles away. One of the ship's boats had been saved from the wreck, damaged but still serviceable for short trips, and was used to ferry the surviving passengers to the safety of the island. This could not be done quickly, and some of the crew waited on the reef for two days, without food or water and exposed to the fierce tropical sun, until all the passengers had been moved. At last everyone reached the little island.

---

20. Pond, "Narrative of the Wreck," 17.

The survivors soon organized a daily routine. They filtered brackish water by placing a barrel saved from the wreck in a hole dug in the sand. Their principal food was what little the island provided: turtle meat and eggs, crabs, and some fish and coconuts. Very little was salvaged from the wreck—one chest of women's clothing, a few tools, and a little flour and other food. "The turtles used to come up on the beach in the night to lay eggs in the sand and the boys would turn them on their backs and go and bring them in the next morning," recalled Charles Logie forty years later. "We built a pen for them and used to kill one each day. There was also a fine grove of cocoanut trees on another part of the reef and we used to grate these nuts and mix the turtle eggs and a little flour that we saved from the ship, and make pancakes."[21] Coconut shells were fashioned into drinking vessels. Rosa Logie kept one of these for the remainder of her life, and this coconut shell is an heirloom treasured by her descendants to this day.

Rosa became ill, but there was little shelter to be had on the small islet where they were now camped until the men built some huts from wood and pandanus leaves. In the meantime, from the salvaged chest of clothing Charles fashioned a large silk skirt into a tent to shelter Rosa and Annie. Despite their troubles, Rosa remained faithful and stalwart. She never forgot the kindness of the Saints and missionaries—in particular Elder John S. Eldredge—while she was ill. Baby Annie crawled around happily, playing in the sand and quite unaware of the dangers she had survived. Apart from minor injuries received the night of the wreck, most of the castaways remained well, though they suffered from boils exacerbated by their unorthodox diet.[22]

After several weeks, the crew managed to repair the ship's boat, and Captain Pond and eight crew members, plus Latter-day Saint

---

21. Charles J. G. Logie, "Local and Other Matters," *Deseret News [Weekly]*, April 23, 1898.

22. Timpson, "Brief History," 2.

convert-missionary John McCarthy, set out on November 20 to row more than two hundred miles to the nearest inhabited islands. Four days later, they reached the island of Bora Bora and reported the tragedy. With the help of the British consul on the island of Rauatei, the captain of the schooner *Emma Packer* was contacted and departed the next day for the tiny island refuge of the stranded *Julia Ann* company. On December 3, two months after the wreck, the castaways were rescued. They disembarked safely in Papeete, the capital of the French Protectorate of Tahiti, on December 19, 1855.

Their troubles were not yet over, however. They had paid their passage to San Francisco and did not have the money to pay again. In desperation, they appealed to both the British and American consuls in Papeete. Peter Penfold, writing to his brother in Australia, reported the result. "The American consul said that he had nothing to do with us, because we were English; and the English Consul said he had nothing to do with us, because we were in an American ship; so we were in a very peculiar situation,—without friends, without money, without home, without clothes, without food, and in a strange land, under the French Government." They could do little to help themselves and their families. "There is but very little work for a man to do in this place," Peter Penfold lamented.[23]

On a remote South Pacific island in the mid-nineteenth century, true Christian charity eventually prevailed. Members of the local Freemasons Lodge, hearing of the survivors' plight, stepped in and cared for the destitute migrants until the consuls received authorization to help their own nationals.[24] Over the next few weeks and months, all the survivors finally found passage aboard vessels bound for California. In March 1856, John Penfold reported that nineteen of the ship's company were still in Tahiti, including Charles, Rosa, and Annie Logie. He wrote to mission president Augustus Farnham in Sydney, "Brother Logie, wife and child is about to sail for San

---

23. Penfold to Penfold, February 17, 1856, 78.
24. Penfold to Penfold, February 17, 1856, 17.

Francisco in about a fortnight."[25] Not until seven months after the wreck—and eight months after sailing from Sydney—did Charles and Rosa Logie reach San Francisco by way of Honolulu.

Elder George Q. Cannon, newly returned from his mission to the Sandwich Islands (Hawaii) and soon to be called to the Quorum of the Twelve Apostles, was presiding over the Church's California Mission, headquartered in San Francisco, and editing a Latter-day Saint journal, the *Western Standard*. Elder Cannon had already published accounts of the wreck from survivors who reached San Francisco earlier. Now he heard the Logies tell their story firsthand, and he presented Rosa with a small pewter teapot in recognition of her bravery in being the first woman to leave the ship and go to the reef. That teapot also is still a treasured family heirloom.[26]

After a few months in San Francisco, Charles Logie was offered work in Carson City, Nevada. There his and Rosa's second child and first son, Charles Joseph Logie, was born on November 18, 1856. The following year the Logies finally reached Utah, where they lived first in Lehi, next in American Fork, and then in Wallsburg, where their third child was born in 1859.

The Logie family moved to American Fork again in 1860, where their friends from the Sydney Branch, Robert and Mary Ann Evans, were now living. They lived at first in a one-room cabin with a dirt roof while Charles worked on the farm of his former missionary friend John S. Eldredge. The following year they bought a one-room house with a lean-to. Here they spent the rest of their lives, and Charles, by now a skilled carpenter, gradually added to the house to make a comfortable family home. An additional eight children were born to them in American Fork, and Rosa experienced the

---

25. John Penfold to Augustus Farnham, March 21, 1856, in *Zion's Watchman* 2, no. 5 (24 May 1856): 70.

26. Timpson, "Brief History," 2.

heartbreak of losing two children—Silas, aged ten, died in 1869, and Emilie, aged two, in 1878.[27]

The Logies never had much in the way of worldly goods, but according to their granddaughter, Laura Clara Logie Timpson, they valued what they did have: "faith in their God, hope in the gospel and their life among the Saints."[28] Nevertheless, life at times was difficult for them, and Charles was grateful to work for eggs, butter, and vegetables. He worked as a carpenter when opportunity offered, gradually developed a business making coffins, and also served as the town undertaker.

The Logies were hospitable, and descendants record that their home was always open to weary wayfarers, as there was no hotel in American Fork at that time. Their home became a regular stopping place for Saints from settlements farther south traveling to and from general conference in Salt Lake City. When all the beds were full, visitors slept on Rosa's floors. Stephen L. Chipman, who boarded with Charles and Rosa for a time, testified of Rosa's homemaking skills and hospitality. "The meals were always . . . well cooked and enjoyed," he said. "It was not the meal alone, but the wonderful welcome you were always sure of . . . that made you love to go there."[29]

Charles Joseph Gordon Logie died in 1903. By that time most of their children were married with homes of their own. To support herself, the ever-resourceful Rosa, now sixty-six years old, turned

---

27. Rosa and Charles's children were Annie Augusta Logie Clark (1853–1938), Charles Joseph Logie (1856–1930), Silas James Logie (1859–1869), Rosa Clara Logie Bennett (1861–1918), Eliza Sampson Logie Bennett (1863–1913), Elizabeth Logie Atkins (1866–1936), Walter Logie (1869–1932), Elenor Logie Gaisford (1871–1933), Georgina Logie Bradley Selson (1873–1940), Emilie Logie (1875–1878), Beatrice Logie Coughlin Lauck (1880–1946). "Rosa Clara Friedlander (1837–1913)," Lineagekeeper's Genealogy, accessed September 24, 2012, http://www.famhist.us/genealogy/descendtext.php?personID=1488&tree=allfam&generations=.

28. Timpson, "Brief History," 3.

29. Timpson, "Brief History," 3.

their home into a boarding house, letting the empty rooms to travelers.[30] She died on June 15, 1913, after a six-month illness and was buried beside Charles in the American Fork cemetery.

At Rosa's funeral, a brief account was given of her early life and the hardships she and Charles had endured for the sake of the gospel. "How much could be said of such lives, vicissitudes, trials, poverty; everything to endure to discourage and dishearten, and through it all faith, hope and courage predominated," the speaker noted.[31] Rosa's obituary in the *Lehi Banner* gave a final glimpse of the life of this stalwart pioneer woman: "Mrs. Logie was a thoroughly good Christian woman and one who had a kind word for all and harsh words for none. She was a devoted wife and mother, a loyal friend and a good neighbor."[32]

Her numerous descendants hold her memory dear. Latter-day Saints throughout the world can ponder the trials that Rosa Clara Friedlander Logie endured for the gospel's sake, marvel at her enduring faith in the face of those trials, and strive to emulate her courage as they face their own different but often no less challenging trials in the twenty-first century.

30. 1910 U.S. Census, American Fork, Utah County, Utah.

31. "Death of Mrs. Rosa Logie," *Lehi Banner,* June 21, 1913.

32. "Death of Mrs. Rosa Logie."

Chapter 15

"Pleasure in Waiting upon Others"

Elizabeth Graham Macdonald (1831–1917)

Lowell C. "Ben" Bennion

Biographical Sketch

During Thomas and Elizabeth Kane's winter sojourn in St. George, Utah (1872–73), they met a charming middle-aged Scottish couple named "McDiarmid" (Macdonald). Using pseudonyms, Elizabeth Kane described her new friends "Maggie" (Elizabeth Graham Macdonald) as a "little" but "still goodlooking" wife and "Hugh" (Alexander Findlay Macdonald) as "a brave looking giant of a husband." Even "after twenty years of wedlock," they acted like "married lovers."[1]

---

1. Elizabeth W. Kane, St. George Journal, 1872–1873, Thomas L. Kane and Elizabeth W. Kane Collection, Holograph, January 21, 1873, pp. 191–92, 218, L. Tom Perry Special Collections, Harold B. Lee Library, Brigham Young University, Provo, Utah. For a published transcription, see Elizabeth Kane, *A Gentile Account of Life in Utah's Dixie, 1872–73: Elizabeth Kane's St. George Journal,* ed. Norman R. Bowen (Salt Lake City: Tanner Trust Fund, University of Utah Library, 1995). Elizabeth gives "Maggie" more pages than anyone else because this

Elizabeth Graham was born on January 12, 1831, in Perth, Perthshire, Scotland, the fifth of ten daughters born to John and Christina MacKenzie Graham. Born in distinctly different regions of Scotland, Elizabeth and her future husband, Alexander, were the first converts in the small southeastern port of Perth.[2] Their marriage in 1851 upset members of the Graham and Macdonald clans as much as their baptism had.[3]

The Macdonalds prepared to migrate to Zion, and despite religious differences with their family members, sailed from Liverpool accompanied by Alexander's father, Duncan Macdonald, and Elizabeth's mother and sister Matilda in March 1854.[4] The group reached New Orleans in May, but many delays kept them from completing their "tiresome journey" overland until September 30.[5] Elizabeth became pregnant en route and gave birth to their first

spirited and "very warm-hearted" Scot had such a fascinating "Mormon love-story" (191, 218).

2. Elizabeth Graham Macdonald, Autobiography, 1875, Holograph, pp. 1, 3–4, Church History Library, The Church of Jesus Christ of Latter-day Saints, Salt Lake City, Utah, hereafter cited as Church History Library. Although covering just the first half of her life, Elizabeth's autobiography remains the best source for sizing up her personality. Alexander's parents moved to Perth from their Highland hamlet of Camusluinie, Kintail Parish, County Ross, when he was still very young. See section on "Alexander Findlay Macdonald, 1825–1903," in *Record of the Descendants of Alexander Findlay Macdonald and Fannie Van Cott,* comp. Taylor O. Macdonald (American Fork, UT: privately printed, 1987), n.p. Fannie Van Cott, whom Alexander married in 1870, was the last of his five wives.

3. Kane, St. George Journal, 192–94, describes the mothers' negative reactions to Elizabeth and Alexander's marriage.

4. Elizabeth's father and Alexander's mother both died in Scotland in 1853, which motivated the living spouses to migrate to Utah with Elizabeth and Alex.

5. Macdonald, Autobiography, 15–18. They traveled in the Daniel Garn Company, leaving from Westport, Missouri, on July 1 or 2, 1854. "Daniel Garn Company (1854)," Mormon Pioneer Overland Travel Database, 1847–68, The Church of Jesus Christ of Latter-day Saints, accessed June 14, 2012, http://mormontrail.lds.org.

child about three months after their arrival in Salt Lake City. They settled in Springville, Utah, the first of many moves that would take them to Provo and St. George, Utah; Mesa, Arizona; Colonía Juárez, Chihuahua, Mexico; and, in her case, back to Salt Lake via Mesa. At times, "little" Elizabeth found herself standing in the shadow or following in the footsteps of her "giant" husband, "Alex Mac."

The Macdonalds' stay in Utah Valley from 1855 to 1872 saw the birth of ten more children—all boys.[6] As if rearing them did not keep Elizabeth busy enough, Alexander added four more wives to the family. Being the first wife, "Betsy" (as friends often called her) was "looked upon as the head of the family."[7] Despite the trials of plural marriage, Elizabeth considered herself fortunate to "have had a husband amongst a thousand" and sister wives who "have ever shown kindness to me."[8]

Alexander's proven skills in building, clerking, and counseling resulted in a call to St. George soon after construction of a temple began there in November 1871. Elizabeth followed a year later and eventually became manager of apostle Erastus Snow's Big House, which was converted into a boarding house for temple construction workers.[9] Completion of the St. George Temple in 1877 gave the Macdonalds little respite from their labors. While her husband and two eldest sons served missions to Scotland, Elizabeth took charge of the farm and families and assisted with temple assignments. Shortly

---

6. Alexander Findlay Macdonald Jr. (1855–1916), Graham Duncan Macdonald (1856–1908), Joseph Booth Macdonald (1857–1942), Aaron Johnson Macdonald (1859–1884), Samuel Whitney Macdonald (1860–1868), Israel Hope Macdonald (1862–1865), Heber Chase Macdonald (1864–1903), Macrae Macdonald (1867–1902), Brigham Alma Macdonald (1868–1869), Smith Macdonald (1870–1870), and Abraham Owen Macdonald (1871–1872).

7. Kane, St. George Journal, 215.

8. Macdonald, Autobiography, 40.

9. "Elizabeth Graham Macdonald," in *Pioneer Women of Faith and Fortitude*, comp. International Society Daughters of Utah Pioneers, 4 vols. (Salt Lake City, UT: Publishers Press, 1998), 3:1845.

after Alexander's return to St. George in 1879, Elder Snow asked him to preside over the Saints in Mesa, Arizona, but Elizabeth stayed behind until 1882. Alexander presided over the Maricopa Stake as its first president (1882–87), while Elizabeth headed the Relief Society when it was organized (1883–88).[10]

To avoid arrest as a polygamist, Alexander left for Mexico a few years before Elizabeth briefly joined him in 1889. Her travel diary makes clear the reasons for her reluctance to stay.[11] She soon returned to Mesa but later moved to Salt Lake City, where she lived at least twenty years before returning to southern Utah.[12] Despite the distance that separated Elizabeth and Alexander from 1890 until his death in 1903, their love for each other never died. She passed away on July 11, 1917, and was buried in Provo beside five of her sons; she was survived by only one of her other six.

LIFE EXPERIENCES

Elizabeth Graham joined The Church of Jesus Christ of Latter-day Saints just a month after turning sixteen and devoted the rest of her life to the faith. How did this petite and spirited Scottish pioneer endure the many trials she faced between her baptism in the River Tay and her death near St. George, Utah, seventy years later? Judging by the forty-six-page autobiography she wrote in 1875, she developed a strong desire to serve, best expressed in her own words: "Ever since I joined the Church, my lot has been cast in places where I have had always the care of a great many more than

10. "Alexander Findlay McDonald," in Andrew Jenson, *Latter-day Saint Biographical Encyclopedia*, 4 vols. (Salt Lake City, UT: Andrew Jenson History Company, 1901–36), 3:557–58; Relief Society Minutes and Records, December 1883, Maricopa Stake, Church History Library; "Elizabeth Graham Macdonald," in *Pioneer Women*, 3:1845.

11. Elizabeth Graham Macdonald, "Diary, 1889 Jan-April," Typescript, 1969, Church History Library.

12. 1910 U.S. Census, Salt Lake City Ward 4, Salt Lake City, Utah; "Elizabeth Graham McDonald," 1917, State of Utah Death Certificate, no. 39.

my own family. In this I have taken pleasure and I can truthfully say, I have always taken more pleasure in waiting upon others than in being waited upon."[13] By examining certain experiences in the places where she lived, one can grasp her commitment to serving others.

As the fifth of ten daughters born to Presbyterian parents rooted in Perthshire, Scotland, Elizabeth wrote, "my opportunities to obtain a Common School education were quite limited." She took action. "My father's family being large, I felt ambitious to aid and educate myself as far as I could, and prepare myself for the duties of life, and, to further this object, I spent my girl-hood in domestic service." Elizabeth also learned how to sew and weave, her father being a tailor and her maternal grandfather "a Gingham weaver."[14]

One evening in late November 1846, a Latter-day Saint elder visiting the Graham house read from Parley P. Pratt's *Voice of Warning*. The tract impressed both Elizabeth and an acquaintance named Alexander F. Macdonald enough that both of them were baptized early the next year.[15] She soon met with persecution, she recounted, "even in my own father's house, where it became so oppressive that in May 1847 I went to Edinbro'." There she was warmly welcomed by district president William Gibson's family and obtained work as a domestic and governess.[16]

Two summers later, her father "came on a visit to Edinburgh" after suffering "a paralytic stroke." He asked Elizabeth to return home with him and to forget past persecutions. Since President Gibson viewed this as "an opening for me to do good," she went back to Perth, where only one person had been baptized since she left. Elizabeth soon attended the baptism of her ailing father and watched him walk home "without the aid of his crutch, and many who knew

---

13. Macdonald, Autobiography, 37.

14. Macdonald, Autobiography, 1–2.

15. Macdonald, Autobiography, 2–4.

16. Compare the somewhat differing accounts in Macdonald, Autobiography, 4–5, and Kane, St. George Journal, 192–93.

him witnessed this blessing. After this, the meetings were crowded to overflowing," and "the Perth Branch soon numbered one hundred and fifty members," including Elizabeth's mother and three of her sisters. At home once again, she wrote, "with my sister Catherine I engaged in the business of Millinery and Dress Making."[17]

In January 1850, after Atlantic seafaring as a shipwright, Alexander received a mission call to his native Highlands.[18] On his way north to Inverness, he passed through Perth and proposed marriage to a surprised but willing Miss Graham. A year later, he visited Perth again, this time to marry her. After an eight-day "honeymoon" spent traveling "from conference to conference among the brethren," Elizabeth moved to Blairgowrie, north of Perth, to live with and work for the family of a Mormon elder named Butters. His wife was not a member but he thought Elizabeth's influence might change his wife's mind about the Church.[19] Elder Butters, a shoemaker, employed and boarded "some fifteen persons, thus making the household labors arduous" even for an experienced domestic like Elizabeth.[20]

A year after the Macdonalds' marriage, the British Mission president, apostle Franklin D. Richards, called Alexander to preside over the Liverpool district, an assignment that finally allowed the young

---

17. Macdonald, Autobiography, 5–8. Catherine strongly opposed the Church at first but later joined it.

18. Alexander was born in tiny Camusluinie, Kintail Parish, County Ross, on the western coast of the Highlands (close to the Isle of Skye), the son of Gaelic-speaking crofters Duncan and Margaret Macrae Macdonald. He became a ship's carpenter in Perth and sailed far and wide for several years before and after joining the Church. A fellow worker introduced him to the Grahams. See Nelle Spilsbury Hatch and B. Carmon Hardy, eds., *Stalwarts South of the Border* (n.p.: Ernestine Hatch, 1985), 445–48, for a summary of Alexander's lifeline that differs in some details from Taylor O. Macdonald's account cited in footnote 2.

19. Kane, St. George Journal, 196–98.

20. Half a year later, she went to work for a family in Arbroath, farther north on the east coast. Macdonald, Autobiography, 8–9.

couple to live together. "We opened our house as a home for the brethren," she recalled, thereby becoming acquainted with numerous American elders and other visitors. For Elizabeth, moving into the "Conference House" also meant preparing meals and cleaning rooms. One Saturday in May 1853, "while performing my household labors, I fell down stairs" and thereafter "endured much affliction." Months later and alone, after asking God for someone to administer to her, she beheld "an aged man standing at the foot of my bed" who blessed her, declaring: "In tears and in sorrow thou hast bowed before the Lord asking for children, this blessing is about to be granted unto thee. Thou shalt be blessed with health from this hour."[21]

Soon after being released from their mission, the Macdonalds boarded the *John M. Wood* in Liverpool with four hundred other Saints on March 12, 1854. Alexander assisted the party's president, Robert L. Campbell, as second counselor.[22] On May 2, "after passing through the ordinary ordeals of an eight weeks' sea voyage," Elizabeth remembered, "we arrived at New Orleans." The "ordinary ordeals" were mostly weather-related, but on calm days Elizabeth may have joined other passengers in making tents and wagon covers for crossing the plains.[23] "We continued our journey . . . up the Mississippi and Missouri," wrote Elizabeth. "Considerable sickness prevailed. . . . We were detained at Quarantine Island, near St. Louis, for several days; when we were released we continued our journey up

---

21. Macdonald, Autobiography, 11–13.

22. The ship's company included Swiss and Italians as well as Britons, but Scots formed the largest single group (167 of 393). See Frederick S. Buchanan, "The Emigration of Scottish Mormons to Utah, 1849–1900" (master's thesis, University of Utah, 1961), Appendix B, 160–65.

23. For more detailed accounts of both the Macdonalds' voyage and their overland trek, consult the Mormon Migration Index, Harold B. Lee Library, Brigham Young University (www.lib.byu.edu/mormonmigration/voyage .php?id=200&q=johnmwood), and the Mormon Overland Travel Database, 1847–68, The Church of Jesus Christ of Latter-day Saints, http://mormontrail.lds.org.

the river on board the 'Honduras,' and finally landed at the General Encampment near Kansas [City] Village." There they waited "nearly two months" for "the purchase of cattle and wagons. . . . During this time quite a number of saints died of Cholera and were buried on the banks of the Missouri." Elizabeth felt "exceedingly thankful to the Lord . . . that we had been preserved upon the sea and upon the river in the midst of disease and death."[24]

The "two yoke of cattle" Alexander purchased early in July "were young, never having been yoked up before." Elizabeth lets readers "imagine the indescribable evolutions of an utterly inexperienced driver and of as utterly unbroke cattle. . . . I know that my extreme anxiety together with my walking made me very tired. It would not have been safe for any of us to have ridden, for the Oxen were not at all particular to keep the road." Eventually "our wild team became so docile that they would come to us at our bidding. They would eat bread and bacon out of my hand, and became so domesticated that I became quite attached to them."[25]

"Before reaching Laramie," Elizabeth reported, "we heard rumors of difficulties with the Indians," prompting her party to pitch camp "in a bend of the Platte" for a while and "guard against an Indian surprise" like the one that had occurred shortly before with "a Company of U.S. troops."[26] Once past Laramie, "we pursued our journey daily without any other incident worth mentioning till . . . we arrived in sight of Salt Lake City." On "the Bench east of the City," they were greeted by a few friends and soon "rented rooms of

---

24. Macdonald, Autobiography, 15–16. By "quite a number," Elizabeth may have meant dozens. William Empey reported the death of "about 200" in the three companies that preceded the Macdonalds'. William Empey to Brigham Young, June 23, 1854, in "Daniel Garn Company (1854)," Mormon Pioneer Overland Travel Database, 1847–68, The Church of Jesus Christ of Latter-day Saints, accessed June 19, 2012, http://mormontrail.lds.org. Cholera was clearly the primary killer.

25. Macdonald, Autobiography, 16–17.

26. Macdonald, Autobiography, 17–18.

Bro. Jacob Houtz and lived on the corner of Emigration St.," where they "remained during the winter."[27]

"By invitation we went to Jacob Houtz' farm and grist mill on Spring Creek, Utah Valley, and engaged to assist in erecting a new grist mill there." Before moving south to Springville, Elizabeth gave birth in Salt Lake to Alexander Jr., which reminded her of "the promise given . . . me by my mysterious Liverpool Visitor." Besides being "busily engaged in farming and in building mills," her husband served as a counselor to Bishop Aaron Johnson and in 1858 was elected mayor.[28] Early the next year, however, Alexander was imprisoned on charges connected with the 1857 killings of three men, the Parrish-Potter murders. Although there was little evidence to indict Alexander, officials took him to Camp Floyd, where he was "placed in solitary confinement . . . [for] nearly two months."[29] While en route to the court at Nephi, Alexander and another prisoner escaped to the mountains and remained in hiding until late October. Thus, for much of 1859 Elizabeth saw little of her husband while caring for four young boys.[30]

"I cannot describe the painful feelings I had under these trying circumstances," Elizabeth wrote. She believed Alexander's unjust treatment had occurred because he was a Mormon:

> This experience taught us that persecution strengthens
> the good and has a tendency to expose and clear off the
> dross. I must certainly state that in persecution, I always felt

---

27. Macdonald, Autobiography, 19.

28. Macdonald, Autobiography, 19–20.

29. Macdonald, Autobiography, 23

30. Elizabeth vividly describes the unnerving events of 1859 in her Autobiography, 20–26. After Alexander returned home in October, Elizabeth recorded that "nothing very particular happened" with regard to his involvement in the court case (26). One historian, in her study of the Parrish-Potter murders, has "seen no evidence" that would "implicate Macdonald." Polly Aird, email message to author, June 6, 2011.

stronger, than when all was peace and quietness. . . . Certain it is that many a member of the church has scarcely known himself to be a Latter Day Saint with full faith in God until he was overtaken by the spirit of persecution from the ungodly; but when such persecution came, the powers of mind became aroused, their faith in the Lord active, the desire to unite with their fellows in adversity made manifest and they have been as ready as any to, if necessary, lay down their lives for the Gospel sake.[31]

As the Macdonalds' lives quieted down, Elizabeth remembered, they "endeavored to complete the house which we had commenced previous to my husband's imprisonment. . . . We were contented, for we realized that as Saints [we] have to be tried in all things."[32] But before completing and living in their "very comfortable dwelling," wrote Elizabeth, "our presence was called elsewhere." In the autumn of 1862, six weeks after Elizabeth gave birth to their sixth son, "we were called to go to Provo. . . . Our hands appeared to be pretty full with our young and increasing family; yet we were all the time blessed with good health among them, for up to this time we had never had an hour's sickness among the children."[33]

During the Macdonalds' decade-long residence in Provo, Elizabeth gave birth to five more sons. While attending meetings in July 1863, Brigham Young's counselor, Heber C. Kimball, stayed with them. "At the dinner table one day," Elizabeth recalled, "the conversation turned upon the subject of my having six sons." When the "jocular" Kimball prophesied their next child would be a boy, their friend Robert Campbell asked, "Sister Mac, if it should be a girl, what then?'" Whereupon Brother Kimball insisted "it would be

---

31. Macdonald, Autobiography, 21, 26–27.

32. Macdonald, Autobiography, 27–28.

33. Macdonald, Autobiography, 28–29. In Provo, Alexander took charge of the tithing department and post office and helped finish the meetinghouse.

a boy and he would see it," which he did a year later, four days after the arrival of son number seven, named of course Heber Chase.[34]

Elizabeth gave birth to four more boys by 1871, but the last three did not live long.[35] In May 1872, Alexander was "called to labor in St. George . . . , to which place he took most of his family. I went to live on our farm near Provo and continued to live there during the summer,"[36] explained Elizabeth Macdonald. She told Elizabeth Kane that "it was not convenient for her to leave their elder boys alone on the farm."[37] In October 1872, Alexander "came north and wished me to get ready to go south with him after Conference was over," Elizabeth wrote. "My son Owen"—just eighteen months old—"was very sick and I feared going from home with him." Nevertheless, she finally agreed to make the journey and at Nephi, "my boy died. This was another great trial to me. I doted on my boy very much, perhaps the more so, because my two previous children had died while very young." Owen was buried in Provo, "five out of my eleven sons being laid side by side."[38]

Elizabeth's trials in Utah Valley make it easy to understand why she took such "great pleasure in this southern country [Utah's Dixie],

---

34. Macdonald, Autobiography, 29–30.

35. Son Israel died as the result of a thigh injury at age two, one son was stillborn, and the other two died in infancy of unspecified illnesses.

36. Macdonald, Autobiography, 34–35. Elizabeth does not specify the nature of Alexander's call to St. George. In late October 1871, however, he had joined Brigham Young's party bound for St. George to dedicate the temple block. Afterwards he helped survey Fort Pearce, fifteen miles southeast of town. George Albert Smith, October 27, 1871, Journal, 1839–1875, Typescript, p.17, Church History Library. The following summer Erastus Snow called Alexander to serve as second counselor in the St. George Stake presidency. James G. Bleak, *Annals of the Southern Utah Mission,* July 13, 1872, Typescript, p. 145, Church History Library.

37. Kane, St. George Journal, 217.

38. Macdonald, Autobiography, 35–36. The five sons were Samuel Whitney Macdonald (1860–1868), Israel Hope Macdonald (1862–1865), Brigham Alma Macdonald (1868–1869), Smith Macdonald (1870–1870), and Abraham Owen Macdonald (1871–1872).

especially in having my family all around me, in the midst of good influences. . . . I prefer it to the north; the people are sociable and kind, and we have no outside element to contend with."[39] In the winter of 1873–74, "we were called to go and take charge of Brother E[rastus] Snow's mansion and open and keep it as a Boarding house for the use of some of the workmen engaged on the St. George Temple." After taking charge of the St. George House, or Big House, as it was called, Elizabeth recorded, "The inmates have varied from thirty to sometimes nearly eighty persons, and though the task is arduous [and my health is poor] I take pleasure in my labors in helping to build a Temple to the Most High in this desert land, where we may receive blessings to fit us for greater usefulness."[40]

"Before closing my record," wrote Elizabeth, "I will briefly review some of my experience and views in connection with the doctrine of Plural or Celestial Marriage." Alexander had married his first plural wife, Sarah Johnson, in 1856, but the marriage lasted only two years, and she had died by 1860.[41] "Three other wives have since been added to my husband's household," Elizabeth recorded.

---

39. The "outside element" in the north may refer to greater Gentile influences, heavier presence of federal law enforcement officials (who were responsible for Alexander's 1859 imprisonment and the later polygamy raids), and the U.S. troops who broke into and damaged the Macdonalds' house in 1870 while Elizabeth and three little ones were there alone. Macdonald, Autobiography, 36.

40. Macdonald, Autobiography, 36–38. The Big House was the same one in which the Kanes had stayed a year earlier. After Brigham Young's party arrived in St. George on November 11, 1874, apostle George A. Smith "engaged two rooms and board in the St. George House Kept by A. F. Macdonald." At midnight, December 31, 1874, George and his wife Bathsheba "received a visit in our bedroom from A F McDonald his wives Betsy and Faney who wished us a happy newyear and treated us to Pie cakes nuts and Wine." George Albert Smith, Journal, 1839–1875, Typescript, pp. 3, 14, Church History Library.

41. W. Aird Macdonald, Notebook, Taylor O. Macdonald Collection, Microfilm of holograph, n.p., Church History Library.

Alexander married Scottish immigrants Agnes Aird and Elizabeth Atkinson on October 22, 1864, and Fannie Van Cott six years later.[42]

> In this Order of Marriage we, as wives have lived mostly together, forming one family household and have striven to do what was right and aid each other. I always had a faculty of creating plenty of work for myself, and have earned quite a reputation for keeping busy others who happened to be near. . . . The rule of our family has been always to attend to family prayer. . . . By attending to our prayers, we received strength from the proper source to remember our covenants and obligations to each other, and to help us to avoid tresspassing upon each other's rights.[43]

Elizabeth admitted to having had many "trials in this Order" but insisted that "the self control I have attained is of more value to me than all I could possibly have obtained by avoiding it." She was sustained through reason and testimony:

> A great deal of good can be done in a family of many wives when the man takes a wise course. . . . I have thought this was not sufficiently realized, and that the actions of some was as much governed by passion as by principle; this the law of God will not allow, hence the failures. . . . I bear testimony that the revelation on Celestial Marriage given through the Prophet Joseph, is from God. In my experience I do know that the blessings and promises contained in that revelation are realized when lived for. . . . Another reason why a plurality of wives is given to worthy men . . . [is] to multiply and replenish the earth . . . and for the exaltation

---

42. Macdonald, Autobiography, 38. Fannie Van Cott was the daughter of John and Lucy L. Sackett Van Cott and a sister of one of Brigham Young's wives, making Alexander and Brigham brothers-in-law.

43. Macdonald, Autobiography, 39.

of all who enter into this holy order; that they may bear the souls of men. . . . Then why should I or any other woman in the Church with-hold this privilege from another because of the feelings of our weak nature.[44]

If "Betsy" had written another autobiography covering the later half of her life, one might admire this petite but intrepid pioneer even more. She saw little of her husband while he was away from 1877 until 1882, first in Scotland and then in the Salt River Valley of Arizona. The quarterly minutes of the Maricopa Stake Relief Society provide only a few glimpses of Elizabeth's activities as president. By the end of her first year, she had "visited all of the branch societies of the Stake," including the one in nearby Lehi headed by sister wife Elizabeth "Lizzie" Atkinson. Elizabeth Macdonald reiterated her belief that developing a silk culture[45] "would be the [best] means of keeping our girls at home away from the Gentiles." She also expressed support for "the mission of our Brethren [prominent among them Brother Macdonald] who had gone to Mexico" to locate places of refuge for polygamous families.[46]

---

44. Macdonald, Autobiography, 38–44.

45. Brigham Young encouraged women to establish home industries to create a self-sustaining economy and supplement income. He considered "locally produced silk as a practical textile and as a light industry that could be maintained at home by women and children." Rarely a lucrative activity, women persisted in the task from leaf to fabric, spinning thread from silkworm cocoons. Elizabeth H. Hall, "Silk Culture," in *Encyclopedia of Mormonism,* ed. Daniel H. Ludlow, 4 vols. (New York: Macmillan, 1992), 3:1314–15; Eliza R. Snow, "Talk Number One: To Every Branch of the Relief Society in Zion," *Woman's Exponent* 3, no. 21 (April 1, 1875): 164–65; Chris Rigby Arrington, "The Finest of Fabrics: Mormon Women and the Silk Industry in Early Utah," *Utah Historical Quarterly* 46, no. 4 (Fall 1978): 376–96.

46. Relief Society Minutes and Records, December 11, 1884, Maricopa Stake, p. 12, Church History Library. She offered no suggestion for how mothers might influence their sons to become something other than freighters and falling into bad company.

In December 1886, Elizabeth, "having recently returned [to Mesa] from a visit to Utah," said she "felt better than she had done for years." She also "spoke of the joy and satisfaction she experienced in her labors in the Temple at St. George, in doing work for the dead of which she had the privilege of doing considerable." Two years later she announced her resignation as Relief Society president, because at last "she expected to leave in a few days to join her husband in Mexico." Imagine the Maricopa sisters' surprise when Elizabeth appeared two months later at their next meeting and spoke of Mexico as "the place for those raising *young* families."[47]

After spending two winter months in Colonía Juárez, "Sis Mac" was more than ready to return to Mesa, having decided, at age fifty-eight, that she had no desire for yet another pioneering venture. The Colonía Juárez Relief Society "got up a surprise party for Bro Mac and myself before leaving."[48] They left together, but he headed for Salt Lake, presumably to attend the Church's general conference. Along the way, Elizabeth "had some very plain talk with Bro Mac on different subjects and especially his concern to me for the past 10 years." She concluded, "We came to a proper understanding and made all things right."[49]

"Mexico is my field of labor," Alexander affirmed, and Elizabeth decided to make Salt Lake City, with its nearly completed temple,

---

47. Relief Society Minutes and Records, December 20, 1888, and March 22, 1889, Maricopa Stake, pp. 61 and 67, Church History Library (emphasis added).

48. Macdonald, "Diary," March 11, 1889.

49. Macdonald, "Diary," March 15, 1889. Elizabeth had undoubtedly felt neglected since Alexander's return from Scotland in 1879, partly because she had seen so little of him, even during their time "together" in Mesa and Mexico. Her sister wife Lizzie succeeded her as stake Relief Society president in Mesa but soon moved to Mexico to join Fannie after the death of their sister wife Agnes when the latter was killed by a hired hand in 1898. Fannie had gone from Mesa to Mexico as early as 1885 and stayed there until the Saints' exodus from Mexico in 1912, but she eventually returned to live with children who had not left Mexico. See Macdonald, *Record of the Descendants,* n.p.

her field of labor.[50] She became a cook and housekeeper in the temple, residing in the "Temple Cottage" just east of Temple Square.[51] That same year Alexander attended the April general conference and stayed with Elizabeth until at least mid-July before returning to Mexico.[52] On July 31, the wife of their son Joseph died in St. George, leaving him with four young children who subsequently moved to Salt Lake to live with Grandma Macdonald. Perhaps that is why she relocated to "a little frame cottage in the rear of 4th Ave. and I St."[53]

As Elizabeth's grandchildren married, they moved out of her house into homes of their own. Sometime after the 1910 census, Elizabeth's failing health apparently led her to live with a grandson and his wife in nearby Sugar House. Eventually she decided to return to the old Macdonald house in Middleton, near St. George,

50. Alexander F. Macdonald to Wallace A. Macdonald, June 7, 1893, Microfilm of holograph, Taylor O. Macdonald Collection, Church History Library. See also letters dated December 16, 1891, and July 11, 1892. Wallace, born in Provo in 1865, wanted his father to move back to Mesa after the 1890 Manifesto; the father kept inviting the son to settle in Mexico. Neither gave in to the other's wishes but nevertheless respected his decision.

51. *Salt Lake City Directory* (Salt Lake City, UT: R. L. Polk, 1897–1899), 437, 497, 549–50.

52. While in Salt Lake, Alexander wrote son Alexander F. Jr. that after attending conference, he was "working in the Temple with E.G. [Elizabeth Graham]." A few months later, he wrote a grandson, "We are entertaining the idea . . . to return for Temple Work at St. George." See letters of Alexander F. Macdonald to Alexander F. Macdonald Jr., April 20, 1899, and Alexander F. Macdonald to Aaron LeClair Macdonald, July 17, 1899, Microfilm of holograph, Taylor O. Macdonald Collection, Church History Library. These and other letters written by A. F. Macdonald while staying with Elizabeth imply both a continuing bond between them and their commitment to performing ordinances in the temple.

53. Lois Richards Hauck, "Addendum to the Biography of Elizabeth Graham Macdonald," Typescript, n.d., p. 3, Church History Library. *Salt Lake City Directory* (Salt Lake City, UT: R. L. Polk, 1910), 700, places her and A. LeClair Macdonald at "rear 371 4th av." but does not list any other boarders.

to stay with Joseph and his second wife.[54] Alexander's "last will and testament" expressed his "desire that in case my wife Elizabeth G. Macdonald should wish to make her home at Middleton and be with our children, that she may be enabled to occupy any dwelling she desires free of any expense."[55]

Although the Macdonalds were determined to serve the Lord in their own fields of labor, primarily living apart after 1889, they seem to have retained a mutual respect and affection, despite time and distance. For her husband's seventieth birthday in 1895, Elizabeth sent him "A Greeting," written with a Scottish flair, to celebrate their long life as husband and wife.[56]

> *Full Seventy Years have passed away*
> *Since first you saw the light of day,*
> *In this Probational State;*
> *Through many a trying scene—you've pass'd*
> *And weather'd many a stormy blast,*
>
> *"Hard Lines" have been your fate. . . .*
> *Short seems the time, but 'tis remote,*
> *Since we agreed to launch our boat*
> *On Hymen's billowy sea:*
> *Whose waves, with a tremendous swell,*
> *Lift folks up, and* down *as well;*
> *Yet, safe and sound are we. . . .*

---

54. Hauck, "Addendum," 4–6.

55. "'Last Will' of Alexander Fin[d]lay Macdonald, 1825–1903," Document 14, Taylor O. Macdonald Collection, Church History Library. His will stipulated that Elizabeth be paid one hundred dollars in gold coin, plus interest, "in satisfaction of a balance of *my note* in her hands."

56. Elizabeth G. Macdonald, "A Greeting," in "Diaries," September 11, 1895, Typescript, Church History Library. Elizabeth had the assistance of her friend Gladys Woodmansee to compose this poem. Taylor Oden Macdonald, email message to Brittany A. Chapman, August 12, 2012.

Our nerves may be the least unstrung
But happily our hearts are young,
If not, they're staunch and true
As in the days of "Auld Lang Sine"
When you exchanged your heart, for mine,
And love entwin'd, the two;

And this you Ken, I love you still!
For well I know, your heart is leal
Faithful, to vows divine;
And crown'd withal, is my delight
That your conceptions of "The Right"
Are in rapport with mine.

Too many wedded ones, we see
Whose views so widely disagree,
Affections cannot thrive,
And wrecked upon this fatal rock,
Love dies—or else receives a shock
Not easy to survive.

And I acknowledge, thankfully,
I'm glad, that unanimity
Of thought, and faith are ours,
Completely, I am satisfied,
That all our vows are ratified
By delegated powers.

What if wide distance parts us twain
Full oft, yet oft we meet again,
For every trouble ends,
Sooner or later, and 'tis true
For every ordeal struggled through
We'll surely have amends . . .

But what are three score years and ten
Only a span, to those who ken;

Of endless time, in store.
Ages and ages, all abune
With blissful love, and glory, soon
As this short life is o'er.

Heaven help us, our children too,
Yea, one and all, that we may do
Our duty, to the end.
And now my Loyal Mate, and Chief,
I must subscribe myself, in brief
Your loving wife, and friend.

Elizabeth closed her autobiography in 1875, sustained to the end of her long life of service with this witness:

> My testimony to-day is, that the system revealed through the Prophet Joseph Smith to this generation, is the power of God unto salvation to every one that believeth and obeyeth; that it is the same Everlasting Gospel of the Father made manifest through His Son Jesus, our Savior, in the meridian of time, and revealed through Joseph. . . . I do firmly believe the day is drawing near when the noble and good of all the earth will embrace in their faith and practice the doctrines and principles revealed through Joseph Smith.
>
> I trust that I may be accounted worthy to dwell with the Saints and merit the blessings promised in the Gospel through the Atonement of Jesus Christ Our Lord.
>
> ELIZABETH G. MACDONALD
> Sᵗ George
> May 18ᵗʰ 1875.[57]

57. Macdonald, Autobiography, 45–46.

Chapter 16

"Place Your Trust in God"

Julia Sophia Raymond McKee (1831–1901)
Jennifer Pratt Reidhead

Biographical Sketch

Julia Sophia Raymond was born February 9, 1831, in Hempstead, Nassau County, Long Island, New York, to Samuel James and Elizabeth Dean Raymond. Julia, her parents, and her only sibling, Benjamin Franklin Raymond, joined The Church of Jesus Christ of Latter-day Saints and in 1845 left their home in New York to join the main body of the Saints. They moved to the small town of Nashville, Iowa, across the Mississippi River and somewhat southwest of Nauvoo and by the fall of 1847 had traveled across Iowa to Council Point.[1]

While Julia lived in Iowa, several significant events occurred in her life. On November 22, 1849, she married Hugh McKee. Her mother became ill and died on November 2, 1850, fifteen months

---

1. Council Point was four miles southwest of Kanesville (Council Bluffs), Iowa.

after giving birth to a baby girl, Harriet Ann, on August 12, 1849.[2] Julia took care of her father, brother, and baby sister (called Ann), whom her father gave to Julia to raise as her own. On December 13, 1851, a daughter, Mary Elizabeth, was born to Julia and Hugh. The child lived only one day.

In June 1852, Hugh, Julia, and Ann—along with Julia's father and brother—traveled with the John Tidwell Company to the Salt Lake Valley, arriving on September 15, 1852.[3] Once they reached the Salt Lake Valley, they settled in central Utah, living in a variety of places, particularly Goshen and surrounding areas. Julia gave birth to five more daughters, all of whom grew up, married, and had families of their own.[4]

In 1886 Julia and Hugh settled in Huntington, Utah, where they lived the remainder of their lives. Julia was the secretary and treasurer of the Relief Society there for a number of years and served as a counselor in the Relief Society presidency for three years.[5] One of their granddaughters wrote about her grandmother, stating she was neat, precise, honest, and kind.[6] She was an intelligent, articulate woman who was called upon to give speeches for Church and civic events.

Hugh passed away on February 2, 1897, and Julia followed on November 12, 1901. They are buried next to each other in the

2. Ruth Hill Brockbank, "Biography of Samuel James Raymond," 1941, Photocopy of typescript, p. 7, Church History Library, The Church of Jesus Christ of Latter-day Saints, Salt Lake City, Utah, hereafter cited as Church History Library.

3. "John Tidwell Company (1852)," Mormon Pioneer Overland Travel Database, 1847–68, The Church of Jesus Christ of Latter-day Saints, accessed April 21, 2012, http://mormontrail.lds.org.

4. Julia Lovira McKee Rudd (1854–1941), Eliza Jane McKee Barnes (1856–1932), Persis Minerva McKee Laird Roberts Horsley (1858–1951), Clarinda Rosella McKee Riley (1861–1930), Louisa Marinda McKee Steele (1863–1903).

5. "Death of Julia S. M'Kee," *Deseret Evening News,* November 20, 1901.

6. Pearl McKee Riley Nielsen McEvilly, "Hugh McKee and Julia Sophia Raymond McKee," n.d., Typescript, private possession.

Huntington Cemetery. Julia's obituary credited her with living "the life of a true Latter-day Saint."[7]

Life Experiences

In November 1892, Julia Sophia Raymond McKee wrote a life sketch for the Young Ladies' Mutual Improvement Association which, according to family tradition, was printed in a publication titled "The Sunbeam."[8] The sketch was written from memory, detailing her life experiences beginning when she was a young girl living in Hempstead, New York. Because the sketch was prepared for young women readers, Julia's comments were written with them in mind. The following is that autobiographical sketch:

> I was born 9 Feb. 1831, at Hempstead, Long Island, New York. My father, Samuel James Raymond, was not a religious man. My mother, Elizabeth Dean, was a member of the Methodist Church, consequently my childhood was nurtured in that persuasion.[9]
>
> While in my 7th year, as I was returning home from sabbath school, I was attracted by seeing a man standing on the frame of a building in the course of erection, and a large concourse of people surrounding him. I heard him prophesy that a disease would come upon the inhabitants of that village which would cause the death of many children, and that not long after, there would be a strange doctrine introduced among them. Many more things he taught the

---

7. "Death of Julia S. M'Kee."

8. Efforts to find the original publication in archives and family records have proven unsuccessful. Creating manuscript newspapers was a popular activity in Mutual Improvement Association groups at that time, and "The Sunbeam" may well have been a manuscript newspaper written and compiled by Julia's local Young Ladies' Mutual Improvement Association.

9. See also Brockbank, "Biography of Samuel James Raymond," pp. 1–2.

people. When he was through speaking he got down and disappeared among the crowd.

Nothing of importance occurred in the village until the winter of my 10th year, when the scarlet fever broke out among the children which caused the death of many of my companions, but the Lord in His goodness preserved me from that disease.

The following summer the village was all excited over the announcement that a Mormon Elder was going to preach in the Bar Room. Thus was the strange prediction fulfilled. I have many times, since [I] became acquainted with the Book of Mormon, wondered whether he was one of the Nephites who never tasted death.

I well remember my father coaxing my mother to go and hear that strange doctrine. Finally she consented to go with him, and it was not long before she embraced the new and everlasting gospel. My father was bitterly opposed to it at first, but it was not long before he too embraced the truth. My companions at school began to ridicule me. They would not associate with me, but told me all manner of stories about "Joe Smith," as they called the Prophet, and the "Golden Bible."

As they would not allow me to join in their amusements I had more time to study; consequently that year I received my certificate to a high school. My parents were not able to send me to New York to a boarding school so that ended my school days.

Four persons were all that joined the Mormon Church at that time. But a year or two later a branch of the Church was organized on Long Island, some six miles from our village, over which my father presided. By this time I was old enough to be instructed in the gospel as it was taught by the servants of God who came to teach us the plan of life and salvation.

I never regretted attending Methodist and Episcopal Sabbath schools, for in them I learned the scriptures. Although I was not taught to believe them correctly, the Lord gave me an understanding heart so that when the gospel was explained to me in plainness I understood it, and on 4 March 1845 I was baptized and confirmed a member in the Church of Jesus Christ of Latter Day Saints by Elder Theodore Curtis.

Shortly after, my father was called to Nauvoo to assist in building the temple. Mother and I went to work at housework to procure means to enable us to gather with the Saints. I arose at four in the morning, prepared breakfast for my little brother, and was at my work at five, staying until nine at night. I worked at a boarding house and was allowed to take the waste pieces of provisions home to my brother. Mother was too far away to come home at nights. The Lord prospered our labors and gave me strength to endure.

With what we earned and received from the sale of our household effects at an auction, we were enabled to undertake our journey to Nauvoo. We bade farewell to [our] native place and my dear aged grandmother, the only near relative we had to leave. She could not be persuaded to leave the graves of her ancestors and come with us on such a long and tedious journey.

We started about the last of October . . . and arrived at Nauvoo on 21 November 1845.

We concluded to reside in Nashville, a small town opposite Nauvoo, where I spent some of the happiest days of my life among the youth of Zion.

But soon it became known that the Saints had

promised to leave Nauvoo in the spring.[10] . . . We remained in Nashville until about the middle of May, when one of the brethren belonging to our company, a stranger, came one afternoon with a wagon and told us that he had come to take us to the camp then forming on Sugar Creek. It was short notice as he wanted to start that night. There was a large Ball that night, and I managed to persuade him to stay all night. I think he spent the most of the night watching me as there had been some girls enticed to stay and their parents could not find them and had to leave them. One apostate offered to find a place for me so I could not be found. I replied that I intended to start in the morning. I did not wish to stay. . . .

The day after we arrived [at Sugar Creek] was Sunday. In the forenoon we were called together for a worship meeting. We had neither meeting house nor bowery but met in the open air, sitting on the ground, and I believe we enjoyed ourselves as well as the Saints do today amidst their abundance, for the Lord was with his people to comfort and strengthen. He certainly did increase our provisions for I never lacked for food, nor did any of the company want for bread. . . . I had no idea where we were going. I had never heard of the Saints going to the Rocky Mountains, but we knew the Lord was our guide, and we were willing to follow our file leader.

When we got within nine miles of Farmington [Iowa] on the Demoins River the brethren took a contract to fence and plow a large farm. That took most of the summer and enabled the sisters who could to go to the town to work to get provisions and clothing. . . . Through the blessings

10. See also Glen M. Leonard, *Nauvoo: A Place of Peace, a People of Promise* (Salt Lake City, UT: Deseret Book; Provo, UT: Brigham Young University Press, 2002), 535–50.

of the Lord we made a living and saved enough to journey on with. It seems a miracle, for I was only a child and all I could get for a week's wages was fifty cents and all mother could get was a dollar and a half.

I enjoyed camp life well that summer, being just the right age to drive dull cares away. We had dancing in camp, on the ground with no roof over our heads. We waxed our floors with shovels and hoes. We held meetings on Sundays and sometimes in the evenings during the week. I made many new friends that summer, though a very few I ever met again after we separated. It seems I was doomed to always make new acquaintances wherever I went.

My father came back and met us just before we started again. He had been in Missouri working at his trade [as a tailor]. . . .

I, with the rest of the family, remained a week in [Mt.] Pisgah, waiting for a brother to get ready to take us to Missouri. Our provisions were getting low, and we had to go some place where we could work for more so we could journey on to Council Bluffs. . . .

The Lord provides for His people. He blessed us with plenty of the comforts of life while we stayed there. . . . We found a family of Latter Day Saints. They had a young girl, and we were not long in forming an acquaintance. While in this place we did not have the privilege of attending a meeting of any kind, but I enjoyed that summer. My friend and I spent many pleasant hours in the forest by the lovely Grand River. Writing of it brings to my mind many pleasant memories of days long past, although my readers no doubt wonder what I found pleasant in a solitary life like that. The Lord blessed me with the spirit of contentment, and I was as happy as girls of sixteen are today.

We stayed in that place until fall, and by that time we had saved quite a supply of provisions, such as wheat, bacon and honey. My father sent to the camp of the Saints for teams to move us to the [Council] Bluffs. . . .

It took three weeks to go from where we were to the Bluffs. We had a pleasant journey. The prairies were grand. We traveled one whole day and saw nothing but grass. When the wind blew gently over it, it seemed almost like a large body of water. We had time to view our surroundings for we did not travel then as they do in these days. There was no railroad in that country as there is today. Horses also were scarce so we had to travel with ox teams, and when we got tired of going so slow we got out of the wagon and walked ahead. That was a rest for us. Some days we traveled by the river and then [saw] large stately trees different from what we see here. Now and then we saw a log house. We passed a few small settlements with a very few inhabitants. . . .

In the fall of 1847 we arrived at Council Point, a small town where the Saints were stopping to prepare for the journey across the plains. The main group were on the opposite side of the river, now known as Florence, Nebraska. That fall Pres. Brigham Young came back from the valley. I was at the conference, held in the tabernacle at Kanesville, when Brigham Young was acknowledged as President of the Church of Jesus Christ of Latter Day Saints, and Heber C. Kimball and Willard Richards as counselors.[11] In the winter of 1847 I made new friends, and some of these I had to part with in the spring. As fast as an outfit could be made up they started. We raised crops and built log houses and made ourselves as comfortable as possible. I spent many pleasant times. We had our dances and picnics and all sorts of recreation, much the same as today, although we did not

11. See also Richard E. Bennett, *We'll Find the Place: The Mormon Exodus, 1846–1848* (Salt Lake City, UT: Deseret Book, 1997), 287–92.

have the riches that we do now. We had our meetings to attend. We had no Sunday Schools or Mutual Improvement Associations.

There were some changes in my life and that of my parents. On the 22 of November 1849 I was married to Hugh McKee. A short time after that my husband went to Missouri to work for teams to take us to the valley. He was gone one year, and in that time I saw hard times. Grain was high, and money scarce, and my father could not always get work. The people that were able to hire had gone on.

My Mother was very sick all winter, and I could not leave home to work. She got well enough through the summer to help me take care of her baby. On 2 November 1850 she took sick about 3 o'clock in the afternoon and died before morning, leaving me the little girl fifteen months old.[12] That was the first real sorrow I had ever known. After the death of my mother I took care of my father, brother, and the little girl, which my father gave me as my own. My husband came home that winter. We expected to go to the valley in the spring, but circumstances prevented us from going until another year. During that time my first child was born, which died in a short time.[13]

In the spring of 1852 we were enabled, by the providences of the Almighty, to leave the states and come to the Rocky Mountains. . . . For the first month it was nice traveling. We had meetings every Sunday. We danced once in a while and often gathered together and sang the songs of Zion. The camp would stop one day every two weeks and repair the wagons, and the women would have a good time cleaning up the wagons and shaking out the dust.

---

12. Brockbank, "Biography," 7.

13. Mary Elizabeth McKee was born on December 13, 1851, and died the following day.

At the end of the month sorrow came in our midst, in the shape of disease and death. Cholera broke out among us, and many were laid in the grave. We had nothing to make coffins with, and the dead were wrapped in a quilt and buried. I well remember seeing three children playing, when one died and the two carried it to the grave. Soon the two were also stricken and carried to the wagon and died in a few hours. It was so fatal that I have seen the brethren walking along by the teams drop down by the road and never get up. The camp would stop a little while until they breathed their last, and then lift them into the wagon, take them to camp at night and bury them. We did not know when we started in the morning whether we would see the sun set or not, although we would be well when we started. When we got further on it became healthy again, and we once more had hope. During all this time neither I nor my family had that dread disease, which I feel to thank my Heavenly Father for.

The rest of the journey we traveled in comfort, although our provisions were getting scarce. We had to do on two meals a day for a week or so. We arrived in Salt Lake City on the 15th of September 1852, making three months in crossing the plains.

After arriving in the valley, the next thing to be done was to find a place for the winter where we could earn a living. We stayed in the city long enough to dine with a family of our acquaintance, and then started south. . . .

We gave part of our team and bought some land. We had hard times that winter. I was taken very sick in December and was not able to sit up until May, and most of the winter my life hung on a thread. My husband could not leave me to hunt work, and we had very little to eat. He and my brother took turns sitting up with me, and during that time I saw but one woman, a Mrs. Bird. The Lord helped us through that winter as He had done before.

In the spring my husband had to go to the field. He would go in the morning, come home once before noon and then at noon get dinner and go again and come home once before night and go again. It was slow work, but he put in ten acres, and that year the grasshoppers took the most of it, but we had enough left for bread.

In the fall we built a new log house. I had regained my health and was able to take my share of the burden. The next June my second daughter (Julia Lovira, 2 Jun 1854) was born. Shortly after we had a very heavy hail storm which took all our wheat, but there was plenty in the valley and we did not want. We went farther south, as far as Spanish Fork and put in a crop. That was the grasshopper year.

We lived on weeds and milk. The Lord blessed us, so that our cows gave more milk, and weeds grew where they had not grown before. All that time my children never asked for bread, and in the fall my third daughter was born (Eliza Jane, 7 Sep 1856). That winter we had a very good time and had plenty to eat and thanked the Lord for His preservation through our hardships. That was the year of plenty.

Our peace did not last long. When we were celebrating the twenty-fourth of July [1857], news came that the United States Army was coming to destroy us. But the Lord ruled things for our good. Some of the brethren camped in Echo Canyon, intending not to let them come in. The people moved south. When they [the United States Army] came, they passed through very peaceable. They did as President Young told, and proved a blessing to the people after in a good many ways.[14]

---

14. A United States Army expedition, led finally by Colonel Albert Sidney Johnston, was dispatched by President James Buchanan to Utah in 1857 to protect

In the fall of 1858 my fourth daughter was born (Persis Minerva, 9 Oct 1858). We felt to rejoice. We had plenty to eat, but clothing was scarce. I had a new lawn dress for Christmas.

In 1861 my fifth daughter was born (Clarinda Rosella, 17 Jan 1861). The following summer the soldiers started back to the states. My husband started with them and some other brethren, expecting to be gone for a year, but the Lord ruled it otherwise. They went as far as Fort Bridger and returned. The [Civil] war broke out between the north and the south and in all probability if they had gone back they would have been mustered [into the army] in the next year.

We rented a farm in Little Salt Creek Canyon. There we remained for five years. During that time I had another [daughter] (Louisa Marinda, 5 Jun 1863). We had very few companions except Indians, and they were very numerous. I sometimes felt afraid when I had to stay alone with the children. My husband burned lime that winter and was gone a good deal. We had plenty of bread but nothing else. For a number of years we had very bad times, scarcely making a living, but the Lord did not forsake us. We lived a long distance from market; that made it hard.

The Black Hawk war broke out.[15] President [Brigham]

---

newly appointed territorial officials amidst concerns of Mormon rebellion against federal authority. The conflict was resolved by negotiation in 1858. William P. MacKinnon, ed., *At Sword's Point, Part 1: A Documentary History of the Utah War to 1858* (Norman, OK: Arthur H. Clark, 2008); Donald R. Moorman with Gene A. Sessions, *Camp Floyd and the Mormons: The Utah War* (Salt Lake City: University of Utah Press, 1992).

15. The Black Hawk War—the "longest, costliest and bloodiest in [Utah] history"—resulted from pioneer settlers' occupation and use of grasslands for grazing cattle, which left the native people without important food sources. The most intense years of the conflict were 1865 to 1867. John A. Peterson, "Living History: Utah's Black Hawk War," *Salt Lake Tribune,* September 2, 2011; John Alton Peterson, *Utah's Black Hawk War* (Salt Lake City: University of Utah Press, 1998).

Young advised us to move closer together. There was a small place called Gardenerville about 3 miles from Goshen, and to this place we moved. The brethren of that place took their teams and hauled our log house to this place and helped to put it up.

We lived in that house three weeks and then the word came that the people must get closer together, so we moved in a house with another family and lived there with them three weeks. At the end of that time we learned the Indians was committing so many depredations that we would not be safe there. We were so few in numbers, my husband concluded to move to Santaquin. By this time it was spring again, and the old log cabin was once more pulled down and moved to Santaquin.

The men had to go to work in the fields. That left the women and children alone, and as our house was all the house among us, a good many families all slept in it. We felt more safe together. Sometimes we had something to eat with our bread, and sometimes we did not. We were blessed with bread that summer. That fall the most of our companions moved back home. We stayed a year and a half. We got a chance to exchange our lot for one in the place we left. So in December 1868 we moved back.

President Young located a town a mile and a half from where we lived that fall, and in the spring they commenced building it up; that made work for the men. The Lord always provides for His people when they try to help themselves.

In 1869 the grasshoppers again made their appearance, doing a great deal of damage, and we lost our grain, but we raised some potatoes and was thankful for that. We were not very well clothed or fed. My younger children went without shoes all winter, and myself, the most of the winter. During that year and the next I saw hard times. Many times through the summer we lived for days on two meals a day, and when my husband came from the field at noon he would take a good sleep and go back to work without dinner.

As most things come to an end, so did the hard times. In 1870 the Tintic mines were discovered and that made labor plenty.[16] Wages were high and there was plenty of grain raised. My husband worked that year in Tintic burning coal. Then we began to live again; we had something to eat and something to wear. From that time forward we did not suffer for the necessities of life. Although we had very little of the luxuries, yet we were blessed, for we had health and strength. . . .

After all I have gone through, I find myself almost alone, only my husband and me enjoy what I call the comforts of life, at the age of 63, in the isolated town of Huntington.

I have given a few incidents of my life, and I hope I have not wearied you. I hope you, my young sisters who read this, will not have to pass through what I have had to pass through. But should circumstances cause that it should be so, place your trust in God, and He will give you strength to bear it as He has me.[17]

---

16. The Tintic mines were located west of Goshen and were developed in part due to the building of railroads north and south through Utah after the completion of the transcontinental railroad in 1869. "Story of the Chief Consolidated Operations in Tintic," *Eureka Reporter,* August 16, 1918.

17. Julia Sophia Raymond McKee, "Autobiography," 1892, Typescript, private possession. Additional autobiographical information is available at the Church History Library.

Chapter 17

"Angels Shall Minister unto You"

Mary Goble Pay (1843–1913)

Christine Banks Bowers, Virginia H. Pearce, and Patricia H. Stoker

Biographical Sketch

William and Mary Penfold Goble had their second child[1] at Brighton, Sussex, England, on June 2, 1843. They named her Mary. The family grew quickly and numbered eight when the Gobles were taught and accepted the restored gospel of The Church of Jesus Christ of Latter-day Saints in 1855.

Like many newly baptized Latter-day Saints, the Gobles immediately began making plans to migrate to Utah. They traveled in the John A. Hunt Wagon Company of 1856, which followed close behind the Martin Handcart Company, and arrived in the Salt Lake Valley on December 11, 1856. Mary lost all of her toes to frostbite, and her rehabilitation was painful and miraculous.

---

1. William and Mary's first child, William (1842–1842), died at the age of seven months.

On June 26, 1859, at the age of sixteen, Mary married a thirty-seven-year-old widower, Richard Pay. Richard and his first wife, Sarah, had traveled on the ship *Horizon* from England with Mary's family and were also part of the Hunt Wagon Company. As the company prepared to leave Iowa City in July 1856, Sarah gave birth to a baby girl. The daughter lived only ten weeks, dying near Chimney Rock, Nebraska. Sarah followed, dying some seven weeks later near Fort Bridger in present-day Wyoming. Her death left Richard alone.[2] Several months after arriving in the Salt Lake Valley, Richard settled in Nephi, Utah, where he and Mary later married on June 26, 1859.

Mary and Richard lived in Nephi for twenty-two years. "When i was married it was hard times," wrote Mary. "My husband Bought a one room adobie house. . . . We had Bed stead, 3 chairs, table, a Box for our flour, our Bed tick we filled with straw. We had 2 sheets, 2 pillow slips, one quilt. . . . We had 3 tin plates, 3 cups, a pan or to, a pot to cook in, and a spider[3] to Bake our Bread in."[4]

Moving from Nephi, Richard and Mary homesteaded 160 acres in Leamington,[5] where they would live for more than a decade. In the Leamington Ward, Mary was called as second counselor in the Relief Society in 1882 and as the first Primary president in 1884, serving in the Primary and Relief Society capacities simultaneously for more than ten years.[6]

------

2. "Hunt Wagon Company Journal," Journal History of The Church of Jesus Christ of Latter-day Saints, December 15, 1856, pp. 29, 36, Church History Library, The Church of Jesus Christ of Latter-day Saints, Salt Lake City, Utah, hereafter cited as Church History Library. Richard and Sarah's daughter, Marinda Nancy, died October 4, and Sarah died November 27, 1856.

3. A cast-iron frying pan, originally made with feet to stand among coals.

4. Mary Goble Pay, Autobiography, 1903, Holograph, p. 109, private possession.

5. Leamington, Millard County, Utah, is located on the Sevier River about thirty miles southwest of Nephi, Utah.

6. Richard Pay and Mary Goble Pay, "A Family Record of Richard Pay," Holograph, p. 19, private possession.

Mary and Richard had thirteen children. Two died at birth: John Henry (1866–1866) and Mercy Mary (1869–1869); Joseph William died at age two (1867–1869); and Sarah Eliza at the age of fourteen (1884–1895). The other nine lived to adulthood.[7]

Richard died in 1893, leaving Mary a widow with seven children still in the home and no means of support. The farm on which they lived provided a very meager living at best, and without a husband, life for Mary seemed grim. Just a little over a year after her husband's death, her oldest living son, George, died, leaving a widow and several young children.[8] Mary's fourteen-year-old daughter, Sarah, died the following year. Mary moved back to Nephi, and later records show that she was married for a short time to Jesse Millgate.[9]

Her attendance at the 1906 reunion of the 1856 handcart companies provided the impetus for Mary to write her remembrances of the trek. This written record by a virtually uneducated woman is a sparse, matter-of-fact, and heart-rending account of faith and tenacity in the face of overwhelming adversity.

Mary Goble Pay died in Salt Lake City at the home of her daughter Marietta (Etta) Bowers, September 25, 1913, at the age of seventy. Her life stands as a testimony to the truth of the restored gospel of Jesus Christ and the price willingly paid by its early converts.

---

7. Richard William Pay (1860–1882); George Edwin Pay (1862–1894); Edward James Pay (1864–1911); Jesse Pay (1870–1960); David Alma Pay (1873–1932); William Goble Pay (1876–1945); Marietta Pay Bowers (1878–1929); Leonard Pay (1883–1958); Phillip LeRoy Pay (1885–1970). Pay and Pay, "Family Record," 17–18.

8. George Edwin Pay died on September 1, 1894. Family records differ on whether he left five or six children. The number six comes from "George Henry Pay: Ancestral File," FamilySearch, The Church of Jesus Christ of Latter-day Saints, accessed February 20, 2012, http://familysearch.org.

9. Mary and Jesse married on September 1, 1897, in Sanpete County, Utah. "Jesse Millgate," Western States Marriage Index, Brigham Young University–Idaho, accessed March 5, 2012, http://abish.byui.edu/specialCollections/westernstates /westernStatesRecordDetail.cfm?recordID=250406.

LIFE EXPERIENCES

Journey to Zion

Mary's journey from England to Utah began at the Bramley-Moore dock in Liverpool, England, on May 19, 1856, as she boarded the *Horizon* in a company of 856 Saints, including her parents and her five younger siblings—Edwin, Caroline, Harriet, James, and Fanny.[10] Mary celebrated her thirteenth birthday shortly before they arrived in America. Her tragedy-laced journey would ask much of a little English girl who had known only the normal adventures and misadventures of childhood until that fateful year.

The Gobles disembarked in Boston on June 30 and traveled by train to Iowa City, arriving on July 8, 1856. "My sister Fanny Broke out with the measels on the ship," wrote Mary. "When we were in Iowa Camp Ground, there came up a thunder storm Blew down our shelter . . . made with hand carts and some quilts. The storm came, and we sat there in the rain thunder and Litning. [My sister got] wet and died the 19 of July 1856. She would have been 2 years on the 23."[11]

William purchased a wagon and supplies, and the Gobles started west with the John A. Hunt Company, a wagon train that was instructed to follow close behind the Martin Handcart Company and stay with the handcart companies should they need help. Mary wrote:

> We got to Counsel Bluffs. I think that was the name. . . .
> Then we started on our jurney of one thousand miles over
> the plains. It was about the first of september.[12] We traveled

10. "Latter-day Saints' Emigration Report," *Millennial Star* 18, no. 34 (August 23, 1856): 542.

11. Pay, Autobiography.

12. The John A. Hunt Company left the outfitting post in Iowa City, Iowa, on August 1, 1856, and arrived in Council Bluffs on August 27. "Hunt Wagon Company Journal," 22.

from 15 to 25 miles a day. We use to stop one day in the weak to wash and rested on sunday, held our meetings, and every morning and night we where called to prayers By the Bugle.[13]

Mary's little sister Edith was born in Nebraska, September 23, 1856.[14] On October 19, a fierce snowstorm hit. Mary recalled:

> We traveled on till we got to the Last Crossing of the platt River. That was the Last walk i ever walk with my mother. We caug[ht] up with the hand cart companys that day. We watched them Cross the River. There was Great Lumps of ice floating down the River. It was Bitter Cold. The next morning there where 14 dead in there Camp through the cold. We went Back to camp went to prayers. They sang Come Come ye saints, no toil or Labor fear. I wonderd what made my mother cry. . . .
>
> We traveled in the snow from the Last Crossing of the platte River. We had orders to not pass the hand cart co. We had to keep close to them so has to help them if we could. we began to get short of food our cattle gave out. We could only travel a few miles a day. When we started out of camp in the morning, the Brethren would shovel the snow to make a track, for our cattle where weak for the want of . . . food as the Buffalos where in Large herds by the Roads and eat all the Grass.
>
> When we arrived at Devils Gate, it was bitter cold.[15] We

---

13. Pay, Autobiography.

14. When writing her life story, Mary combined the events of Edith's birth during the night of September 23 and the first snowstorm. The Hunt company journal indicates that the weather on the morning of September 24 was "cold and frosty." The first snowstorm was recorded on October 19. "Hunt Wagon Company Journal," 27, 32.

15. Robert T. Burton of the rescue company recorded a temperature of eleven degrees below zero at Devil's Gate on November 6, 1856. Robert T. Burton, Diaries, 1856–1907, Holograph, November 6, 1856, Church History Library.

Left Lots of our things there. . . . We stayed there 2 or 3 days. While there an ox fell on the ice, and the Brethren Killed it, and the Beef was Given out to the camp. We made soop of it. My Bro James eat a hearty supper. Was as well as he ever was wen he went to bed. In the morning he was dead.[16]

I got my feet froze and Lost all my toes. My Bro Edwin got his feet froze bad. Sister Carrie [Caroline] feet where froze. It was nothing but snow. We could not drive the pegs in our tents. Father would clean a place for our tents, put snow around to Keep it down. We were short of flour, But father was a good shot. They called him the hunter of the camp. So that helped us out. We could not Get a enough flour for Bread, as we Got to a quarter lb per head a day. So we would make it Like thin Gruel. We called it skilly.

Well there was 4 companies on the plains.[17] We did not know what would become of us, when one night a man came to our camp telling us there would be plenty of flour in the morning, for Bro Brigham had sent men and teams to help us. There was rejoiceing that night. Some sang, some danced, some cried. Well, he made a Living santy claus. I have forgotten his name, but never will i forget how he Looked. He was covered with the frost. His beard was Long and all frost. His name was Eph[raim] Hanks.[18]

---

16. James, just four years old, died November 6, 1856. Although the Hunt Company journal does not specifically mention James Goble's death, the journal does record that the group arrived at Devil's Gate on November 5 and "resumed their journey" on November 9. Mary's Autobiography records that James's death occurred while at Devil's Gate. "Hunt Wagon Company Journal," 35; Pay, Autobiography, 102.

17. The Martin and Willie handcart companies, as well as the Hunt and Hodgett wagon companies, traveled more or less together, sometimes getting separated and strung out along the trail, as so often happened with emigrant companies crossing the plains.

18. Pay, Autobiography, 101–3. The Hunt Company journal for October 28

The companies remained trapped by snow, inching forward when possible. Mary recounts:

> We had been without water for several days just drinking snow water. The captain said there was a spring of fresh water just a few miles away. It was snowing hard, but my mother begged me to go and get her a drink. Another lady went with me. We were about half way to the spring when we found an old man who had fallen in the snow. He was frozen so stiff we could not lift him, so the lady told me where to go and she would go back to camp for help, for we knew he would soon be frozen if we left him. When she had gone I began to think of the Indians, and looking and looking in all directions, I became confused and forgot the way I should go. I waded around in the snow up to my knees, and I became lost. Later when I did not return to camp, the men started out after me. It was 11:00 o'clock before they found me. My feet and legs were frozen. They carried me to camp and rubbed me with snow. They put my feet in a bucket of water. The pain was terrible. The frost came out of my legs and feet but not out of my toes. [19]

---

records: "Brothers Joseph W. Young and two other brethren arrived in camp in the evening from the Valley. This caused a general rejoicing ~~generally~~ throughout the camp, though the tidings of the snow extending westward for forty or fifty miles, was not encouraging. The handcart companies had been supplied with food and clothing and the condition of the wagon companies would be reported to the Valley speedily, as the brethren traveling ~~in that company~~ with teams were also getting short of provisions." "Hunt Wagon Company Journal," 33.

19. "Life of Mary Goble Pay," Typescript of autobiography, p. 2, private possession. The company journal entry for November 1 indicates that the trail they were traveling "led through poisonous creeks of water," which would account for Mary's mother sending her for fresh spring water. "Hunt Wagon Company Journal," 34.

Edith, Mary's six-week-old sister, died November 3 at Grease-wood Creek for "want of nourishment."[20]

> When my little sister died . . . , Brother [Richard] Pay help my Father when she was Burried by the road side.[21] I felt i could not Leave her for i had seen so many graves open by the wovles, and the team had got quite away when my Father came Back for me. I said, Oh i cannot Leave her to be eat by the wolves; it seem so terrible.[22] But he talked to me, and we hurried on.[23]

The Goble family finally arrived in the Great Salt Lake Valley just short of seven months from the day they left their homeland. Mary Penfold Goble, Mary's forty-three-year-old mother, died eight miles before reaching the valley.[24] Mary remembered:

> We arrived in Salt Lake City 9 o clock at night the 11 of Dec 1856, 3 out of the 4 [children] that was Living froze, my mother dead in the wagon. Bishop Hardy had us taken to a house in his ward, and the Brethren an sisters fetch us

---

20. Pay, Autobiography, 101. Mary's autobiography states that Edith died at Sweetwater, but the company journal records that "the infant child of William Goble" died at Greasewood Creek on November 3 at 9 o'clock P.M. "Hunt Wagon Company Journal," 34.

21. Mary wrote that Richard Pay, whom she would later marry, "could not get any one to dig the grave [of his wife Sarah]. So he started to dig it himself, when my Father came and helped him." Pay, Autobiography, 105.

22. See also Pay, Autobiography, 105.

23. Pay, "Life," 5.

24. En route to Zion, the following Goble family members died: Fanny, age twenty-three months, died July 19, 1856, in Iowa City, Iowa; Edith, age six weeks, died November 3, 1856, at Greasewood Creek in what became Wyoming; James, age four, died November 6, 1856, at Devil's Gate, which also later became part of Wyoming; Mary Penfold Goble, age forty-three, died December 11, 1856.

plenty of food. We had to be careful and not eat to much as it might Kill us as we were so hungry.[25]

Early next morning Bro. Brigham Young and a doctor came. . . . When Brigham Young came in, he shook hands with all of us. When he saw our condition, our feet frozen and our mother dead, tears rolled down his cheeks.

The Doctor wanted to cut my feet off at the ankles. But Pres. Young said, No, just cut off the toes, and I promise you, you will never have to take them off any farther. The pieces of bone that must come out will work out through the skin themselves. The Doctor amputated my toes using a saw and a butcher knife.[26]

The sisters were dressing mother for her grave. My poor father walk in the room where mother was, then back to us. He could not shed a tear. When our feet was fix, they packed us in to see our mother for the last time. Oh, how did we stand it. That afternoon she was burried.[27]

Life on the Frontier

The decades following the Saints' arrival in Utah included times of peace and times of tension between the settlers and the native peoples. Now married and living in Nephi, Mary recounted:

A[t] night our cattle, sheep were Brought home, and we were all Lock inside the fort for safety from the indians. There were gaurds at Both the gates to see no one came in or went out of the gates. They were Locked at 8 o clock every night; if you did not get in By than, you were Locked out. We were a happy Band of Bro an sisters. We felt safe Locked

25. Pay, Autobiography, 103.
26. Pay, "Life," 3.
27. Pay, Autobiography, 103.

inside the fort walls. We would spend our winters having house partys. We had good times. We were all united. . . .[28]

Pres. Brigham Young advised all that Could to Learn the indian Language, so we Could talk to them, and to be kind to them, feed them, and they would respect us.[29]

There were a small tribe of indians called pagwats[30] that stayed around Nephi. There Cheifs name was pauvania. Him and his squaw was very friendly to the white people. Many a time has she brought Letters for us, and she would take messages for us. She would help me wash and pick wool, and she Learned me to talke there Lanugage. . . . She was honest. . . .

One day I was dressing my baby and 2 of the Boys where playing on the floor when the Door opened and two Indians came in. One was pauvania, and one was the meanest Looking Indian I have ever saw. They started to talk. He said, Let's Kill them; see there are 4 scalps. The old Cheif said, No, you cannot kill them. He talked a Little while trying to get his consent, but when i Looked at that chief, i knew he was my true friend. He said, You cannot hurt them, for she and her husband are my true friends. He [the other Indian] got mad, and he said, I would like to cut her throat anyhow. Than I answerd him. I tell you he was a scart Indian, for he didnot know i knew what he said. He stood ramming his Gun. I told him to go; he was to mean for anything. The old Chief Laughed, mad[e] fun of him, because he did not now i understood him. Well, i tell you, i Loaded

---

28. Pay, Autobiography, 109–10.

29. Pay, Autobiography, 105.

30. Ute Indians were "scattered over the land in family groups or bands. . . . Each band traveled over a wide but certain familiar area. . . . The Sevier Lake Utes called themselves Pahvant, which means 'close to water.'" Mary may have been referring to this group. Clifford Duncan, "The Northern Utes of Utah," in *A History of Utah's American Indians,* ed. Forrest S. Cuch (Salt Lake City, UT: State Division of Indian Affairs/Utah State Division of History, 2000), 174.

him [Pauvania] down with something to eat because he saved my Life and my Babes. After, it was proven the Indian was one that helped Kill a family of 6 in thistle Kanyon. . . .

One time when the Boys were fetching sheep for the 24 July, we herd there were 8 indians in Dog valley. They were very hostile. I tell you we were afraid. There were Richard an George and one of there friends, J Carter. We thought sure the indians would get them. All we could do was to pray for the Lord to protect them. Well it came 9 clock at night; we could not rest. When we heard the Boys singing it was a moon light night. I said to them, Did you see any indians in dog valley? Why we did not Come that way, Richard said. We got to a road [and] turned of[f] throug[h] spring Kanyon. Something said go that way. I said that was answer to prayer. The Lord did protect you.[31]

One day when the [Black Hawk] war[32] was about over, my husband and one of the Boys where in Salt Creek kanyon with the sheep. They saw 6 Indians on horseback Coming to there camp. One was B[lack] Hawk with 5 of his warriors. He thought his time was Come sure, but the Cheif told him and his braves were wyno, Good. They were very hungry and wanted a sheep. He told them they Could get one. They went into the herd, shot one of the best, and eat every bit of it but the skin. That night they staid by the camp fire. B Hawk said you need not be afraid of us any more. He said, I am sick of Blood. Look at me. The Great Cheif Brigham Young told me if i shed the mormons blood i should wither

---

31. Pay, Autobiography, 106, 113.

32. The Black Hawk War—the "longest, costliest and bloodiest in Utah history"—was named for the Ute leader Mary mentions in her account. It resulted from pioneer settlers' occupation and use of grasslands for grazing cattle, which left the native people without important food sources. John A. Peterson, "Living History: Utah's Black Hawk War," *Salt Lake Tribune,* September 2, 2011; John Alton Peterson, *Utah's Black Hawk War* (Salt Lake City: University of Utah Press, 1998).

and die. I am going up to see the Great Cheif Brigham once more. And then i am going to were i was Born, and i will die. He did not Live more than 2 or 3 weeks after. . . .

One day when our trees where starting to bear, Little John and his sqaws came to our house for some peaches. My husband gave them some. The next day they came again. My husband was away from home. There was a tree [of peaches] they wanted. I told them they could not have them, for i wanted them myself. He told his sqaws to go get them, for i would be afraid to stop them. I knew what he said. I told him, As sure as you go, i will fecth you of[f] the Lot. He Laughed [and] told them to go. They went. He sat down under the tree; his squaws and his Boy were picking the fruit. I gather up a stick when they saw me coming they got out of the tree tumbled over one another, indian [Little John] and all. Oh he was mad. He said the white man had taken the Land and water away from them. All that was here belong to them.

He did not come to our house till the spring. Then he came in Laughing, wanting to shake hands, asking us if we were tecabo friendly. My husband told him he didnot know. He wanted to shake hands with me. He said, Brave squaw not afraid. We shook hands with him and he went of[f] Laughing. He behave his self after that. . . .

I could relate Lots of more Circumstances But we followed pres youngs advice, Be good to them. Feed them; do not fight. An indian never forget a kindness; they never forget a wrong. They are truthful. If they say they will do a thing, they will do it. I Remember my husband ask one of them if he had seen his oxen. He told him if he would get them for him he would pay him. The next morning it rain hard but he was there with the oxen. It was storming hard but he said, I told you i would Bring them; i have Brougth them.[33]

---

33. Pay, Autobiography, 109, 111.

Reunions

As decades passed, reunions were held for the companies who had crossed the plains together. The first one Mary attended was in October 1906. While in Salt Lake City for this Jubilee reunion, she went to see her mother's grave.

> It was the first time i had seen it, for when she was
> Burried, our feet were so bad we coud not go to the funeral,
> and the move came and we moved south to Nephi. No one
> noes how i felt as we stood there by her grave. . . . I thought
> of her words: Polly [a nickname for Mary], i want to go to
> Zion while my Children are small so as they can be raised
> in the gospel of Christ, for i know this is the true Church.[34]

These reunions provided a space where the Saints could renew friendships and reflect on their experiences. "Have been to our re-nion," wrote Mary. "Had a good time. Told of incidents of our trip over the plains. It made us feel bad. It brought it all up again. Is it wise, yes, for our Children to see what there parents passed through for the Gospel."[35]

Night Visions, Dreams, and Death

In 1893, after returning from a trip to the Manti Temple, Richard suddenly became ill and died after only a few days. Mary was devastated by his death and struggled to understand how she would be able to raise her large family alone.

In her 1895 patriarchal blessing, Mary was told, "Angels shall minister unto you and your husband also shall visit you in your night visions and dreams and comfort your heart as he is laboring in

---

34. Pay, Autobiography, 108.

35. Pay, Autobiography, 112.

the ministry in the spirit world. . . . Therefor be patient in your trials and afflictions and no good thing shall be with-held from you."[36]

Mary wrote:

> At the time . . . my husband died . . . I was Left With 9 children [2 married]. I couldn't see Wherein the Lord was Justified in taking my Husband an Leaving me With so many mouths to feed an hardly any means of Support. It didn't just seem right. I became almost bitter. . . . The Bishop an His counselers came to See Me an said, "It was the Lord's Will." I was so angry, I grabbed the Broom an chased them from my yard. I was Bitter toward the church—my Neighbors, the Lord, even to staying away from church. An then one night I was Laying not a sleep But Pondering— when my Husband stood Beside me, an He an I talked face to face. He told me that It was the Lord's Will that He had Been taken an that He Was Building a Home for us in Heaven an would not come back on Earth if He could. He told me not to worry, that He would always Be With me, and that soon Edward and Jesse [her sons] Would secure Work an would Support the family. . . . He Left me then an the Bitterness left my Heart. I began to attend church. I loved my neighbor an ask the Lord's forgiveness for ever doubting His Wisdom—Soon my Boys were Working an Supporting me an my family.[37]

Mary also secured work nursing the sick and "assisted with many births and gave assistance to the town doctor, who regarded her services as extremely valuable."[38]

---

36. Mary received this patriarchal blessing from Jacob G. Bigler in February 1895 in Nephi, Utah. It is on file at the Church History Library.

37. Mary Goble Pay, interview by Phillip LeRoy Pay, transcr. Leon R. Pay, pp. 1–2, Family Records, photocopy in possession of authors.

38. Phillip LeRoy Pay, "Dreams of Mary Goble Pay," Typescript, p. 2, photo-copy in possession of authors.

Mary told her children of several more visits her husband made to her in dreams, detailing the progress on their "house." Phillip LeRoy Pay recorded:

> I was the youngest child, 13 in number, and about two years after I was married my mother took sick. She was living with my sister, Etta [Marietta Bowers], at the time. One morning she called my sister and said, "Last night your father came to me and took me and showed me the house. It is all finished with furniture and everything. My, it is a wonderful home. He said, 'Now all the children are married and don't need you, why not come here with me?' I told him I would. So tomorrow he is coming for me and I am going. So you tell the boys if they want to see me to come tomorrow."[39]
>
> My Sister tried to talk Her Out of it By saying she was just dreaming. But Mother insisted she had not been asleep an Was Wide awake all the time, an she wanted all her Boys called an to Be there before 10 AM. My sister Contacted all Our family, an when we all arrived. Mother told us the above Incident—an that she was going with Our father to Live With Him. . . . She wanted us to know that she an Our father would Be waiting for us, an she wanted us to Live clean Lives and Obey the commandments of the Lord so we could come and all live together again, an that she wanted us all to come. Then Her Happiness would be Complete—but if we didnt all Come she would Be filled with sorrow.
>
> Then Just a few minutes Before 10 AM she Looked about—Smiled a Beautiful Smile—gave a sigh an passed on. It was September 25, 1913.[40]

39. Pay, "Dreams," 1.

40. Phillip LeRoy Pay, interview by Leon R. Pay, Holograph, pp. 3–4, Family Records, photocopy in possession of authors.

Chapter 18

"WE ARE BLESSED AS SISTERS"

SARAH ANN NELSON PETERSON (1827–1896)

Jennifer L. Lund

BIOGRAPHICAL SKETCH

Sarah Ann Nelson was born February 16, 1827, in upstate New York—by her own account "the second Norwegian born in America."[1] Just two years earlier, her parents, Cornelius and Kari Hesthammer Nelson, along with Sarah's older brother and three sisters,[2] had traveled to America in the first organized immigration from Norway. Sarah spent her early childhood in New York before moving in May 1836 with her widowed mother to a new settlement on the Fox River in LaSalle County, Illinois.[3] Both of these

---

1. Sarah A. Peterson to Rasmus B. Anderson, April 17, 1895, as quoted in Rasmus B. Anderson, *The First Chapter of Norwegian Immigration (1821–1840) Its Causes and Results,* 4th ed. (Madison, WI: printed by author, 1906), 407.

2. Two additional siblings were born in the United States after Sarah was born, making a total of seven children.

3. In addition to the autobiographical sketches featured here, Sarah's life is recounted in detail in Anthon H. Lund, "A Noble Life," *Latter-day Saints' Millennial*

colonies—the first two Norwegian settlements in America—had been founded by her uncle Cleng Peerson.[4]

The arrival of Mormon missionaries in the Fox River settlement in 1842 and her subsequent baptism meant that Sarah was also among the earliest Scandinavian converts to The Church of Jesus Christ of Latter-day Saints.[5] She demonstrated her commitment to her newfound faith when in 1849, at age twenty-two, she bade her family good-bye and joined an emigrating company bound for Utah. Sarah was not the only one to make the journey alone. Twenty-five-year-old Canute Peterson, a friend of the family, was

---

Star 58, no. 27 (July 2, 1896): 426–31, which informs most other sketches. Additional biographies include Anthon H. Lund et al., eds., *Scandinavian Jubilee Album* (Salt Lake City, UT: n.p., 1900), 194; Susa Young Gates, "Mothers of Our Leaders in Israel," *Relief Society Magazine* 3, no. 5 (May 1916): 246–53; Kate B. Carter, ed., "Sarah Ann Peterson," in *Heart Throbs of the West,* vol. 2 (Salt Lake City, UT: Daughters of Utah Pioneers, 1940), 317–18; A. B. Anderson, "Pioneer News and Views," *Lehi Free Press,* May 19, 1947; "Sarah Ann Nelson Peterson," in *Pioneer Women of Faith and Fortitude,* comp. International Society Daughters of Utah Pioneers, 4 vols. (Salt Lake City, UT.: Publishers Press, 1998), 3:2383–84. Background on the emigration experiences of her parents comes from J. Hart Rosdail, *The Sloopers: Their Ancestry and Posterity* (Broadview, IL: Norwegian Slooper Society of America, 1961), 12–29.

4. Cleng Peerson (1782–1865) is sometimes referred to as the father of Norwegian-American immigration. He traveled widely in America, identified a potential settlement site, encouraged his countrymen to emigrate, and founded a total of four Norwegian settlements in the United States. For more information, see Alfred Hauge, *The True Saga of Cleng Peerson,* trans. John Weinstock and Turid Sverre (Dallas: Norwegian Society of Texas, 1982).

5. A broadside published in 1925 for the centennial of the first Norwegians in America recognizes Sarah Ann Nelson Peterson and her husband, Canute Peterson, as two of the first three Norse in Utah. Arnt-Engh, "The First Norse in Utah" (1925), Church History Library, The Church of Jesus Christ of Latter-day Saints, Salt Lake City, Utah, hereafter cited as Church History Library. For background on Latter-day Saint proselytizing among Norwegians in Illinois, see Keith A. Erekson and Lloyd D. Newell, "'A Gathering Place for the Scandinavian People': Conversion, Retention, and Gathering in Norway, Illinois (1842–1849)," *Mormon Historical Studies* 1, no. 1 (Spring 2000): 21–36.

also part of the Norwegian company. The couple was married en route on July 2, 1849.

After a brief stay in Salt Lake City, they settled in Lehi, Utah County. Sixteen years later they made a final move to Utah's Sanpete County when Canute was called as bishop of Ephraim. During those years, Sarah gave birth to nine children, seven of whom lived to adulthood. The family was further enlarged when Canute married two plural wives, each of whom bore several children.

Much of Sarah's life was defined by her husband's responsibilities as a Church leader, first as a missionary in Scandinavia, then as Ephraim's bishop, Scandinavian mission president, and Sanpete Stake president. Sarah too was called to lead. She served as president of the Ephraim Ward Relief Society from 1869 to 1880 and as a counselor in the Sanpete Stake Relief Society presidency from 1880 until her death on May 20, 1896.

LIFE EXPERIENCES

By the time Sarah sat down to write the first of two brief life sketches, she was mindful of her role in the founding generation of Scandinavians in America. Her account published in Edward W. Tullidge's *Women of Mormondom* in 1877 featured her Norwegian heritage. Eliza R. Snow had written a personal appeal urging that Sarah "get up some interesting items . . . relate incidents that have come under your observation and also those of note related by your husband."[6] Sarah dutifully complied, and the published sketch is included here almost in its entirety.

Eighteen years later, Sarah corresponded with Rasmus B. Anderson, who published excerpts from three of Sarah's letters in *The First Chapter of Norwegian Immigration*. One long selection and a few shorter ones are featured here.

------

6. Eliza R. Snow to Sarah A. Peterson, n.d., Holograph, p. 2, Peterson Family Papers, circa 1844–1957, Church History Library.

Sarah's status as the daughter of original immigrants made her a particularly influential contributor to Anderson's volume. In addition, she was married to Canute Peterson, another prominent Norwegian. In recognition of her position, Sarah notes that her son was "the first Norwegian male child born in Utah" and her daughter was "the first Norwegian female child born in Lehi, Utah." Anderson completed the litany by naming Sarah as the first Norwegian schoolteacher in America, an accomplishment which Sarah herself downplayed.[7] "It did not require much education to teach those country schools," Sarah recalled. "I had some scholars who were from twenty to forty years old. They came to learn the English language."[8]

Sarah lived a remarkable life, yet she wrote little about her own experiences. Following are two autobiographies used to create a single life narrative, interspersed with selections from family members. Finally, excerpts from the diary she kept from January 1, 1890, to July 30, 1893, round out her life story.

I was born in the town of Murray, Orleans county, N. Y., February 16, 1827. My parents, Cornelius and Carrie Nelson, were among the first Norwegians who emigrated to America. They left Norway on account of having joined the Quakers, who, at that time, were subject to much persecution in that country. In the neighborhood was quite a number of that sect, and they concluded to emigrate to America in a body.[9] As there was no direct line of emigration between Norway and America, they purchased a sloop, in which they performed the voyage.[10] Having been raised on the coast,

---

7. Sarah A. Peterson to Rasmus B. Anderson, March 9, 1895, and April 17, 1895, as quoted in Anderson, *Norwegian Immigration,* 402, 406–8. Anderson credits Sarah with being the first Norwegian to teach school in America, 95.

8. Peterson to Anderson, April 17, 1895, 407.

9. Here "neighborhood" refers to the region around Stavanger on the west coast of Norway. Rosdail, *Sloopers,* 9–11.

10. A sloop is a small sailing vessel better suited to coastal fishing than voyages

they were all used to the duties of seamen, and found no trouble in navigating their vessel. They also brought a small cargo of iron with them, which, together with the vessel, they sold in New York, and then moved to the northwestern portion of that State, and settled on a wild tract of woodland. Eight years afterwards my father died. I was at that time six years old. When I was nine years old my uncle went to Illinois, whence he returned with the most glowing accounts of the fertility of the soil, with plenty of land for sale at government price. The company disposed of their farms at the rate of fifty dollars per acre, and again moved from their homes, settling on the Fox River, near Ottawa, Ill. Here, when fourteen years of age, I first heard the gospel, and at once believed in the divine mission of the prophet Joseph; but on account of the opposition of relatives, was prevented joining the church until four years later.[11]

In the spring of 1849 I left mother and home and joined a company who were preparing to leave for the valley. On our way to Council Bluffs I was attacked with cholera. But there was a young gentleman in the company by the name of Canute Peterson, who, after a season of secret prayer in my behalf, came and placed his hands upon my head, and I was instantly healed. Two weeks after our arrival at the Bluffs I was married to him.[12]

---

on the open sea. The sloop, *Restauration,* was fifty-four feet long by sixteen feet wide and carried fifty-two immigrants. Ingrid Semmingsen, *Norway to America: A History of the Migration,* trans. Einar Haugen (Minneapolis: University of Minnesota Press, 1978), 10.

11. When Sarah was endowed in 1852, she listed the date of her baptism as April 1845, three years after she first heard the missionaries. Endowment House Register, Book A, 45, Special Collections, Family History Library, The Church of Jesus Christ of Latter-day Saints, Salt Lake City, Utah, hereafter cited as Family History Library.

12. Sarah A. Peterson, quoted in Edward W. Tullidge, *The Women of Mormondom* (New York: Tullidge & Crandall, 1877), 465–66.

Sarah's brief telling of her bout of cholera belies her precarious situation. Cholera was the leading cause of death on the overland trails in the mid-nineteenth century, and half of all untreated victims died. The disease, caused by water-borne bacteria, was particularly virulent along transportation routes. Victims typically suffered from vomiting, acute diarrhea, dehydration, and severe intestinal cramping. Symptoms came on quickly, often running their course in a matter of hours until death came as a relief.[13] Sarah provides little detail about her illness, but her husband, Canute, relates a much fuller account in his own biographical narrative:

> A journey of about two hundred miles brought us to Burlington, Iowa. We found the city deserted, with the exception of the ferryman, and a few guards who were left to watch the city. The streets and porches had been strewn with new lime, because of the great cholera epidemic.
>
> We passed out of the city as quickly as we could and camped about eight miles from there on a beautiful little creek.
>
> When we came to Chardon Point, Iowa, Sister Sarah Ann Nelson was seized with a violent attack of cholera. The sisters did all they could for her relief, but it was of no avail.
>
> I became impressed to go down into the woods on the creek and pray to the Lord for her recovery.
>
> Here I earnestly besought the Lord that He would spare her life, and I became so filled with the Spirit of the Lord that I thought I hardly touched the ground while going from the place of prayer to the wagon.
>
> When within a few rods of the wagon, I could hear her groan. I went to the side of the wagon nearest to her head,

---

13. A cholera epidemic began in the United States in 1849. Shane A. Baker, "Illness and Mortality in Nineteenth-Century Mormon Immigration," *Mormon Historical Studies* 2, no. 2 (Fall 2001): 84–86.

put my hand between the wagon cover and the wagon box, and placed my hand on her head and silently rebuked the Destroyer.

She immediately straightened herself out of the cramp, smiled, and told the Sisters, "I am healed."

She was well aware whose hand it was that had touched her. She had the disease no more.[14]

During Sarah's illness, Canute Peterson realized he loved the young woman he had known since his youth. As the company crossed Iowa, the two young people courted and decided to marry. Canute was twenty-five and had little to offer his bride other than a meager traveling outfit and "his honest heart."[15] On July 2, soon after arriving at the Missouri River, the couple was married by apostle Orson Hyde at camp five miles east of Kanesville, Iowa.[16] Two weeks later, they set out for the West.

We joined Ezra T. Benson's company, and arrived in Salt Lake City on the 25th of October, and spent the winter following in the "Old Fort." In 1851 we removed to Dry Creek, afterwards called Lehi. My husband was among the very first to survey land and take up claims there. In 1852 he was sent on mission to Norway. During the four years he was absent I supported myself and the two children.[17]

Now twenty-five and pregnant, Sarah bade her husband goodbye. During his absence, she worked the farm, often by herself, gave

---

14. Canute Peterson, "The Story of Canute Peterson As Told to His Daughter Carrie," *Instructor* 81, no. 4 (April 1946): 174. Peterson dictated his narrative to his daughter Carrie Peterson Tanner in 1900. Earlier manuscript and typescript versions differ only slightly from the published version used here.

15. Lund, "Noble Life," 428.

16. Peterson, "Story of Canute Peterson," 174–75.

17. Peterson, quoted in Tullidge, *Women of Mormondom,* 466.

birth to a baby girl, and endured uncertainty, tensions with native people, and famine. Drought, accompanied by grasshopper invasions, devastated several harvests.[18] On May 6, 1855, fellow Lehi resident John Nield noted in his diary, "grasshoppers rampant. Taking everything green Looks bad for us."[19] A few weeks later, Heber C. Kimball commented in a letter to his son that the fields in Utah County "are pretty much desolate."[20] A few fields, however, were spared, including Sarah's. Lehi historian Hamilton Gardner retold the story as related to him by one of Sarah's daughters:

> Owing to the absence of her husband on a mission, the responsibility of tilling the land fell upon Mrs. Peterson. She was unable to obtain assistance so attempted the planting of the crop herself. In furrows made with a hoe, she planted the precious kernels of wheat and because of her anxiety to perform the work well, she covered them deeply with soil. An acre of land was utilized in this laborious manner. Because of the lateness and depth of planting, the wheat did not show above the ground until after the departure of the grasshoppers, so that when the other fields were barren and waste, that of Mrs. Peterson was covered with a luxuriant growth. Sixty bushels of wheat was the generous reward bestowed by Mother Earth, in addition to sixty bushels of corn and some potatoes. With these, this good lady was able

---

18. D. Robert Carter, "Fish and the Famine of 1855–56," *Journal of Mormon History* 27, no. 2 (Fall 2001): 97–99; Davis Bitton and Linda P. Wilcox, "Pestiferous Ironclads: The Grasshopper Problem in Pioneer Utah," *Utah Historical Quarterly* 46, no. 4 (Fall 1978): 340–42.

19. Eva Elenor Nield Franck, "Extracts from the Journal of John Nield," May 6, 1855, Typescript, p. 11, Church History Library.

20. Heber C. Kimball to William Kimball, May 29, 1855, in Journal History of the Church of Jesus Christ of Latter-day Saints, May 29, 1855, p. 2, Church History Library.

to provide, during the following winter, for seven orphans, and to give generous aid to numerous neighbors.[21]

On Canute's return from his mission in 1856, he penned a letter to Sarah from Fort Laramie, giving an account of his successful emigrating company and issuing a good-natured challenge, "Now if you can beat that I think you have done well."[22] Arriving in Lehi, he was pleasantly surprised. Not only had Sarah sustained her little family and cared for others, but her hard work had paid off, and they were "in a much better condition financially than when he left."[23]

Sarah's narrative turns next to plural marriage. When Eliza R. Snow invited Sarah to contribute a biographical essay to *Women of Mormondom,* she noted, "They want particularly the testimonies of the sisters how they have lived polygamy—whether their hearts have been broken by it—whether they were forced into it &c."[24] Sarah obliged:

> In the fall of 1857 my husband added another wife to his family; but I can truly say that he did not do so without my consent, nor with any other motive than to serve his

---

21. Hamilton Gardner, *History of Lehi* (Salt Lake City, UT: Deseret News, 1913), 88–89. This is the earliest written account of the preservation of Sarah's wheat. Of the daughters, Sarah A. Peterson Lund is the most likely informant, since her husband, Anthon H. Lund, provided other information for Gardner's volume. Sarah preserved some of the wheat and presented it to Canute when he returned from his mission. They kept the wheat, which Canute dubbed "Salvation Wheat," as a memento of Sarah's resourcefulness. In accordance with his wishes, the bottle was placed in Canute's coffin when he died. Bertie Peterson Beal to Carrie Peterson Tanner, July 13, 1939, as cited in Carrie Peterson Tanner, "Story of the Life of Canute Peterson As Given by Himself and by Some Members of His Family," Typescript, p. 63, author's possession.

22. Canute Peterson to Sarah A. Peterson, August 13, 1856, quoted in Tanner, "Story of the Life," Appendix: Letter 9.

23. Lund, "Noble Life," 429.

24. Snow to Peterson, p. 2.

God. I felt it our duty to obey the commandment revealed through the prophet Joseph, hence, although I felt it to be quite a sacrifice, I encouraged him in so doing. Although not so very well supplied with houseroom, the second wife and I lived together in harmony and peace. I felt it a pleasure to be in her company, and even to nurse and take care of her children, and she felt the same way toward me and my children. A few years afterwards my husband married another wife, but also with the consent and encouragement of his family. This did not disturb the peaceful relations of our home, but the same kind feelings were entertained by each member of the family to one another. We have now lived in polygamy twenty years, have eaten at the same table and raised our children together, and have never been separated, nor have we ever wished to be.[25]

While Sarah admits that she felt plural marriage "to be quite a sacrifice," she very carefully explains the motivation for Canute to take a plural wife, stressing her own sense of duty and obedience. Sarah was clearly an active participant in the decision, and it was likely her commitment and unfailing kindness and compassion that helped to make their family relationships agreeable and even pleasant.[26]

The Petersons' Lehi farm prospered, and Canute was well respected in the community where he served as a counselor to Bishop David Evans. Their large home was open to the many Scandinavians traveling between Salt Lake and the southern settlements.[27] Even

---

25. Peterson, quoted in Tullidge, *Women of Mormondom,* 467.

26. Canute Peterson married Gertrude Maria Rolfson (1830–1913) on November 9, 1857, and Charlotte A. Eckstrom (1844–1934) on February 2, 1867. Canute Peterson Family Group Sheets, Family History Library; Death Certificates, Utah State Archives, accessed November 5, 2011, http://archives.utah.gov /research/guides/death.htm.

27. Canute Peterson Family Group Sheets; Lund, " Noble Life," 429.

though the territory was experiencing renewed Indian tensions, it seemed as if the days of pioneering were behind them. Then came the call for Canute to move to Ephraim in Sanpete County, where he was to serve as bishop. Sarah recalled:

> We lived in Lehi until 1867, when my husband was called to go to Sanpete, and we now reside at Ephraim, one hundred miles south of Lehi. At this time the Indians had become very hostile, and war was raging between them and the settlers. Many people were killed, and the most of their cattle and horses were either stolen or killed. Under these trying circumstances Mr. Peterson was called to take the lead as bishop of this place. A bishop with us takes the lead in temporal as well as in spiritual affairs. The first thing he did was to send teams and guards to bring the settlers from the smaller settlements, where they were not able to protect themselves. A fort was built of stone, and men were put on guard to protect the people. From that time but few people were killed, and scarcely any cattle were stolen.[28] In one of the raids our son Peter with others went up in the mountains to recover some horses, but the Indians lying in ambush shot at the men. Our son had his horse shot from under him, and he and his men were glad to get back with their scalps.[29]

---

28. Consolidation of the settlement into the fort actually occurred in 1866, before Canute Peterson arrived on the scene; however, Canute was involved in the 1867 evacuation of the Sevier Valley settlements to Sanpete County. See Albert C. T. Antrei and Allen D. Roberts, *A History of Sanpete County*, Utah Centennial County History Series (Salt Lake City: Utah State Historical Society and Sanpete County Commission, 1999), 77–78; John Alton Peterson, *Utah's Black Hawk War* (Salt Lake City: University of Utah Press, 1998), 329–35.

29. This incident occurred in July 1868. Canute Peterson, Niels C. Anderson, George P. Jensen, and Peter C. Peterson, Deposition, October 21, 1897, Typescript, p. 2, United States Court of Claims, Canute Peterson vs. the United States and Ute Indians, Church History Library.

This was continued a little over two years, but finally the Indians saw that they were outgeneraled. Ten of their chiefs came down from the mountains and stopped in front of our gate. We were very much surprised, not knowing their intentions. My husband went out to meet them and asked them what they wanted. They dismounted, and said they wanted to talk. He invited them to come in and at once sent for two interpreters. After they had eaten a hearty dinner at our table, my husband asked them if they felt like fighting. They said "No!" they felt good and wanted to smoke a pipe of peace. After this matters were talked over and an agreement of peace was made, which has not been broken since. My husband is now known among them as their "White Father." Their chiefs frequently come to visit us.[30]

Local tradition holds that it was Sarah's homemade dumpling soup that helped bring about lasting peace.[31] Whether or not that claim is true, Sarah had a profound effect on her fellow Saints in Ephraim and throughout Sanpete County. After the Relief Society was reorganized, Sarah was chosen in 1869 as the first president of the newly formed Ephraim Relief Society. Under her leadership, the sisters raised substantial funds, which were put to good use. They built a two-story building on Main Street, renting out the first floor and using the second as a meeting hall. Sarah vigorously championed the gleaning and storing of wheat and oversaw the construction

---

30. Peterson to Anderson, March 9, 1895, quoted in Anderson, *Norwegian Immigration,* 403–4. General peace talks in August 1868 resulted in an agreement between Black Hawk and other Ute chiefs and the Indian superintendent to end hostilities. Bands of warriors then visited individual settlements to negotiate local peace treaties as described in Sarah's account. While some raiding continued until 1872, Ephraim residents considered this treaty as marking the end of Indian-settler conflict. Peterson, *Black Hawk,* 350–52.

31. Grace Johnson, *"Brodders and Sisters"* (Manti, UT: Messenger-Enterprise, 1973; repr. 1979), 50–52.

of a granary as insurance against hard times—something she herself knew only too well. She was perhaps best known for encouraging the sisters to dedicate the eggs their hens laid on Sundays to charitable works. Even the chickens yielded to her persuasion and "seemed to lay more eggs on Sunday than on any other day in the week!"[32]

Sunday eggs were so successful that the practice spread to other settlements. Following Sarah's lead, women consecrated the eggs that were traditionally reserved to provide themselves with a little spending money. In Ephraim, the funds raised from Sunday eggs and other donations sustained the poor, supported missionaries in the field, assisted converts from Europe to emigrate to Utah, and contributed to construction of the Manti Temple.[33] When Tullidge published Sarah's autobiography in 1877, he noted that under her leadership the Ephraim Relief Society had disbursed $11,000 to charitable works, the equivalent of more than $230,000 in 2010 United States dollars.[34]

After being called as a counselor in the Sanpete Stake Relief Society presidency in 1880, Sarah continued her labors in behalf of her sisters and the causes for which she felt most passionate, particularly the storing of grain. While she once noted, "I think it is good times for we have plenty to eat and wear," she wanted to make sure that the sisters never forgot that "hard times" could be just around the corner. She repeatedly urged, "We ought to prepare ourselves for whatever awaits us."[35] Despite her concern, Sarah had a naturally cheerful disposition, and she counseled the women to appreciate

---

32. Lund, "Noble Life," 430.

33. Lund, "Noble Life," 430; Jill Mulvay Derr, Janath Russell Cannon, and Maureen Ursenbach Beecher, *Women of Covenant: The Story of Relief Society* (Salt Lake City, UT: Deseret Book, 1992), 104.

34. Tullidge, *Women of Mormondom,* 467; Samuel H. Williamson, "Seven Ways to Compute the Relative Value of a U.S. Dollar Amount, 1774 to present," MeasuringWorth, accessed March 16, 2012, http://www.measuringworth.com /uscompare/.

35. Relief Society Minutes, September 22, 1893, Sanpete Stake, Church

their circumstances. "We are blessed as sisters," she acknowledged, "that we have the privilege of meeting togather where we can partake of spiritual things as well as Temporal."[36] On another occasion, she encouraged the young women to gain a testimony: "We must be humble, fast and pray in order to obtain it. We do not all need the visiting of angels, but we should know within our own hearts that the gospel is true."[37] She admonished all to be obedient, noting that "it makes us feel better when doing some noble act."[38]

Sarah's own life was filled with noble acts as she often attended at a sickbed, assisted in childbirth, or comforted those who grieved. Life was also filled with the mundane—cooking meals, washing clothes, watering the garden, and hosting a houseful of boarders as well as a constant stream of visitors. At times Sarah assumed responsibility for the family's farm, business dealings, and finances, particularly when Canute was serving as a missionary, first for four years in the 1850s and then for another two as Scandinavian mission president in the 1870s. In preparation for their family's move to Ephraim in 1867, Sarah stayed behind in Lehi to settle their affairs while Canute prepared a home in Sanpete County. Canute wrote from Ephraim: "Sarah you are the One that I look for to sand [send] me all that I need up here, this summer and allso to seport [support] the Family at Home, for you are *Harnesst* [harnessed] up *next* to *me* to *work* for *us All*." He then continued with an admonition, as well as his perspective on their plural marriage: "Now Girls be Pashent and

History Library; Relief Society Minutes, September 14, 1894, Sanpete Stake, Church History Library.

36. Relief Society Minutes, June 8, 1894, Sanpete Stake, Church History Library.

37. "Minutes of Quarterly Conference of the Y.L.M.I.A.," *Young Woman's Journal* 1, no. 2 (November 1889): 51.

38. Relief Society Minutes, March 22, 1895, Sanpete Stake, Church History Library.

all will be rit [right] for I have not done onley what the Lord wanted me to do for to try us all. Probly this is the thing that will save us."[39]

Sarah apparently did not appreciate the comparison to a work horse. Her side of the correspondence no longer exists, but judging by Canute's conciliatory response, Sarah was heartbroken. She doubted his love for her, as well as her own ability to overcome feelings of jealousy and heartache.[40] Despite Sarah's disdain, the metaphor is perhaps appropriate. She and Canute really were equally harnessed in building both the Peterson family and the kingdom of God.

Much of Sarah's resilience in the face of challenges came from her ability to recognize the humor in nearly any situation. She was quick to laugh and to regale listeners with stories of her own predicaments. Family lore tells of her nearly paralyzing fear of both Indians and being alone. When Canute was on his first mission to Scandinavia, she faced her most dreaded fears day after day. On one occasion, she saw two Indians approaching her cabin. She quickly bolted the door, grabbed two-year-old Peter, and cowered under the bed. The men rapped at the door over and over, but Sarah, her heart pounding, did not answer. Finally, one of the men pushed an arrow through a knot hole in the door, knocking out the rag Sarah had carefully stuffed in the hole. He then bent down and peered into the cabin. Little Peter shouted out, "Peek-a-boo." The chagrined Sarah opened the door and gave the men the flour they requested. When they were gone, Sarah crumpled to the floor in laughter and relief.[41]

Late in life, Sarah kept a diary. The entries are brief, but they

---

39. Canute Peterson to Sarah and Maria Peterson, June 5, 1867, Peterson Family Papers, ca. 1844–1957, Church History Library.

40. Canute Peterson to Sarah Peterson, June 12, 1867, Peterson Family Papers, ca. 1844–1957, Church History Library.

41. Edith P. Christiansen, *As unto the Bow: Canute Peterson from Norway to America,* 2nd ed. (Provo, UT: printed by author, 1976), 47–48.

give a sense of her duties and concerns. Here is a selection from a typical month's record from June 1890 when she was sixty-three:

> Father [Canute] went to the [Salt Lake] City. . . .
>
> 8 had a short visit from Sister Zina W. Card
>
> 11 Bro Preston called
>
> 13 Started in company with Sister [Mary Isabella Hales] Horn[e], Stevens, Sister [Ellen Lee] Jakeman, Johon to drive to go to sisters conference at Fairview
>
> 15 went to Indian Oley [Indianola] organised relief cociety and y. L. M. [Young Ladies Mutual] then to Millburn organised Relief Society
>
> 16 we organized Relief Society [at] Mt pleasant and went on to Spring City. Held meeting and came home held 7 meetings all felt well Sister Horn[e] went hom[e]
>
> 17 wen[t] to the [Manti] Temple Baptised for my cousin Sousan and 12 others
>
> 18 Stayed at home and water[ed]. . . .
>
> 21 Sister [Mary Ann Price] Hyde came. . . .
>
> 26 we had a jubilee Manti and Ephraim Sunday Schools
>
> 27 Bro and Sister [George] God[d]ard Stayed with us all night
>
> 28 Erastus Willardson home from a mission to Scandinavia. We went a few miles and met him
>
> 28 hauling Lusurn [lucerne] [42]

On occasion, the diary reveals Sarah's deep affection for her sisters in the gospel, such as in this entry from November 5, 1891: "Sister Hyd and [Elizabeth] Allred came and met with [us] in meeting we had joyful time. Sister Hyde spoke in toungs [tongues] the Pres interpeted."[43] In a few instances, such as one from May 3,

42. Sarah Ann Nelson Peterson, Diary, June 1–30, 1890, Photocopy of holograph, private possession.

43. Peterson, Diary, November 5, 1891.

1890, Sarah's sense of humor emerges as she paints an entertaining scene on a trip to the theater with Canute and her two oldest grandchildren:

> Canut and me went to the show and maria [Gertrude Maria Rolfson Peterson] stayed home Sarah ["Sazie" Peterson] went out two with John Jensen and so did Ethel with Tony [Lund].
>
> Sazie just holerd and laughed so did Ethel but Canut went too sleep.[44]

Sarah's diary omits her own reaction to the show but instead focuses on her grandchildren, whom she found so engaging, and her husband, who nodded off, much to her amusement or chagrin. This attention to others is typical of Sarah's own life; her attention was repeatedly turned outward. When she died on May 20, 1896, after a long battle with stomach cancer, the eulogies recounted her selfless service to others. Artist and writer C. C. A. Christensen, an old friend of nearly forty years, stepped out of his journalist's shoes and spoke personally in summing up her life: "She was, in my view, as close to perfection in this life as a mortal can come: noble, devoted, resourceful, free from vanity, diligent and God-fearing, frugal toward herself, but generous toward those in need, and her greatest pleasure was when she could contribute to making others happy, or at least to lightening others' sorrows and losses—such was our Sarah."[45]

---

44. Peterson, Diary, May 3, 1890.

45. C. C. A. Christensen, "Death," trans. Michele McNabb, *Bikuben,* June 4, 1896.

Chapter 19

"EYE TO EYE IN FAITH AND SCIENTIFIC KNOWLEDGE"

ESTHER ROMANIA BUNNELL PRATT PENROSE (1839–1932)

Laurel Thatcher Ulrich

BIOGRAPHICAL SKETCH

In a speech given in Ogden, Utah, in 1879, Romania Pratt roused her audience with a powerful image: "Knowledge feeds and fattens on itself."[1] That was her way of saying that the more a person learns, the more she is able to learn. Her own life exemplified that concept. Born in Washington, Indiana, on August 8, 1839, the daughter of Luther Ball and Esther Mendenhall Bunnell, Romania was privileged to study in her teens at the Female Seminary in Crawfordsville, a pioneering school for girls.[2] Inspired by the presence of nearby Wabash College, the Female Seminary offered a

---

1. "Dr. Romania B. Pratt," *Woman's Exponent* 8, no. 1 (June 1, 1879): 251. The concept, if not the exact sentence, was widely known. See, for example, George Gore, *The Art of Scientific Discovery* (London: Longmans, Green, 1878), 294: "Knowledge begets knowledge, as wealth begets wealth, and he who possesses much can with the greater facility obtain more."

2. Romania B. Pratt Penrose, Memoir, 1881, Photocopy of holograph, pp. 1–2,

rigorous curriculum with courses in ancient and modern history, English composition, physiology, algebra, and a kind of astronomy that contemporaries called "uranography."[3]

Although migration to Utah in 1855 interrupted Romania's formal education, the courses she had taken in Crawfordsville provided the foundation she built upon years later when Brigham Young urged the Relief Society to send women east to study medicine. She became the first of several Latter-day Saint women to graduate from the Woman's Medical College of Pennsylvania. Her life experiences, as well as her faith in God, propelled her. Married at nineteen, Romania had given birth to seven children by the time she was thirty-four. Two of those children, including her only daughter, died in infancy. She wanted to prevent other women from losing their children. In her view, educated women made better mothers, and she devoted her life to that conviction.[4]

Early Latter-day Saints were often rightly suspicious of secular medicine. In the 1830s and 1840s, so-called "regular medicine" often relied on extreme blood-letting and the administration of harsh drugs like the mercurial compound calomel. Church leaders urged Latter-day Saints to rely instead on mild herbs and faith. But by the 1870s, both medicine and leaders' attitudes toward it had changed. Even Brigham Young, who had once said that he could put all the

Church History Library, The Church of Jesus Christ of Latter-day Saints, Salt Lake City, Utah, hereafter cited as Church History Library.

3. Pat Cline, ed., *Montgomery County Legend and Lore* ([Crawfordsville, IN]: Montgomery County Historical Society, 1988), 161–62.

4. Brief modern biographies of Romania Pratt include Claire Noall, *Guardians of the Hearth: Utah's Pioneer Midwives and Women Doctors* (Bountiful, UT: Horizon Publishers, 1974), 100–114; Christine Croft Waters, "Romania Pratt Penrose: To Brave the World," in *Sister Saints*, ed. Vicky Burgess-Olson (Provo, UT: Brigham Young University Press, 1978), 341–60; Shana Montgomery, "Esther Romania Bunnell Pratt Penrose (1839–1932): An Uphill Climb," in *Worth Their Salt, Too: More Notable but Often Unnoted Women of Utah*, ed. Colleen Whitley (Logan: Utah State University Press, 2000), 29–39.

knowledge doctors had in a "knut shell and put it in my vest pocket, and then I would have to hunt for it to find it," believed there was value in the new scientific training.[5] This did not mean abandoning spiritual forms of healing. It meant putting faith to work in order to advance knowledge of the human body.

Romania embraced the new emphasis. Returning from Philadelphia in 1877 with her M.D. degree in hand, she expressed hope for medical advancement in Utah. "The resources should be equal to all the ills the flesh is heir to, and spirit too, if we could only grow eye to eye in faith and scientific knowledge," she wrote.[6] The autobiography she composed in 1881, as well as the essays and speeches she wrote during the same period, attest to her yearning for both spiritual and scientific knowledge. They also reveal some of the difficulties she faced both in Utah and in eastern colleges and hospitals. In the east she was an anomaly because of her religious faith. In the west she stood apart because of her secular education. Fortunately, she was sustained by a community of Latter-day Saint leaders committed both to the Church and to the advancement of women.

She composed her memoir as a contribution to the Relief Society's "Jubilee Box." In honor of the fiftieth anniversary of the organization of the Church, the Relief Society gathered memorabilia and sealed it in boxes meant to be opened fifty years later at the Church's centennial. Romania closed her memoir hoping she might live "to witness the opening of this Jubilee box and rejoice with my children and children's children and all the Saints of the most High

---

5. Historian's Office (1842?–1972), June 18, 1861, Reports of Speeches, 1845–1885, Holograph, Church History Library; Linda P. Wilcox, "The Imperfect Science: Brigham Young on Medical Doctors," *Dialogue: A Journal of Mormon Thought* 12, no. 3 (Fall 1979): 26–36. For an overview of this transition, see Lester E. Bush Jr., *Health and Medicine among the Latter-day Saints: Science, Sense, and Scripture* (New York: Crossroad, 1993), 89–100.

6. Romania B. Pratt, "Correspondence," *Woman's Exponent* 6, no. 4 (July 15, 1877): 30.

God."[7] Remarkably, she got her wish. She died on November 9, 1932, at the age of ninety-three, having outlived three of her children and both of her husbands: Parley P. Pratt Jr. (1837–1897), who was the father of her children and whom she divorced in 1880; and Charles W. Penrose (1832–1925), whom she married in 1886. Charles, a writer and educator remembered for his hymns, was serving as a counselor in the First Presidency at the time of his death.[8] Her granddaughter Edna Pratt Sutherland lovingly preserved her memoir.

Over her long life, Romania Bunnell Pratt Penrose served the Latter-day Saint community as a daughter, wife, mother, teacher, physician, writer, editor, lecturer, woman suffragist, Church worker, and earnest advocate for human rights. The selections below come from her 1881 memoir and from articles and speeches she composed at about the same time.

LIFE EXPERIENCES

Memoir of Romania B. Pratt, M.D.
Salt Lake City, March 19, 1881

Dr. Romania B. Pratt, daughter of Luther B. Bunnell and Esther Mendenhall Bunnell, was born in the town of Washington Wayne Co. Indiana, August 8th 1839. My mother embraced the gospel when I was three years old— my father three years later. My parents gathered with the saints in 1846 just before they left Nauvoo, and travelled with them into Winter Quarters, but on account of the very delicate health of my mother, father returned to the settlements. I well remember of investigating with childish wonder and eagerness the mysteries of the Nauvoo Temple, from

---

7. Penrose, Memoir, 26.

8. Romania B. Pratt Penrose, Family Record, ca. 1924, Photocopy of holograph, n.p., Church History Library.

the white marble font on the backs of white marble oxen in the basement to the wondrous bell in the belfry. . . . While in Nauvoo Father, mother and I received our Patriarchial blessings from John Smith, uncle of the prophet Joseph. Great things were promised us all which if we live for them we will receive. My father finally returned to the home of his father, where he purchased a farm, upon which he placed mother and her children and then went to California during the Gold fever prevailing at that time.[9] He died there just as he contemplated returning home.

All my childhood days, until I was sixteen years of age, was spent in school, when my mother in 1855 again gathered with the saints. I attended the Female Seminary in Crawfordsville, Indiana, and no doubt had I remained, I should have obtained a very finished education; but my blooming womanhood began to draw around me admirers which warned mother to flee from Babylon before I became fastened by Gentile bonds. I do not remember of having any other faith than that of the true and everlasting gospel. I was not baptized until we were on our journey to Salt Lake City, May 1855.

The journey across the plains with ox teams was a summer full of pleasure to me;—the early morning walks—gathering wild flowers, climbing the rugged and oftimes forbidding hills—the pleasant evening gatherings of the young folks by the bright camp fire. . . . I well remember how I sped up the east side of the Little Mountain with fleet footsteps and anxious heart to get the first peep at the Great City of the Saints. With lightening glances I rapidly swept the whole valley north and south but no city could I find; my disappointment was extreme. I looked for bristling

---

9. The Bunnells resided in Clear Creek, Warren County, Ohio. 1850 United States Federal Census.

spires and flashing metallic cupolas which I had been accustomed to see when first coming into sight of other cities.
After a long but fruitless search for the city some one came
to my relief and called my attention to a small collection of
black spots indicating houses. . . . The year we arrived was
one of famine and tis needless to recount the sorrows and
disappointments common to all. Through the blessing of
our Father who has promised to care for the widow and the
fatherless we did not suffer from hunger. Now for the first
time in life did I face its stern realities. . . .

After my father's death, a guardian was appointed to
take care of the property left us, and he not believing in the
Latter Day work would not let us have any means "to come
among the Mormons," saying they would at once take it all
from us, and thus we were in a measure penniless when we
arrived. I taught school the greater portion of my time. . . .

I was married to Parley P. Pratt son of the Apostle
Parley—February 23ʳᵈ 1859, and to us were born seven
children. . . .

December 1873 I left my children with my mother
and went to New York City, with the intention of studying
medicine. The first six weeks in New York was spent assisting Mr. Pratt in proof reading his father's autobiography.[10]
After it was ready for the press, I entered a medical college.
It was late in the winter, and I merely learned that term how
to proceed in my studies. Of course I took a back seat, but
all my faculties were on the "qui vive" to learn all I could. I
shall not soon forget my extreme confusion on being asked
a question during a quiz by a professor who for the moment
forgot I was a new student—, nor the mischievous smiles
of the students, but my revenge was more than complete

10. *Autobiography of Parley Parker Pratt . . . His Life, Ministry and Travels,* ed.
Parley P. Pratt Jr. (New York: Russell Brothers, 1874).

at the beginning of the next term in witnessing their astonishment because of my advancement. During the summer
vacation while they were recreating, sea-bathing and visiting
with friends, I daily plodded studiously up the rugged hill
of knowledge; reciting as a private student every day to the
professor of physiology. . . . I was well prepared to enter the
winter term of 1874 & 5, and made rapid progress in my
studies. . . .

The summer vacation of 1875 & 76 I returned to Salt
Lake City and once more had the joy of the society of my
children and the Saints. . . . In the fall of 1875 I started
for Philadelphia to enter the Medical College for Women to
finish my medical education. I spent this winter as the one
before in attending lectures, clinics, and dissecting. The days
all seemed so much alike that it was as one long day. After
the spring term a situation in the New England Hospital
for Women and children in Boston was proffered me which
I most gladly accepted. The practical experience I gained
while there has been of incalculable value to me. I experienced the greatest pleasure in my duties. . . .

With the autumn leaves came the opening of another
winter term in college, and I hastened back to Philadelphia
to enter upon my last course of lectures. This was a winter
full of work, for in addition to the regular studies, I had my
thesis to write. At last the winter's days were over and those
who successfully passed their examinations stood on the
heights of the rugged hill we had been climbing, waving joy-
fully the flag "Excelsior". On March 15th, 1877 one of the
most eventful days of my life arrived—my graduation day.
Dressed in black and with throbbing hearts we repaired to
Association Hall—the house was crowded full of interested
friends and spectators, but alas! few were mine. A stranger in
a strange land, beside being almost a "hiss and a byword" on
account of my religion. Nevertheless after we had received

our diplomas and a present of the code of Medical Ethics, I received two beautiful bouquets and a book from friends.

Now that I had really passed the golden gate, stern reality and responsibility began to rudely stare me in the face—but I was not yet ready to begin practice. I had not yet learned enough about the eye and ear, for I designed to prepare myself as a specialist in this department. I remained in Philadelphia and attended two courses on the eye . . . [and] a course of lectures on the ear. . . . After finishing these courses of study, I went to Elmira Water Cure by special request of John W. Young—, son of Pres. Brigham Young.[11] I remained at Elmira about a month, and then I set out for Bloomington, Indiana, where my sister resided, who was near her accouchement and I had promised to attend her. . . .

On my route from Elmira to Bloomington, I visited all the noted Water Cures with letters of introduction and also Niagara Falls. At Clifton Springs, the most noted as well as most extensive, I was very cordially received by the proprietor and lady assistant.

I spent a week at Clifton, and during the time Mr Foster—, the proprietor—, asked me if I knew I was near "Mormon Hill" [Cumorah]. With a surprised delight, I said I did not, when he turned to the lady assistant and proposed a visit to the hill, saying his carriage was at our disposal. With many thanks we accepted the visit, and next morning early found us on our way. After a pleasant ride of nine miles we came to a lone bluff or immense mound in the midst of a plain. After placing our horse and buggy in the hands of a farmer living at the foot of the Hill—we commenced what

---

11. Elmira Water Cure, a resort located in Elmira, New York, was devoted to healing patients through prescribed "baths" and massage. Pratt, "Correspondence," 30.

was to me a sacred journey. How can expression be given to the sacred awe pervading the soul as one nears the hallowed ground, where of a certainty we know that angels trod,—perhaps your foot may press the very footprint of a celestial being. Slowly and deeply impressed, I assended the sacred mount accompanied by the other ladies who had no impression of awe or solemnity of the occasion. As we neared the summit, a flock of sheep were grazing quietly but fled at our approach, and soon we stood on the top of that memorable hill which has been the theatre of many a severe conflict, physically between mortals, and spiritually between the angels of light and darkness.

As we sat on the brow of the hill I mentally offered up a prayer asking our Father to so bless me that I might fully appreciate the privilege I then enjoyed and also the great privilege we enjoyed by possessing the Book of Mormon. We are yet so nearly children that we scarcely begin to realize what great things the Lord has done for us in these last days. Oh! that we could arise and shake off this mantle of darkness that we might commune with the angels of light that our onward and upward stride might be swifter.

I had now been from home nearly two years, and none except those having experience can know my joy when I felt I really was homeward bound. The journey was long and wearisome, though of only a few days. I arrived home September 18th 1877 and found my home still, quiet and empty,—but hearing voices in the orchard, I wandered back and found my dear faithful mother and two youngest children gathering fruit. My heart was pierced with sorrow when my little ones opened wide their eyes in wonder and with no token of recognition of their mother. I wept bitterly that I had been forgotten by my babes. Very soon all my dear children were gathered around me, and we soon renewed old acquaintances and affections.

After a short rest I began giving free lectures in the Exponent Office to all ladies interested in medicine.[12] I also was soon called into practice when care and responsibility was my portion. . . .

In the spring of 1878 I taught a class in anatomy and physiology and soon after commenced teaching classes in Obstetrics by urgent request of the presiding sisters who travelled much among the settlements and knew the great lack of knowledge in this branch of medicine—and I have steadily taught class after class until the present time and expect to continue so long as it is needful. . . .

I cannot close without making mention of the many spiritual feasts and pleasant reunions enjoyed by the sisters from time to time. One was held in an upper room of the house of Mrs. Emeline B. Wells, editor of the Exponent— the ladies present were as follows: Eliza R. Snow Smith, Elizabeth Ann Whitney, Mrs M. I. Horne, Mrs Zina D. Young, Mrs Bathsheba Smith——, Mrs. Sarah M. Kimball, Mrs Hannah T. King, Mrs S. M. Heywood, Mrs. Elizabeth Howard, Mrs Emeline B. Wells, Mrs Lydia Wells, Mrs Hannah Pidcock and myself. I never witnessed such a rich flow of the spirit of God as was manifested on that occasion. Sister Snow Smith spoke in tongues and gave each one present a rich blessing—Sister Whitney sang a song of Zion in the pure language—Sister M. I Horne also sang in tongues. Sister Zina Young gave the interpretations of all. Each lady present spoke (not in tongues) by the power and spirit of the Holy Ghost, and we truly had a time of feasting the soul and rejoicing. . . .

---

12. A popular place for women's groups to meet, the *Exponent* office was a rented space used by Emmeline B. Wells to edit the *Woman's Exponent* (1872–1914), a semi-monthly newspaper published by women for women. Sherilyn Cox Bennion, "The *Woman's Exponent*: Forty-two Years of Speaking for Women," *Utah Historical Quarterly* 44, no. 3 (Summer 1976): 222–39.

Who, after tasting the truth as revealed in these last days, could go back into the darkness of the world? It is better to brave all the ills the flesh is heir to in the light of the Gospel than to possess all the world in its darkness.[13]

Why Medical Knowledge Matters, 1879

If medical knowledge to a certain degree was a part of every daughter's education, she would be far better fitted to fulfill her future destiny as wife and mother, and she would know more about the infant on her bosom than that it is a little form of throbbing clay and that she loves it; and there might be fewer little mounds in the "City of the Dead". . . .

I do not by any means depreciate sound practical experience, for it is of great value, and in newly settled countries it is often an imperative duty for those having the nerve and natural ability, to reach forth and assist suffering humanity; but whoever finds it her lot to fill such a responsible and important position in a community, should feel it an incumbent duty to thoroughly prepare herself at her earliest opportunity for such an important work. Some may say if we live right we will need no doctors, which is theoretically true, but where is there one who can live in this fallen estate without hygienically or physically making a mistake or mishap sometime? Nature herself often makes most grevious errors entirely incapable of spontaneous or natural rectification, requiring the most cultivated skill to meet the emergency.

Our reason, the greatest gift of God to man was given us for cultivation and our life here on earth presents a series of opportunities of transforming circumstances into eternal knowledge. Progress is the keystone of heavenly thought

13. Penrose, Memoir, 1–6, 10–26.

and plan, and for an individual to live and die without the world being the better for it, comes short of the object of their existence. True knowledge no matter of what science or art is given man of God, and every acquisition which advances us one step should only broaden our reason and strengthen our belief (which is simply physical knowledge) in the existence of God, and of our unbounded obligations to him. True medical knowledge can never corrode the soul or unfit us for usefulness in any way. It is said in Holy Writ that "faith without works is dead," and it is a matter of correct observation that good intelligent common sense work is very frequently a most excellent subordinate to faith. [14]

Standing Up for Women's Rights

The pioneers of all innovations have been strong, or never would the walls of traditions and old customs have been broken down and swept away, and a smooth path beaten for the feet of weaker ones to follow. When great ends are to be achieved, a persistence and perseverance of purpose without a shadow of turning is the only means of gaining victory. What is this spirit of the 19th century, that is inspiring men as well as women with a determined spirit of resistance. Which says we are all equally the children of the God of this earth and He created it for us all to enjoy. Is it not the innate spirit of Justice. . . .

Many thousand women earn their own living and many earn it for their families also doing the same work as men with only half the wages. Many women are equally capable of filling a number of lucrative offices which now are only eligible to men, where their work is not heavy and would

---

14. Romania B. Pratt, "Work for Women," *Woman's Exponent* 7, no. 21 (April 1, 1879): 217.

seem in the fitness of things more suitable to women than men. Why not let capacity and ability be the test of eligibility and not sex? Power is held in respect, and when women hold the ballot they will command more deference then, in virtue of that power, than they do now through the mere sentiment of chivalry. It is affirmed by the great workers in suffrage that the greatest opposition to the cause is the apathy and indifference of women themselves.[15]

In an 1889 essay published in the alumnae magazine of the Woman's Medical College, Romania said that while her associations with male physicians in Utah had always been cordial, she sometimes felt a certain "spice of contempt—a feeling that I am somewhat out of my sphere."[16] With grace and energy, she persisted in her chosen work. By adding knowledge to faith, she not only enlarged her own sphere but helped to inspire, heal, and strengthen others.

---

15. Romania B. Pratt, "Some Reasons for Women Studying Politics," *Woman's Exponent* 18, no. 6 (August 15, 1889): 46–47. This is from a speech Romania gave at a meeting of the Utah Woman Suffrage Association on July 19, 1889.

16. Romania B. Pratt, "Medical Report from Utah," *Alumnae Association of the Woman's Medical College of Pennsylvania* (Philadelphia, 1880), 41.

Chapter 20

"Give Our Creator
the Thanks Due to Him"

Emeline Grover Rich (1831–1917)

Rosaland Thornton, Deborah R. Otteson, and Teresa S. Rich

Biographical Sketch

Emeline Grover was born in Freedom, Cattaraugus County, New York, on July 30, 1831, six months after her parents, Thomas and Caroline Whiting Grover, joined The Church of Jesus Christ of Latter-day Saints. Her early life mirrored the history of the Church as her family moved from New York to Ohio, then to Missouri, and finally to Nauvoo, Illinois. In October 1840, Emeline's mother died about a week after giving birth to a little girl, who also died, leaving her father with six daughters under the age of twelve. Emeline, the second oldest, was nine.

Thomas soon married a widow with three children. As Emeline later said, "[With] nine small children in one house with one room in it, we soon discovered that we were to[o] thick to thrive well."[1]

---

1. Emeline Grover Rich, "A Biographical Sketch of Emeline Rich," 1883, in Emeline G. Rich Journal, 1881–1886, Holograph, p. 242, Church History

She chose to live and work in other Nauvoo homes, including that of Charles C. Rich.

In February 1846, when it was apparent the Saints could not stay in Nauvoo, fourteen-year-old Emeline consented to marry Charles and became his fifth wife. Less than two weeks after her marriage, the Rich families left Nauvoo in the bitter cold. It was a long, rainy, muddy wagon trip through Iowa, with little food and clothing.

At Winter Quarters, in part because there was a shortage of men after the Mormon Battalion left on its march west, Emeline and other young women learned how to drive ox teams. Despite Charles's position as company captain, Emeline drove an ox team more than one thousand miles west to the Salt Lake Valley, arriving October 2, 1847. In the 1850s, she bore two daughters during three years she spent in San Bernardino, California, a Latter-day Saint community whose members were eventually recalled during the Utah War. Reflecting upon her time there, Emeline wrote, "To me it was a Paradise. I spent the happiest part of my life in that lovely valley."[2] Other than that California interlude, Emeline spent the seventeen years after her arrival in the West living in Centerville, Utah. During this time, she struggled to support herself and her young children while Charles was on a mission to Europe. She described those years as some of her hardest.

In 1864, Charles was called to settle the Bear Lake Valley in

---

Library, The Church of Jesus Christ of Latter-day Saints, Salt Lake City, Utah, hereafter cited as Church History Library. The Emeline G. Rich Journal, 1881–1886, includes both diary entries and Emeline's autobiography. The pages of the journal are not numbered; however, each page is headed with a preprinted date, one page representing one day of the calendar year, making a total of 365 pages. The page number in each Emeline G. Rich Journal citation numerically represents the preprinted day of the year for a given date (i.e., January 1 is page 1, February 1 is page 32, February 2 is page 33, and so on). The preprinted date does not correspond with the actual date of Emeline's journal entries.

2. Rich, "Biographical Sketch," 247–48.

Idaho Territory. All of his families went with him. Winters there were long and severe, cutting off the settlement from the outside for six months at a time. Emeline had six children when they moved and two afterward, including one born prematurely in Logan, Utah, as she was returning to Idaho from a conference in Salt Lake City.[3] In addition to being a fine seamstress, Emeline served more than thirty-five years as a physician, midwife, nurse, dentist, and druggist.

After a series of strokes, Charles died in 1883, leaving Emeline a widow at age fifty-three. She continued to live in Paris, Idaho, working as one of the few medical practitioners in the Bear Lake Valley. By age seventy-five, she was often asked to relate her memories of Joseph Smith the Prophet and the early days of the Church.

Emeline raised her eight children to adulthood, and they became successful, exemplary men and women in the Church and in society. On May 14, 1917, she died in her home in Paris at age eighty-six, "having been ill only a few hours."[4]

LIFE EXPERIENCES

In 1881, Emeline Grover Rich celebrated her fiftieth birthday in Paris, Idaho. Her husband, apostle Charles C. Rich, had been absent from her home on many occasions during their marriage but was present for this special event. As Emeline offered remarks, shared her testimony, and thanked the family, Charles "shed tears of joy" and afterward counseled their children "to never let an opportunity of this kind pass without celebrating it in this . . . way."[5]

Emeline and Charles's oldest son, Thomas, had been killed three years earlier in a fall from his horse.[6] Their two daughters, Caroline

---

3. "A Biography of Emeline Grover Rich with Sketches of Her Eight Children," comp. Rich Family Reunion (unpublished manuscript, 1954), 38, Church History Library.

4. "Biography of Emeline Grover Rich," 19.

5. Rich, Journal, 39.

6. "Biography of Emeline Grover Rich," 21.

and Nancy, had each married. And their five living sons—Landon, Samuel, Heber, Joel, and George, ages twelve through twenty-three—were still living at home. At this time of her life, Emeline was a busy, hard-working mother, physician, and friend. She was a tall, well-built, serious-minded, dedicated woman with a strong conviction of the reality of God.

In 1864, the Rich families had obeyed the call to settle in the Bear Lake Valley, enduring the "Northern Wilderness." This was another test of her willingness to obey Church counsel, but it was the beginning of her last home and the first time she could feel really "rooted."[7] Her log home in Paris, Idaho, was replaced later with a nice brick one. A family biography recorded:

> It was Emeline's skilled hands assisted by others that made the first American flag to float over Bear Lake. The occasion was the 4th of July, 1864. Sarah Jane, . . . daughter of [Charles's] first wife, contributed some red-and-blue cloth she had been saving for a dress. Emeline donated her own white petticoat for a background. . . . She said years later with a twinkle in her eye: "My petticoat floated over Paris for days."[8]

From her youth, Emeline helped care for the sick and deliver babies, feeling these were opportunities life had provided her to help others. Her life sketch recounts:

> While in Nauvoo as a young girl she was taking a large bucket full of green peas to a store to trade for a piece of factory-made cloth for an apron (a luxury in those days). On her way she met Patriarch Joseph Smith, Sr. . . . [He] thought she was bringing the peas to him. He thanked her, told her she was a good girl and offered to give her a

7. "Biography of Emeline Grover Rich," 10–11.

8. "Biography of Emeline Grover Rich," 12.

blessing. She was surprised, crestfallen but without hesitation gave up the peas. Whereupon Patriarch Smith laid
his hands on her head and gave her a patriarchal blessing.
Among other things, he portrayed many of the actual happenings in her later life, promised her she would have a large
family and become a noted nurse and woman physician in
the hands of the Lord in saving, restoring, and bringing into
the world many souls. She thanked grandpa Smith and returned to her home both elated and disappointed. However,
the patch yielded another bucket of peas later, and she got
her apron after all.[9]

Emeline's skill to heal was refined in her own family as she
nursed her children through "considerable sickness." "Strange to
say," wrote Emeline, "although inexperienced myself in the treatment of . . . diseases, I saved my own, and in consequence of which,
I was called on by *many* to treat their families, and I can say truthfully (by the help of the Lord) that I did not loose a single case." She
was later "called and Set apart to treat the sick, both temporally and
spiritually."[10]

For many years Emeline worked "gratis . . . without charging
people."[11] As time passed, Emeline desired to have more training.
She reasoned:

> My labors had so much increased in this line, that it
> ingrossed the greater part of my time, and it became neces-
> sary to "make charges," and in order to do so, One must
> be duly qualified and armed with a small piece of "Sheep
> Skin" [medical diploma]. . . . About the year 1879 there was
> establis[h]ed in Morgan City, Utah. A Medical College by
> Prof. [William] Kohler of Phil[adelphia], Pa. But it was like

9. "Biography of Emeline Grover Rich," 12–13.

10. Rich, "Biographical Sketch," 253–54.

11. Rich, "Biographical Sketch," 253.

a great many other institutions "Short lived." It answered the purpose for me admirably. I have often thought that it was organized especially for my benefit.[12]

Emeline wrote of this training:

Since my Collegiate Study I find myself much more competent, and efficient in practice, scarcely ever meeting a case in practice that really puzzles me. In all of these things, I cheerfully acknowledge the hand of the Lord, realizing that he has overruled things for my best good. I know that I have, through the blessing of the Lord been an instrument in his hands of doing much good among the sick. I feel safe in making this assertion that I have (with the help of God) saved hundreds of lives. . . . Knowing this, who can say that the office of a Physician is not an honorable calling? Although not a pleasant one, nor one to be envied. But such seems to have been destined for me. I commenced as nurse when but nine years of age and have been in "the school" for 35 years, and do not hesitate to say that as . . . good results have attended my practice as any practitioner that has ever come under my observation, not only is this *my* testimony but it has been the testimony of *hundreds* and for this reason I feel no dellicacy about saying this much in *my own behalf.*[13]

On returning to Paris from medical school in 1880, she resumed her practice, along with her regular duties with her family. Her husband, Charles, had a paralytic stroke a few months after her return, and she helped with his care for many months, both in Paris and in Salt Lake City.[14]

---

12. Rich, "Biographical Sketch," 254.

13. Rich, "Biographical Sketch," 255–56.

14. For an account of her experience nursing Charles, see Rich, "Biographical Sketch," 256–60.

After his condition stabilized, her priority became the education of her children. In 1881 she took her five sons to Provo, Utah, to attend Brigham Young Academy. For the next two years, she rented out her Paris home and arranged for the care of her ranch and animals. While in Provo, Emeline took in boarders and practiced medicine. She and the boys returned to Paris for the summers.[15] The first summer back from Provo, she received many calls for assistance:

> As soon as I was fairly settled, I took Mr. Rich to care for, but owing to the calls on me to practice among the different settlements I could not keep him long at a time, but have taken care of him in turn with his other wives, in addition to other duties. I have to study continuously in order to be prepared to meet the *demands* of the proffession. Scarcely a day but that I have to practice or give advice in a proffessional way.[16]

The journal she kept in Provo while her sons attended Brigham Young Academy provides insights into her daily life:

> [December] 21st [1881] Housework continued, cooking and cleaning. Night comes, 'am tired but feel as though I am engaged in a good cause. Never enjoyed myself better. I feel as though the Lord opens the way for me day by day, and although tired and weary at night, I allways feel refreshed when morning comes, and it seems as though I am blessed in very deed. . . .

> Feb 13th [1882] I love to do good to my fellow creatures, but it wears on me, and causes great anxiety of the mind. But I realize that the Lord has given me this blessing [medical skill], and he will hold me responsible for the use or

---

15. Rich, Journal, October 1, 1881, 3; Rich, "Biographical Sketch," 261–62.
16. Rich, "Biographical Sketch," 266.

abuse of so great a gift. And I have long since made up my mind, that so long as he will give me health and strength, and blesses my labors as he has done thus far, I will endeavor to do all that I can for suffering humanity. . . .

[January] 13th [1883] . . . I am so tired of this monotony. It might be worse, and I will not complain, for we are well and doing well but a great deal of sameness in our every day life, and we are so constituted that we love excitement and variety. But I am here for the purpose of educating my boys, and they are progressing . . . Therefore I will be content, and ask the Lord to bless us, and open the way for us to prosecute our studies and plans. . . .

[January] 16th [1883] . . . Will spend the evening writing and reading medicine, which affords me much pleasure as it diverts my mind from the daily cares of life, and replenishes my knowledge of medicine, so that while I am resting from practice I am increasing in knowledge.[17]

In the spring of 1883, Emeline returned to Idaho and cared for her husband, Charles C. Rich, who had been living in turn with his three wives in Paris. After three years' illness, Charles "quietly expired" on November 17, 1883, "with his family and a few friends surrounding his bed side," wrote Emeline.[18] By that stage of Emeline's life, most of her sons worked in various places and were home in Paris part time. Emeline's son Landon was serving in the Southern States Mission, and her daughters lived close by. She was often host to many who were in Paris for district court, conference, or reunions. Warm-hearted Emeline was willing to help when needed, as her journal entries demonstrate:

17. Rich, Journal, 6–7, 17–18, 72–73.
18. Rich, "Biographical Sketch," 266.

Dec. 1st [1884] . . . Retired at an early hour completely tired and wishing in my heart that folks would call in the day time if they *must* call. But such is not often the case—I had on *this* occasion, got into a sound slumber when a knock at the door with a call of "aunt Emeline" aroused me saying come quickly to Alice. She is in labor. She whom we all thought was at deaths door from neuralgic rheumatism, had been bed ridden for two years; Well "such is life." I dressed my self and away I went at breakneck speed, not expecting to find a baby tho', but at the expiration of 5 hours and 30 minutes I delivered my lady of a daughter weighing . . . 4 lbs. Spent an hour or two with mother and babe to make my self sure that they *could* and *would survive* and then came home to rest again . . . busied my self with domestic labors until evening when I visited my patients found them weak, of course but doing well all things considered.[19]

Emeline's journal furnishes other examples of her courage and determination. A journal entry of May 26, 1886, relates: "Was Telephoned to come to St Charles immediately.[20] . . . Started with horse and buggy . . . found their hired girl Caroline Jensen Suffering with quinsy, throat swelled shut. I wrapped the blade of my hernia knife, leaving the point bare, compressed the tongue with spoon handle, and with great caution, introduced the knife and made an incision in the tonsil, which discharged freely and gave immediate relief. She was soon able to take nourishment, the case has progressed favorably."[21]

From that time until she was almost seventy-five years old, a span of some twenty years, Emeline labored for the relief of others, whether in Provo, Bear Lake Valley, Logan, or the Snake River

---

19. Rich, Journal, 191–92.

20. St. Charles, Idaho, is eight miles from Paris.

21. Rich, Journal, 333.

Valley. She felt it was her obligation as a doctor to always go when called or needed, whatever the time or place.

Emeline had more to occupy her time than just caring for her patients. She had to fit her medical practice in with the demands of everyday life in a late nineteenth-century Latter-day Saint community. Her journal entry for December 15, 1893, illustrates how busy she was even after Charles's death:

> I hardly have time to be lonesome. Have so many chores to do—four pigs to feed—two cows to feed and to milk—chickens Turkeys and lamb to feed and water. Am now knitting some mittins for Landon—Stocking for Nancy piecing calico quilt and a silk crazy ~~silk~~ quilt—i.e. I busy my self with these things when I've leisure time to spare. It is wonderful the amount of work one pair of hands can do in the course of a winter.[22]

Emeline was fortunate to attend the dedications of the Logan and Salt Lake Temples. The Logan Temple was the second built in the west, and Bear Lake residents had contributed for years to its construction. "As it is a privilige *not likely* to be enjoyed but once in a lifetime, think I will improve the opportunity," wrote Emeline on May 11, 1884, before attending the Logan Temple dedication on May 17. On the day of the dedication Emeline wrote:

> At 10.30 oclock, there were convened in the temple, 1600 Souls. Services commenced by Singing, and the dedicatory prayer read by Prest. John Taylor. . . . After meeting the congregation were allowed to go through the building led by Prest Taylor and the twelve. They marched

---

22. Emeline Grover Rich, Diary, 1892–1893, Holograph, pp. 110–11, Church History Library.

two abrest. after we had viewed the interior, *So grand,* we marched down the hill, thoroughly tired.[23]

Later, she was able to serve in the Logan Temple for eight winters.[24]

The Salt Lake Temple had taken forty years to complete, and Emeline probably thought she would never live to see it finished. At age sixty-two she was thrilled to be invited to the dedication. Her journal recites her experience:

> [April] 4th [1893] Started 6 A.M. for Salt Lake to attend the Dedicatory Services of the Temple. . . .
>
> 6th . . . To describe the beauty and grandure of that Holy temple is far beyond my power. The Services were *great and mighty.* Prest. Wilford Woodruff read the Dedicatory prayer—aged as he is—with a full round distinct voice. He also talked to the saints in his usual pleasant and encouraging manner—after which the audience were call'd upon . . . to rise upon their feet and Shout Hosanna—Hosanna—Hosanna—to God and the Lamb Amen—Amen—Amen repeated 3 times. . . . During the Services in the morning the wind blew a perfect hurricane unroofing houses and uprooting trees, etc. but all was quiet within. When the congregation emerged from the Temple all was serene & quiet. Although there was so many thousands of people in Salt Lake City—there was a reign of peace and quiet prevailed.[25]

Emeline's medical practice slowed as she aged, and she spent time visiting her children in Logan, Utah, and in the east Snake River Valley of Idaho in Idaho Falls, Sterling, Pingree, and Blackfoot.

---

23. Rich, Journal, 163–64.

24. "Biography of Emeline Grover Rich," 17.

25. Rich, Diary, 1892–1893, 78–79.

She attended Church meetings regularly and hosted many people from out of town. She was asked to speak at an Old Folks party and in other meetings about the rise of the Church, as well as about events that had transpired in the early days of this Church, all of which she did "to the best of [her] ability."[26] She wanted to avoid the cold weather of Bear Lake in the winters; she would leave for a week or two but then insist on going home despite the cold.

Emeline, concerned for her children's welfare, decided to invite her sons, now aged thirty-seven through fifty-three, to "a conference" on November 26, 1902. "Sam had a nice dinner Served," Emeline recorded, "after which we repaired to the Parlor and there talked until midnight. Subject discussed was principally the drink habit which was acknowledged and *covenanted* to forsake, each one promising to abstain from for one year after a good many resolves among themselves."[27]

Another experience occurred in the late winter in Bear Lake and showed Emeline's continued desire to reach out to others. She wrote in her journal:

> [March] 28th [1904] Am busy making preparations to entertain the widdows of 1st ward . . . mostly old ladies and living alone. [The] 30th is the day Set for our "widdows convention" althoug[h] the weather is cold and stormy, and *mud* very deep—we expect to bring them in with Sleighs.
>
> 29th Nancy . . . came to assist me . . . as my strength was not what it once was—73 years of hard service has had a telling

---

26. Emeline Grover Rich, Diary, 1900–1903, Holograph, p. 51, Church History Library.

27. Rich, Diary, 1900–1903, November 26, 1902, 139–40. On the history of the Latter-day Saint health code known as the Word of Wisdom, see Paul H. Peterson, "An Historical Analysis of the Word of Wisdom" (master's thesis, Brigham Young University, 1972). It took generations before compliance with this code became general among the Saints.

effect on me, but I have had a desire to give the widdows a benefit in the shape of a feast, for many years. . . .

30th . . . Gathered at 2 P.M. Sat down to the table at 3 pm (26 in number) I never saw a happier lot of folks assembled. . . . After dinner the company repaired to parlor where we had a genuine feast of songs, recitals, Speeches etc. . . . We passed refreshments around until some of the most aged began to feel as though they wanted to be taken home. The boys . . . hitched up their sleigh and drove them home as they got ready one by one. All seem'd happy and *more* than satisfied with their afternoon convention.[28]

In 1909, a large reunion was held to commemorate the one-hundredth anniversary of Charles C. Rich's birth. Emeline spoke at one of the meetings, and she ended her comments by stating, "I trust that the Lord will bless us that we may die full in the faith of the gospel is my prayer, Amen."[29] Heber, one of Emeline's sons, spoke of her at the reunion: "I love my mother equally with my father, never has she taught me a principle that was not right, never has she placed before me an example that was not worth[y] of emulation."[30]

Emeline Grover Rich, mother of eight and grandmother of forty-nine, passed away on May 14, 1917, at the age of eighty-six, after a very brief illness.[31] She was buried beside her husband in Paris, Idaho. An entry written by Emeline at the end of 1893 offers insight into her deep determination to live a faith-centered life:

28. Emeline Grover Rich, Diary, 1903–1909, March 28–30, 1904, Holograph, Emeline G. Rich Autobiography and Diary, Church History Library.

29. "Minutes and Transcript of the Speeches of the Rich Reunion," 1909, Photocopy of typescript, 21, Church History Library.

30. "Minutes and Transcript," 16.

31. "Biography of Emeline Grover Rich," 19.

This life is made up of ups & downs. I have struggled hard to rear my family. Spared no pains to the accomplishment of my duty in their behalf. Have watched and prayed over them by night and day, least after all my feeble efforts in *their behalf* they might go astray or deny the faith of our Gospel. Many a day and night have I travelled through storms that were too severe for the Sterner Sex, to wait upon the sick . . . for the *good* I *could do* in relieving the sick and suffering humanity. . . . The Lord has blessed me abundantly in the performance of my profession. I have Spent the proceeds of my labors in educating my children for their advancement and in so doing have had but one object in view i.e. that they might make good noble men and women, ornaments in society—and in their turn might be able to transmit to their posterity an imperishable legacy.

I am not ashamed of my examples set for children to imitate—feeling that in my humble career through life, I have done the best I could according to my judgment. . . .

My-self and family I consider have great reason to feel thankful to our Heavenly father for his kind protecting care throughout the year past. . . .

Doubtless we do not at *all* times stop to consider from whom these blessings flow—or, to give our Creator the thanks due to Him.

As this is the last of the old year 1893, I feel to pen a few of my considerations and grateful feelings and thoughts on this subject—knowing and realizing that a New Year is approaching—but just how the close of the same will find us we *cannot say.*

Still we plod along—Struggling with what *almost* seems to be *fate,* and oft times forgetting, or neglecting to pray to our father—realizing that we *are* dependent upon Him for all we have and are—Knowing as we do, that he answers our prayers and never forsakes us when we call on Him in sincerity and *worthily*. *Yes* that is the *word, worthily*.

How often do *I* call on him, when I fear I would be accounted unworthy? perhaps, [when] prompted by selfishness. Well we are but mortal, and why should [we] wish to be otherwise in this probationary state? . . .

This is a *right good* world—have no fault to find with it, my only regrets are, that I cannot bring myself *square up* to the line of what I would like to do—but, I mean to persevere while "Life endures" And if at the close of the coming year I can see that I have gained one point, or overcome one of *my* faults—Shall feel well repaid.

E. G. RICH[32]

32. Rich, Diary, 1892–1893, December 31, 1893, 116–20.

Chapter 21

"For the Best Good of the Children"

AURELIA READ SPENCER ROGERS (1834–1922)

RoseAnn Benson

BIOGRAPHICAL SKETCH

Aurelia Read Spencer was born October 4, 1834, in Deep River, Middlesex County, Connecticut, to Orson and Catherine Curtis Spencer. In 1840 Aurelia's parents joined The Church of Jesus Christ of Latter-day Saints, and in 1841 the family moved to Nauvoo, Illinois. After the martyrdom of Joseph and Hyrum Smith, the family left their brick home in Nauvoo to head west with the Saints. The family had traveled only thirty miles when Catherine died at age thirty-four, leaving six living children and her husband to continue west without her. At Winter Quarters, Orson built a log cabin for his children in preparation for his leaving on a three-year mission to England, where he presided over the British mission and was editor of the *Latter-day Saints' Millennial Star*, an official Church publication in Britain.[1]

---

1. The *Millennial Star* was published from 1840 to 1970, at which time it

Although their neighbors helped look after the children, Aurelia's fourteen-year-old sister, Ellen, acted as mother. During this time, severe weather killed most of their cows, the money their father sent for provisions never arrived, and the children subsisted on cornmeal and water until Wilford Woodruff heard about their plight and provided temporary relief. The children left Winter Quarters for the Salt Lake Valley in June 1848 with a company led by Brigham Young. During the trip, thirteen-year-old Aurelia became acquainted with twenty-one-year-old Thomas Rogers, who three years later would become her husband.

Aurelia was educated at the University of Nauvoo,[2] where her father taught; Louisa Barnes Pratt's school in Winter Quarters; Hiram Clawson's writing school; and the University of Deseret in Salt Lake City, where her father was first chancellor. She learned from other women to make dresses and became skilled at sewing and jewelry-making to earn money. On March 27, 1851, she married Thomas Rogers and moved sixteen miles north of Salt Lake City to the newly settled community of Farmington. Theirs was a two-room log home roofed with willows, a dirt floor covered with handmade carpet, and a view of the Great Salt Lake. Aurelia bore twelve children, five of whom died at young ages.[3]

As her own family grew, her concern for the spiritual development of children caused her to ponder how to help build testimony in the rising generation. In consequence, as directed by the First Presidency and general leaders of the Relief Society, she developed

---

was replaced by the *Ensign*. Stanley A. Peterson, "*Millennial Star*," *Encyclopedia of Mormonism*, ed. Daniel H. Ludlow, 4 vols. (New York: Macmillan, 1992), 2:906.

2. The University of Nauvoo, an ambitious undertaking, initially operated without buildings and never fully developed because of vigilante actions against the Saints. Glen M. Leonard, *Nauvoo: A Place of Peace, a People of Promise* (Salt Lake City, UT: Deseret Book; Provo, UT: Brigham Young University Press, 2002), 193–94.

3. Aurelia Rogers, *Life Sketches of Orson Spencer and Others, and History of Primary Work* (Salt Lake City, UT: George Q. Cannon & Sons, 1898), 163–64.

the first children's Primary Association, an organization she felt was divinely mandated.

Aurelia lived all of her married days in Farmington, Utah, where she died on August 19, 1922.

Life Experiences

While visiting Salt Lake City in 1866 as a young mother, Aurelia met President Heber C. Kimball. She recorded that he spoke with her and "seemed to read me like a book, and to understand my inmost thoughts." He spoke a little of her future, saying that "I did not begin to know what was before me; but [he] told me to continue as faithful as I had been, and all would be well, for there was a great work for me to do."[4] Many years later, she concluded, "With all the difficulties encountered, I have indeed had joy in my Primary labors; and feel that it was this work that President Heber C. Kimball saw when conversing with me."[5]

In providing a personal sketch of the creation of the Primary Association, Aurelia Rogers described some of the children in her Farmington community as being "allowed to be out late at night," some even deserving the designation "hoodlum." In addition, some children were guilty of "carelessness in the extreme, not only in regard to religion, but also morality." She identified the exhaustion of parents who had been driven out of Illinois and suffered persecution of every kind and now could barely provide sustenance for their families as the cause for negligence in training their children. Nevertheless, she refused to allow that as an excuse or apology for a lack of spiritual upbringing in what she considered "the most sacred duty of parentage."[6]

Aurelia's concern for the upbringing of youth and especially young boys continued, and she sought resolution. She wrote:

4. Rogers, *Life Sketches,* 165.

5. Rogers, *Life Sketches,* 233.

6. Rogers, *Life Sketches,* 205–6.

I had children of my own, and was just as anxious as a mother could be to have them brought up properly. But what was to be done? It needed the united effort of the parents, and, as is often the case in a community, some of them were careless. A fire seemed to burn within me. . . . The query then arose in my mind could there not be an organization for little boys wherein they could be taught everything good, and how to behave. This was in March; a few weeks later Sister Eliza R. Snow Smith and Sister Emmeline B. Wells, from Salt Lake City, came to Farmington to attend a Relief Society Conference.

After meeting was over, and when on their way to the depot, these sisters . . . stopped at my home for a short call. The topic of our conversation was the young people, and the rough, careless ways many of the young men and boys had at the time. I asked the question, "What will our girls do for good husbands, if this state of things continues?" Sister Eliza seemed deeply impressed with the question; and then I asked,

"Could there not be an organization for little boys, and have them trained to make better men?"

She was silent a few moments, then said there might be such a thing and that she would speak to the First Presidency about it.[7]

Eliza presented the idea to John Taylor, the senior apostle and soon-to-be president of the Church, and others of the Quorum of Twelve.[8] After they approved the proposal, Eliza wrote a letter

---

7. Rogers, *Life Sketches*, 207–8.

8. Rogers, *Life Sketches*, 208–9. Eliza remembered asking "Mrs. R. if she was willing to take the responsibility and labor on herself of presiding over the children of that settlement, provided the Bishop of the Ward sanctioned the movement." Eliza omits presenting the idea to members of the Quorum of Twelve. Instead, she states that "directly after arriving home, I wrote the Bishop, and by return Mail

explaining the matter to Bishop John W. Hess of the Farmington Ward. Soon, Bishop Hess met with Aurelia, and after they had "talked awhile on the subject," he asked her if she "would be willing to preside over an organization of the children."[9] Up until this point, girls had not been mentioned, and her focus had been on an organization for the young boys. Almost immediately Aurelia realized, however, that the organization would not be complete without the young girls.

With no directions from a presiding organization or personal academic training, it was motherhood and divine assistance that taught Aurelia what to do. "While thinking over what was to be done for the best good of the children," Aurelia related, "I seemed to be carried away in the spirit, or at least I experienced a feeling of untold happiness which lasted three days and nights. During that time nothing could worry or irritate me; if my little ones were fretful, or the work went wrong, I had patience, could control in kindness, and manage my household affairs easily. This was a testimony to me that what was being done was from God."[10]

Over a year after Aurelia's initial inspiration and questions regarding children, the first Primary Association was organized. At a public meeting on Sunday, August 11, 1878, Bishop Hess set

---

received from him a very satisfactory response, in which he, (Bishop [John] Hess) not only gave his permission but hearty approval accompanied with his blessing. I then informed Mrs. Rogers that she might consider herself authorized to proceed, and organize in Farmington, which she did." Eliza R. Snow Smith, "Sketch of My Life" [1885], in *The Personal Writings of Eliza Roxcy Snow,* ed. Maureen Ursenbach Beecher (Salt Lake City: University of Utah Press, 1995), 37. In a journal entry dated July 10, 1878, Emmeline B. Wells recorded that Aurelia "talked to us about an Association for little boys. . . . We all spoke to Bishop Hess and he approved & on the way home on the train we decided to go to [President John] Taylor and take the matter before him." Jill Mulvay Derr, Janath Russell Cannon, Maureen Ursenbach Beecher, *Women of Covenant: The Story of Relief Society* (Salt Lake City, UT: Deseret Book, 1992), 118.

9. Rogers, *Life Sketches,* 208–9.

10. Rogers, *Life Sketches,* 212.

apart Sister Aurelia Rogers and two counselors, Louisa Haight and Helen M. Miller, to preside over a Primary Association in Farmington. The minutes of the organizational meeting call for the "Primary Mutual Improvement Association to include children of both sexes from six to fourteen years of age."

At that meeting Aurelia testified, "I believe the Lord is preparing the way and blessed is the name of the Lord. . . . Over one year ago B[isho]p. Hess called the sisters together, feeling that the young people were being led astray, and threw the responsibility upon the sisters to look after their daughters. I felt then if he had called the Brethren together also, to advise together with them it would have been better." Aurelia's greatest concern was for the boys and young men, the future "Elders in Israel, who are running in the streets, their mothers hardly able to control them. . . . While they are running loose, the Adversary will feel that he can instill into their tender minds *such* influences that in their youth will make them subject to him. But I feel that in this he will be baffled. But he will not cease his efforts." Nevertheless, she was certain that "when children are taught in the right way they will notice the course of their parents more and more. When asked if I would lead out in this movement I felt that I could not refuse. . . . My intentions are to speak and act with the Spirit of the Lord." She concluded with the desire that all "pray to the Lord to bless those in Authority with wisdom to direct aright" the new Primary organization.[11]

The Primary was now established, and work began in earnest. Although Aurelia's initial feelings about the new association had brought "untold happiness," she wrote:

> One thing that seemed strange to me, was, that after the organization [of the Primary] I was nearly overcome by the opposite power, and was sunken, as it were, into the

11. Primary Association Minutes and Records, August 11, 1878, Farmington Ward, Davis Stake, Church History Library, The Church of Jesus Christ of Latter-day Saints, Salt Lake City, Utah, hereafter cited as Church History Library.

very depths of misery; I felt my unworthiness so keenly that I could scarcely attend to my duties; and went to my meetings weeping by the way, being humbled to the very earth. . . . I had been made to feel my entire dependence on God the Eternal Father.[12]

Nine days later, on August 25, the children were called together for the first time.

The object of the meeting was explained to them, and another one appointed. . . . And from that time on, our meetings were held every Saturday at 2 p. m. in the meeting house. . . . When the children came to understand the motives which prompted the calling of their little meetings, they seemed elated with what was being done for them. . . .

It would be impossible for one who had never experienced anything of the kind, to imagine our feelings as we stood before an audience of children who had come there to receive instructions from us. We were very weak indeed, but felt to lean upon the Lord in all humility.[13]

The leaders felt that Primary meetings were a school for themselves as well as for the children. They felt their entire dependence on the Lord to assist them and enlighten their minds by the Holy Spirit "that they might be in very deed teachers of life and Salvation unto the children committed to their care."[14]

After seven years as Primary president, Aurelia lamented.

With all my anxiety and labor to get the boys to attend meeting, [I] had, in a measure, failed. This tried me very

12. Rogers, *Life Sketches*, 214.

13. Rogers, *Life Sketches*, 214–15; Primary Association Minutes and Records, August 25, 1878, Farmington Ward, Davis Stake, Church History Library.

14. "Sketch of the First Primary," Primary Association Minutes and Records, 1878, Provo 4th Ward, Utah Stake, Church History Library.

much, for these Associations were instituted for the good of the little boys especially, and when but few came to meeting, and it seemed hard to interest them, at times I was quite discouraged. I felt to blame the parents, particularly the fathers, and thought if they were more interested their boys could be spared from work, and encouraged to attend their meetings. With these feelings I made up my mind not to worry any more, but leave them in the hands of the Lord, and when He saw fit to wake the people up things might be different.[15]

As Primary Associations grew in wards and stakes throughout the Church, Aurelia recorded that in April 1880, Eliza R. Snow came to her and said "it was thought best to have some one appointed to preside over all the Primary Associations in the [Utah] Territory . . . and asked me whom I would propose to fill the office." Upon a few moments' reflection, Aurelia said "the name of Sister Louie B. Felt came to my mind." Sister Eliza confirmed that Louie was also her choice—a witness, wrote Aurelia, that "satisfied me that Sister Felt was the one to hold that important office." In first meeting Louie B. Felt, Aurelia had "an unusually warm feeling of sympathetic friendship" toward her. "When [Louie] was chosen to preside over all the Primary Associations, some persons thought it was my place to hold that position. But I wish to say here, that I never had a moment's jealousy over anyone holding office; for no person will ever take my honors from me; I shall have all that I deserve."[16]

After nine years as president of the Farmington Primary Association, Aurelia was released in 1887 from her ward responsibilities; however, she continued in her calling as the Davis Stake Primary president.[17] She was honored throughout her lifetime by her

---

15. Rogers, *Life Sketches*, 230.

16. Rogers, *Life Sketches*, 222–23.

17. Aurelia was appointed as Davis Stake Primary president on July 16, 1880. Rogers, *Life Sketches*, 224, 235.

own Farmington Primary children, her Primary coworkers, and the general Primary presidency. Anna C. Tanner, one of the children in that first Primary offers insight to what Aurelia accomplished:

> As children, we were very proud to have our own little meetings, for even then did we know that the interesting moral stories and encouraging words of Sister Rogers and her co-laborers made it easier for us to be obedient, to resist temptation, control our tempers, and keep the Sabbath day holy.
>
> The joy that we realized in becoming acquainted with the Spirit of God, the simple but honest resolutions that entered our minds, cannot be too highly appreciated. I think that I speak for all faithful members of the Primary, when I say that much of our happiness and prosperity, and ambition to become good and useful, is due to the valuable instructions and encouragement received in the Primary Association.
>
> Who of us have forgotten the impressive lessons taught us on the Word of Wisdom? The result of which is that whole families, grown, half-grown, and little sons and daughters can be found now, in which none use tea or coffee. Some have never tasted it, nor any kind of liquor; even in medicine it is refused. How many of us received our first lesson in singing in the Primary Association, and with what pride did the little boys, dressed in uniform, show their skill in playing the flute, etc.? No one will forget the first carpet made by the patient fingers of the little Primary girls. And the lessons of industry that were taught us in the bean patch will long be remembered with pride and pleasure. The concerts and fairs were our delight.

What a broad field of usefulness was presented to us, but still so gradually was it opened to our view that every new feature brought with it renewed ambition.[18]

A later tribute attested:

Sister Aurelia S. Rogers heeded the inspirations of her heart and there came into existence the Primary Association, an organization we love so much. Had she not trusted in God, how much she never could have known or realized. This is true of every living soul—the difference in calling and reward is in kind and not degree.

Who can measure the joy and satisfaction of Sister Rogers' heart today when she understands that by one of her important obediences to the inspirations of her Maker, she can again serve His purposes. . . . She is so great, and yet so humble; so worthy, and yet so modest, we are happy to honor her. And for all us Primarians, God bless our own Aurelia S. Rogers. May she live her days in continued service and joy.[19]

After her release from her ward Primary calling, Aurelia often accompanied Zina D. H. Young, Eliza R. Snow, and others to Relief Society, Young Ladies' Mutual Improvement Association, and Primary Association meetings throughout Utah.[20] In 1894 she was elected as Davis County delegate to attend the National American Woman Suffrage Convention in Atlanta, Georgia, traveling by train with Emmeline B. Wells, president of the Utah Woman Suffrage Association, and the Utah County delegate, Marilla Daniels. They also traveled to Washington, D.C., to attend the second triennial

18. Rogers, *Life Sketches,* 261–63.

19. Adelaide U. Hardy. "Librarians' Department: Aurelia S. Rogers," *Children's Friend,* September 1919, 358–59.

20. Rogers, *Life Sketches,* 247–54.

congress of the National Council of Women.[21] Although her work in the women's suffrage movement was important, Aurelia's great contribution to the Church was her gift of the Primary organization.

On October 4, 1897, the day after general conference and the eve of her birthday, Aurelia attended a special meeting for all the Primary officers of all the stakes of Zion and was honored by general Primary president Louie B. Felt and her counselors. The crowning surprise was a statement read by Joseph H. Felt of the George Q. Cannon & Sons Publishing Company, "announcing that arrangements had been made with them, by the General Board of the Primary Association for the publishing of Sister Aurelia Spencer Rogers' book," *Life Sketches of Orson Spencer and Others, and History of Primary Work,* which contained her own life story, as well as the story of Primary.[22] Aurelia declared, "It seemed to me then that the Lord had opened up the way for the publishing of my book in the most pleasing and satisfactory way possible. How could the Primary Association have better expressed great love for me than by this ready and cheerful compliance with the request to aid in the accomplishment of this work?"[23]

Aurelia's conclusion to her book recounted her testimony:

> By a careful reading of the pages I have written, it will be seen that my blessings have exceeded all my trials. Yet of some of my greatest blessings, I have said but little; perhaps too little, I almost think, when I realize my causes for gratitude. . . . And I wish to bear my testimony, that with all that

---

21. Rogers, *Life Sketches,* 301–7; "Convention in Atlanta," *Woman's Exponent* 23, nos. 15–16 (February 1 and 15, 1895): 236–37; Susa Young Gates, "Utah Women at the National Council of Women," *Young Woman's Journal* 6, no. 9 (June 1895): 391–425. The National American Woman Suffrage Convention took place from January 31 to February 5, 1895, and the National Council of Women from February 18 to March 2, 1895.

22. Rogers, *Life Sketches,* 322–27.

23. Rogers, *Life Sketches,* 328–29.

the members of our family have passed through, I have not doubted the truth of the Gospel which I have embraced, and feel that I have great cause to be zealous in testifying that I do know that God lives, and that the Church of Jesus Christ of Latter-day Saints is His true Church.

The one time in my life, which has been referred to, when my children were taken from me by death, and I did almost question the existence of a God, was momentary. The words of my father comforted me, and the seeming doubt when cleared away never returned.[24]

Aurelia Read Spencer Rogers died at age eighty-seven and was buried in the Salt Lake City Cemetery. Her grave marker reads "Primary Mother."

---

24. Rogers, *Life Sketches,* 330–31.

Chapter 22

"GOD IS EVER JUST AND KIND"

MARGARET CONDIE SHARP (1839–1928)

Emily B. Farrer

BIOGRAPHICAL SKETCH

Margaret Condie[1] was born November 19, 1839, in Clackmannan, Clackmannanshire, Scotland, to Thomas and Helen Sharp Condie. She was the fifth of twelve children; only six of her siblings lived to adulthood.[2] Margaret was baptized into The Church of Jesus Christ of Latter-day Saints in 1848 before she turned nine.[3] In 1849, the family started their journey to Utah to join the Saints. They were passengers on the ship *Zetland* and arrived in

---

1. She was sometimes called Maggie.

2. Gibson Condie, Reminiscences and Diary, 1865–1910, Microfilm of holograph, pp. 1, 6–7, 11, 15–16, 23, Church History Library, The Church of Jesus Christ of Latter-day Saints, Salt Lake City, Utah, hereafter cited as Church History Library.

3. Margaret Condie Sharp, "Margaret Condie Sharp," in *Genealogical Surveys of LDS Members,* comp. Genealogical Society of Utah, vol. 27 (Salt Lake City, UT: 1924–1929), Microfilm of holograph, p. 380, Family History Library, The Church

New Orleans on April 2, 1849. They then traveled by steamboat to St. Louis, where they lived one year.[4]

In St. Louis, Margaret's older sister Janet married Joseph Sharp, who was also from Clackmannan. Janet and Joseph went west in the spring of 1850, joining a company led by Joseph's brother John.[5] The rest of the Condie family then migrated to Council Bluffs, Iowa, where they lived for two years. During these years, the family suffered much loss. Margaret's mother was pregnant three times, yet only one of the babies survived. Additionally, Margaret lost a sister, Mary, to cholera.[6]

Crossing the plains, thirteen-year-old Margaret and her family were part of the Thomas C. D. Howell Company. They left Council Bluffs on June 7, 1852. Margaret recounted that she "walked barefooted more than half the way" and "arrived in S.L. City Sept. 8, 1852."[7]

On March 13, 1857, Margaret, age seventeen, married Joseph

---

of Jesus Christ of Latter-day Saints, Salt Lake City, Utah, hereafter cited as Family History Library.

4. "Margaret Condie," Mormon Migration Database, Brigham Young University, accessed April 24, 2012, http://lib.byu.edu/mormonmigration /index.php. Margaret's brother Gibson Condie wrote an autobiography that contains a detailed account of their journey. Condie, Reminiscences and Diary, 26.

5. Joseph and Janet were married on August 28, 1849. Gibson Condie's autobiography states that in St. Louis the Condie family found some of their old acquaintances from Scotland. The Sharps were among these acquaintances. Condie, Reminiscences and Diary, 26; "John Sharp Company (1850)," Mormon Pioneer Overland Travel Database, 1847–68, The Church of Jesus Christ of Latter-day Saints, accessed April 24, 2012, http://mormontrail.lds.org.

6. Mary was not yet three years old. Sharp, "Margaret Condie Sharp," 380; Condie, Reminiscences and Diary, 27.

7. "Thomas C. D. Howell Company (1852)," Mormon Pioneer Overland Travel Database, 1847–68, The Church of Jesus Christ of Latter-day Saints, accessed April 24, 2012, http://mormontrail.lds.org; Sharp, "Margaret Condie Sharp," 380.

Sharp as his second wife.[8] By this time, Joseph and Janet had four children. Almost two years later, Janet gave birth to another baby and died two days later, leaving Margaret to care for Janet's five children.[9] Ten months later, in 1859, Margaret gave birth to her first child, Agnes. Margaret later had two more children, Joseph in 1861 and Cecilia in 1863. Just months prior to Cecilia's birth, Janet's eleven-year-old daughter, Helen, died. She was followed two days later by Margaret's firstborn, Agnes, who was almost four years old.[10] In 1862, Joseph took a third wife, Janet Smith, who did not bear children in that union.[11]

In September 1864, Joseph was returning to Utah as captain of the Sharp and Spencer Freight Train, supervising the transportation of merchandise across the plains. Overstraining himself by heavy lifting, Joseph died of a ruptured blood vessel in Wyoming. Margaret became a widow after only seven years of marriage and at age twenty-four was left with six young children.[12]

Margaret recorded that from the time of Joseph's death, she "earned my own living and supported my family and also my dead

8. Condie, Reminiscences and Diary, 43.

9. John C. Condie (1850–1921), Helen Condie (1852–1863), Mary Jane Condie (1854–1937), Margaret Ann Condie (1857–1932), Janet Condie (1859–1941).

10. Condie, Reminiscences and Diary, 27. Margaret's biological children were Agnes Sharp (1859–1863), Joseph Condie Sharp (1861–1934), and Cecilia Sharp Baker (1863–1933).

11. Condie, Reminiscences and Diary, 54. After Joseph's death, Janet Smith (1846–1939) appears to have married James Crystal (1839–1924). The couple had two children. "Janet Smith Crystal," 1939, State of Utah Certificate of Death, no. 170.

12. Joseph died on September 7, 1864. "Died on the Plains," *Salt Lake Daily Telegraph,* September 9, 1864; Ruth J. Martin, comp., *Twentieth Ward History, 1856–1979* (n.p., 1979), 48. More details about his death, including journal excerpts from members of the freight company, can be found at "Sharp and Spencer Freight Train (1864)," Mormon Pioneer Overland Travel Database, 1847–68, The Church of Jesus Christ of Latter-day Saints, http://mormontrail.lds.org.

sister's children. . . . I have nursed the sick, doctored them, and acted as Accoucher."[13] She was a devout temple worker and participated in Relief Society and in other organizations, including Daughters of Utah Pioneers and the Genealogical Society of Utah. She died in Salt Lake City on June 22, 1928, at the age of eighty-eight.[14]

LIFE EXPERIENCES

The following pages are from Margaret's writings, mostly from her diary. She kept records of her income and expenditures, including donations, home repairs, groceries, and vacations. She also recorded interesting information she learned. Her diary was organized topically, in the main, but it has been reorganized here to chronologically sketch a clear picture of her inspiring and industrious life.

Autobiography

[I] was baptized when eight years old in Scotland, the land of my birth, just before coming to America with my parents and brothers and sisters, in 1849. . . . Crossed the plains in 1852. . . . We lived in a dugout the first year, and then I helped make the adobes to build us a house. Subsisted on roots, and fought grasshoppers during the famine of '53.

I was married to Joseph Sharp in 1857 and was left a widow in 1864. Since which time I have earned my own living and supported my family and also my dead sisters children, five in number. . . .

Was a member of the first organization of the Relief Society in the 20th ward, also acted as teacher in same organization for eleven years, as secretary 23 yrs until I moved from ward. Was also Coun[selor] to Sister Toone in the

---

13. Sharp, "Margaret Condie Sharp," 380. *Accoucheur* is a French word meaning midwife.

14. "Margaret Condie Sharp," 1928, State of Utah Death Certificate, no. 1057.

Primary Association three or four years, and am now a worker in the Salt Lake Temple.

Selected Passages from Diary Book[15]

When Father lived in Scotland he Kept a large store.[16]

1857 Johnston Armey [Johnston's Army] Came to Salt Lake City. Joseph Sharp[17] was a volenteer to stop it from coming in the City. Joseph my husband [went] with a message from Brigham Young (than governor of Utah). Went to Captain Alaxandre[18] of the Arme[y] [and] delivered the message, he escaped with his Life, Captain swore at Brigham.[19]

1862 22 April <u>Mesilanious</u> S.L. City

---

15. Margaret Condie Sharp, Diary, 1872–1928, Holograph, Margaret Condie Sharp Papers, J. Willard Marriott Library Special Collections, University of Utah, Salt Lake City, Utah.

16. Sharp, "Margaret Condie Sharp," 380.

17. Margaret's husband.

18. Probably Colonel Edmund Brooke Alexander.

19. Sharp, Diary, 151. According to the *Twentieth Ward History,* "During the very severe winter of 1857–58, at the time of the Johnston's Army 'invasion of Utah', Brigham Young decided that he must send a message to the U.S. Army Commander camped near the burned Fort Bridger. He met Joseph and Adam Sharp [Joseph's brother] on the street and told them he wanted someone to take the message. They inquired, 'How soon do you want us to leave?' He replied, 'As soon as you can get ready. How about tomorrow morning.' They told him they would be ready in one hour. Ready they were and picked up the letter at the office of the First Presidency. . . .

"When they reached the army encampment, it was late afternoon. The soldiers had tents with warm fires and they had a hot meal ready to be served. But the soldiers did not invite the two Mormons to come in out of the wintry blasts. . . . The two Sharp brothers were left to care for themselves as best they could. . . . Some of the soldiers gathered around them and poured out many vile names expressing themselves concerning the character of the Mormons. As soon as they received the written answer to Brigham Young's message, they jumped onto their horses and galloped away, returning to Salt Lake City safely." Martin, *Twentieth Ward History,* 49.

Female Relief Society Organization of first meeting of 20th Ward. Margaret L. Smoot (in her home) President 1 Coun. Jane P. Sharp 2nd coun. Ann Savage. Bishop John Sharp & Bro. William Allen Coun-Presided. Sister Shutlen Secretry. Treasure[r]—Elizabeth Ramsey. Eliza R. Snow & Zina Young members. Margaret C. Sharp chosen 1st member in August 1868 became a Teacher Acceten [assistant] in that 11 years. Till March 9th 1880 was set Apart secretry held that Position 23 years. Jane Miller now President 17 August 1894 a New Organization of Society. Again Jane Miller P[resident]. 1st Vice P. Rhoda Owen 2 vice P Elizibeth Hanford Secretary Margaret C. Sharp Treasure[r] Lula G. Richards.[20]

June 26, 1863 Helen died. Agnes died two days after Helen.[21] There father was teeming in Carson Valley City when they died. And he went in a tranee [train] & saw the 2 children. . . .

Prize Poatry [Poetry]

A tina [tiny] feather from the wings of Love
Dropt into the secred [sacred] lap of mother hood.[22]

April 1864 Joseph Sharp[23] my husband to the States. When returning home Sept. 7th 1864 died at Willow Springs [Wyoming]. 3 hundred miles from S.L. City. Aged

---

20. Sharp, Diary, 39.

21. Ellen was the daughter of Janet and Joseph Sharp; Agnes was the daughter of Margaret and Joseph.

22. Sharp, Diary, 152.

23. "Joseph engaged in the quarrying and freighting business. He was an extremely strong and powerful man. It is said that he could hold a fifty pound weight at arms length for one minute and could shoulder 150 pounds of wheat with his feet together. As a freighter, he journeyed many times back and forth across the plains." Martin, *Twentieth Ward History*, 47.

34 years & 60 days. H[e] was Born in Alloa, Scot[land] July
8th, 1830.24

This is all Margaret wrote of her husband's death. Margaret's
brother Gibson Condie, however, recorded details about this time
in Margaret's life:

> My sister Margaret raised all the children and [was] a
> mother to Janet['s] children. She passed thru great trials
> and afflections. Sometimes she thought she could not en-
> dure the trials, even her friends relations her husbands side
> would like to take everything what was left and leave her
> destitute. They did not give a word of comfort To cheer her
> up, while she was very sick. One day Sister Eliza Snow with
> Sister Smoot took a walk together. When they came to my
> Sister['s] house [in the] 20th ward, she felt impressed to Call
> in. My mother was in the house at the time attending to
> margaret at the time. Sister Snow, had never been in the
> house before, she did not [know] that margaret was sick.
> She was led by the spirit of the Lord. She laid her hands
> upon Margaret['s] head and Blessed her, that she should live
> and the angels of God would preserve her, and her enimies
> would not have any powers over her, and she would conqi-
> uor her enimies. Her words, seemed to strenghend her faith
> and she began to amend from that time, and prospered. She
> also Blessed my Mother.25

---

24. Sharp, Diary, 152.

25. Condie, Reminiscences and Diary, 54–55. For further context on the
practice of blessing, see Jonathan A. Stapley and Kristine Wright, "Female Ritual
Healing in Mormonism," *Journal of Mormon History* 37, no 1 (Winter 2011):
1–85.

Aug. 17 1872 Rented her house. To: Kilpatric rec[eived] $5.^{00}.[26]

1873 Tithing Paid $2.00.[27]

1875 For Annie Sharp made [k]Nitted 7 Pair of Socks.[28]

[18]77 Raised Silk Worms Rec 2.^{00}. raised currants 1.65.

1877 Cecilia [daughter] learned straw braiding hats 3 months of Mrs Rumells.

1877–8 Cecilia to University S[c]hool.

" 78 Sept 26 Cecilia taught School with T. B. Lewis 1 year & a ½.[29]

1879 Waiting o[n] Sickness received $60.^{00} 50.[30]

1879 Joseph [son] to University s[c]hool for the year 40.70.[31]

1881 Eliza R. Snow chosen Pres. by Brigham Young of all Relief Societies in Worald [world].[32]

---

26. Sharp, Diary, 1. Kilpatric is the first boarder of approximately forty-five that Margaret recorded from 1872–1897.

27. Sharp, Diary, 84. This is the earliest Margaret recorded tithing; it is also the smallest amount. Throughout her diary she lists tithing paid in other years.

28. Sharp, Diary, 1875, 22. Making socks was one of Margaret's sources of income. In subsequent years, she recorded several other ways she generated income, including selling potatoes and chickens and making temple clothing. See Sharp, Diary, 22.

29. Sharp, Diary, 22, 51.

30. Sharp, Diary, 16. This is the earliest Margaret recorded practicing medicine; 1924 was the last date (Diary, 159). Throughout her diary she listed treating such problems as cough (8), noises in ear (8), obstetrics (17), heart trouble (26), womb trouble (26), and consumption (26). She also listed medicines and treatments she used. For obstetric care, the least she earned was two dollars; the most, twenty dollars (17). Although she documented the names of many patients and medicines, she recorded only one cure: "Cure for Poison Ivy Kimney Kneck Bark Steep & rub, the tea weark drink it" (160).

31. Sharp, Diary, 49.

32. Sharp, Diary, 155. Eliza R. Snow (1804–1887) became general president of the Relief Society on June 19, 1880. In 1868 Brigham Young had asked Eliza R.

[1881] Ironed & Washed 14 days [Received] 13⁰⁰.

1884 Feb 12 Joseph received a Patent from Washington he helpt to Envent.

April 2 1884 [Joseph] Bought a Bycical [bicycle] Paid 9000 about the first in the City.[33]

1884 October 18 To Yallo Stone [Yellowstone]. . . .

1885 Janar[y] 4ᵗʰ Cecilia at Teachers Assosiation & Coressponding Comittie to the Teachers of S. Lak[e] County in the Colums [columns] of the school journal.

April 24 (28) 1885 Cecilia chosen Second Councelor to Siste[r] Toone Primary.

June 16 1885 Cec[ilia] rescited [recited] in young Ladies festivel.

1886 Sep. 19 Hyrum Classon Invited Cecilia to [s]peak in 12 Ward to the young peeople Sundy night.

1886 Cecilia Birth day Prescindia Kimball & Sister Highby blessed her. S. Higbey spoke in tongues on her head.

1886 Nov. 2 Zina Young said Cecilia would receive the gift of Tongue's.[34]

1888 Dec. 25ᵗʰ F[rederick] E[llis] Barker asked for Cecilia hand in marrage.[35]

1889 Quilts made M C Sharp & Cecilia . . . Total 53.[36]

Snow to establish ward Relief Society organizations throughout the Church, but her official call as Relief Society general president did not occur until after his death. "Salt Lake Stake Relief Society Conference," *Woman's Exponent* 9, no. 3 (July 1, 1880): 21–22.

33. Sharp, "Diary," 1884, 22, 49.

34. Sharp, Diary, 51.

35. Sharp, Diary, 51. Margaret recorded Cecilia's wedding expenses at a total of $80.55 (Diary, 5).

36. Sharp, Diary, 156. Margaret lists a quilt made for Joseph F. Smith. Also, one of her quilt blocks can be found on the Twentieth Ward Friendship Quilt made by the Relief Society sisters of the Salt Lake Twentieth Ward, 1860–1870.

1890 April 9th [Joseph] Left for a mission to Scotland 8 day[s] before set apart & ordained a Seventy. Babtized 16 people Abro[a]d.[37]

[18]90 Give to Missionars [Missionaries] & Charity

"To Bro Jenkenson2.00

"Old Ladyalso . . .

"A Poor Man[38]

April 6 1893 The Weather was Blustrey. Windy rain snow that day. While Pres. Woodruff was giveing dedecatery [dedicatory] Prayer the Storm seamed to peirce the Temple wal[l]s & the quails swarmed the Pinica alles [pinnacles].[39]

1893 Made & Sold Endowment Apron 2.00.[40]

A Trip to the 1893 Chicago World's Fair

In conjunction with the Chicago World's Fair, the Mormon Tabernacle Choir arranged a grand concert tour, performing in Denver, Kansas City, St. Louis, Chicago, and Omaha.[41] About four hundred people, including choir members, made the round trip, and Margaret was among them.

1893 August 29 To Worald Fair

Tusday Tabernical [Tabernacle] Choir Ticket 70.00

Pioneer Memorial Museum, International Society Daughters of Utah Pioneers, Salt Lake City, Utah.

37. Sharp, Diary, 49.

38. Sharp, Diary, 22. Margaret made many donations to the poor and needy throughout her life.

39. Sharp, Diary, 53. The dedicatory services she mentions are those for the Salt Lake Temple.

40. Sharp, Diary, 22.

41. Utah Territory World's Fair Commission, *Utah at the World's Columbian Exposition* (Salt Lake City, UT: Salt Lake Lithographing, 1894), 47.

Mrs. Kate Grosbeck my Companion in Carr [car]. Other Expences 14.50

Mrs. Pierce & May Jane along. Presedent W. Woodruff & Joseph F. Smith, G. Q. Cannon. 4.00^{00} in all. 11 of the grandest carrs that ever left the West. Choir 200^{00} & 50 singers. My car named Evenston in going Sherman [Wyoming] the highest point East of Lar[a]mie. Am[e]s Mountain is 8 thousan[d] feet 51 feet abov[e] S.L. City. Dined in WinSo [illegible].

1893 Was at Temple block Jackson County. [Choir Director Evan] Stephens, Choirs and P[res]. Wo[o]druff sto[o]d on rock. We felt we were o[n] sacred g[r]ound. After to Hendrickites Church. Eston then Oh My Fathe[r]. Traveled of Missipei [Mississippi] in St Louis Dined their [there] 400 ^{00}. Sat down had ~~twelve~~ 8 cour[se] for din[n]er & each had half spring chicken on plait [plate]. Moser Hotele. Went through St Louis Cemetery 6 miles from centey [center] of City. Named Bellfaunt[aine] 3^{00}.60 acres of Grave yard Flower gardens. To Chicago next the tranys [trains] & low railways, clim[b]ing stairs, Pusshing your way through Crowdes was tiring. Rode to Columbian Center. Saw Mico Centeral [Central] Hotle. Michigan Lake 80 milles [miles] acrose [across]. Bought a trinket from a Black girl. . . . Festivel Hall where the Tabernical Choir had their consted [contest][42] held is a mile around it & holds 100 & 40 thousand People Standing room price 1^{00}. Saw Washington Secretary. It is 100^{00} years Old & Chair a[nd] cradile [cradle] belong to 5 generations in Presidents Adams family. Saw California tree in Diameter 14 feet acrose, a stair way in centre of tree. 3 alligatre [alligators] 13 ¼ feet long. At contest judjes [judges] said they were spell bound

---

42. The Mormon Tabernacle Choir participated in a national choir contest on September 8, 1893, receiving the second place award. Commission, *Utah,* 59–62.

to heir [hear] the Mormans sing. Stevans said the mormans wone [won] the Prize but got the 2nd P[lace].

One moving side walk[43] it Projected in Michigane Lake Saw a Bon[n]et Worn in 1828 Like a scope. Saw a Piller of Salt Called Lots Wife. From China a red bulb flower made 50 years ago. A <u>Doll</u> made in 1797. Thursday 200 & 75 thousand people that day in fair. Saw a Rushian [Russian] Ladies Suit & Sabels furres [furs] & satan [satin] dress on Dumma [dummy] Costing 15$\frac{00}{}$. Dress woven Like the <u>rainbow</u>. Saw house built with corn & cobs, also orang[e]s house. Independance Bell with the crack. Weighs 1,000 & 3½ Pound. Fire works go in Michigan Lake like serpants fireworks of all the Presedents of the United States. Oct 30 1893 Worald fair grounds toorn [torn] up.[44]

1895 [Woman's] Exponant 1\frac{00}{}$.[45]

1895 Donated to Temple $3.25.[46]

1897 July 24 Utah Celebrated its 50 years. Utah Celebration was the Grandist in America.[47]

1903 8 July moved in 18th Ward. 20 Ward Soci[e]ty gave me a Party & give me a coppey of Reselution of Respect in a Frame by B[r]o. Savage also a ring with 3 Diamonds & Pearls.[48]

---

43. Moving walkways, the predecessor of modern horizontal escalators, made their debut at the 1893 World's Fair.

44. Sharp, Diary, 55–56.

45. Sharp, Diary, 7. The *Woman's Exponent* was the unofficial organ of the Relief Society. Margaret also recorded purchasing the *Woman's Exponent* in 1891 for $4.20 (page 32).

46. Sharp, Diary, 1895, 7. Margaret recorded making many donations to the Relief Society, to the poor, to children and grandchildren, and to others.

47. Sharp, Diary, 27.

48. Sharp, Diary, 39.

19/04 August 3 to 5ᵗʰ Warr [war] started in Germania, France Belg[i]um & Others Mexico. Fredie in Germ[a]n[i]a.⁴⁹

19[0]4 Sept 27ᵗʰ Recome[n]d For 18ᵗʰ Ward. Also a Teacher. & blesed to wash and anoi[n]te.⁵⁰

Feb 1ˢᵗ 1905 Joseph C. Sharp Arressted Emery Marten & A. E. Thamer in Naveda [Nevada] Reno, County boodlers. The steal was the grea[te]st in the Stat[e] of Utah over 50⁰⁰⁰ Stolen. Caught through Joseph's vigelance & cliver [clever] work.⁵¹

1905 M.C. Sharp Admitted to Daughter of Pianeres [Pioneers] to Enter 50ᶜᵗˢ.⁵²

1906 April 16ᵗʰ Admited to Repears [Reapers'] Club on social (50ᶜᵗˢ).⁵³

1906 Bishop Clauson & Ray Whiting 1 coun[selor] set me a Part to Wash and Ano[i]nt the sisters.⁵⁴

1907 July 17 M.C. Sharp was apointed Chaplin to S. Lake County Daughters of Pianers. Minie James President.⁵⁵

---

49. Sharp, Diary, 149.

50. Sharp, Diary, 39. Margaret was a long-time temple worker and recorded many, perhaps all, the sisters for whom she performed temple ordinances (pages 30, 160). She also wrote that she made twenty-four endowment aprons from 1889 for individuals, members of the Twentieth and Eighteenth Wards, and for the temple (page 157).

51. Sharp, Diary, 160.

52. The Daughters of Utah Pioneers was founded to honor and preserve the histories of Utah's pioneers. Membership is limited to descendants. Sharp, Diary, 155.

53. Sharp, Diary, 2. The Reapers' Club (1892–1912) was a women's literary organization founded by Emmeline B. Wells and dedicated to the "social and intellectual development" of its members. "Utah Federation of Woman's Clubs," *Woman's Exponent* 25 (June 1, 1896): 1; Sharon Snow Carver, "Salt Lake City's Reapers' Club," *Utah Historical Quarterly* 64 (Spring 1996): 108–20; "A Historic House," *Woman's Exponent* 21 (December 15, 1892): 92.

54. Sharp, Diary, 39. Also in 1906, on January 26, Margaret received a patriarchal blessing from James H. Martineau, private possession.

55. Sharp, Diary, 155.

1907 Lectured to Daughter of Pionere's said the Pione[e]rs Expoditoins. Traveled 13 hundred Miles to come to the mountains When Mosas [Moses] & his company only travled one hundred & 50 miles strait acrose. Spoke of 3 great women croseing [crossing] the plains. One was ~~Nancy~~ Marey Chandler.[56]

1908 Nov 3rd [Joseph] Sworen in as Sherriff of Salt Lake County.[57]

1909 Feb. 5th Paid ten dollars for Life membership In genological [Genealogical] Society. M C. Sharp.[58]

1910 May 31st Paid 30⁰⁰ for a Wash[ing] Machine.[59]

1911 Mrs. [Lydia Mamreoff von Finkelstein] Mountford's Lecture. . . . She spoke of People paying there Taxes in Jeruselam rich & Poor all anxious to pay an honast Taxes. . . . Madam [Mountford] was in the [home where] Mary lived. Also was on the hill (Mesha) & Pinical [pinnacle] Where the Saviour was Tempted by the Divel (Mesha). One side of the hill was full of holes Like honey-Come. . . . The other side of hill toards the bottom grew all kinds of flowers. . . . The Evil one thought he could decieve Jesus—but he could not be tempted by him.[60]

1912 January 9th Went to Center Ward Talked to R. Society on Obstetricts.[61]

---

56. Sharp, Diary, 27.

57. Sharp, Diary, 153. Margaret records Joseph as being sworn in as sheriff two additional years: 1909 (2) and 1910 (153).

58. Sharp, Diary, 155.

59. Sharp, Diary, 73.

60. Sharp, Diary, 150. On Lydia Mamreoff von Finkelstein (Madam Mountford), see Thomas G. Alexander, *Things in Heaven and Earth: The Life and Times of Wilford Woodruff, a Mormon Prophet* (Salt Lake City, UT: Signature Books, 1991), 324–28.

61. Sharp, Diary, 60.

1913 Sept. 3ʳᵈ Edna Smith Put me head of the 1ˢᵗ roome in Temple.[62]

1914 Pres. Woodrow Wilson's Wife [Ellen Louise Axson] died August 6ᵗʰ.[63]

1918 July 26ᵗʰ Insighn [Ensign] Stake got up the Selibretion [celebration]

The Pianeers Came in 1847 to S. Lake Valey. Now they are Celebrateing [celebrating] it 1918 July 26ᵗʰ making it 71 years since they came to Valy. MC. Sharp & Lucille[64] went to Insign Peak. Present About 20⁰⁰ People there. Program. Bid. Young Prayed grandson of Brigham Young. 1ˢᵗ Counsoler to stake James Knight spoak[e]. Sang "Come Let us Anew."

Sang Mary Romney Ross "O Yea Mountain High" Apostol Orson Whiteny [Whitney] spoke on the Bible quoting relating to these last days of Isai[a]h & Insign Peak & Brig. Young saying this was the Plase for the Saints to Dwell. Joseph Smith in vision saw this Valley & took a glass of water in his hand said, the pure cold water in the streems he saw & the mountains & the Saints would Dwell in peace. But after a whil[e] they wou[l]d have Trouble. Said this [w]hole Valey was a arm of the Picific Ocian, a Long time ago. Sometim[es] on th[e] sidies [sides] of the mounta[i]ns would find shells. Ascalanta [Escalante] & his compa[n]y first found this valey But did not come in it himself. Jim Bridger said this valley could not rais[e] anything it was so dry & crickets are so plentifull & relaited about the saints driven from Navoue [Nauvoo] with 5\000 people &

62. Sharp, Diary, 63. Edna Lambson Smith (1851–1926), also a temple worker, was the fourth wife of Joseph F. Smith. Designated president of the women workers in the temple, she may have had responsibilities similar to those performed today by a temple matron or her assistants.

63. Sharp, Diary, 149.

64. Most likely one of her granddaughters.

goverment wanted 5\00 of mon [men] to go to Mexico [the Mormon Battalion] & the men Had to go & figh[t] them & women & children drove the cattle to the valy.[65]

1920 Total [tithing] for 1920 paid $171[00].[66]

1923 April 6[th] 23 years M.C. Sharp have been a Temple worker.[67]

1924 January 7[th] Had my up[p]er Teeth mad[e] over cost $15[00].[68]

1924 August 8[th] Lotte Deston treated for Cancer in hand give 1[00].[69]

1928 Janu[a]ry 13
Zion Co[o]perative Mir Instit[ut]ion stock $1[00]
100[50]
Paid Tithing 15$[70]

Itoms of Intrist[71]

Coal is wood Composed of roots, Bark, Leaves, Stumps. Al[l] Buirred [buried] in Earth Thousands of years.[72]

I am that I am. Means for Ever & for Ever
Body & Spirit mean the soul.[73]

---

65. Sharp, Diary, 147.

66. Sharp, Diary, 88.

67. Sharp, Diary, 97.

68. Sharp, Diary, 98.

69. Sharp, Diary, 159. This is the last entry in Margaret's diary regarding medical work.

70. Sharp, Diary, 83. This is the last date Margaret recorded anything regarding stocks and dividends; it is also the latest dated entry in her diary. She died five months later.

71. Sharp, Diary, 152.

72. Sharp, Diary, 3.

73. Sharp, Diary, 30.

June 21 or 22 midnight longest day Dec. 21st shortest day[74]

　　Don't Cul[ti]vate Evil thoughts
　　Niver [Never] Harbor an Impure Desire
　　Evil thinking & speaking make scars on you[r] soul
　　Like a burn that disfigures your body.
　　God said be yea perfect as I am In this Sphere on Earth
　　as He is in Heaven Perfict.[75]

Although Margaret suffered much loss, particularly in her younger years with the deaths of her sister, children in her care, and her husband, she maintained her faith until the end of her life. Her spirit could have been crushed by her hardships, but she carried on. Eventually life got better, yet she did not grow complacent. She showed her dedication to the Church by always paying tithing, by serving in the Relief Society and in the temple, and by living the Word of Wisdom.[76] And she reached out to others by sharing her talents and meager financial resources.

In 1881, when her mother died, Margaret wrote a poem. Although it was not about herself, it expresses Margaret's own testimony of faith:

> *Our mother has gone to rest,*
> *Away from care and pain,*
> *To mingle with the blest,*
> *Till the Savior comes again. . . .*
> *Six children she has left behind,*
> *To mourn their mother dear;*

---

74. Sharp, Diary, 153.

75. Sharp, Diary, 160.

76. In 1927, Margaret's granddaughter Gladys Barker Westwood wrote an article about Margaret's health habits, which align with the Word of Wisdom. Gladys Barker Westwood, "My Grandmother, by Her Granddaughter," *Correct Eating*, January 1927, 30–31, 56.

But God is ever just and kind
To those who will Him fear.
And she will conquer death,
And be to them restored,
Crowned with the victor's wreath,
Forever with the Lord.[77]

Margaret died June 22, 1928, in Salt Lake City at the age of eighty-eight.

---

77. Condie, Reminiscences and Diary, 1883.

Chapter 23

"THE LORD HELPS US IN SMALL THINGS AS WELL AS LARGE"

RACHEL EMMA WOOLLEY SIMMONS (1836–1926)
Laura F. Willes

BIOGRAPHICAL SKETCH

Rachel Emma Woolley was born on August 7, 1836, in East Rochester, Columbiana County, Ohio. Her Quaker parents, Edwin Dilworth and Mary Wickersham Woolley, had moved from Pennsylvania to eastern Ohio in 1832 to homestead new land. Rachel was the first daughter and third child born to them. Missionaries of The Church of Jesus Christ of Latter-day Saints reached East Rochester in 1837, and first Mary and then Edwin were baptized by the end of the year. Rachel, less than two years of age when her parents were baptized, belongs to the first generation raised with a lifelong influence of the restored gospel.

In 1839 the family gathered to Nauvoo, Illinois. There Rachel celebrated her eighth birthday. In 1846 the Woolleys were driven from Nauvoo with other Saints, spent two years at Winter Quarters, and in 1848 crossed the plains to Utah with Rachel driving a horse-drawn buggy all the way. When they arrived in September, Salt Lake City became Rachel's permanent home.

In 1851 Rachel, then fifteen, married Joseph Marcellus Simmons, twelve years her senior. Joseph was on his way from Massachusetts to the California gold fields when he was converted to the Church in Utah. Five years later, in 1856, Joseph married Rachel's younger sister Henriett (Nett) as a plural wife. The marriage of Joseph and Rachel lasted for more than twenty years, when Joseph's sudden death left Rachel a thirty-five-year-old widow with ten children, ages six months to nineteen years. To support her family, she took a course in obstetrics and practiced midwifery for almost forty years, delivering hundreds of babies, including most of her own grandchildren, great-grandchildren, and a nephew, Spencer Woolley Kimball, who became the twelfth president of the Church.

When Rachel died in 1926 at age ninety, she had ten children, seventy-four grandchildren, and 123 great-grandchildren. A grandson paid this tribute: "She did not seem to be subject to the distractions and vicissitudes of life, but was always calm, kind, loving and sympathetic." She lived a life of "courage, dignity and honor."[1]

LIFE EXPERIENCES

"S. L. City May 13th 1881 At this late time of my life, being in my 45 year, I feel impressed . . . to keep a journal," wrote Rachel Emma Woolley Simmons in a new leather-bound diary. "I do this for my own satisfaction . . . and knowing it will be a pleasure to my children to look at and read, no matter how little merit it may contain, or how poorly done, they will cherish it. Not for great or noble deed, or sacrifices made for others, But they will like it to read

---

1. Joseph Willes, "Brief Biography of Rachel Emma Woolley Simmons," ca. 1947, Typescript, pp. 1, 83, Church History Library, The Church of Jesus Christ of Latter-day Saints, Salt Lake City, Utah, hereafter cited as Church History Library.

Just because it was Mother."² So began nearly a decade of Rachel Emma Woolley Simmons's record keeping. Within the pages of her first journal, she also wrote an autobiography. Excerpts from both reveal the vibrancy of her wit and her wisdom, rich experience, and foundation of religious devotion.

Nauvoo

The Woolley family arrived in Nauvoo in 1839. Rachel recorded: "The ague was so prevalent, that our family . . . were sick. I can remmember, being in our trundle bed with my brothers, and all shaking untill it seemed as if our teeth would come out. The chill would last for hours, then the fever, was just as hard as the chill. There was no one to wait upon us but uncle John, and in time he was taken sick so father had to pay a man a bit or 12¹/² cents for every pail of water that was brought into the house. . . . But all things come to an end, the ague with [the] rest."³

A Strong Will

Rachel's schoolteacher, of English extraction, taught the class to repeat the alphabet, pronouncing the letter "L" with an "H" in front. Rachel refused to repeat it, saying, "My mother has taught me not to say naughty words."⁴

"Our chills must have come back, for we were on the steamboat . . . when I felt the chill coming on," she wrote. "I jumped out of the b[e]rth, and stamped my feet and said most emphatacaly, three

2. Rachel Emma Woolley Simmons, Journal, vol. 1, Holograph, pp. 2–3, Rachel W. Simmons Collection, Church History Library.

3. Simmons, Journal, 1:6–7.

4. Rachel Emma Simmons Willes, "Biography of My Mother, Rachel Emma Woolley Simmons," 1925, Typescript, p. 1, private possession.

times I won't have another chill, and I did'nt, nor hai'nt had one of that kind up to the present time."[5]

Joseph Smith

While the Woolleys lived in Nauvoo, Joseph and Hyrum Smith were frequent visitors at their home.[6] Rachel recalled:

> The intimacy existing between my parents and Joseph and Hyrum Smith continued as long as they lived. I think Br Joseph, must have been very easy to approach, for . . . [he] was always kind and fatherly. Many times I've sat on his lap.
>
> In those day it was the custom to ride, on horseback for pleasure. . . . One day Br Joseph and his wife Emma was waiting for father and mother, at our house to . . . go for a ride. Father was shaving. . . . There was some disturbance in the street and we all went to the windows to see what it was. I was leaving the window as Father was going and he held the razor very carelessly in his hand. I run against the point of it, and cut a gash in my forehead. The blood flowed friely. . . . I have the impression that, Br Joseph bound up my head with his handkerchief. . . . I carried the scar for many years but it is now lost in the wrinkles of age and care.[7]

Rachel was seven when the Prophet was martyred. She said, "I went with my uncle Sammuel to see [Joseph and Hyrum] . . . laid in state at the mansion house, although I was but a child the solemnity of the occasion made an impression on me that I never forget."[8]

---

5. Simmons, Journal, 1:8–9.

6. Willis, "Biography of My Mother," 1.

7. Simmons, Journal, 1:17, 24–26.

8. Simmons, Journal, 1:29.

Baptism in Nauvoo

Rachel's determination comes through in her recollection of her Nauvoo baptism: "On the seventh of August [1844] . . . I was eight years old, and through the teaching of my parients I could hardly wait to be baptized. . . . I didn't give father any peace until he hitched up the buggy and took me down to the [Mississippi] river and baptized me."[9]

Crossing the Plains

"We left winter quarters in the begining of May, 1848," Rachel wrote of her family's journey across the plains to the Salt Lake Valley. "We had three wagons and a light spring wagon, for mother to ride in as her health was rather delicate at that time. . . . I had to drive the buggy. I did so in fear and trembling, as one of the horses was very vicious. She used to kick up dreadful until she would kick the end board of the wagon all to pieces, but it made no difference I had to go at [it] the next day just the same."[10]

Rachel turned twelve on the trail. She collected buffalo chips to burn in the campfires. Once, the buffalo chips "were very thick in a certain place close to the road. . . . I thought I was in luck, but I soon found out the cause. I was picking up as fast as I could when all at once I heard the rattle of a snake. I looked to see in what direction it was and there he was in a hole almost at my feet. I did not stop for any more chips at that time. That was the second escape I had of being bitten by a rattle snake. . . . I acknowledge the hand of the Lord in it."[11]

Some landmarks planted themselves in her memory. "I remember . . . [crossing] Rocky Ridge," she wrote. "I was driving as usual, and to make matters worse we had an old pig, that was in trouble

---

9. Simmons, Journal, 1:30.

10. Simmons, Journal, 1:40–41.

11. Willes, "Brief Biography," 10.

that day, and she had to ride in the buggy, as Father was very anxious to save the little pigs, but they all died in consequence of the rough road. . . . That night I was so completely tired out, with the road and the frisky horse."[12]

Arrival in the Salt Lake Valley

After traveling through high mountains, Rachel and her family approached the end of the trail, finally emerging from the Wasatch range:

> With what gladness we got our first glimpse of the valley. We camped just at the mouth of emigration Canyon, in the afternoon to wash and fix up a little before meeting our friends that had preceded us, the year previous. Uncle John had been here a year, and ~~had~~ was living in the fort. . . . His wife had supper ready, corn, cucumbers and other vegetables, and I have no doubt, but what we did justice to that supper being the first, in a house for five months. . . .
>
> Father and the boys went right to work making adobe's for a house, and before the winter set in, he had . . . put up two rooms, so that we were very comfortable, took the wagons to pieces, and made floors. The roof was made of brush with dirt thrown on. For doors we had blankets hung up. Mother and Ellen [plural wife] each had a wagon bed set at the doors so they could step right in to them, for bed rooms. . . .
>
> Of course father and the boys were not idle, so our circumstances improved.[13]

---

12. Simmons, Journal, 1:48–49.

13. Simmons, Journal, 1:50–54.

Marriage

Rachel's writings include an account of events that led to her marriage, beginning with her chance meeting of one of the many California-bound gold miners who passed through the Salt Lake Valley:

> In the year of 1850 I met my fate, but it took me some time to find it out. His name was Joseph Marcellus Simmons. He had started for California to dig gold . . . [but he] stopt here to replenish [his] stores of provisions. He got interested in mormonism and remained. . . . Joseph came to mother and asked her to take him for a boarder. . . . He told me afterwords that he had a motive in staying, he said he loved me, the first time he seen me, and came with the determonation to make me his wife.
>
> We were married on the 18 of December 1851 in what was called the Warm Spring Bath House. It was at that time the largest and best adapted for large parties, as well as the fashionable place. I had as nice a wedding as could be had in those days. . . . After the guests had all arrived, we were told to come . . . and take our places in the middle of the hall. . . . Br Brigham Young married us. . . . After the cerremony we had supper, then danced until allmost morning. ~~It was just gett~~ We went home to father's and continued to live there for three years untill Joe built our own little house.[14]

Rachel and Joseph were sealed when the Endowment House was completed in 1855 on Temple Square in Salt Lake City.[15]

---

14. Simmons, Journal, 1:55–58, 62–63.

15. Before the Salt Lake Temple was completed in 1893, several buildings were used for the administration of temple ordinances. In Salt Lake City, one such building was the Endowment House, which was in operation from 1855 to 1889. LaMar C. Berrett, "Endowment Houses," in *Encyclopedia of Mormonism,* ed. Daniel H. Ludlow, 4 vols. (New York: Macmillan, 1992), 2:456.

Soon after we were married Joe joined the Deseret Dramatic Association, the first one of the kind in the Valley. (I forgot to mention what his employment was, Just before we were married he went to work in the ~~tithing~~ Presidents [Brigham Young's] office as a clerk, and continued to work there for many years.) Of course it took him away a great deal at night to rehearse and get ready to play. I didn't like it at first but one can get used to all most any thing.[16]

A Sister Wife

"I was always taught to respect poligamy," Rachel wrote, "and I believe in the principle as strong to day as at any time of my life and I hope my children will not only believe but practice it, and do so in the spirit and meaning thereof, and if they do so there will a blessing follow." Rachel left a straightforward account of her husband taking a second wife—Rachel's younger sister—and how the sister wives got along: "Joe married Henriett[17] Aug 21, 1857. She came home to live with me, where with the exception of a few months she has lived ever since, and I think that we have lived as peacefully as two women could under the circumstances."[18]

Church Attendance

In the early days after the Saints settled the Salt Lake Valley, they attended Sabbath meetings on Temple Square. Rachel wrote this account of attendance at those meetings:

I used to go to the theatre every night nearly . . . [but I also went to meeting], nearly every sunday Joe used to go

---

16. Simmons, Journal, 1:63.

17. Spelled Henriett in Rachel's journal but also spelled Henriette and Henrietta elsewhere.

18. Simmons, Journal, 1:71–72.

always, he had a certain place in the old tabernacle, and every one in those days [k]new it, and it was left for him, so that shows a pretty good record, in going to meetting.[19]

Death of Her Husband

Not long after Rachel joined other women of Utah in casting votes for the first time, she also became a widow. She recounted:

The Monday before [Joe] died was the first time the women of Utah ever voted.[20] Nett and I went across to the city hall and voted and when we came back [five minutes later] . . . he took a very bad spell. I think he was struck with death then, but he didn't die until [two days later]. . . . There [were] sixteen of us in the family [so . . . we] were out of everything. Father had to get us things to go to the funeral. . . . [Later] I was fortunate enough to get the boys [employment] in Walker Bro's Store. . . . I can truly say that the Lord has been a husband to the widow and a father to the fatherless. I acknowlage His hand in all these things.[21]

Midwife

At the request of one of Utah's leading women, Rachel agreed to take medical training, which provided her with a profession so she could support herself:

---

19. Simmons, Journal, 1:75–76.

20. Rachel was mistaken; Utah women voted for the first time on Monday, February 14, 1870, two years before Joseph's death on Wednesday, February 14, 1872. Thomas G. Alexander, "An Experiment in Progressive Legislation: The Granting of Woman Suffrage in Utah in 1870," *Utah Historical Quarterly* 38, no. 1 (Winter 1970): 20–30.

21. Simmons, Journal, 1:87, 89, 92–93.

In the spring of [18]74, sister Zina D Young came to
me and wanted me to attend a course of lectures on obstetrics given by Dr. Mary Barker. . . . I told sister Zina I
couldn't do so for I hadn't the means, but she said there was
two appointed from each ward, and the relief scociety's of
each ward was to pay for the lectures, she insisted so that I
consented, but I borrowed the money, as I dont like to be
under obligation to the public in that manner. I attended
the lectures there was about thirty in the class. Soon after I
commenced to practice. . . . I continue to practice yet and
will do so until I have an income that is sufficient to keep
me without if the Lord is willing for I ask His blessing on
all I do.[22]

In 1883 Rachel noted: "I paid to the Relief Society twenty one
dollars and a half, to day being money I borrowed to attend a course
of lectures, on midwifery. . . . I looked upon it as a loan and as such
paid it."[23]

Midwives attended women during childbirth and also stayed
with the new mothers for several weeks until they could be up from
bed. Once when nursing two patients at the same time, Rachel
wrote: "I had a hard time of it for a couple of weeks. I was going
night and day. . . . All together I was away seven weeks. I recieved for
my services ninety four dollars."[24] Her patients lovingly called her
"Aunt Rachel."

Rachel was dedicated to her calling as a midwife. On one occasion, she wrote: "I have been the instrument in the Lords hand of
bringing two children into the world to day. . . . I hope the Lord will

---

22. Simmons, Journal, 1:96–98.

23. Rachel Emma Woolley Simmons, Journal, vol. 2, June 30, 1883,
Holograph, pp. 94–95, Rachel W. Simmons Collection, Church History Library.

24. Simmons, Journal, October 22, 1882, 2:59.

bless me in the future as he has in the past, for I realize that without his help I can do nothing. His is the honor and the glory, for all the work of my hands."[25]

One Christmas her children had given her a beautiful woolen paisley shawl. Often at a delivery there was no layette; Rachel often used her shawl to wrap the infant. She penned a tribute to this shawl, calling it her "old and honored friend." She wrote, "You have ministered to the aged and given warmth to the newly born. You have been at my side through many a hard fought battle, always ready to serve."[26]

Word of Wisdom

In the early days of the Church, adherence to the Word of Wisdom, the revealed law of health for the Saints, was encouraged but not required. Like many first-generation Church members, Rachel struggled to obey the law:

> Dec 24 [1881] It is just one year to day since I commenced to keep the word of wisdom in regard to drinking tea and coffee, so far I take credit to myself, that I have been able to over come the temptation many times. I hope the Lord will continue to bless me. I desire to keep the word of wisdom, that I may have more faith, and a better grace to call on the Lord, in sickness, and that I may have the blessings that He promises to them that will keep it.[27]

> June 18 [1883] To day is wash day. I thought when I was getting breakfast, I didn't feel well [and] I would make a cup of coffee to help me through with my washing, but the

---

25. Simmons, Journal, February 1, 1883, 2:69.

26. Willes, "Brief Biography," 34.

27. Simmons, Journal, December 24, 1881, 2:18.

thought came to me instantly "why not trust to the Lord, instead of the coffee." I did and got through splendidly felt better than I had for some time. I know the Lord helps us in small things as well as large if we will trust Him.[28]

Old Folks Excursion

Rachel participated in Utah's annual Old Folks Day, which honored elderly members of the community.[29] She recorded an 1882 Old Folks excursion in Salt Lake City:

> It was the greatest affair. . . . There were a thousand and forty-eight old people over seventy. Those that did not live in the city were brought here on the cars and . . . provided with homes with the Saints. There was a Jubilee in the Tabernacle and a free theatre. . . . There was a dinner given at Liberty Park. It was estimated there were thirteen thousand in the Park that day, met to enjoy themselves and make it pleasant for the old folks. All my family was there. . . . There were races run by the old men and prizes given to some. One old lady got a dollar for having a bonnet that was twenty years old and in a good state of preservation. A dollar was given to an old man for getting up and making the fire in the morning for his wife for more than sixty years. I think a dollar is not enough for such goodness. [Another man] got a dollar for living peacefully with his mother-in-law for twenty-five years. It seems almost incredible, but he is a man of truth.[30]

---

28. Simmons, Journal, June 18, 1883, 2:89–90.

29. Joseph Heinerman, "The Old Folks Day: A Unique Utah Tradition," *Utah Historical Quarterly* 53 (Spring 1985): 157–69.

30. Willes, "Brief Biography," 42.

Holidays

Holidays were a time of celebration. Rachel recorded:

Nov 30 [1882] This has been Thanksgiving day. I had a family dinner and about eight or ten invited guests . . . all together there was thirty eight sat down to table. We had music and singing in the evening . . . a splendid time. . . .

Dec 24 This is christmas eve we have been filling stockings. There is 22 pair hanging up to be filled—no small chore but a very pleasant one. . . .

Dec 25 Well christmas is nearly over . . . there was a good deal of fun an[d] excitement in the morning when [we] opened our parcels. . . . I acknowledge we have been greatly blessed both spirtualy and temporally. The Lord has been mindful of us. . . .

Dec 28 I am very busy getting ready for company on New Years day. I have in vited some of the brethren and their wives of the ward. . . .

Jan 1 1883 Every thing is in readiness for my company dinner at 3 o clock. I am cooking three turkies six chickens and other things . . . Well the day is over and it has been a success in every way. . . . There was forty persons ate dinner.[31]

Death of Missionary Son

Rachel, already a widow, came to know the joys of having her sons serve missions and the sorrow of having a missionary son die. Regarding the missionary call of her fourth son, Edgar, she wrote:

Feb 21 [1889] Edgar recieved a notice to day to go on a mission to Turkey to which he has responded to without the

---

31. Simmons, Journal, 2:62–65, 67.

least hesitation although it is a long way from home, but it gives joy to know he is willing. I shall miss him more than I can express, but he is a servant of the Lord and must do His bidding before all other things.[32]

A short time later, Rachel's fifth son, Louis, was called as a missionary to Holland. "He accepted just as willingly as Edgar," wrote Rachel, "for which I feel truly thankful. It would be a source of grief to me were any of my boys to refuse to go when the Lord calls them."[33]

Both sons were away from home at the same time. In Turkey just ten months, however, Edgar contracted smallpox and died. He was buried in Aintab. Rachel's grief was almost overwhelming. Within months she stopped writing in her journal, though she was only fifty-four and would live another thirty-six years. She never wrote about Edgar's death. Possibly it was just too painful to write, and after time had eased the wounds, she was out of the habit of journal keeping. As a result, she left no written feelings about the Manifesto of 1890, which led to the discontinuance of plural marriage, a principle to which she was wholly dedicated; the completion of the Salt Lake Temple in 1893; her oldest daughter Lucy's death in 1904; or World War I, which raged from 1914 to 1918—although she experienced all these events. Yet her deep faith and devotion to the Church and her family remained intact.

Later Years

On November 30, 1926, the day Rachel died, her family gathered in preparation for her to receive a priesthood blessing. She whispered, "Tell Oliver in his prayer for me not to ask the Father to permit me to stay longer—I am ready and wish to be gathered

---

32. Simmons, Journal, 2:206–7.

33. Simmons, Journal, June 7, 1889, 2:209.

home."[34] She died shortly thereafter. A descendant described her thus: "She was a noble woman, brave, self-sacrificing, hard working, loving and true to every principle of the gospel; teaching by precept and example all those with whom she came in contact."[35]

Testimony

Rachel left a written record that has allowed later generations to read her testimony of God and her hopes for her family:

> I feel, that I want to live nearer the Lord than I have ever done. We all have need to, for the time is drawing near when the line will be drawn, and all that are on the Lord's side will be set apart from the wicked. . . . It is my prayer by night and by day that [my children] may prove faithful to the gospel to the end.[36]
>
> I can truly say that so far in my life there has not been a principle revealed that I have not recieved without a doubt of its truth, and I know if we live, so that we can keep the spirit of the Lord, with us, we will never doubt, any thing that he may reveal to his people.[37]

It also gave them an example of how to handle hurt caused by someone else's actions and how to keep it in perspective:

> It will soon be a thing of the past. I will let pass with it all the tangled ends, vexations, and the ups and downs of the past year, bear in memory only the ups. . . . Life is like the weaver's net, which has both bright and grey threads.

34. Willes, "Brief Biography," 81.
35. Transcribed in Willes, "Brief Biography," 82.
36. Simmons, Journal, January 1, 1883, 2:68.
37. Simmons, Journal, May 19, 1883, 2:75.

The grey ones serve to make the bright ones still brighter, so let it be.[38]

Her journal ended this way:

Jan 1 [1891]. Another year has begun. I wonder what it has in store for me, of good or ill, I trust that whatever it bring, I shall have grace to bear, ever seeking to keep the spirit of the Lord with me strive to overcome my weaknesses and do what good I can, and make a better record than I have the past year, Amen.[39]

---

38. Willes, "Brief Biography," 75.
39. Simmons, Journal, 2:212–13.

Chapter 24

"Peace Be with You"

Bathsheba Wilson Bigler Smith (1822–1910)
Heidi S. Swinton

Biographical Sketch

Thousands filled the Salt Lake Tabernacle to attend the funeral of Bathsheba Wilson Bigler Smith, matron of the Salt Lake Temple and fourth general president of the Relief Society. Fondly called "Aunt Bathsheba," she had died five days earlier, on September 20, 1910. Her funeral was the first held in the Tabernacle for a woman officer of The Church of Jesus Christ of Latter-day Saints. It replaced the usual Sabbath meeting.[1]

"Following her was a chain of good works," eulogized President Anthon H. Lund of the First Presidency. "A crown of righteousness awaits her, we feel she was a woman of God."[2]

---

1. Emmeline B. Wells, "A Loving Tribute," *Woman's Exponent* 39, no. 3 (September 1910): 18; "Body Lies in State at Family Residence," *Deseret Evening News*, September 14, 1910.

2. "Impressive Services," *Woman's Exponent* 39, no. 3 (September 1910): 21.

Bathsheba, the daughter of Mark and Susannah Ogden Bigler, was born in Shinnston, Harrison, Virginia,[3] on May 3, 1822, the eighth of nine children. She had a happy childhood on a large and prosperous farm. Her father and a few neighbors employed a teacher intermittently, and Bathsheba "made the most of those school days," which, to her, "seemed all too short."[4]

Joining the Church in 1837, the Biglers sold their prosperous three-hundred-acre farm to join the Saints in Missouri. They arrived to face persecutions and violence, which soon drove them to refuge in Illinois. Despite her poverty, Bathsheba endeavored to beautify her surroundings, a talent she expressed in both poverty and wealth.

She married George A. Smith, a member of the Quorum of the Twelve Apostles and cousin of Joseph Smith Jr., on July 25, 1841. They had three children.[5] The Smiths lived at the heart of Church society, first in Nauvoo and then in Salt Lake City. Her eighty-eight years were marked by the sorrow of losing loved ones,[6] the harshness of the pioneer trail, settling a desert, and long separations from her beloved husband.

Bathsheba was a charter member of the Nauvoo Relief Society, the youngest married woman in the group. She received temple ordinances in Nauvoo in 1843 with the Prophet Joseph Smith

---

3. Present-day Shinnston is in West Virginia. During the Civil War, what is now West Virginia seceded from Virginia in 1861 and was admitted to the Union as a new state in 1863.

4. "Bathsheba W. Smith Autobiography," ca. 1875–1906, Typescript, ed. Alice Merrill Horne, p. 3, Church History Library, The Church of Jesus Christ of Latter-day Saints, hereafter cited as Church History Library.

5. George Albert Smith Jr. (1842–1860), Bathsheba Kate Smith Merrill (1844–1920), and John Smith (1847–1847). Zora Smith Jarvis, comp., "Genealogy of George A. Smith and Bathsheba W. Bigler," in *Ancestry, Biography, and Family of George A. Smith* (Provo, UT: Brigham Young University, 1962).

6. Her son George was murdered by Navajo Indians at the age of eighteen while on a mission to the Moqui Indians.

presiding.[7] She served as general president of the Relief Society from 1901 to 1910, as a board member of the women-run Deseret Hospital and a founder of its nursing school, and as a women's suffrage leader. She served in the Endowment House in Salt Lake City for seventeen years[8]; in the St. George, Manti, and Logan Temples; and as matron of the Salt Lake Temple.

Bathsheba was a noble figure in the community, known for her homemade silk dresses, her distinctive lace mantilla, and her peaceful presence. A frequent visitor to homes of fellow Saints throughout Utah Territory, she left their company with her signature farewell, "Peace be unto thee, Peace to this house."[9]

LIFE EXPERIENCES

Bathsheba Wilson Bigler was reared in Virginia's genteel southern culture and was a joyful, dignified, and thoughtful woman. She recalled:

> From my earliest remembrance I was religiously inclined and loved honesty, truthfulness and integrity. I attended to my secret prayers, studied to be cheerful, industrious, clean and I was opposed to rudeness. I often attended meetings of different religious sects but did not see much difference in them.
>
> When I was in my fifteenth year some Latter-day Saint elders visited our neighborhood. I heard them preach and believed what they taught. I accepted the Book of Mormon

7. Wilford Woodruff, December 1843, *Wilford Woodruff's Journal, 1833–1898,* ed. Scott Kenney, 9 vols. (Salt Lake City, UT: Signature Books), 2:332.

8. Before temples were completed, other buildings were dedicated for the administration of temple ordinances. In Salt Lake City, one such building was the Endowment House, which was in operation from 1855 to 1889. LaMar C. Berrett, "Endowment Houses," in *Encyclopedia of Mormonism,* ed. Daniel H. Ludlow, 4 vols. (New York: Macmillan, 1992), 2:456.

9. Wells, "Loving Tribute," 17.

as a divine record and Joseph Smith as a prophet of God. I knew these things to be true by the Spirit of the Lord, which I received in answer to prayer.

On the 21ˢᵗ of August 1837, I went down into the waters of baptism. I felt to rejoice and firmly believed that I was accepted as a member of Christ's kingdom. A part of my experience as a member of the church was that most of my young acquaintances and companions began to ridicule me. The spirit of gathering came upon me and I begged to be allowed to go with my sister Nancy and her family, for they . . . were preparing to go to the center stake of Zion in Missouri. The boon was denied. This caused me to retire feeling most sorrowful. While silently weeping and pondering upon my great desire, I heard a voice saying, "Weep not Bathsheba, for you will go to Missouri in the Fall." I believed what I had heard.[10]

This prophecy came to pass, and Bathsheba's family departed for Far West, Missouri, in the fall. Bathsheba described the early stages of the journey as "novel and romantic," but the nearer the Biglers approached their destination, the more hostile the people became.

I saw thousands of mobbers arrayed against the Saints. I heard their shouts and savage yells when Joseph and his brethren were taken into their camp. I witnessed much, very much suffering which was brought upon our people by those lawless men.[11]

"In those distressing times," Bathsheba reflected, "the Spirit of the Lord comforted and sustained me. I had an abiding testimony that we were being persecuted for the Gospel's sake and I took care

10. Smith, "Autobiography," 4.
11. Smith, "Autobiography," 6.

to exhort those older Saints about me that though many of us might be called on to lay down our lives, the Gospel must survive."[12]

During the long march to refuge in Quincy, Illinois, Bathsheba's father fell ill; he died just weeks after arriving in Illinois. In the spring of 1840, her family settled in Nauvoo, where she "had many opportunities of hearing Joseph Smith preach and endeavored to profit by his instructions. I received many testimonies to the truth of the doctrines he taught."[13] She also gained a deep love and respect for Emma Smith, his wife.

Four years earlier, in Virginia, Bathsheba had met the young missionary George A. Smith. Once in Missouri, she had promised to "keep his cabin":

> On the 25th of July 1841, I kept this promise and was married to George A. Smith youngest member of the Twelve. . . . Before my marriage I had not heard from the man I loved since he left for his mission to England until one day Lorenzo Snow joined him in London and gave him news of me and my family. One day a neighbor came to our house showing a letter addressed to Bathsheba W. Bigler and post-marked Liverpool. He held the letter high to tease me, but knowing well who had written my name, I danced and sang for joy.

Before George returned from his mission, he had sent six letters to Bathsheba that she "tucked away among [her] precious belongings."[14]

At a feast celebrating their marriage, Bathsheba's father-in-law, John Smith, promised her and George the blessings of Abraham,

---

12. Smith, "Autobiography," 6–7.

13. Smith, "Autobiography," 7.

14. Smith, "Autobiography," 8.

Isaac, and Jacob, but Bathsheba confessed she "did not understand the import of that blessing so well then" as she did in later years.[15]

Brother Joseph gave them a small log house and a lot in Nauvoo. "My husband fixed up the place as best he could; but after all, it was the worst looking house we had yet lived in . . . however, [it] had the desirable qualities of neither leaking nor smoking."

Their first child, George Albert Smith Jr., was born July 7, 1842. Bathsheba wrote, "Words are feeble to express my joy."[16] Other blessings followed.

> We were blessed by receiving our endowments and were sealed under the holy order of the Celestial Marriage which order is for time and eternity and was revealed July 12, 1843.
>
> I heard the Prophet charge the Twelve with the duty and responsibility of administering the ordinances of endowments and of sealing both for the living and the dead.
>
> My husband and I met with Joseph and many others in a room dedicated for the purpose and prayed with them repeatedly.[17]

In the spring of 1844, with tensions at fever pitch in Nauvoo, George left to proselyte in Illinois and surrounding states. On June 27, 1844, a mob murdered the Prophet Joseph and his brother Hyrum, who were incarcerated in Carthage Jail. Bathsheba wrote to her husband:

> My Dear Husband I sit down this morning to let you know we are all well, and in as good spirits as could be expected considering all things. We have strange times since you left. You will no doubt hear before this reaches you,

---

15. Smith, "Autobiography," 9.

16. Smith, "Autobiography," 10.

17. Smith, "Autobiography," 11.

of the death of our beloved Breathren Joseph and Hirum Smith.

She described the return of the bodies, adding, "Such a day of mourning never was seen. It paines me to write such a painfull tale, but the Lord has comforted our harts in a mesure."[18] Years later, that day still haunted her: "I cannot think of it without experiencing again, those days of anguish and horror and mourning."[19]

Amidst the crisis of Joseph's death, and shortly after George's return, "a daughter was born to us and we gave her the name Bathsheba." In Nauvoo, Bathsheba wrote:

> The spirit of resentment gave way to mourning, from which the people emerged more hopeful and more determined that Truth should triumph. The Twelve, who were acknowledged as the presiding quorum of the whole church, immediately exercised all their influence to finish the Temple and the Nauvoo House in accordance with the Revelation of January 19, 1841.[20]

But violence against Church members continued. Some, burned out of their homes, fled to Nauvoo for shelter. The Smith house was "filled with refugees."[21] With every means available, George helped forward work on the temple, and in 1845, thousands received the endowment. Bathsheba remembered:

> I officiated for a time as priestess. Mr. Smith and I believed firmly in Joseph Smith as a Prophet of the Most

18. Bathsheba Smith to George A. Smith, July 6, 1844, in Kenneth W. Godfrey, Audrey M. Godfrey, and Jill Mulvay Derr, *Women's Voices: An Untold History of the Latter-day Saints, 1830–1900* (Salt Lake City, UT: Deseret Book, 1982), 131.

19. Smith, "Autobiography," 11–12.

20. Smith, "Autobiography," 12.

21. Smith, "Autobiography," 13.

High. We believed that he had sealed his testimony with his blood I became thoroughly convinced as well as my husband, that the doctrine of "plurality of wives" as taught by Joseph the Prophet, in our hearing, was a revelation from God and having a fixed determination to attain to Celestial Glory, I felt to embrace every principle, and that it was for my husband's exaltation that he should obey the revelation on Plural Marriage, in order to attain to kingdoms, thrones, principalities and powers, firmly believing that I should participate with him, in all his blessings, glory and honor.

In accordance with this purpose I had in the last year [in Nauvoo], like Sarah of old, given to my husband five wives—good, virtuous, honorable women who had gathered to Zion without their families.[22] Four of these women were considerably older than I and two of them older than my husband. They were all deeply religious. I was young, only twenty three years old and Mr. Smith but twenty eight, though I believe we were mature for our years, on account of experiences gained amid the perilous times through which we had already passed. I was proud of my husband and loved him, and knowing him to be upright in all things, a man of God, and believing that he would not love them less because he loved me more, I had joy in testimony that what I had done was acceptable to my Father in heaven.[23]

Bathsheba's departure from Nauvoo was but a footnote in the greater drama; the moment defined the faith that had sustained her through much travail:

On the 9th of February 1846 . . . my husband took

---

22. Lucy Meserve (1817–1892), Nancy Clements (1815–1847), Zilpha Stark (1818–1878), Sarah Ann Libby (1818–1851), Hannah Maria Libby (1828–1906), and Susan Elizabeth West (1833–1926). Jarvis, *Ancestry, Biography, and Family.*

23. Smith, "Autobiography," 13–14.

me and my boy of three and a half years and my little girl of one and a half years . . . and we crossed on the ice, the Mississippi River and turned our faces toward the wilderness in which we were to seek out an abiding place.

We left a comfortable home, the accumulations of four years of labor and thrift and took away with us only a few much needed articles such as clothing, bedding and provisions. We left everything else behind us for our enemies. My last act in that precious spot was to tidy the rooms, sweep up the floor and set the broom in its accustomed place behind the door. Then with emotions in my heart which I could not now pen and which I then strove with success to conceal, I gently closed the door and faced an unknown future, faced a new life, a greater destiny as I well know, but I faced it with faith in God and with no less assurance of the ultimate establishment of the Gospel in the West and of its true, enduring principles, than I had felt in those trying scenes in Missouri. I, a girl of sixteen, had at that time declared to the weeping saints, around the death-bed of David Patten, that God had established His church with the promise it would never be thrown down and I testified that though we might all of us be called to give up our lives, yet the Kingdom of God should stand and His people would be preserved. Now I was going into the wilderness, but I was going with the man I loved dearer than my life. I had my little children. I had heard a voice, so I stepped into the wagon with a certain degree of serenity.[24]

The refugees settled in what became known as Winter Quarters. George built four cabins and a dugout for his families. Because of scant food supplies, scurvy ravaged the makeshift settlement. The Smith family was not exempt. Bathsheba's mother, Susannah, age

24. Smith, "Autobiography," 14–16.

sixty-one, died March 11, 1847; Bathsheba's sister wife Nancy Clement and her young child also died that spring. In April, Bathsheba gave birth to a second son, John. Her record of his birth is brief and telling: "The child lived but four hours."[25] He was her last child and was buried next to Bathsheba's mother.

George rode in the first company to the Salt Lake Valley, led by Brigham Young. He returned to his families eight months later, delighted that "they had found a place in the heart of the Great Basin, beyond the Rocky Mountains so barren, dry, desolate and isolated," a perfect setting for the Saints to be alone.[26] Bathsheba recorded:

> June 20th, Wednesday [1849]. Winter Quarters is behind us. I have left the graveside of my dear mother and infant John at Winter Quarters and we now turn our faces toward Zion, in the valleys of the mountains.[27]

The Smith party consisted of four wagons. Bathsheba did her best to make the wagon a home with feather beds, pillows, quilts, cushioned chairs, carpets, and animal skin rugs. She even hung a looking glass. She recalled:

> At last, worn and weary, we reached Zion's gathering place. But ah! How thankful to have left far behind us our persecutors. To clasp the hand of dear and trusted friends, and sit down in a place of peace. These thoughts filled me with joy unspeakable.[28]

George put up walls for an adobe home, but the work was interrupted when he received a call in December 1850 to establish

---

25. Smith, "Autobiography," 18.

26. Smith, "Autobiography," 19.

27. Bathsheba W. Smith, "Day Book," June 20, 1849, Typescript, in "Bathsheba W. Smith Autobiography," ca. 1875–1906, p. 43, Church History Library.

28. Smith, "Autobiography," 28.

a settlement two hundred and fifty miles south. He took his wife Zilpha with him. Bathsheba described it as "the saddest day I had yet seen."[29]

Her home being unfinished, she and the children moved in with Father John Smith and, in addition to helping with the housekeeping, assisted him in recording patriarchal blessings. She worked hard to improve her situation:

> I saved religiously and my thrift brought results. Soon I had doors and windows in my house. On the 20th of March 1851, four months after Mr. Smith went away into Dixie, I moved into my own house. There were two fireplaces and a bake-oven, five twelve light windows. . . . it seemed almost a palace.[30]

At the April 1854 general conference, George was named Church Historian. The Smith family moved into the Historian's Office in Salt Lake City, which was a portion of a home set aside for that purpose until 1856, when a separate building was constructed across from Brigham Young's office.[31] George traveled extensively, going back and forth to southern Utah and settling Utah County, where he moved wives Lucy and Hannah. He served in the territorial legislature and led a delegation to Washington, D.C., as well as one abroad to the Holy Land.

In addition to her regular household routine, Bathsheba did carding, spinning, dying, weaving, and cutting and making of household articles and clothing. Her early training in Virginia made her particularly adept at such handwork. At her side were often her sister wives, visiting one another:

---

29. Smith, "Autobiography," 29.

30. Smith, "Autobiography," 29.

31. Howard C. Searle, "Historians, Church," in *Encyclopedia of Mormonism*, ed. David H. Ludlow, 4 vols. (New York: Macmillan, 1992), 2:590.

I have respect for my husband's wives. They have all
lived with me, if only for a short time. We have toiled and
suffered together, and have had joy in each other's society.
Our faith is the same, our anticipations are the same. I love
their children, from the little child to the grown up man
and woman. I rejoice with them in their prosperity and sorrow with them when they are overtaken by bereavements,
disappointments and trials of life.[32]

She too faced heartbreak. "I let my only son go to preach life
and salvation to [the Indians] and he lost his life." Although her
son was killed by some of the native people he was sent to teach,
Bathsheba testified in a Relief Society conference: "Nothing has
struck me more forcibly than the converting of the Indians. I have
great sympathy for them. . . . I believe [my son] is preaching to them
yet in the spirit world."[33] His remains—only three bones and a lock
of hair—were retrieved from a hastily dug shallow grave.

In October 1869, President Brigham Young named George A.
Smith as his first counselor, and Bathsheba found herself traveling
the territory and speaking to the Saints.[34]

The two spent several winters in St. George with President
Young. The warmer weather no doubt helped George, who suf-
fered from poor health. Returning to Salt Lake from St. George in
February 1875, he took cold after preaching in the evening.

He coughed badly all the way home [to Salt Lake] and
was much fatigued when arrived on the 19th. . . .
His cough racked him at night. I had nursed him and at
his request prayed for his recovery repeatedly though night

---

32. Smith, "Autobiography," 41.

33. Emmeline B. Wells, "A Beloved Mother in Israel," *Woman's Exponent* 31,
nos. 23–24 (May 1903): 90.

34. One listener observed that Bathsheba "is a believer in short speeches and
practises what she teaches." Wells, "Beloved Mother in Israel," 90.

or day. On April 24ᵗʰ we were greatly alarmed. President
Young telegraphed every station on May thirtieth to pray,
on the Sabbath following for his restoration. He rallied. His
family and friends now assisted me in caring for him. He
slept little and his suffering though at times severe, is endured with patience and fortitude.

On the last day of August, "he felt that his time had come." He
spoke to Bathsheba of what lay ahead.

> He was reconciled to die if the Lord so willed that he
> had no regrets for the past and nothing to dread in the fu-
> ture. The next morning we walked into the front parlor and
> he sank into a chair and expired. I could not think of my-
> self. I loved him more. He was now through; his head lay
> on my bosom; good angels had come to receive his precious
> spirit; perhaps our sons, prophets, patriarchs, saints beloved
> were there! But he was gone—my light, my sun, my life,
> yes, almost my God! But mine is not to mourn, but to pre-
> pare to meet him.[35]

In the years that followed, Bathsheba worked daily in the temple
and found great solace in that service. She acknowledged, "That
seems to be my calling."[36]

President Joseph F. Smith called Bathsheba as Relief Society
general president in November 1901. She succeeded her dear
friend Zina D. H. Young, to whom she had been a counselor since
1888. In a written address to the Relief Society on January 1, 1902,
Bathsheba set the course for a new century of Relief Society:

> With the dawn of this New Year's day, I send greetings
> to the noble band of Relief Society workers throughout the

---

35. Smith, "Autobiography," 42.
36. Wells, "Beloved Mother in Israel," 89.

world. Let us go forth at this hour with renewed resolutions to take up the work of relief and improvement with a strong purpose and with even more faith and love and unity than we have ever enjoyed.

Let forgiveness and charity be our bond.

Let love and cleanliness and order rule in every home that our children may not desire to leave the fireside for idle pleasures.

And, dear sisters, seek to bind your society with hoops of love and union.

Let not harsh words pass our lips nor yet any envious nor unkind thought enter our hearts. Read often First Corinthians, thirteenth chapter, that we may seek more ardently the spirit of charity. Be prayerful and seek earnestly to improve.

Be not carried away with vain social pleasures and the foolish fashions of the hour.

Make yourselves beautiful; be gentle and womanly.

The Prophet Joseph addressing the sisters at the first meeting (the organization of this society, March 17, 1842, Nauvoo, Ill.) said: "This society of sisters might provoke the brethren to good works in looking to the wants of the poor, searching after objects of charity, and in administering to their wants, and to assist by strengthening the virtues of the community." When I heard these words from the lips of the prophet, a little of the greatness of the work to be done by the Relief Society came before me, and I have never felt to shirk the duties devolving upon me either as a member or an officer of this association.

I feel that I have been blest in my labors while ministering to the sick and unfortunate and have experienced much joy in Relief Society work, and I feel to promise similar

blessings to those who lovingly and faithfully take up a part
of their labor of relief.

Peace be with you.

BATHSHEBA W. SMITH,
President of the Relief Society
in all the world.[37]

In her nine years as president, she implemented mothers'
classes to teach children "ideas of life, of right, of duty, of pleasure,
of usefulness."[38] She taught that a good Relief Society meeting is
"only a means and not the end of this work." She called for meetings to be "helpful, elevating, practical," designed to promote "order,
cleanliness, the virtues, spirituality, and uniting the home circle in
intelligence, love and harmony."[39] She raised funds for a Woman's
Building to be constructed near Temple Square, a dream which was
not realized until 1956.[40]

In 1903 she and her counselors encouraged the sisters to honor
the founding of the Relief Society and "make it a day of rejoicing
and of gratitude that the Lord inspired the Prophet Joseph."[41] She
declared:

---

37. Bathsheba W. Smith, "Greetings to Relief Society," *Woman's Exponent* 30,
no. 9 (January 1902): 67.

38. "General Instructions to the Relief Society," *Woman's Exponent* 31, nos.
15–16 (January 1903): 61.

39. Bathsheba W. Smith, "The Officers of the Relief Society," *Woman's Exponent*
35, no. 9 (May 1907): 68.

40. Property promised for a Woman's Building was used instead for a Bishop's
Building, which was completed in 1910 and included offices for the Relief Society,
Young Women, and Primary auxiliaries. The Relief Society Building across from
Temple Square was completed in 1956. Jill Mulvay Derr, Janath Russell Cannon,
and Maureen Ursenbach Beecher, *Women of Covenant: The Story of Relief Society*
(Salt Lake City, UT: Deseret Book; Provo, UT: Brigham Young University, 1992):
174–77, 467n76–77.

41. "The Seventeenth of March," *Woman's Exponent* 31, nos. 19–20 (March
1903): 76.

I want to see the young mothers and grandmothers join this Society and learn from the older ones. . . . It is the oldest Society organized by the Prophet Joseph, and what could be greater and nobler than trying to carry out his wishes?[42]

In one of her last missives to the sisters of Relief Society in 1910, just months before she suffered the stroke from which she never recovered, she wrote:

My heart is with you in these labors of love so diligently and faithfully fulfilled by our sisters of the Relief Society in localities where they reside. Would I could take each of you by the hand and converse with you. . . . In the vision of my mind I follow you as you go on your errands of mercy and charity and from my heart I bless you with the blessing of a mother in Israel; and I pray that your work may seem light and not burdensome, and the rich outpourings of the Holy Spirit may buoy you up when days seem dark, and life's pathways long and lonely.

I exhort you to keep the commandments of the Lord and teach by example as well as by precept, and never grow weary in well doing, pray without ceasing, uphold those who preside over you and remember the words of the Savior, "Inasmuch as ye have done it unto one of the least of these, ye have done it unto me," and now peace, joy and love be and abide with you always is my prayer for all those engaged in this glorious organization of the Relief Society.[43]

At the death of this "noble and queenly woman," the members of the general board of the Relief Society declared in resolution their

---

42. "General Relief Society Conference," *Woman's Exponent* 32, no. 5 (October 1903): 37.

43. "Greeting and Congratulations," *Woman's Exponent* 88, no. 6 (January 1910): 41.

"love and high esteem for her, whose life was our great example and whose death is our great sorrow." They proclaimed, "May her beautifully completed life be upheld as a beacon and inspiration to the generations yet to follow."[44]

44. "Resolutions of Respect in Honor of President Bathsheba W. Smith," *Woman's Exponent* 39, no. 3 (September 1910): 21.

Chapter 25

"'Tis No Easy Thing to Be a Saint"

Anstis Elmina Shepard Taylor (1830–1904)

Andrea G. Radke-Moss

Biographical Sketch

Anstis Elmina Shepard was born on September 12, 1830, in Middlefield, Otsego County, New York, the daughter of David Spaulding and Rozella Baily Shepard. Elmina (or Mina) was the eldest; she had two younger sisters, Ann and Hannah.[1] Her parents were devout members of the Methodist Episcopal Church, and Elmina was raised in that faith. At age twenty, Elmina officially joined the Methodists and "during some six years was a zealous and consistent member of the same."[2]

---

1. Elmina's parents lost their first child, Alfred, in infancy.

2. Augusta Joyce Crocheron, "Elmina S. Taylor," in *Representative Women of Deseret: A Book of Biographical Sketches to Accompany the Picture Bearing the Same Title* (Salt Lake City, UT: J. C. Graham & Co., 1884), 48. See also Susa Young Gates [Homespun, pseud.], "Our Picture Gallery: Biographical Sketcht [sic] of Mrs. Elmina S. Taylor, President of the YLMI Associations," *Young Woman's Journal* 2, no. 1 (October 1890): 3.

As a child, Elmina had been "spiritual minded," but still "numerous things perplexed her."[3] She had always desired baptism by immersion, considering it "the pattern set by our Savior," but she finally settled on "sprinkling." Even as a baptized Methodist, her doubts continued, for, she recalled, "there were many doctrines and tenets with which I never was satisfied, and when I went to my minister to have them explained I was more beclouded and found myself more in the dark than before; though I sought to the Lord earnestly to be guided aright."[4]

While employed as a schoolteacher, Elmina was introduced to The Church of Jesus Christ of Latter-day Saints and was baptized on July 5, 1856. Less than two months later, on August 31, 1856, Elmina married another local convert, George Hamilton Taylor. Within three years, they decided to move to Utah, following the overland trail in 1859 from Omaha to Salt Lake City, where they resided from then on.

George and Elmina started a successful lumber company in Salt Lake City. The Taylors had seven children, three of whom died in infancy or early childhood.[5] While raising her family, Elmina also served in numerous Church callings, including as secretary of the Salt Lake City Fourteenth Ward Relief Society and first counselor in the Salt Lake Stake Relief Society presidency. The culmination of her life's Church service, however, came in 1880, when she was called and sustained as the general president of the Young Ladies' Mutual Improvement Association, a position she held until her death on December 6, 1904.

---

3. Susa Young Gates, *History of the Young Ladies' Mutual Improvement Association* (Salt Lake City, UT: Deseret News Press, 1911), 91.

4. Crocheron, *Representative Women*, 48.

5. George Shepard Taylor (1860–1924), Frank David Shepard Taylor (1862–1914), Lydia Rosella Taylor (1864–1867), Elminnia Mae Taylor (1867–1867), Clarence Warren Taylor (1869–1930), Almira Mae Taylor Nystrom (1871–1959), and Eugene Shepard Taylor (1874–1874).

LIFE EXPERIENCES

Diploma in hand, Anstis Elmina Shepard became a school-teacher at age sixteen. In 1854, she took a teaching position in Haverstraw, New York, two hundred miles from home. In spite of frail health and a shy nature, Elmina demonstrated independence and eagerness to fill any responsibility.

Haverstraw proved a defining period for Elmina. There she became friends with Latter-day Saint elder John Druce and his family. "For a long time they never mentioned religion to us, fearing to frighten us away," wrote Elmina, "but one night, just as I was leaving, [John Druce] asked me if I would read some Mormon books. I answered, 'Oh, yes! You know the Bible says prove all things and hold fast that which is good.'"[6] Druce gave her some Church literature, which she "scanned with a prayerful heart, and a sincere desire that her mind be led aright."[7]

Her conversion came through thoughtful study, inquiry, prayer, and the gentle reassurances of the spirit. She recalled:

> Before opening the books I bowed before the Lord and fervently implored Him to give me His spirit that I might understand if they were true or false. My interest was awakened, and the more I investigated and compared the doctrines with the Scriptures, the more I was convinced of their truth. I fought against my convictions, for I well knew how it would grieve my dear parents to have me unite myself with that despised people; and I also thought I should lose my situation which was a very lucrative one. However, I could not silence my convictions, and as the promise was given, 'If you obey the doctrine, you shall know whether it is of God or man'; I went forth and was baptized July 5th 1856. When I was confirmed by the laying on of hands I

6. Crocheron, *Representative Women*, 49.

7. Gates, *History of the YLMIA,* 92.

received the testimony of its truth which I have never lost from that day to this.[8]

While in Haverstraw, she met George Hamilton Taylor, who had also joined the Church through his acquaintance with the Druces. George and Elmina were married on August 31, 1856, by apostle (later Church president) John Taylor.[9] Soon after their marriage, the couple returned to upstate New York to visit her grandparents, where they had another marriage ceremony. George later remembered, "However wrong it was from a religious stand point, our motives were good, as we wished to conciliate them, and take away some of the sting of our joining an unpopular people."[10]

Joining the Edward Stevenson Company in June 1859,[11] Elmina got her first real taste of the hardships of traveling to Zion while journeying from Quincy, Illinois, into Missouri. She noted in her diary, "I never spent such a Sabbath, as many as 2 or 3 hundred people came to look at us as though we had horns."[12] Leaving from

---

8. Crocheron, *Representative Women*, 49.

9. The circumstances of their courtship and betrothal are worth some description here. Impressed by Elmina's "vivacious disposition" and the fact that she was always able to "'hold her own' . . . in any company," George became "very much interested in her." However, he felt "timid . . . and so fearful of being refused, that when in the company of both [Elmina and her cousin Kate McLane]," he paid attention to Kate more than Elmina. "I did not act thus to deceive Miss McLane, but as a blind to cover my real feelings from Miss Shepard." When he finally proposed to Elmina, Kate felt that she had been deceived and "soon left Haverstraw. . . . George and Elmina never heard from her again." *Autobiography of George Hamilton Taylor* ([Salt Lake City, UT]: privately printed, 1949), 11–12.

10. *Autobiography of George Hamilton Taylor,* 15.

11. Elmina arrived in the Salt Lake Valley in late September 1859. "Edward Stevenson Company (1859)," Mormon Pioneer Overland Travel Database, 1847–68, The Church of Jesus Christ of Latter-day Saints, accessed July 3, 2012, http://mormontrail.lds.org.

12. Anstis Elmina Shepard Taylor, Diary, May 8, 1859, Holograph, Anstis Elmina Shepard Taylor Collection, 1844–1956, Church History Library, The

Winter Quarters in 1859, Elmina and George shared their ox-drawn covered wagon with "a young man who was mentally handicapped, an asthmatic English widow, a thirty-year old German woman who spoke no English, and an older single woman."[13] This combination was extremely trying for Elmina, who remembered the trip as a "long tedious journey."[14] Besides disagreements with traveling companions, Elmina experienced tensions with her own loving husband, mostly due to his sickness, or, as she described on June 22, 1859, "many things to trouble & annoy us."[15]

1859 Diary

Elmina's 1859 diary reveals much about the difficulties of bringing together people of significant differences into a community of Saints and also about her constant personal concern for becoming a more agreeable, Christian woman:

> May Saturday 14 Landed at Omaha City. A dazzling rain & obliged to remain out in it from seven till ten A.M. Held a meeting & enjoyed the spirit of God. I do not marvel that people call us a singular people, for we can rejoice even amid difficulties, dangers & trials. Went to the Seaman's, very worthy but poor people.

> May Sunday 15 'Tis no easy thing to be a saint. Walked some distance expecting to be taken to Florence; but no, we were obliged to remain till another team were sent for us. A most dismal, gloomy day! No one came for us & we must remain where we are.

Church of Jesus Christ of Latter-day Saints, Salt Lake City, Utah, hereafter cited as Church History Library.

13. Janet Peterson and LaRene Gaunt, *Keepers of the Flame: Presidents of the Young Women* (Salt Lake City, UT: Deseret Book, 1993), 7.

14. Crocheron, *Representative Women*, 49.

15. Taylor, Diary, June 22, 1859.

May Monday 16 Remained at Omaha until 12 P.M. then started for Florence. Several families in one house but I will endeavor to suit myself to circumstances & be as happy as I can.

May Tuesday 17 This morn had a few unpleasant words with Sister Barrows. 'Tis more than I can bear, to be intruded upon. Washed & exceedingly fatigued. Read a letter from Sister Billa to-day. She thinks me unkind to my best friends. I will endeavor to watch myself.

May Wednesday 18 Not well. Somewhat discouraged, but I know the Lord has blessed us & I believe He will. . . .

June Thursday 23 George more impatient & fretful to me than I ever saw him before, but I pray God to forgive him & help me to be patient, loving & kind. Moved out to Camp. Walked about 3 miles for the first: very much fatigued. . . .

July Friday 1 All passed off pleasantly till we camped & each & all seemed to have a good spirit, but when we reached camp & all too much fatigued to move, then each felt cross & ill-tempered & said words which never should have been spoken.

July Saturday 2 Sick in body & mind. If I were not so sensitive I might not feel unkind words as I now do, but I will endeavor not to use them to others. God help me to do right! Traveled 12 miles & then washed, baked &c &c. Tired but more calm in mind.[16]

The Taylors arrived in the Salt Lake Valley in September of 1859 and finally settled in the Fourteenth Ward to begin their family and a successful lumber enterprise. Soon after their arrival in Utah, they were rebaptized, received the endowment, and were

16. Taylor, Diary, May 14–18, June 23, July 1–2, 1859.

sealed by Brigham Young in the Endowment House.[17] George and Elmina had seven children, three of whom died young, leaving them to raise three boys and a girl to adulthood. After deciding twenty years earlier to accept the principle of plural marriage, they agreed to a second wife, and George married Louise (Louie) Foote in 1877. The long years between the Taylors' initial testimony of polygamy and the actual practice gave them time "to know it and be prepared for it." George admitted that "[w]e had rather polygamy were not a principle of our religion, yet we knew the principles we had embraced were true, and as that came from the same source we could not reject it."[18] In 1885, George married a third wife, Ella Susannah (Nellie) Colebrook, an English widow, and in 1886, he was jailed for about six months for practicing polygamy.[19]

Elmina ardently defended plural marriage as a true principle in both public and private. She was forty-seven years old when George married nineteen-year-old Louie but recorded, "We are like sisters . . . and there has never been the least unkind word or thought between us." Elmina described their family as having "all lived under the same roof, and eaten at the same table, ever in the enjoyment of peace and harmony."[20]

---

17. Peterson and Gaunt, *Keepers of the Flame*, 8. In the early days of the Church, members were often rebaptized as a symbol of rededication to the gospel. Paul H. Peterson, "Rebaptism," in *Encyclopedia of Latter-day Saint History*, ed. Arnold K. Garr, Donald Q. Cannon, and Richard O. Cowan (Salt Lake City, UT: Deseret Book, 2000), 984–85. Before temples were completed, other buildings were dedicated for the administration of temple ordinances. In Salt Lake City, one such building was the Endowment House, which was in operation from 1855 to 1889. LaMar C. Berrett, "Endowment Houses," in *Encyclopedia of Mormonism*, ed. Daniel H. Ludlow, 4 vols. (New York: Macmillan, 1992), 2:456.

18. *Autobiography of George Hamilton Taylor*, 13–14.

19. Peterson and Gaunt, *Keepers of the Flame*, 10.

20. Crocheron, "Elmina S. Taylor," in *Representative Women*, 50; Gates, "Our Picture Gallery," 4.

Notwithstanding her testimony, Elmina did not shy away from some frank observations about plural marriage. Once, after taking tea at "Br Sharp's sec[ond] wife's," Elmina called her "the only intelligent wife he has. Very pleasant."[21] And following one riding excursion with "Sr. George A. Smith" [Bathsheba W. Smith], Elmina shared part of the conversation between the two first wives: "She does not think that a first wife must learn to not love her husband before she can be happy in plurality. You know that is what Sr. [Phebe Carter] Woodruff tried to teach me."[22]

Plural marriage appears to have done little to lessen George's and Elmina's own marital affections and mutual love. In 1878, George was called on a three-year mission to England, and Elmina stayed home to care for their four children, her own father and sister, and George's second wife, Louie, along with Louie's new baby. She managed George's business while also fulfilling multiple Church callings and continuing to endure chronic physical pain. During those years, Elmina and George exchanged tender and affectionate letters, and Elmina used her diary as a kind of long letter to her absent husband, revealing an intimacy that had endured the trials of pioneer life, long separations, and plural marriage.

1879 Diary

(1879) July 4 . . . After dinner I went to bed & thought to sleep a part of the time away. I dreamed that you had come & I was cuddling close by your side with my hand clasped in yours & I felt very happy, but the waking was desolate. Geo [oldest son] has not enjoyed his 4th. In the evening he took me & the little ones riding. Saw fire works in every direction. . . . Geo said you need not think every one as dull as we are. I says no 'Tis not every body that hasn't got a father.

---

21. Taylor, Diary, July 31, 1879.

22. Taylor, Diary, August 6, 1879. The marriage of first wife Bathsheba W. Smith to George A. Smith was well known for its loving and affectionate character.

A good ending to the day for we received your unexpected letter, a good idea but it will be a long time before we get the next.[23]

Child-rearing, domesticity, and elder care dominated most of Elmina's energies in the 1860s and 1870s. But she also found time for dedicated and time-consuming Church service, usually in simultaneous callings. A selection of Elmina's 1879 diary entries from that summer reveals not only her tireless occupation for the work but a bit of foreshadowing of service soon to come as the president of the Young Ladies' Mutual Improvement Association:

> 30th [June]. Visited at Sr. Haywood's in company with Sr. E. R. Snow, M. Hyde, S. M. Kimball, M. Horne & others. Most pleasant. Sr. Snow clasped me in her arms & said she always felt like blessing me all over because I am such a faithful worker in the kingdom. I fear I do not merit it but will strive to in the future.
>
> 19th July. Attended Meeting. Altho very warm, yet had a very excellent meeting. Speaking in tongues & interpretation.
>
> Sat. 16th [August] Attended 14th Ward Meeting. Srs Horne & Kimball present, who gave a very interesting account of their northern trip. An excellent spirit prevailed. It can truly be said that the women of Zion are alive to the work in which they are engaged.[24]

Elmina's interactions with women in leadership positions afforded her the opportunity of inclusion in the upper crust of Salt Lake society. After attending a meeting of the Fourteenth Ward Relief Society, she confessed—with almost schoolgirl-like excitement—her pleasure at having friends of high status:

---

23. Taylor, Diary, July 4, 1879.

24. Taylor, Diary, June 30, July 19, August 16, 1879.

Aug. 30th. Sewed, baked &c. Attended 14th Ward Meeting. Good instructions & spirit there. Sr Snow who has not been with us of late, was present & occupied some time. Srs Minerva Snow & Sr Ivins of St. George were also there. After meeting was dismissed Sr S. M. Kimball invited Srs Miner Snow & Ivins to go home with her and said I wish all you good sisters to go too. Sr. Eliza says [come] along, for I wish to be included in that crowd, so several of us went. Sr. Eliza, Sr. Horne, B. Smith, R. Grant, Minerva Snow & Sr Ivins. Br. Snow's son (half brother to your Moroni brought me home, so you see if you are getting to like the company of the dignitaries; I too am associating on warm terms with prophets & apostles wives & sons.[25]

In 1880, Elmina experienced a turning point in her Church service when she was called to be the first general president of the Young Ladies' Mutual Improvement Association. Following a conference of women called by President John Taylor for organizing the women of the Church into three auxiliaries (Relief Society, YLMIA, and Primary), a group of women met at Bathsheba W. Smith's home for noon dinner. During the mealtime discussion, Eliza R. Snow looked at Elmina and said, "Well, Sister Taylor, have you chosen your counselors?" Caught in surprise, Elmina replied: "For what?" Sister Snow declared, "We have decided to make you president of the Mutual Improvement Associations in all the Church."

"I shall not act," retorted the woman who had shrunk from publicity all her life. "I cannot act in that capacity." However, with the wise arguments that always convince a Saint who desires to be one, Sister Taylor's scruples were overcome, and she was voted in at the afternoon meeting.[26]

---

25. Taylor, Diary, August 30, 1879.

26. Gates, *History of the YLMIA*, 85–86. Eliza R. Snow was sustained as the second general Relief Society president and Louie B. Felt as the first general president of the Primary on the same day.

As the first general president of the YLMIA, Elmina brought limited experience at visiting and attending meetings, but she was thrown in at the deep end without any resources necessary for meeting the needs of thousands of young women.[27] Together with her counselors, Elmina built a program from scratch that included a YLMIA general board, extensive travel to attend stake conferences and visit youth throughout the Church, correspondence with stake and ward YLMIA leaders, and other administrative responsibilities.[28] During the first ten years, Elmina managed "between three and four hundred visits . . . traveling thousands of miles, mostly by team; and visiting some of the nearby stakes two or three times a year in addition to the regular scheduled visits."[29]

What the YLMIA still lacked was its own publication, a central and unifying periodical whereby the board could communicate efficiently with young women and their leaders throughout all the Latter-day Saint settlements. To that end, Susa Young Gates, daughter of Brigham Young, felt inspired to start a monthly magazine for the YLMIA as an important venue for conveying gospel and secular teaching, homegrown poetry, literature, and news. Susa received immediate encouragement from the First Presidency and Elmina and her counselors to create the *Young Woman's Journal,* published between 1889 and 1929.[30]

---

27. Elmina also benefited from supportive and energetic counselors—her longtime friend Margaret Y. (Maggie) Taylor, wife of President John Taylor, and Martha Horne (later Tingey), the daughter of her friend and ward Relief Society president Mary Isabella Horne. Gates, *History of the YLMIA,* 86, 88; Peterson and Gaunt, *Keepers of the Flame,* 12. Maggie Taylor resigned in 1887 after the death of her husband and was succeeded by Maria Y. Dougall, one of Brigham Young's daughters and counselor in the first Young Ladies' Cooperative Retrenchment Association in 1870.

28. Gates, *History of the YLMIA,* 87–88; Peterson and Gaunt, *Keepers of the Flame,* 12–13.

29. Gates, *History of the YLMIA,* 87–88.

30. Petrea Kelley, "Young Woman's Journal," in *Encyclopedia of Mormonism,*

Although off to a shaky financial and editorial start, the *Young Woman's Journal* persisted in fits and starts through the 1890s. From the very beginning, Elmina was a hands-on participant in the publishing process, which inevitably led to clashes at times with Susa's forceful editorial style. True to form, however, Elmina managed to moderate both women's strong wills with her own patient, soft touch. After one particular misunderstanding, Elmina wrote to Susa:

> Now, although I was much wounded by the contents and the spirit of the letter you sent me, I hold no hard feelings against you, for I fully realize that your feelings have been very much tried, and under excitement or great pressure we often say and do things which we would not under other circumstances. Let it pass.[31]

The correspondence between Elmina and Susa reveals much about the intensity of work required to publish a monthly magazine and represent the YLMIA in the national arena while also trying to balance that work with their private lives, including addressing health problems and maintaining personal relationships.

Two 1895 Letters

S.L.C. 1-1-95
Mrs. Susa Y. Gates.
My Dear Friend:—

Permit me to wish you a Happy New Year, and may the year that is just ushered in be filled with more of joy, peace and happiness than any of its predecessors have been, and

---

ed. Daniel H. Ludlow, 4 vols. (New York: Macmillan, 1992), 4:1615–16; Lisa Olsen Tait, "The *Young Woman's Journal* and Its Stories: Gender and Generations in 1890s Mormondom" (PhD diss., University of Houston, 2010).

31. Elmina S. Taylor to Susa Young Gates, December 18, 1891, Holograph, Susa Amelia Young Gates Papers, ca. 1870–1933, Church History Library.

may our power for good and usefulness be increased, as day by day rolls on, is my prayer for you.

I have not heard how you are progressing, but I do hope you are quite well & strong again!

Next Monday, at 2 P.M. the General Board hold their usual monthly meeting at my house, and I would be much pleased, if you have anything prepared for the [National] Council [of Women][32] if you would forward it to me by that time, as we would like to look over and discuss all papers which are to be read there. . . .

I was at the Juvenile Office yesterday and tried to see Br. [Abraham H.] Cannon in regard to issuing our Journal on time, but did not see him. I am receiving letters frequently, inquiring what is the matter with our Journal & I have not received either No 2 or 3. Of course they are out now, but late.

They informed me that they had not sufficient copy for the Jan. No. Please send on some if you have it. It is now late, and I will close.

Lovingly yours,
ELMINA S. TAYLOR

Salt Lake City, Jan. 27th/ 95
Mrs. Susa Y. Gates;—

Dear Susa:

Your package was duly delivered this morning. I have been out in the snow storm all the afternoon, and now at

32. Elmina represented the YLMIA at the second triennial meeting of the National Council of Women, an organization that served as a central umbrella to unite women's associations throughout the United States. The Council convened in Washington, D.C., from February 12 through March 2, 1895. A number of Utah women, including Elmina, presented papers at the convention. "The National Council of Women," *Woman's Exponent* 23, no. 13 (January 1 and 15, 1895): 228; "The National Council," *Woman's Exponent* 23, no. 17 (April 1, 1895): 244.

9 p.m. have taken my pen to trace a few lines to you. You ask about Monday. We had a pleasant meeting, but the papers were not ready. . . .

I think you need have no fear that they will not be alike.

Dear Susa, the article you wrote for me does not entirely fill the bill but I cannot tell how to improve it. Oh, dear me! How I wish I was smart and could write. Last night I laid awake most of the time worrying. Oh, Susa dear! How I do wish you could go in my place [to the triennial session of the National Council of Women], since you seem to have such a desire. If it were left to me I would step aside for that purpose, and I know you would enjoy it more than I will, and reap greater benefit from it too. How I wish we had the funds to take and give to you for that object. You have earned it over and over again, at our hands, but still we have it not. Speed the time when the Journal will be a source of revinue to its editor! Yet, even if you had the money I fear the trip would be too much for you at this time.

Mrs. [Rachel Foster] Avery has sent the same request to every one in both organizations [Relief Society and YLMIA] who are down on the program for paper or speech.

I return to you the paper in regard to suffrage. It is not thought best to agitate the subject much at the present time. Especially would it be very unwise to publish anything in our Journal. I have consulted others on the subject, and this is the decision.[33]

Will you be able to come up to our monthly meeting, the first Monday in Feb.? We shall be very pleased with your

---

33. While Latter-day Saint women leaders were mostly staunch supporters of woman suffrage, Elmina is here demonstrating some caution on the subject. In 1895, Utah applied for statehood, and some feared that a strong call for woman suffrage might jeopardize Utah's chances for congressional acceptance of its bid. As it turned out, Utah gained statehood in 1896 with a constitution that included full suffrage for women.

presence. Sr. Wells and company expect to leave for Atlanta [to the National American Woman Suffrage convention] on the 21st inst^{34} We will go on the [1]0th or 11th I presume.

Good night, and may God bless us all, and fully prepare us for all that lies before us.

Yours most sincerely.
ELMINA S. TAYLOR.

P.S. I take pleasure in informing you that the Young Woman's Journal is out. And I have received the first form of the Feb. No.

E.S.T.

In addition to the successful launching of the *Young Woman's Journal,* Elmina's YLMIA leadership achieved other significant milestones, laying important foundations for future Church youth programs. In 1890, Elmina held the first Churchwide conference for young women and, six years later, the first joint YLMIA and YMMIA (Young Men's Mutual Improvement Association) conference in 1896. During Elmina's tenure, weekly Young Ladies' meetings were formalized, and official class curriculum was created beginning in 1893.[35]

Elmina was not an ardent and vocal feminist like some of her Relief Society and YLMIA contemporaries. Instead, she advocated young women's advancement through secular and religious education, self-improvement, and righteous living.[36] She preached that "it

---

34. The National American Woman Suffrage convention was held in Atlanta, Georgia, from January 31 to February 5, 1895. Delegates representing the Utah Woman Suffrage Association included Marilla Daniels, Aurelia S. Rogers, and association president Emmeline B. Wells.

35. For a summary of Elmina's achievements as YLMIA president, see Peterson and Gaunt, *Keepers of the Flame,* 13–16.

36. In a letter dated May 5, 1902, the president of Latter-day Saints' University asked for the YLMIA board's support in a domestic economy training course, noting the "interest which the M.I.A. general board and aides have always taken in

is not the outward appearance but the forces which gather within the soul that go to develop the individual." Elmina hoped to "cultivate every gift and grace of true womanhood. . . . To this end every effort is made to induce independent thought, study, individuality and progress."[37]

In 1891 the YLMIA was accepted, together with the Relief Society, as a member organization of the National Council of Women (NCW) and, soon after, the International Council of Women (ICW). Elmina became an "ex-officio vice president of the organization."[38] This was a beneficial association that allowed Latter-day Saint women opportunities to overturn negative stereotypes held by their non-Mormon contemporaries. It also provided the YLMIA engagement in some of the most important issues of the day for women, including woman suffrage and the international peace movement. Throughout these years, Elmina maintained correspondence with the likes of Susan B. Anthony (president of the National Woman Suffrage Association), Rachel Foster Avery (founder of the ICW and secretary of the NWSA), and May Wright Sewall (president of the ICW). Fully appreciative of Latter-day Saint women's contributions to the work of the ICW, Sewall complimented Elmina on YLMIA involvement in peace demonstrations, stating, "I have an almost unlimited admiration for the zeal and the executive energy of your association."[39]

Besides attending numerous meetings of the National Council of Women and International Council of Women throughout the

---

these matters." In 1898 Elmina's general board created a traveling lending library to promote literacy for young women in outlying areas. Linda Thatcher, "The Traveling Library in Utah," *Utah Libraries* (1987): 4, 6–7.

37. "Report of the Young Ladies' Mutual Improvement Associations of Utah," *Young Woman's Journal* 2 (May 1891): 383.

38. Gates, *History of YLMIA*, 93.

39. May Wright Sewall to Elmina Taylor, December 2, 1901, Holograph, Anstis Elmina Shepard Taylor Collection, 1844–1956, Church History Library.

1890s, perhaps Elmina's most important appearance at a national meeting came at the World's Congress of Representative Women, held in conjunction with the Chicago World's Columbian Exposition in 1893. Elmina received authority from the First Presidency to "preach, teach, and expound the Scriptures and the doctrines of the Church of Jesus Christ of Latter-day Saints," officially representing the Church as she was "brought into association with preachers of other denominations and especially with those of her own sex."[40] Despite her sometimes debilitating fear of speaking in front of crowds, Elmina presided and spoke at the well-attended YLMIA conference session.[41] The World's Congress offered an unprecedented opportunity for Elmina and her counselors to share Latter-day Saint ideals taught to young women on politics, education, and motherhood, while also strengthening their relations with other national women leaders.

Elmina Taylor served as president of the YLMIA until her death on December 6, 1904. During her tenure, the organization became foundationally solid and "admirably martialed," with a vibrant publication and flourishing membership; its "power for good was acknowledged as paramount in Israel."[42] Never resting on the laurels of her long years of service, Elmina sought others' advice right up to the end. When pressed about introducing new "Mother's lectures" into the YLMIA testimony meetings, Sister Taylor humbly deferred: "My reply—Must consult with my counselors."[43]

---

40. Wilford Woodruff, George Q. Cannon, and Joseph F. Smith to "To Whom It May Concern," May 8, 1893, Holograph, Anstis Elmina Shepard Taylor Collection, Church History Library.

41. World's Congress of Representative Women, "Department Congress of the Young Ladies' National Mutual Improvement Association: Program of Exercises," May 19, 1893, Anstis Elmina Shepard Taylor Collection, Church History Library.

42. Gates, *History of YLMIA*, 94. From 1890 to 1900, YLMIA membership increased from 8,000 to 20,575 members in the United States, Canada, Mexico, England, New Zealand, and Hawaii. Peterson and Gaunt, *Keepers of the Flame*, 15.

43. Taylor, Diary, October 21, 1904.

Just before her death at age seventy-four, Elmina completed a diary that showed in many ways how she had come full circle through her life's work as a loving wife, mother, grandmother, and friend; as a tireless and humble leader of LDS young women; and as someone who still sought to achieve a peaceful, Christlike life. She was remembered for her "unselfish devotion, her zealous labors, her sweet disposition, and her tender solicitude in [young women's] behalf." Few women could have achieved what she did "in organizing, in cementing a strong sisterhood, and in training the young women of Israel."[44] But perhaps the greatest valedictory is the one she gave herself on her last birthday:

> My 74th birth-day. It does not seem possible that I have lived so many years. I have endeavored to make a good record and my Heavenly Father has been very kind to me. May my record always be as good.[45]

---

44. "Death of Elmina S. Taylor," *Improvement Era* 8, no. 3 (1905): 219.

45. Taylor, Diary, September 12, 1904.

Chapter 26

"I Believe in Women,
Especially Thinking Women"

Emmeline Blanche Woodward Wells (1828–1921)
Carol Cornwall Madsen and Cherry B. Silver

Biographical Sketch

Emmeline Blanche Woodward was born in Petersham, Worcester County, Massachusetts, on February 29, 1828, auguring an exceptional life for the seventh child and fifth daughter of David and Diadama Hare Woodward. She was privileged to attend school until the age of fourteen and then followed her mother and three younger siblings into The Church of Jesus Christ of Latter-day Saints. A year later she married James Harris and moved with him and his parents to Nauvoo, Illinois, where she met Joseph Smith shortly before his death. She never forgot the experience and drew on it often when she became one of the last people alive to have known him.

After Joseph's martyrdom in 1844, the elder Harrises left the Church, Emmeline's newborn son died, and husband James left

---

"I believe in Women, especially thinking women" is from Emmeline B. Wells [Blanche Beechwood, pseud.], "Why, Ah! Why," *Woman's Exponent* 3 (September 30, 1874): 67.

Nauvoo to find work and never returned. In 1845 Emmeline became a plural wife of Newel K. Whitney, with whom she had two daughters, and traveled with the Whitney family to Utah in 1848. She became an enduring friend of Newel's wife Elizabeth Ann Whitney, who gave Emmeline her great love of Relief Society. After Newel K. Whitney's unexpected death in 1850, Emmeline taught school to support herself and her two daughters, and in 1852 she became the seventh wife of Daniel H. Wells, with whom she had three more daughters.[1]

An ambitious writer from childhood, in 1872 she became a frequent contributor to the newly established Latter-day Saint women's newspaper, the *Woman's Exponent,* which she edited from 1877 to 1914. Besides her editorials, she contributed poems, articles, and short stories, eventually publishing a volume of her poetry, *Musings and Memories,* in 1896. It was reissued in 1915.

Active in public life, Emmeline became a leader in the female suffrage movement and led the Utah Woman Suffrage Association's successful effort to include women's suffrage in the Utah state constitution in 1895. She also led the Relief Society into membership in the National and International Councils of Women and became friends with Susan B. Anthony, Elizabeth Cady Stanton, and many other national women's leaders. In defending the women of her church in Washington, D.C., Emmeline met many senators and congressmen and visited with three United States presidents.

In 1877, when she became editor of the *Woman's Exponent,* Brigham Young asked her to lead a grain-saving mission for the Church. Using the network of Relief Society sisters, Emmeline ignited the interest of women in this project through the *Exponent,* and the project became one of the charitable causes of the Relief

---

1. Emmeline's children were Eugene Henri Harris (1844–1844), Isabel Modalena Whitney Sears (1848–1941), Melvina Caroline Blanch Whitney Dunford Woods (1850–1940), Emma Whitney Wells (1853–1878), Elizabeth Ann "Annie" Wells Cannon (1859–1942), and Louise Martha "Louie" Wells Cannon (1862–1887).

Society.[2] For twenty years, Emeline was general secretary of the Relief Society, serving under Eliza R. Snow, Zina D. H. Young, and Bathsheba W. Smith. Emmeline became general president of the Relief Society in 1910 at the age of eighty-two and presided for eleven years until shortly before her death in 1921.

She was highly honored in her later years, her birthdays marked by public celebrations drawing hundreds of people. She received an honorary doctorate of literature degree from Brigham Young University in 1912 and was privileged to unveil the Seagull Monument on Temple Square the following year. At her death on April 25, 1921, flags on Church buildings were hung at half-mast, and she was honored with a funeral in the Tabernacle, where she was remembered as "one of the finest products of Mormonism."[3] On the centenary of her birth, the women of Utah memorialized her contributions to the advancement of women by commissioning a bust of her, sculpted by Cyrus Dallin, which was placed in the rotunda of the state capitol. It reads profoundly but simply, "A Fine Soul Who Served Us," a fitting tribute to a woman who dedicated her life to serving women and her Church.

LIFE EXPERIENCES
Autobiographical Writings in the Woman's Exponent

Emmeline Wells employed several literary forms—articles, short stories, poetry, and fiction—to write her life experiences, often under the name "Aunt Em." Most of these autobiographical writings were based on her New England childhood. Besides many reminiscences published in the *Woman's Exponent*, Emmeline also wrote a twenty-eight-chapter autobiographical novel entitled "Hephzibah,"

---

2. Emmeline B. Wells, "Sisters Be in Earnest," *Woman's Exponent* 5 (October 15, 1876): 76.

3. Charles W. Nibley, in Amy Brown Lyman, "Funeral Services of President Emmeline B. Wells," *Relief Society Magazine* 8, no. 6 (June 1921): 358.

serialized between 1889 and 1890 in the *Exponent*. In it, Emmeline narrated her own baptism through the heroine Hepsie:

> Two powers were warring with her, one said "Obey your mother, go down into the waters of baptism in the little brook that always seemed a sanctuary," the other said "do not heed the sayings of your mother or the Elders, a brilliant future awaits you, you must not make this sacrifice." This and much more the tempter whispered in her ear. When the time came she went with the others who had gathered at Mrs. H's down the hill to the edge of the water or ice, and as she stood there all the time the same subtle powers were striving with her. Two or three of the chief men of the village came and spoke to her "Are you doing this of your own free-will and choice?" she only replied in monysyllables and heeded not the crowd, the wind blew fierce and whistled down through the hemlock grove above a sort of chant, it soothed her, she felt the sympathy it brought, it was like a strain of rare old music, and it gave her fresh courage, seven had already been immersed and her name was called, some one took hold of her arm—it was one she had known and reverenced, one who had been specially kind to her, the father of her dear friend and champion, Jane—the most influential man in the County—"Hepsie he said come away you are but a child, you must not make this great sacrifice"—the sentence was unfinished,—Hepsie saw the Elder standing in the icy stream waiting for her—she went towards him it was but a step—her heart gave a great sob—the words were pronounced with great solemnity, in a moment it was over,— the crowd dispersed, and the little band of men and women had gone up one after another when the ordinance had been performed, to the house to change clothing. Hepsie was the last—and silently she returned to the house and was soon ready seated with the others for confirmation. It had been

an exciting time, Hepsie's mother, cool and collected as she had always seemed, had been very nervous, lest at the last moment Hepsie should waver and refuse as some others had done after having come prepared to go into the water. Hepsie did not at all comprehend the situation, she had no conception of the obstacles that would beset her path more and more from this time forward.[4]

Nauvoo and Joseph Smith

After she was baptized, Emmeline joined the Saints in Nauvoo, where she first saw the Prophet Joseph Smith greeting new arrivals at the dock. She continued to bear witness of his influence throughout her life.

As we stepped ashore the crowd advanced, and I could see one person who towered away and above all the others around him; in fact I did not see distinctly any others. His majestic bearing, so entirely different from any one I had ever seen (and I had seen many superior men) was more than a surprise. It was as if I beheld a vision; I seemed to be lifted off my feet, to be as it were walking in the air, and paying no heed whatever to those around me. I made my way through the crowd, then I saw this man whom I had noticed, because of his lofty appearance, shaking hands with all the people, men, women and children. Before I was aware of it he came to me, and when he took my hand, I was simply electrified,—thrilled through and through to the tips of my fingers, and every part of my body, as if some magic elixir had given me new life and vitality. I am sure that for a few minutes I was not conscious of motion. I

---

4. Emmeline B. Wells, "Hephzibah XIV," *Woman's Exponent* 18 (February 1, 1890): 132.

think I stood still, I did not want to speak, or be spoke to. I was overwhelmed with indefinable emotion. . . .

. . . The one thought that filled my soul was, I have seen the Prophet of God, he has taken me by the hand, and this testimony has never left me in all the "perils by the way." It is as vivid today as ever it was. For many years, I felt it too sacred an experience even to mention. . . .

I heard him preach all his last sermons, and frequently met him and shook hands with him, and always felt in my inmost soul, he is indeed a man unlike all others.

In the Prophet Joseph Smith, I believed I recognized the great spiritual power that brought joy and comfort to the Saints. . . . He was beyond my comprehension. The power of God rested upon him to such a degree that on many occasions he seemed transfigured. His expression was mild and almost childlike in repose; and when addressing the people, who loved him it seemed to adoration, the glory of his countenance was beyond description. At other times the great power of his manner, more than of his voice (which was sublimely eloquent to me) seemed to shake the place on which we stood and penetrate the inmost soul of his hearers, and I am sure that then they would have laid down their lives to defend him. I always listened spellbound to his every utterance—the chosen of God in this last dispensation.[5]

Relief Society

From Nauvoo, Emmeline trekked with others to Winter Quarters and on to the Salt Lake Valley. Through writing and public speaking, Emmeline became an advocate for the capabilities of Latter-day Saint women:

5. Emmeline Blanche Wells, "Joseph Smith, the Prophet," *Young Woman's Journal* 16 (December 1905): 555–56.

The organization of the Relief Society in Nauvoo, Ill., in March, 1842, opened perhaps one of the most important eras in the history of woman. It presented the great woman-question to the Latter-day Saints, previous to the woman's rights organizations, which have created such extensive agitation of the subject since, in America, Great Britain, and Europe. The question did not present itself in any aggressive form as woman opposed to man, but as a co-worker and helpmeet in all that relates to the well-being and advancement of both, and mutual promoting of the best interests of the community at large. It has given to woman, in its rise and progress, influence on almost all subjects that pertain to her welfare and happiness, and opportunities for expressing her own thoughts, views and opinions; all of which has had a tendency to make her intelligent in regard to matters which before were considered incompatible with "woman's sphere," and unintelligible to her "weaker" mind.

Through these organizations an immense work has been done in developing the faculties and capabilities of woman, that never could have been effected except through some permanent organization, or association, for mutual help, benefit, and interchange of ideas.

The developments and progression made since the commencement of these [Relief] societies, which exist now throughout the extent of the settlements of the Latter-day Saints, was not dreamed of in the beginning. They are educational in the most general sense; all subjects, religious, moral and mental, in their various bearings, are discussed, and instruction is given on all matters pertaining to life, health and happiness. One of the strongest features of this remarkable organization is the cultivation of the gift of faith. That great power has been manifested under the hands of sisters in administering to the sick is a fact to which many can testify; and is not this one positive proof that the Lord recognizes them and approves of their labors in this direction? Is there anything more heavenly than to give comfort and relief to the sick and distressed? We think not.[6]

Education for Women

Given the need to financially support herself most of her life, Emmeline championed the wisdom of education for her daughters and other young women:

> Objectors to equal opportunities for education of the sexes, and to woman's suffrage argue that woman's delicacy will be soiled by studying in the same classes with men; and that she will come in contact with rough men at the polls; yet their wives, daughters and sisters may go to balls and parties with neck and arms bare, and waltz and polka with men, and they seldom think it indelicate, because, forsooth, it is the fashion, and custom has made it popular; and the newspapers will speak of the fascinating Miss, or Mrs. So and So, and her elaborate costume, while it denounces in strongest terms and holds up to ridicule noble-minded women, who are laboring heart and soul for the elevation of their sex, and the good of humanity.
>
> Men will be men, and women will maintain their identity "While life and thought and being last, or immortality endures," there need be no fear on that score. Men are not usually frightened to let women carry about great bundles of sewing, for which, in many large cities, women only earn a bare pittance, scarcely enough to keep the wolf from the door—that is womanly work; but let her dare talk about voting, or securing equal wages with men for the same

6. [Emmeline B. Wells], "Women's Organizations," *Woman's Exponent* 8 (January 15, 1880): 122; Jonathan A. Stapley and Kristine Wright, "Female Ritual Healing in Mormonism," *Journal of Mormon History* 37, no. 1 (Winter 2011): 1–85.

amount of work faithfully executed, and she must expect to be cried down as lacking in womanliness, or propriety.

Women should be themselves in all that the word implies, but they should have every avenue for learning open to them, that they may have a better and more practical knowledge of the conditions of life. Every mother should become intelligently acquainted with her own physical and mental nature, her life-powers, her nerve forces, before she takes upon herself the sacred obligations of motherhood, and identifies herself with a new life. Enlightened motherhood is one essential element wanted to lay the foundation for a purer and better race of people.[7]

Congress and the President

In 1879, Emmeline B. Wells and Zina Young Williams represented Utah at the meetings of the National Woman Suffrage Association in Washington, D.C., where they lobbied congressmen and even the president of the United States, Rutherford B. Hayes, for repeal of antipolygamy laws. Emmeline recounted:

> We cannot tell you now just how we managed to see everybody we wanted to see, and say what we wanted to say, but we will pass on to the White House (at some future time we will tell you about the receptions) and our interview with President Hayes. His Excellency made the appointment himself, and after we had given him a few facts in relation to the condition of this people, and what was likely to be the consequences of severe and harsh measures, he remarked that he had never before considered the subject in the light we had presented it, and he felt it was of too much importance to trust to memory, and desired us to make a similar

---

7. [Emmeline B. Wells], "Womanliness," *Woman's Exponent* 8 (December 1, 1879): 100.

statement in writing, which we prepared and placed in His Excellency's hands before leaving Washington. We also had the pleasure of a private interview with Mrs. Hayes. . . . To our party she was kindness personified; she listened attentively to all we had to say in regard to the circumstances of our people, and her womanly sympathies were very perceptibly aroused.[8]

Despite his show of sympathy, President Hayes later in the year called for stringent enforcement of antipolygamy laws against the people of Utah. Emmeline expressed shock and betrayal in her editorial of December 1879:

We do not believe him to be hard-hearted, or unfeeling, but the continual howlings of those who are seeking to destroy the peace and prosperity of the Latter-day Saints has had its effect upon the rulers of the country. We earnestly and solemnly beseeched him, as the Chief Executive of this great nation, and the father of its people, to consider well the nature of the persecution aroused against this people by

---

8. [Emmeline B. Wells], "Visit to Washington," *Woman's Exponent* 7 (February 15, 1879): 194. Female journalists observed the efforts of Emmeline and Zina: "They were both of them women of culture, well dressed and well appearing. Mrs. Wells was a lady of perhaps fifty, with a pleasing, intellectual face. Mrs. Williams was young and very good looking. They were both Mormons, apparently from devout, religious belief, and . . . have presented their views with force and clearness." Lillie Devereux Blake, "The Women of Utah. Mrs. Blake's Analysis of Their Plea for Polygamy," *[New York] Evening Telegram*, February 11, 1879. Reprinted in *Woman's Exponent* 7 (March 15, 1879): 212.

"But the beauty of the interview to me was when the two Mormon ladies laid their case before the President and he showed such kindly sympathy with them when they proved what misery would follow in Utah the enforcement of the act of 1862 against polygamy." Augustine Snead [Miss Grundy, pseud.], "Mormon Ladies Calling at the White House," *Philadelphia Times,* January 19, 1879. Reprinted in *Woman's Exponent* 7 (March 15, 1879): 212.

the ministers and women of the nation whose petitions were pouring into Congress from all quarters. . . .

We argued that it was impossible for His Excellency to comprehend the strength of the affection which exists in Patriarchal Mormon families—of husband and wives for each other, of the father for all his children; and also, we would most respectfully suggest that before you countenance any measures taken to destroy the happiness and prosperity of the Mormon people you would become familiar with the record of the Latter-day Saints, and in judging them, not only be guided and dictated by the highest and finest sentiments of humanity; but with the reflection that upon the annals of this nation will be engraven the record of your decision in a matter which involves the life, liberty, and happiness of many thousands of loyal citizens of this Republic. It is impossible to state, in so small a space, the arguments presented, or the pen picture drawn for His Excellency, of the disastrous effects which must follow a decision such as has been urged by the Anti-polygamy party. The Latter-day Saints know to what terrible straits they would be driven, if compelled to submit en masse to the rigid enforcement of any harsh measures, such as are now being agitated. It is too hideous a picture to contemplate, therefore we will leave it for the present, knowing there is a God who has said to his opposers in times past, "Thus far shalt thou go and no farther."[9]

Poetry

From childhood Emmeline aspired to be a poet but often struggled in her multifaceted life to find time to express her poetic sentiments. She reflected:

9. [Emmeline B. Wells], "President Hayes and a Part of His Message," *Woman's Exponent* 8 (December 15, 1879): 108.

To have the desire, the longing to write, the intense fascination, to be able to skim through the clouds of fancy and weave a golden web of fine spun threads, of which each one is like a jewel radiantly set, is something no one ever can comprehend, save one of these same fanciful, poetical scribblers, who live in a world of their own creation, and only come down from the towering heights of fancy, when they are hungry, cold or wretched. Such is the poet's workshop, not what it really is but what it seems to him. Amethyst[10]

The publication in 1896 of *Musings and Memories,* a compilation of 130 of her poems, was a milestone in Emmeline's life. Most of the poems fall into one of three categories: paeans to nature's lessons, tributes to friendship, and assurances of eternal reward for enduring faith. One popular poem, however, lies outside these categories. "The Wife to Her Husband" is a love poem, which causes one to wonder to which of her three husbands it might have been addressed:

The Wife to Her Husband

It seems to me that should I die,
And this poor body cold and lifeless lie,
And thou should'st touch my lips with thy warm breath,
The life-blood, quicken'd in each sep'rate vein,
Would wildly, madly rushing back again,
Bring the glad spirit from the isle of death.

It seems to me that were I dead,
And thou in sympathy should'st o'er me shed
Some tears of sorrow, or of sad regret,
That every pearly drop that fell in grief,
Would bud, or blossom, bursting into leaf,
To prove immortal love could not forget.

---

10. Emmeline B. Wells [Amethyst, pseud.], "The Poet's Workshop," *Contributor* 4, no. 7 (April 1883): 273.

I do believe that round my grave,
When the cool fragrant evening zephyrs wave,
Should'st thou in friendship linger near the spot,
And breathe some tender words in memory,
That this poor heart in grateful constancy,
Would softly whisper back some loving thought.

I do believe that should I pass,
Into the unknown land of happiness,
And thou should'st wish to see my face once more,
That in my earnest longing after thee,
I would come forth in joyful ecstasy,
And once again gaze on thee as before.

I do believe my faith in thee,
Stronger than life, an anchor firm to be;
Planted in thine integrity and worth,
A perfect trust implicit and secure;
That will all trials and all grief endure,
And bless and comfort me while here on earth.

I do believe who love hath known,
Or sublime friendship's purest, highest tone,
Hath tasted of the cup of ripest bliss,
And drank the choicest wine life hath to give,
Hath known the truest joy it is to live;
What blessing rich or great compared to this?

I do believe true love to be
An element that in its tendency
Is elevating to the human mind
An intuition which we recognize
As foretaste of immortal paradise,
Through which the soul will be refined.[11]

---

11. Emmeline B. Wells, "The Wife to Her Husband," *Musings and Memories,*
2nd ed. (Salt Lake City, UT: Deseret News, 1915): 266–67.

Through her writings and through the organizations and other public activities that consumed her life, Emmeline continually strived to advance the cause of women, especially Latter-day Saint women. She represented women in national and international forums, defended their religious practices, led them in winning greater political voice, and ministered to them through her Relief Society leadership roles. That her work in their behalf was recognized and valued is evident in the many tributes and honors she received in her later years. All spoke to the fact that she was indeed "a fine soul who served us."

Chapter 27

"The Lord Has Remembered His Handmaiden in Her Affliction"

Helen Mar Kimball Whitney (1828–1896)
Jay A. Parry

Biographical Sketch

When Helen Mar Kimball Whitney was a child, she prayed privately that the Lord would protect her from a threatened spanking, and her mother's heart was softened The Prophet Joseph Smith wept when he heard the story. "He told the brethren that that was the kind of faith they needed—the faith of a little child, going in humility to its Parent, and asking for the desire of its heart."[1] Such faith was a hallmark of her entire life.

Helen Kimball was born in Mendon, Monroe County, New York, on August 22, 1828, to Heber C. and Vilate Murray Kimball, the third of ten children. She was their only daughter to survive.[2]

---

1. Orson F. Whitney, *Life of Heber C. Kimball,* 2nd ed. (Salt Lake City, UT: Stevens & Wallis, 1945), 69–70.

2. Todd Compton, *In Sacred Loneliness: The Plural Wives of Joseph Smith* (Salt Lake City, UT: Signature Books, 1997), 487–88.

Her parents joined the Church of Christ, later renamed The Church of Jesus Christ of Latter-day Saints, in 1832 when she was three years old; she was later baptized by Brigham Young in the ice-filled Chagrin River.[3] "I had longed for this privilege," recalled Helen, "and though I had some distance to walk in my wet clothes I felt no cold or inconvenience from it."[4]

Helen was a young participant in many of the early trials of the Church: She fled with her family from Missouri after Governor Lilburn Boggs's extermination order, walking much of the way in a freezing winter. They helped to settle Nauvoo, Illinois. She participated in plural marriage as a wife of Joseph Smith and later, after she married Horace K. Whitney (son of Newel K. and Elizabeth Ann Smith Whitney) as his first wife, she consented to his taking additional wives. Helen and Horace enjoyed the blessings of the Nauvoo Temple before fleeing the city and living for a time in Winter Quarters near the Missouri River. They trekked across the American plains to the Great Basin to pioneer in Utah. In Salt Lake City, as a daughter of a member of the First Presidency, Helen often moved in the inner circles of society. She was a friend or close acquaintance of most of the leading men and women in early Utah history.

She eventually became the mother of eleven children.[5] One of her sons, Orson F. Whitney, served as a member of the Quorum of the Twelve Apostles from 1906 until his death in 1931. Helen was a prolific author, publishing her memoirs in five series in the *Woman's Exponent,* as well as two pamphlets in defense of plural marriage; she

---

3. Compton, *Sacred Loneliness,* 490.

4. Helen Mar Kimball Whitney, "Life Incidents," *Woman's Exponent* 9, no. 22 (April 15, 1881): 170.

5. Helen Rosabelle Whitney (1847–1847), William Howard Whitney (1848–1848), Horace Kimball Whitney (1849–1849), Vilate Murray Whitney (1853–1870), Orson Ferguson Whitney (1855–1931), Elizabeth Ann Whitney Paton (1857–1905), Genevieve Whitney Talbot (1860–1901), Helen Kimball Whitney Bourne (1862–1927), Charles Spaulding Whitney (1864–1886), Florence Marian Whitney Dinwoodey (1867–1930), Phoebe Isabel Whitney (1869–1874).

also kept an almost-daily diary for the last twenty-two years of her life.[6] With such a full and meaningful life, however, she was anxious that her accomplishments not be exaggerated. Reading in a newspaper the death notice of a friend, she wrote, "I hope no praises will be sounded over my head that I have not richly earned."[7] After a short illness, Helen Mar Whitney Kimball died November 13, 1896.

LIFE EXPERIENCES

Helen suffered many trials during her life: chronic illness, depression, the challenge of sharing her husband with other wives, and pressing financial difficulties during the years of her widowhood.[8] But some of her greatest trials came from the death of loved ones. An older sister died before Helen was born, and of her eight other full siblings, five preceded her in death—all of them younger than

---

6. The pamphlets were *Plural Marriage As Taught by the Prophet Joseph: A Reply to Joseph Smith, Editor of the Lamoni (Iowa) "Herald"* (Salt Lake City, UT: Juvenile Instructor Office, 1882); and *Why We Practice Plural Marriage* (Salt Lake City, UT: Juvenile Instructor Office, 1884). The *Woman's Exponent* series were titled "Early Reminiscences," 8:188–89; 9:5, 10; "Life Incidents," 9:18, 25–26, 38–39, 42, 59, 66, 82, 90, 98, 111–12, 114–15, 126, 130–31, 138, 154, 169–70, 177, 186; 10:6, 9; "Scenes and Incidents at Nauvoo," 10:26, 34, 42, 50, 58, 66, 74, 83, 93–94, 97–99, 106, 114, 122, 130, 138, 159–60, 162, 178, 185–86; 11:26, 39–40, 50, 70–71, 74, 82, 90, 98, 105–6, 130, 138, 146, 153–54, 161–62, 169–70, 177–78, 186; "Marriage to Horace K. Whitney," 12:81–82; "Our Travels Beyond the Mississippi," 12:102–3, 110–11, 117–18, 126–27, 135–36, 138, 161–62, 170, 182, 186; 13:2, 10, 18, 49–50, 58, 65–66, 75, 87, 91; and "Scenes and Incidents at Winter Quarters," 13:98, 115, 131, 139, 151, 162, 170; 14:11, 18, 30–31, 53–54, 57–58, 66, 78, 82, 98, 105–6, 118, 138, 146; 15:6–7, 18; all published from May 1880 to August 1886.

7. Charles M. Hatch and Todd M. Compton, eds., *A Widow's Tale: The 1884–1896 Diary of Helen Mar Kimball Whitney* (Logan: Utah State University Press, 2003), 575.

8. Hatch and Compton, *A Widow's Tale*, 8–13, 19–24.

she was.[9] Joseph Smith, her beloved prophet and at least nominally her husband, was murdered in 1844.[10] She wrote of other losses:

> I lost three babes before I kept any, (two boys and girl). My first to live was Vilate, she grew to womanhood and was taken. Orson F. was my next, who has been appointed Bishop of the Eighteenth Ward. I had four more daughters, then a son, my last a little girl who died at five years of age; being eleven in all. My parents have left me and my heart has been wrung to the utmost, yet I have said—Thy will O God, be done. Persons have sometimes wondered at my calmness and endurance, but I think they would not had they passed through the same experience.[11]

She outlived six of her eleven children. She also lost her husband, Horace, in 1884, a dozen years before her own death. As his health began to fail, she and her sister wife Mary gave him nearly constant care. During this time she kept a journal of her experiences and feelings. Some of the entries about her widowhood are particularly poignant:

> Monday [November] 24th [1884]. . . . The morning after Horace's death I felt for the first time that he had really departed, having nothing to do but sit down to breakfast,

---

9. Stanley B. Kimball, *Heber C. Kimball: Mormon Patriarch and Pioneer* (Champaign: University of Illinois Press, 1986), 311; Compton, *Sacred Loneliness,* 487.

10. Helen became a plural wife of Joseph Smith in May 1843, just one year before his death. See Richard Lloyd Anderson and Scott H. Faulring, "The Prophet Joseph Smith and His Plural Wives," *FARMS Review of Books* 10, no. 2 (Provo, UT: Maxwell Institute, 1998), 79–81; Compton, *Sacred Loneliness,* 14, 486–501.

11. Helen Mar Kimball Whitney, quoted in Augusta Joyce Crocheron, *Representative Women of Deseret: A Book of Biographical Sketches to Accompany the Picture Bearing the Same Title* (Salt Lake City, UT: J. C. Graham & Co., 1884), 114.

the thought that there was nothing else for me to do—that every morning it had been my first care to wait upon him, wash his face & hands & prepare him some breakfast—of late, had been till ten o'clock before I could take my own. and now there was nothing for me to do. I had to leave the table & go out to give free vent to my feelings. Orson & Zina[12] came down in the evening. O. asked me what we expected to do for a livelyhood. I told him I knew not, but trusted that the Lord would still provide in some way. . . .

Monday Nov [Dec.] 1st Feel no better. . . . Am weighed down to the very earth—still, the Lord is my friend. . . .

Sunday [December] 7th. I slept but little last night. Spent it in prayer for grace & strength to bear, & forbear & to rise triumphant above my temptations, & that which would mar my peace, if possible, & sicken me of life. Sister Lucy came near night to stop all night—had a pleasant visit—She said my sad countenance haunted her all night, & she feared that I would sink under my feelings if I didn't try to shake them off. . . .

Saturday [March] 7th [1885] . . . My mind troubled over many things—how we are to do. . . . Oh! how I feel my loss—my widowhood. I wept & prayed the Lord to help us in our spirit, and to make me willing to yield up, what to me has been a haven of rest. . . . My comfort and quietness sacrificed to gain a livlihood. . . . Received an invitation to a surprise on Sister Rachel Grant, her birthday Went at 6 o'clock—had a very pleasant time.[13]

Yet despite all her experience with death, Helen was unprepared

---

12. Zina "Zine" Beal Smoot Whitney (1859–1900), wife of Helen's son Orson F. Whitney.

13. Compton and Hatch, *Widow's Tale*, 48–49, 50–51, 74.

for the loss of her son Charley (Charles Spaulding Whitney), who died by his own hand in August 1886. He was twenty-one years old. Helen recorded in her journal the pain of the first weeks after that loss:

Salt Lake City, Tuesday [August] 10th[14]
Weakened in body & sad at heart—

Oh, what a change has been wrought in my house since I left it for the purpose of visiting at Bear Lake then go to Temple in Logan to work & get renewed in body & in mind—Another earthly prop removed—Why and wherefore is all unknown, only to Him who giveth and taketh away:—blessed be his name—He knows my heart, & that I have asked for nothing so much as the eternal salvation of my children; that before they should be left to do any thing that would cut short their glory He would take them to Himself—And that I have held them upon the "Alter" that nothing should stand between Him & me, whom I will love though He slay me—

Wednesday 11th. Granate—Wasatch. One week ago tomorrow I returned from Meadowville Bear Lake—When at Kaysville Sol[15] saw Bro Henry Grow who came onto the Car, and thinking him more experienced than himself Sol charged him to break to me the horreble news of my Charley's death, all of which he'd been able to keep from me by watchful care—telling every one on the train . . . not to speak of it, his mother being on the train. And the papers were being read all around me containing an account of the

---

14. The sequence of dates in this journal entry is somewhat out of order. Helen records her thoughts and experiences on August 10 and 11 and then backtracks to August 8. When she reaches August 11 again, she makes a second entry for that date.

15. Solomon F. Kimball (1847–1920), Helen's younger brother.

dreadful act,[16] but which I'd had no thought of wanting to read—Poor Sol went in jeoperdy. . . . The thought of breaking the news to me almost overcame him as we were drawing near the City—

Bro. Grow broke it to me as Carefully as possable, but I insisted upon his telling me the whole truth, when he said he did not think I'd find my boy alive, and then he told me the facts and even more, adding a poisoned dart which pierced me deeper than death could do if it came in any common form—I could not believe that Charley was dead—it seemed like a dream that I must awake from—But, Oh it was a bitter reality, and in my silent agony I wondered what I have done, or what I had left undone, or if I was doomed to suffer this that I could know how to feel for others under like trials who's suffering I could not know in any other way. How I cried to the Lord to help me bear it if needful, & acknowledge His hand in C's taking his own life. I could not weep but Oh the agonizing thought—how a boy like him could have given way—what could have brought him to commit such an act? Had all my prayers for his eternal salvation fallen to the ground unheeded?

When arriving at the Depot I was hardly able to walk. . . . [Two men] nearly carried me to the Hack [carriage], & helped me in with my Orson's[17] assistance. . . . We were driven to my home of wretchedness, and to my

---

16. "A Horrible Tragedy," *Deseret Evening News,* August 4, 1886; "Suicide of C. S. Whitney," *Deseret Evening News,* August 5, 1886; "C. S. Whitney Suicides," *Salt Lake Tribune,* August 5, 1886. Helen had only hours to comprehend the news of Charley's death before he was buried. "Fragments," *Deseret Evening News,* August 6, 1886, explains that "Sister Helen Mar Whitney reached home from the north last evening. Four o'clock this afternoon was the hour set for the funeral of her son, Charles S. Whitney."

17. Orson F. Whitney (1855–1931), Helen's fifth child. He was the bishop of Helen's ward for twenty-eight years before being called as an apostle in 1906.

surprize it was surrounded, & filled with sympathetic & anxious friends. My children strove with all their might to be calm for my sake.—As soon as all was quiet Orson, Sol, & George[18] administered to me. Sol anointed my head—He wept, & could hardly speak. Orson then gave me a great blessing—many wonderful things were pronounced upon my head.—

Orson had previously offered a prayer, & all present thought it the greatest they had ever heard—The first thing he'd said—when we were on the way from the Depot was that Charley was not accountable for the act, and he had gained this testamony by fasting & prayer. I told him if I could know this I would never murmor. He propesied that I should know it & that very soon. . . . Orson said he knew Charley was innocent, and he thought Bro. Grow had little wisdom or good sence to add needless suffering to my stricken heart—Sol felt the same & blamed himself for asking Grow to break the news to me. I told them not to blame him, as I believed it to be so, for it would help to lighten the blow, & If I could but know that Charley was not guilty of this, or of putting an end to his earthly existence—I'd not mourn for him now, if I could only know that he'd done nothing to lesson his eternal salvation, & if I had not heard this I should no doubt have mourned more deeply his loss. . . . When on my couch alone tears came to my relief, and I vented my anguish. How often I silently cried from the depths of my soul—My God—My God— My God, why is this and what have I done to merit so bitter a punishment at thy hand?—have mercy and help me to bear it and to "kiss the Rod".—Oh that I could know that

18. Likely George Thomas Bourne, husband of Helen Kimball, Helen Mar's eighth child.

my boy was worthy to be among the sanctified I would not utter a murmoring word.

Sleep came to my relief towards daylight. But when I saw the form of my Charley stretched in death, in an instant I was overwhelmed, & cried aloud—This was the first time and the last, though my sorrow has been deep and unspeakable. And yet with all I have been blessed and felt that the Lord had not forsaken me—Friends by hundreds have given me their prayers, & words of consolation have poured in as a healing balm—and the greatest of all my children that are left me have repented and confessed their sins & that this has brought them to see how far they were from the Lord, & that He had chastened them for this cause— How little I thought how they were to be chastened, when I was predicting it. I felt for a time that I would pray only the "Lords Prayer" in the future. But "the Lord works in a misterious way his wonders to perform." Every one acquainted with Charley testafy to his purity of mind, and that he was unconscious at the moment he killed himself. This fact is bourn out by his turning to the Lord & being more attentive of late. to his spiritual duties—. . . & the very day, within a few moments of committing the tereble act he was talking of & urging B. Young[19] to intercede for him to go as his companion on a mission to New Zealand . . . , which was the last subject that occupied his mind or he talked upon. . . .

Mary and Phebe Kimball[20] each offered me a black

---

19. Brigham Willard Young (1860–1887) was a son of Lorenzo Dow Young (1807–1895) and Hannah Ida Hewitt (1839–1888). He was a close friend of Charley. Brigham died less than a year later while serving as a missionary in New Zealand.

20. Mary may be Mary Cravath Whitney (1838–1895), Helen's sister wife. She may also have been one of the plural wives of Heber C. Kimball: Mary Ellen Harris Able Kimball (1818–1902) or Mary Houston Kimball (1818–1896). Phebe

dress—I accepted Mary's. They & many more were over-whelming in kindness and sympathy—The day follow-ing a room full of Sisters came by appointment to com-fort me. . . . Every one spoke with the exception of Mary Whitney[21]—the girls & Will Richards. . . . The spirit of God burned in their hearts, and some very glorious prom-ises were made to me—After they had all spoken I was invited to speak—Having intended to I arose & spoke at some length—much of the time tears flowing down my cheeks, & my words were so affecting that they were all in tears—Sister Elmira Taylor & others with my girls were sob-bing aloud before I closed—I never remember of speaking my feelings with such freedom and I could have continued had I thought it wisdom. . . .

Sunday the 8th. My girls, all but Lillie,[22] went to meet-ing with Sol & myself—also George Bourne. And Lulu Musser[23] came & accompanied us. I felt that the Lord had brought them to His feet in a very strange and unlooked for manner.

Monday the 9th. Helen[24] received a letter from Zina urging her to come to Granite[25] with baby & said Orson would

---

Kimball may have been Phebe Judd Kimball (1837–1909), wife of Heber Parley Kimball (1835–1885), who was one of Helen's brothers.

21. Mary Cravath, Helen's only living sister wife, married Horace on December 1, 1856.

22. Elizabeth Ann "Lillie" Whitney Paton (1857–1905), Helen's sixth child.

23. Louisa ("Lulu" or "Lu") Stenhouse Musser Barton (1865–1940) appears to have been Charley's girlfriend and perhaps fiancée. Her father was T. B. H. [Thomas Brown Holmes] Stenhouse (1824–1882), a prominent Mormon apostate.

24. Helen Kimball (1862–1927), Helen's eighth child.

25. This is an invitation to go on a camping trip.

be down the day following & wanted me to return with him. . . .

Wednesday 11th. Took breakfast & said good bye. Sol & Orson carried our bedding, etc to the Street Car, and my spirits were much improved by the excitement, and the consoling words from Orson which flowed from his lips from the time we started till we were met by Zina & Racie[26] as the Train stopt at this little Eden, which Gen[27] & I had no idea existed in this region—Quiet—peaceful with none to molest or disturb our thoughts, or conversation. . . .

. . . Orson read to us from Book of Mormon. We spent a very pleasent day hearing it, & teachings from him. . . . Every morning as the thought of my loss, & the facts flashed upon me the feeling that came over me was like I was disolving—each portion of my body sepparating—lasting longer every day till I came here.—The excitement of getting ready, and the conversation has broken the spell, or power that was gaining ground. . . .

Thur. 12th. . . . After breakfast I took quite a strole up the steep mountain, at the foot of which we are stopping— came to a large rock in the path of there knelt & prayed 2 or 3 times—climbed up & went still higher till I came to three flat rocks, where I knelt again, & when I'd prayed twice the rain beginning to fall I went down. . . .

Saturday 14th. Packed up every thing to return to the City this afternoon—I took one more walk up to the 3 rocks and offered up prayers & thanksgiving to the Most High. . . .

Friday 27th. I am troubled in mind over Gen's running so much with the unbelieving fearing she is loosing the taste of

---

26. Horace Newel "Racie" Whitney (1880–1908), Orson's oldest son.
27. Genevieve "Gen" Whitney (1860–1901), Helen's seventh child.

the Holy spirit that she had gained since the chastening rod has fallen heavily upon us. . . .

Sunday, 29th. My body was too feeble to walk to meeting. While we were at breakfast I spoke to Gen upon the subject that I'd desired to for days—I told her I thought it wrong for her to be going with Ed Talbot, and fooling him along.[28] . . . To my utter astonishment she, in answer to my questions, acknowledged that they were engaged to each other. I was as much astonished at this as I was at the news of Charley's committing Suicide. . . . I was dumbfounded, & heart broken & returned to my room—there I prayed and wept the best part of the day to the Lord that He would have mercy on us, & help me to acknowledge His hand in this as well as all other things. . . . Gen came to my room & put her arms around me & cried bitterly saying she wished she'd died when she was so sick since she saw how I took it, and begged me not to feel so. But my bitterness she cannot know. . . . Oh, how long have I prayed that the Lord would send some man to her that she could love & respect, & would be truly a savior on Mount Zion, and why should my prayers be in vain? I feel that I am a mourner indeed. But though my sorrows are keen the Lord will not withold His mercy from me when I've tried so hard to serve Him— and to bring my children to His feet—. . .

Monday 30th. Another day of lementation & my eyes are sore with weeping—Sol informed Orson of my second trouble. . . . At evening, Lulu Musser came down, & in talking with her I rose above my present sorrow & preached to her all the evening. She & Helen were sitting under the

28. Gen married Edward Lee Talbot (1862–1925), who was not a member of the Church, on December 29, 1886. They lived for a time with Helen, helping with household labor and expenses.

sound and tears were plentiful in the midst of our conversation. Lulu could not believe that Charley shot himself intentionally or that they could ever be with each other again, as I'd told her it would be her privilege if she'd live for it. I gave her a key that would open the doar that she feels she can never hope to enter.—to pray the Lord to assist her, no matter how few & simple her words, & she would find Him ready & willing to teach her the way to Heaven. She had not prayed for a year or more & thought it no use now— Her sorrow she said was deeper because she had caused Charley so much anoyance, & greef—by rejecting his religious teachings &c. She made humble confessions, & I told her that I had said that if he had married her in her state of mind probably she never would have been converted, & that his being taken might prove her salvation, as well as others. She would give any thing now, she said, if she'd felt then as she had since his death. . . .

Thursday [September] 2nd. Took a slight addition to my cold—The weather still stormy & cold without—My heart is melted, and tears flow spontaniously till my eyes are sore with weeping. O, that I may not fail, & become discouraged in the midst of this battle of life and sorrow of which no one knows the depth but the Lord, & His Angels that have charge of me and my household.—

Friday 3d. Weather fine. Commenced to write an article for Ex.[29] expressive of gratitude for the kindness shown me by the Brethren & Sister in the midst of my troubles which has been to me like "oil poured upon the troubled waters." . . .

Sunday 12th Spent a strange night not easily eradicated from my memory—Slept good the forepart of the night & dreamed something interesting. . . . Got up & dressed me,

---

29. *Woman's Exponent.*

though I felt sick—my head aching—as it had, all night. And while washing face, & cleaning my teeth I prayed to myself . . .—I then bowed in prayer before going out, after being called to breakfast—

I had dreamed of being with Charley—Father, & Brigham Young & others with a great deal more which I could not remember but knew that they were more than commonly interesting from the time that I'd first dropped to sleep—When I went out & saw the table ready, the first thing that struck me was the vacant chair at the head of the table, & Charley not there to fill it, when I burst into tears & went back & fell on the Lounge, telling Gen who followed me not to wait for me. This occurence with others that transpired during the morning I have only a dim recollection of.[30]

Despite her many struggles and heartaches, Helen retained a lifelong faith in the goodness of the Lord and in his promises to her. On December 18, 1884, not quite a month after the death of her husband, Horace, she recorded in her journal:

I feel still more that the Lord has remembered his handmaiden in the days of her affliction & that His promises will not fail—that my last days should be the best. My treasures are laid up in heaven, where, I've been told, that I should be enthroned in the presence of God, and also that here I "should be honored of God and by man," and no power should stay the blessings pronounced upon my head by my

---

30. Hatch and Compton, *Widow's Tale*, 176–80, 183–87, 190–91. Nearly a year after Charley died, Helen learned more about the likely circumstances of his death. She was comforted to hear that he had probably shot himself by accident, rather than as an intentional act. See Hatch and Compton, *Widow's Tale*, 241; M. Russell Ballard, *Suicide: Some Things We Know, and Some We Do Not* (Salt Lake City, UT: Deseret Book, 1993).

dear father in my Patriarchal blessing, & at various times. But O, how weak & unworthy I feel, and dependent upon His arm to lead me and to sustain me in the midst of this dark world of sorrow and disapointment.[31]

Two years later, weighed down by the normal burdens of life as well as recurring sickness, she wrote of a priesthood blessing she received:

Thursday, [April] 8th [1886] . . . Orson & Bro. Donolson[32] were here. . . . Bro D. gave me a blessing, and revealed such great & marvalous things to me concerning myself, & made such promises, & predictions of things present, and things to come, and what I should accomplish in this life that I felt that the Lord had heard my petitions, for I'd been praying and weeping over the things that were weighing me down. . . . All the glorious things spoken to me over-whelmed me with gratetude to the Giver of all that is good & exalting. I was told that I would have trials and some things to meet that would trouble me—. . . but that I would overcome them.[33]

This heartfelt expression seems to encapsulate the experience of Helen Mar Kimball Whitney. Her life brought many occasions for "praying and weeping over the things that were weighing [her] down." Yet she continued to return to feelings of "gratetude to the Giver of all that is good & exalting." This faithful woman—subject to chronic sickness, depression, and heartache—remained steadfast to the end when, no doubt, she enjoyed a happy reunion with those many loved ones who had preceded her in death.

---

31. Hatch and Compton, *Widow's Tale,* 54.

32. John Donaldson was a friend of Orson.

33. Hatch and Compton, *Widow's Tale,* 148.

Chapter 28

"ALL IS WELL AND PEACE WITH US DWELLS"

CATHERINE ELIZABETH MEHRING WOOLLEY (1826–1880)

Jay G. Burrup

BIOGRAPHICAL SKETCH

Catherine Elizabeth Mehring, daughter of Henry and Anna Hurst Mehring, was born in Earl Township, Lancaster County, Pennsylvania, on November 19, 1826. Her father was a farmer, and her mother died in 1834 when Catherine was about seven and a half years old. Her father later remarried.[1] Unfortunately, little is known about Catherine's early life.

Catherine's uncle and aunt, John and Barbara Mehring, were converts to The Church of Jesus Christ of Latter-day Saints and moved to Nauvoo, Illinois, in June 1845. Catherine apparently

---

1. Samuel A. Woolley Family Bible (1848), Church History Library, The Church of Jesus Christ of Latter-day Saints, Salt Lake City, Utah, hereafter cited as Church History Library. Irene Mercer Anderson, "Catherine Elizabeth Mehring Woolley," Typescript, p. 1, Pioneer Memorial Museum, International Society Daughters of Utah Pioneers, Salt Lake City, Utah, hereafter cited as Pioneer Memorial Museum.

accompanied them; she did not intend to stay long because she took with her only a small amount of clothing. Her stay in Nauvoo was extended, however, when she was baptized a member of the Church on July 6, 1845, and began working as a housemaid for the William Mendenhall family.[2]

The prosperous Edwin D. Woolley family, Quaker converts from Pennsylvania, soon learned of Catherine's efficient domestic abilities and offered her employment. Edwin's younger brother Samuel Amos successfully convinced Catherine to accept their offer. Through this introduction Samuel and Catherine courted, fell in love, and eventually wed on May 21, 1846, in Nauvoo.[3]

The couple's first child, Samuel Henry (nicknamed "Bub") was born September 29, 1847, in Winter Quarters, a Latter-day Saint settlement in what later became Nebraska. He was the first of eleven children born to the couple: Three children were stillborn, and three died in their early twenties.[4]

Samuel, Catherine, and Bub joined the 1848 Brigham Young emigration company and arrived in Salt Lake City on September 21

---

2. Anderson, "Catherine," 1; General Church Recorder, Far West and Nauvoo Elders' Certificates Collection, 1837–1838, 1840–1846, Church History Library. The latter volume contains lists of Church members who arrived in Nauvoo beginning in 1841 and those baptized in the city. It also includes a list of persons received in Nauvoo by recommendation certificate or letter, 1843–1846. Entries state that Catherine and her aunt and uncle registered their recommends in Nauvoo on June 14, 1845.

3. Samuel A. Woolley Family Bible; Anderson, "Catherine," 1–2.

4. Catherine and Samuel's children were Samuel Henry Woolley (1847–1870), Mary Pamelia Woolley Fletcher (1849–1915), Rachel Anna Woolley Vance (1852–1872), Catherine Adella Woolley Eardley (1857–1939), Susan Calista Woolley Reese (1858–1926), Amos Mervin Woolley (1860–1949), Clara Ela Woolley Coombs (1862–1932), Cyrus Leo Woolley (1865–1889), Stillborn (1867–1867), Stillborn (1868–1868), Stillborn (1869–1869). Claud Lincoln Russell, Samuel Amos and Catherine Elizabeth Mehring Woolley Family Group Record, private possession. In diary entries Catherine referred to son Samuel Henry as Bub.

of that year.[5] In 1850 Samuel was called to serve a colonizing mission in Parowan, Utah. Catherine remained in Salt Lake City during the several months that Samuel spent in southern Utah. In 1852 Samuel was called to serve a proselytizing mission in India, where he remained until 1856.[6]

Catherine and Samuel corresponded as frequently as possible while Samuel was in India. The stress of being a temporary single parent surfaced in an undated note Catherine sent to Samuel from Bub, who was then about seven years old: "Dear father, I will mind my Mother, and not run with bad boys, nor use bad words. I will love my sisters and not quarrel with them, and I will pray for my father and mother and do as she tells me. Dear father I will not run away from my mother to do eny thing bad. I love you pray and want to see you." Catherine finalized the note, "this is word for word as your son has dictated."[7]

In 1857, about a year after Samuel's return from India, the Utah War began, and the Woolleys migrated south to Parowan, where Samuel set up a business making jugs, pails, barrels, and tubs from local cedar wood. The family lived there for two years and then returned to Salt Lake City.[8]

A year after Catherine's father died in Pennsylvania in 1860, Samuel went east on business and to collect Catherine's inheritance. She issued Samuel strict instructions that she wanted a changeable

---

5. "Catherine Elizabeth Mehring Woolley," Mormon Pioneer Overland Travel Database, 1847–68, The Church of Jesus Christ of Latter-day Saints, accessed April 16, 2012, http://mormontrail.lds.org.

6. "Eighth General Epistle," *Deseret News [Weekly]*, October 16, 1852; Anderson, "Catherine," 8; Florence Woolley Russell, "History of Samuel Amos Woolley: Pioneer of 1848," Typescript, p. 2, Pioneer Memorial Museum.

7. Catherine and Samuel Henry Woolley to Samuel A. Woolley, ca. 1854, Holograph, Samuel A. Woolley Letters, 1854–1864, Church History Library.

8. Russell, "History of Samuel," 3.

silk dress pattern and a gold watch and chain before he used any of the money for other purposes.[9]

In 1864 Samuel began serving as bishop of the Salt Lake City Ninth Ward, a position he held for thirty-six years. Catherine was called to serve as the Relief Society president in 1868 and served until 1870.[10]

Samuel married a plural wife, Frances Ann Phillips, in 1867. For a time the two wives lived in the same house, but that arrangement did not work out well; Samuel relocated Frances and her family to a separate home nearby.[11] Several years after Catherine's death, Samuel married another plural wife, Elizabeth Ann Stephenson.[12]

After years of failing health, Catherine died on September 3, 1880. Samuel recorded in his diary after her passing, "She has suffered very much for the past 3 years & a half, but now sleeps in peace free from pain."[13] He summarized her life in an obituary he wrote for the *Deseret News:* "She was a kind friend, an affectionate wife and a loving mother, and lived and died in the full faith of the gospel. She truly did forsake father, brother, sisters, and friends for Christ's sake and the gospel's . . . and continued firm in the faith to the end."[14] At her funeral, Presiding Bishop Edward Hunter and

---

9. Russell, "History of Samuel," 3. The 1860 U.S. census mortality schedule for East Earl Township, Pennsylvania, states that Catherine's father, Henry Mehring, died in May 1860 of typhoid fever.

10. Manuscript History and Historical Reports, Ninth Ward, Liberty Stake, 1864, 1868, Church History Library.

11. Margaret Wilson Jorgensen, "Catherine Elizabeth Mehring Woolley," Typescript, p. 11, Pioneer Memorial Museum.

12. Elizabeth and Samuel were married on October 28, 1885. "Samuel Amos Woolley," Family Pedigree, New FamilySearch, The Church of Jesus Christ of Latter-day Saints, accessed on April 16, 2012, http://new.familysearch.org.

13. Samuel A. Woolley, Diary, 1879–1881, September 3, 1880, Holograph, p. 127, Church History Library.

14. "Died," *Deseret News [Weekly],* September 8, 1880; "Obsequies," *Deseret Evening News,* September 6, 1880.

Elder Joseph F. Smith spoke of Catherine's faithfulness and urged those attending to follow her example.

Life Experiences

Catherine Mehring Woolley's diary entries from May 1848 to January 1850 reveal a frank and candid account of a woman's perspective of the challenges of overland pioneering and life on the western frontier. She faithfully kept a record of her travels west and her first years helping her husband establish their young family in Utah. The location of her original journal is unknown, but her words are preserved because a descendant allowed its contents to be published serially in the *Salt Lake Telegram* in 1935. Catherine begins:

> Early in May, 1848, we prepared for the journey to the valleys of the Rockies. One hundred wagons were in the company headed by President Brigham Young. . . . We were assembled about four miles out of Winter Quarters, ready to start for Elk Horn river 12 miles distant, as soon as Brigham Young's family arrived. They came into camp about dusk the 26th of May, 1848. . . .
>
> Sunday, 28th. . . . made arrangements for Elizabeth [Calvert][15] to go with us to the mountains.
>
> Tuesday, 30th. Arranged the companies for our journey. Fell out of my wagon, was injured some, but able to get around. I was prayed for immediately, and I think that helped me.
>
> Wednesday, 31st. Laid by, and did some washing and ironing and fixing up. . . .

---

15. Unmarried and apparently traveling alone, twenty-two-year-old Elizabeth Calvert (1826–1885) was likely hired domestic help. She may have exchanged her labor for provisions, wagon space, and protection along the trail. After reaching the Salt Lake Valley, Elizabeth married Isaac Chase. "Elizabeth Calvert," Mormon Pioneer Overland Travel Database, 1847–68, The Church of Jesus Christ of Latter-day Saints, accessed April 25, 2012, http://mormontrail.lds.org.

6th. Mrs. Groves fell from her wagon and was run over, breaking her leg. . . .

9th. Traveled 18 miles. Oliver Duncan got his leg broken; fell out of his wagon. . . .

Thursday, 15th. . . . Samuel on guard. Andrew Garver did a great kindness: brought a waterproof cloak and cap for Samuel so he won't get wet. Raining and very dark tonight. Samuel's partner lazy; went to bed and left S. A.[16] all the work to do. . . .

July 1. (At Cold Spring.) John Webb shot two buffaloes to-day. Samuel A. brought one of them to the wagon. It was a sight to see, took four yoke of oxen to drag it into camp. We are overloaded with buffalo meat this evening. Went to see Elizabeth Foster and Mary Sheppard. Sister Pratt went along. At Platte river again. This is the last timber we will see for two hundred miles, no more wood: buffalo chips our only fuel for cooking. . . .

Tuesday, July 4th. Nothing to celebrate with, only corn-dodger and buffalo meat. . . .

Sunday, 9th. Remained in camp. Had meeting at 7 o'clock this evening. Wrote a letter to Elizabeth Hurst; sent it by some folks on the other side of the river from the valley. . . .

Wednesday, July 12th. Did not get started very early this morning. There were wagons to mend. Hard dragging this day. Came to Cable's [Cobble] hill. Aunt Minnie and I walked about two miles; went on top of the bluff to see Chimney Rock. We met 18 wagons from the valley this evening all in good spirits. Twelve miles today, camped. Lots of Indians: they are noble looking fellows. . . .

16. Catherine frequently refers to her husband, Samuel, as "S. A."

Wednesday, 19th. (near Scott's Bluff)—I got some books from Franklin today to read; read four today . . .

Saturday, July 22d—Traveled 15 miles. Today we passed Fort Laramie. I went in to see the old station trading house. . . . There is a grave in one of the rooms. . . .

Sunday, 23d—We are right in between the bluffs, and they look mighty blue to me. I feel terrible lonesome. Samuel is off fishing; Arthur herding; Elizabeth ironing, and I am baking. Samuel caught fourteen fish; gave E. D.[17] five, Ellen two for their supper . . . Susan Snively, Emily Free and Margaret Alley stopped in to see me this afternoon. I treated them with saleratus beer . . . I took Bub [about ten months old] and went to see Mrs. Bullock; she played the accordion for him; he was much pleased with the music; it was charming . . . Prayer meeting in the corral.

27th. (House creek or Heber's spring)—There are a great many wild currants along the road; had some for pies. I don't feel very well. E. D. is nearly dead with colic. . . .

August 1, 1848—Samuel, Bub and I went after gooseberries; found as many as we could eat; got supper, then went to the party.

3d. . . . Hazy Stout lost one of his oxen; died; and widow Smith lost one. . . . Mother Angell rode with me this afternoon; spent a pleasant time. One of Sister Ashby's girls got run over; fell out of the wagon. . . .

6th. Elizabeth ironed and I baked, and mended the boys' clothes. Samuel and Frank were on the island; got currants; I baked them into pies . . . James has the toothache; I made a poultice for him to put on his face. . . . spent the evening in singing. . . .

17. Edwin D. Woolley, Samuel's older brother.

12th—S. A. and I went on Independence rock; left our names there on the rock; there were a great many names written there. Passed the Devil's Gate: it was a curiosity to see. . . .

15th—Elizabeth washed and ironed. I made a pair of shoes for Bub. The hunters came home this evening; got one buffalo; made a bonnet for Bub.

16th—Samuel and the boys took care of the meat and the rest went hunting; shot three more buffalo; sent a man for a wagon to bring them to camp; he got lost, but came in at 3 A.M. . . .

22nd. There is neither grass, wood nor water (in the past 16 miles). Churned this evening. E. D.'s girl [hired help] ran off this morning and has not returned. All right this evening, except Julia Baldwin running away.

Wednesday, 23rd. Horace Whitney's child died last night, and E. D.'s girl not back this morning, so I let them have Elizabeth and will try to do my own work.

24th. E. D.'s sow had three pigs, but they are all dead; wolves got one of them. . . .

Sunday, 27th. Porter Rockwell gave me a piece of buffalo meat. I baked some mince pies. Brother Smoot took dinner with us. Maria Angell called to see me. S. A., E. D. and Mr. Canada [Kennedy] went out hunting. I did some baking, but was hardly able to do it. Sister Rachel Emma[18] came to stay all night with me. The wolves are howling around our wagon; it almost makes one think we are in the wilderness! . . .

---

18. The daughter of Edwin D., twelve-year-old Rachel Emma Woolley, is Catherine's niece. See chapter 23 herein.

[September] 9th. Traveled 15 miles to Fort Bridger. Crossed Black's Fork four times. . . . Hard on cattle's feet, so many stones in the river bed. Camped near where we crossed. Some Indians and traders here. We traded some buffalo meat for a pair of moccasins. All's well.

Sunday, 10th. Did not travel today. Cattle are tired; thought best to lay by. Did some baking and some washing and ironing. Mended some stockings. Got supper. Mary sent me a currant pudding; it was first rate. Samuel did some trading; got a pair of moccasins for me and two pairs for Bub. Franklin and I traded; mine were too heavy and his not heavy enough. Got my work done and to bed. . . .

16th. Did some washing and baking. B. Young's company passed today; stopped here for noon. Mr. and Mrs. Young and Mrs. Cobb took dinner with us. I made some tea for the girls. Samuel and the boys went after hops and service berries. Sister [Margaret] Garns died today; they intend taking her to the valley for burial. . . .

Thursday, 21st. This morning we had a shower of rain. Got up at 5 o'clock to get an early start to go to the valley. Crossed the mountain and traveled about five miles until noon. Overtook E. D. had dinner, then started for the valley. Got to the fort [in Salt Lake City] at 3 o'clock, and camped near John Woolley's. All hands took supper with them this evening. Found them all well and in good spirits; only their little boy is not very well. . . . Spent the evening there, then went to our wagons and got ready for bed.[19]

---

19. "In the Beginning: Diaries of Mormon Pioneers," *Salt Lake Telegram,* January 7, 1935; "In the Beginning: Catharine [sic] Woolley in Action," *Salt Lake Telegram,* January 8, 1935; "In the Beginning: Near Scott's Bluff," *Salt Lake Telegram,* January 9, 1935; "In the Beginning: Mrs. Woolley at Ft. Bridger," *Salt Lake Telegram,* January 10, 1935; "In the Beginning: Salt Lake City at Last," *Salt Lake Telegram,* January 11, 1935.

The grueling overland trek to the Salt Lake Valley was completed on September 21, 1848. Her entries continue thereafter and supply a fascinating glimpse of life in the fledgling frontier city:

Monday, September 25. Packed up my things. Samuel got the oxen and took our wagon up to John's; set the [wagon] boxes off the wheels and put up our tent back of their house. . . . We are fixed up quite comfortably with two wagon boxes and a tent. . . .

Sunday, October 1. Samuel went to herd and I got ready for meeting, but Samuel did not get back until after meeting time, so I could not go, no one to leave Bub with. I took off my best clothes and stayed home. Then the two Misses Neff and Miss Dilworth came and spent the evening; had some hot sling and pie. . . .

Saturday, 7th. Did some baking, then cleaned my wagon boxes, caught two mice in my boxes: they ate some cloth and brown muslin. . . .

Saturday 21st. I did my baking and scrubbed some of my boxes. Lovina Harper came and cut two dress linings for me. I then went over to Riter's and got ten pounds of meat. Samuel came home. . . .

November 1st. I did some sewing and baking. Samuel worked around home. Mrs. Ensign sent me some turnips and beets for some saleratus. Paid Elizabeth Calvert 25 cents for washing. Lent Auntie a teakettle, she sent me beets for some milk. I ate corn dodger at Maria's today at noon, and it was first rate. . . .

2nd . . . Samuel has the toothache yet. Made a poultice for his face, then doctored Bub. . . .

Sunday, 12th . . . S. A. went to the sawmill to get his house logs ripped in two.

13. S. A. went to haul his house logs from the mill to the lot; came home at noon: had the toothache, went to Mr. [Willard] Richards to get it drawn; and he broke it off and that made it worse than ever. I got supper and then made a poultice for Samuel's face.

Tuesday, 14th. Went out to the lot to take S. A.'s dinner; found him busy, and having the toothache. . . .

15th. Mrs. Van Fleet and Mrs. Whitesides came to spend the evening. I got supper. Then Horace Whitney and Porter Rockwell came, ate supper, then Porter went for Mr. Baird to play on the violin and Mr. Whitney sang. We all went into John's room after they were through singing. We had a dance, then dismissed.

Thursday, 16th. Unpacked my dishes to let Aunt Eliza have them; she brought a piece of beef for me to roast for the party. Worked around all day, then got dressed for the wedding. S. A. came home and got ready and then went to Mr. Riter's where the ceremony was performed. The bride and groom were Mr. Francis F. Hammond and Miss Mary Jane Dilworth.[20] Mr. H. C. Kimball did the performance. Had a splendid supper and all went right. Brother Kimball spoke a little while, then the party turned into a dance. We staid until 12 o'clock then came home. . . .

21st. . . . This day we moved into our house. Got all out of the Fort until dark. Put up quilts at the door and around the side of the wall to keep the cold out until Mr. Woolley can get it chinked and dob[be]d.

[2]2nd. . . . Samuel sawing out the windows; got two done. I did some baking both bread and mince pies. . . .

---

20. See chapter 7 herein.

Thursday 23rd. Samuel got his windows done, and I put in the glass. . . .

24th. S. A. chinked and "dobd" the house, and Bub and I went to the Warm Springs to baths, along with Mrs. Woolley and her children; had a pleasant time. . . .

[December] 3d. S. A. went to meeting. Came home with the teethache. E. D. came and brought us two letters, one from my sister and the other from Mr. Briton . . . Had to pay $1.10 postage, but did not begrudge it. . . .

Tuesday, 5th. Samuel nearly crazy with his teeth. . . . I worked around all day at one thing or another; too cold to do much of anything.

6th. Samuel took so bad with his teeth that I had to go for Mary, and Maria and John came. But it seemed to get worse all the while, so John went after President Young, but he could not come, but told us to give him tincture of lobelia and it would stop the pain. By spells he was cramped . . . his hands all up together so he could not move. John went after the doctor, but found him not at home. . . . Albert Dewey and wife were here upon the count of the cold, for they lived in a tent. So we all joined together and fixed us some hot teas for Samuel and got him in a sweat; and so he got better from that hour and rested pretty well. . . .

Sunday, 24th. I finished my baking and got ready for the party.

25th. Christmas. S. A. took the things out of the house. . . . We had dinner ready until 3 o'clock, and the company here, had seventeen couples to eat, besides E. D. and children, Betsy, Samuel, and I. Got dinner over, then went in the house and took a rest; had refreshments at 8 o'clock, and at 1 and 3. The company was very quiet and did well, had a fine dance.

26th, clear and cold. The company left this morning after sunrise. Then we went to work and cleaned up the things and sent the borrowed dishes home . . . All well this evening, only I am very tired.

[January 1, 1849] Welcome, happy New Year: may peace and health, may joy and love and prosperity this house attend, and all that dwell therein may share the blessings of another year, while slowly it rolls around. Received a compliment from Dr. (Willard) Richards with joy; and a few lines from friend Jane, which was a token of friendship and love. Maria Dewey spent the day with me. I made a cap for her, and had the toothache all the time. . . .

[March] Friday, 9th. I helped Maria clean up her things then went to sewing. Mrs. Woolley gave me a paper of needles. Samuel came home from the canyon with the toothache. I went home and made a fire and got some cloves to put in his tooth, then went again to John's and took supper, then came home for S. A.'s tooth ached too hard to stay. I made him caian [cayenne] tea and bathed his feet. S. A. went to bed. I did some sewing then got ready for bed. . . .

July 1, 1849. S. A. went to meeting, then came home and went to water his lot. The United States mail came in today, and a great many emigrants for the gold mines.

2d. Mr. Ford came and cut out two pairs of shoes for us. E. D. went to the office, got a letter for me which was from my cousin in Pennsylvania and it gave me some unpleasant news which was the death of my dear sister and grandmother. . . .

Tuesday July 24. The people were awakened by the roar of the cannon and then saluted by the brass band. We all got ready and went to the stand to spend the day; took our dinners along; it is two years ago this day that the first presidency and pioneers came into the valley . . . President B. Young and H. C. Kimball and others entertained the community with speeches; and there were 24 Silver Grays with staves in their right hands and with tassels on; and 25 young gents dressed in white bearing a copy in their right hands and a sword in their left; and they held a banner in their hands which had written on it in large print: "Lion of the Lord," and they sang a song which had a chorus in these words: "None with us can be compared for we're of the root and branch of Joseph the bright and glorious morning star; for we are the true born sons of Zion." And there were 24 young ladies dressed in white bearing in their right hand the Bible and in the left the book of Mormon and the lines on their banner were: "Hail to Our Chieftain." The sight was splendid, but the oppression of the sun was very great; but still they have the bowery fixed so most of the people were in the shade. . . . It was 6 o'clock when the feast broke up. This was a great (day) long to be remembered among the saints and others who were present to the scenery. . . .

Sunday, August 5, 1849. I got dinner for two gentiles; got 50 cts. for it. . . .

Sunday, 12th. S. A. watering, and went to the emigrant's camp. I staid at home all day and got dinner and supper for two of the emigrants; got 75 cents apiece for it. . . .

August 16th. S. A. and I went to the hay lot this morning and put up what was dry; then he cut some grass and brought it home. . . .

Sunday, October 21st. S. A. went after some hay and Mary went to meeting and I stayed at home. The Mormon companies had quite a snowstorm at the Pacific Springs which was very hard on their teams; and so all the spare teams and men are called on to go and help them over the mountains. . . .

27th. I worked in the garden some, putting away potatoes and beets, etc. S. A. came home with the lumber then ate supper then went and met George A. Smith's [emigrant] company and drove a team to his father for him. . . .

October 29, 1849. S. A. helping Brother Bailey to unload his wagon and then Brother B. helped him dig at his cellar. I received a few presents from my father and a few from some of my cousins in the east; they sent them by Brother Bailey's and a great many others sent things by them for their relations. . . .

[December] 10th. S. A. at home, for I was sick all night and was confined to my bed in the morning; brought birth of a young daughter [Mary Pamelia]. Mother Angell and Aunt Eliza and Mary Wooley were with me the most part of the day. Dr. Richards sent for Mother Angell for Jane was very sick the same as myself, but there was no help for her; she left this world and took her abode with the Saints above who went to their homes in former days. May happiness be her lot and joy and peace attend her days. . . .

December 31, 1849. S. A. went to the canyon after a load of wood for Samuel Ensign. I did some knitting; Mary ironed some and did the housework. Eliza A. Malin called. All as usual the last evening in 1849.

January 1, 1850. Tuesday. Fair. Welcome New Year's morn; happy days were spent in the past and bygone year, and blessings from above were realized by Saints who dwell on earth, but yet my faith is thus, and prayers and hope, if we faithful prove, that we'll more blessings get in the new, sweet coming year. Samuel around home this day. We had an invite to take tea this evening, but my health would not permit it. I spent my New Year's day at home with my sweet little babe to rest upon my knee. All is well and peace with us dwells. Amen.[21]

---

21. Catherine E. [Mehring] Woolley, "In the Beginning: Salt Lake City at Last," *Salt Lake Telegram,* January 11, 1935; "In the Beginning: Early days at Salt Lake," *Salt Lake Telegram,* January 12, 1935; "In the Beginning: Christmas Joys and Sorrows," *Salt Lake Telegram,* January 21, 1935; "In the Beginning: A Party for Brigham Young," *Salt Lake Telegram,* January 22, 1935; "In the Beginning: Many Winter Chores to Do," *Salt Lake Telegram,* January 23, 1935; "In the Beginning: Crops and Emigrants," *Salt Lake Telegram,* January 26, 1935; "In the Beginning: The Harvest Days," *Salt Lake Telegram,* February 4, 1935; "In the Beginning: Autumn Tints," February 5, 1935; "In the Beginning: Another Baby," *Salt Lake Telegram,* February 6, 1935. J. Cecil Alter borrowed Catherine's diaries from her son Amos Mervin Woolley and transcribed and published them in a serialized newspaper column. Despite numerous attempts by Woolley family members to locate the original diaries since 1935, the diaries' whereabouts remain unknown to the author.

Chapter 29

"Truth Is What My Soul Craves"

Emily Dow Partridge Young (1824–1899)
Sherilyn Farnes

Biographical Sketch

On Friday, September 7, 1877, Emily Dow Partridge Young wrote in her diary, "As Benjamin Franklin bottled the lightning, so I will have to bottle my thoughts metaphoricaly speaking by writing them down, for . . . they fly away like so many frightened birds, and I will have to use pen ink and paper as a trap, to hold them, untill they can be used."[1] Emily succeeded in "bottling" many of her thoughts, "trapping" them for posterity and others who would receive her legacy of faith and fortitude.

Emily Dow Partridge was born on February 28, 1824, in Painesville, Geauga County, Ohio, to Edward and Lydia Clisbee Partridge.[2]

---

1. Emily Dow Partridge Young, Diary and Reminiscences, September 7, 1877, Holograph, p. 58, Church History Library, The Church of Jesus Christ of Latter-day Saints, Salt Lake City, Utah, hereafter cited as Church History Library.

2. Edward Partridge Jr. Genealogical Record, 1878, Holograph, p. 64, Church History Library. Today Painesville is in Lake County, which was formed in 1840

When she was six years old, her family joined The Church of Jesus Christ of Latter-day Saints. Within a year, her father had been called as the first bishop of the Church,[3] and her family had moved to the frontier town of Independence, Missouri. While in Missouri, she and her family, along with many other Saints, were driven from more than one home.[4] Later in life, when she recalled her Missouri experiences, she wrote of January 1839 in Far West:

> The city was under martial law. . . . Many of the saints were short of bread stuff. We had a little corn meal but no flour. Mother hulld wheat to eke out our bread. . . . Well these were some of the good old mobocratic times, of my childhood days.[5]

After being expelled from Missouri, the Partridges settled in Nauvoo, Illinois. While there, Emily's older sister Harriet and their father passed away in May 1840. In 1843, Emily and her sister Eliza both married Joseph Smith as plural wives. After the martyrdom, Emily married Brigham Young, with whom she had seven children: Edward Partridge (1845–1852), Emily Augusta (1849–1926), Caroline Partridge (1851–1903), Joseph Don Carlos (1855–1938), Miriam (1857–1919), Josephine (1860–1912), and Laura (1862–1862).[6]

Although she at times struggled with being a wife of the man who was president of the Church, territorial governor of Utah, and

---

from several townships in northern Geauga County. See 1820 U.S. Federal Census, Painesville, Geauga County, Ohio.

3. Doctrine and Covenants 41:9.

4. Emily Dow Partridge Young, "Autobiography of Emily D. P. Young," *Woman's Exponent* 13, no. 13 (December 1, 1884): 102; Emily Dow Partridge Young, "Incidents of the Life of a Mormon Girl," Holograph, p. 1, Church History Library.

5. Young, "Incidents," 166.

6. Edward Partridge Jr., Genealogical Record, 65.

husband of multiple wives, she shouldered much of the responsibility of raising her children and drew strength and comfort from her faith as well as from her children and, later, her grandchildren. As she reflected on her life in her advanced years, she wrote in her autobiography, "The Lord in mercy withholds the future from our gaze, or that portion that would cause us unhappiness, and gives us strength to bear the reality when it comes, even that which we could not bear in anticipation."[7] Emily Dow Partridge Young remained true to the gospel until the end, passing away on December 9, 1899.[8]

Life Experiences

Emily Dow Partridge Young's personal writings include a diary and several autobiographical works. One of her autobiographical writings appeared in a series of issues of the *Woman's Exponent* in 1884 and 1885. With the first installment appeared this preface:

The following sketch of the life of one of our faithful sisters, told in her own plain unvarnished style, will be doubly interesting to our readers because of the graphic manner in which she describes the most thrilling and pathetic incidents that have ever transpired in the history of the Latter-day Saints. We commend and recommend it to our readers as one of the most interesting pen pictures we have ever read.[9]

Emily was surprised to open the *Exponent* and find her writing inside. She described her feelings in her journal:

Dec I see in the Exponent, De 1st, Sister Wells has started my auto biography. I did not expect to see it in this number and it almost took away my breath. Two spirits have been influencing me since I have been writing, one

7. Young, "Autobiography," 102.

8. "Wife of Brigham Dead," *Salt Lake Tribune,* December 10, 1899.

9. Young, "Autobiography," 102.

tries to shame me out of it, by showing me my weaknesses, and sometimes I have almost given it up, the other says go ahead and do the best you can, never mind what people say, let those that can, do better, and so I have kept on.[10]

Emily's motivation to write came because she wanted people to know and remember what the early Saints of the Church went through. She was anxious that a record be kept of the atrocities committed by Missouri mobs, in part because she had a firm sense of justice. Emily was young when the Saints were driven from Missouri and only partially understood the gravity of the situation that in later years she would comprehend more fully. In 1881 she wrote:

> We were bundled into a waggon with what little we could carry with us and started for—well, any where, out of the state of Missouri. We were set down on the banks of the Missisippi river opposite Quincy to await an opportunity to cross over. . . . Now my home was in a tent on the banks of the Mississippi river, instead of the Missouri, as it was a few years ago, in 1833. Being a child, I could not sense the awful reality of our situation, as older people did. . . . I sometimes look back upon those scenes with horror, and wonder how the saints did continue to endure, time after time such heartless cruelties. . . . It will not be very long, and there will be none left, living upon the earth, to bear witness against the horrid deeds of the Missouri mob. But the records of their wicked deeds remain and that will condemn them. They, yet, will have to foot the bill, with interest.[11]

As long as she lived, Emily felt compelled to bear her witness of the persecutions that she and other early Saints experienced. After

---

10. Young, Diary, December 1884, 185.

11. Young, "Incidents," 167–68.

reading Parley P. Pratt's *Autobiography*,[12] Emily wept and recorded these lines:

> Many incidents Br Pratt speaks of (although I was a child) I well remember. From the time we went to Jac[k]son county and Clay, Caldwell and from that time till his death. Those things connected with the body of the church; I have witnessed with my own eyes, an[d] heard it spoken of at the time. Many of them I have experienced my self, being with and identified with this church since I was seven years old; almost from its commencement.[13]

She had her own share of persecutions both in general and specifically, as she recalled losing one of her pets to the mob in Far West:

> A party of the mob came to fathers correll [corral] and right before our eyes, shot down a young two year old heifer; not so much as saying, "by your permission" The heiffer was one that father had given to me when it was very small and it was my pet. I felt very sorry to see it killed; but the saints children must suffer persecution in silence as well as their parents.[14]

Child though she was, she recognized that she was powerless to stop the mob from taking food from them. She wrote, "I remember seeing [my mother] make some pumpkin pies, using corn meal for the crust; I suppose she thought the corn dodger and pumpkin sauce

---

12. *Autobiography of Parley Parker Pratt . . . His Life, Ministry and Travels*, ed. Parley P. Pratt Jr. (New York: Russell Brothers, 1874).

13. Young, Diary, August 27, 1877, p. 51.

14. Young, "Incidents," 165–66.

would taste better to the children if it was made in the shape of, and called a pie."[15]

When Emily was sixteen years old, her father—Bishop Edward Partridge—met an early death.[16] To help support her family, Emily sought work outside the home and secured a position helping Joseph and Emma Smith with their children. "They gave me the privilege of attending a school that summer, taught by Brother and Sister Howard Coray,"[17] wrote Emily. "This was the last of my going to school. What little education I have got I received in the log cabin schools, as we were roaming about, being driven from place to place; but I have gained an experience that money cannot purchase."[18]

One of the trials Emily struggled with was loneliness. She re-called in her memoirs more than once the loneliness she felt as a young plural wife with a small child, often separated from her mother, sisters, and brother. After a prolonged absence en route to Utah, Emily briefly rejoined her family in the temporary Iowa settle-ment of Mt. Pisgah. She recalled:

> My sisters, Eliza and Caroline, went on with the com-
> panies, and as my baby was very sick at the time it made me

---

15. Emily Partridge Dow Young, "Autobiography of Emily D. P. Young," *Woman's Exponent* 14, no. 4 (July 15, 1885): 26.

16. "When I look back and remember the great responsibility that rested upon my father as first Bishop—his poverty and privations, and the hardships that he had to endure, the accusations of false brethren, the fault-finding of the poor, and the persecutions of our enemies—I do not wonder at his early death." Emily Dow Partridge Young, "Autobiography of Emily D. P. Young," *Woman's Exponent* 13, no. 19 (March 1, 1885): 145.

17. See the chapter on Martha Jane Knowlton Coray in the eBook edition of this volume.

18. Young, "Autobiography," *Woman's Exponent* 14, no. 5 (August 1, 1885): 37.

feel very lonesome to see them all go and leave us, so few, alone in the wilderness.[19]

In her diary, she recalled sitting with her baby in Sugar Creek camp "without home or friends."[20]

Emily found comfort and happiness in her family and experienced bouts of loneliness as her children grew and began to leave home. Yet she allowed her hardships to temper her feelings toward others. She wrote in her diary one evening:

> The girls have invited a few of their associates to spend the evening. They are sometimes rather noisy, but I have spent so many lonely hours or, years, myself, that I may be a little over indulgent to my children. I cannot withold any reasonable pleasure.[21]

She remembered the tragedies of her youth, and her struggles did not cease in adulthood. In her diary, she reflected:

> July 29th 1881 Sunday. Today I'v been thinking, thinking, thinking my mind goes back to days gone by and what do I find, can I find anything so pleasant that I could wish to live it over again or even to dwell upon it in thought, with any degree of satisfaction? No I cannot. My life has been like a panorama of disagreeable pictures. . . . I ask myself what great or good thing have I done that I should hope for better things in the next world—or what great trial or exploit can I recount like many others perhaps, that will bring honor and greatness. I can only sum it up in one word, and that is I am a "woman" or if that is not enough I am a "mother" and still

---

19. Emily Dow Partridge Young, "Autobiography of Emily D. P. Young," *Woman's Exponent* 14, no. 5 (August 1, 1885): 38.

20. Young, Diary, February 15, 1897, p. 253.

21. Young, Diary, December 28, 1874, p. 8.

more I am, as the world calls it, I am a "spiritual wife" of
early days, when public opinion was like an avalanch burying all such beneath its oppressive weight. Some will understand ~~me~~ what it is to be a woman, mother, or an unloved
"spiritual wife."

Aug 1ˢᵗ 1881 Yesterday I was in a dark mood. Today I am
looking for the bright spots, although they may be few and
far between they should not be overlooked and among my
greatest blessings I class the fates that I am a mother, and
was a spiritual wife.[22]

Emily chose to press forward, despite her trials. She wrote about
daily events, and her journal glimmers with humor and inquisitive
thought. For instance, at Brigham Young's seventy-sixth birthday
dinner at the Lion House, someone asked him what resurrected beings eat. He replied, "They eat angels food." Emily drily commented
in her diary, "We were all just as wise then as we were before" but,
her curiosity piqued, "it set me to thinking, is not all that is on this
earth typical of heaven, also what is heaven. The Lord made this
Earth and pronounced it good: if it was freed from sin and death,
would it not be heaven in very deed, would not its beautiful luscious
fruits be good enough for angels?"[23]

In her later life she described a large protest meeting she attended on November 16, 1878, held to oppose federal antipolygamy
legislation and sentiment:

> Being seated in the second circle; and surrounded by
> "mormon wives" evry other one haveing a baby, and the rest
> having two; I was unable to hear much that was said.
>
> However I was pretty well charged with the spirit of the
> meeting; and ocupying an exalted position in the house, I

---

22. Young, Diary, July 29, 1881, and August 1, 1881, pp. 154–55.

23. Young, Diary, June 1, 1877, pp. 31–32.

could look down upon the sisters, and commune with them in spirit.[24]

An aspect of Emily's character that helped her endure was her active interest in the world around her. She often recorded ideas, not only daily happenings, in her diary. For instance, one day she recorded:

Apr 22nd 1877 We all beleive that God created the souls of mankind, now the question arises in my mind "did he oraganize our souls out of the raw materiel bringing them into form, as a child ~~would~~ does mud babies? . . . God has in reserve gifts and graces, which he bestows upon his creatures, according to his great wisdom. Now after organizing souls he gives them their agency, and makes them accountable beings, capable of doing good or evil, which they must chose for themselves, but as they have no experience, they are as apt to choose the evil as the good, but after doing wrong and suffering the consequences that natuaraly follows they have taken one step in knowledge and are better prepared to dissern between right an[d] wrong. And as evrything is known by its opposite, a great amount of experience is necessary, and a great amount of suffering, before souls can be made perfect. . . . As their existence rolls on, and they grow and increase in knowledge more is required at their hands, and as they are faithful over the little they have received God bestows upon them other gifts and graces but if they are slack and abuse the gifts they have received, they loose instead of gaining hence the great difference that we see existing among mankind. The Lord says

24. Young, Diary, November 16, 1878, p. 101. About fifteen hundred women attended the mass meeting held in the Salt Lake Theatre, where "no gentlemen were admitted except reporters." "Woman's Mass Meeting," *Woman's Exponent* 7, no. 13 (December 1, 1878): 97–99, 102–3.

he is no respecter of persons, and we can see the truth of this saying, as all are created after the same plan, possesing the same attributes . . . and all receive the same instruction, and care from their maker, and it rests entirely with themselves whether they improve or not, and if they do not, they have nobody to blame but themselves for God is just as willing to bless one, in doing the works of righteousness, as another, his designs in their creation, is to exalt them to be Gods, to become equal with himself, he has given them all the attributes necesserary to begin with, and he will add to them here a little, and there a little, according to their faithfulness. . . .

. . . Gods work is one of progression, and its study is one of interest and usefulness, easy to be understood when we have the light of the Holy Spirit to inspire our minds and to open the eyes of our understanding to see truths as they actualy exist. Truth is what we want, however strange it may be. . . . Then let us divest our minds of bigotry, and suffer our hearts to become enlarged, that there may be room to receive the beautiful truths of science, which are Gods plans or laws by which he works, and controls all that belongs to him, both in Heaven and on this Earth.[25]

Yet the knowledge she valued most was her testimony of the gospel. She reflected on the sacrifices her family had made for the gospel and concluded:

There is nothing in this life too dear to sacrifice for the hope that our religion gives us. One of my uncles wrote to my father, as follows,—"You say, 'the world, with all its pomp and show, looks very small in your eyes,' I have evry reason to beleive this, from the manner of disposing of your ~~farm~~ property, particularly your farm, which I learn you

25. Young, Diary, April 22, 1877, pp. 22–24.

have received a fifteen years old horse for." The world cannot understand us, or our religion.[26]

One of the tenets of Emily's faith was that God would protect her and her family from evil, although not always from physical hardship. She wrote, "[God] will take us through the fire unscathed, as he has done heretofore."[27] She believed that "if we will place ourselves under his guidance he will lead us on from step to step, from one grade to another untill we obtain perfect bliss."[28] She testified, "I have no fears for the Lord will help those that trust in Him."[29]

Emily recognized, however, that trust in God did not preclude hardship in life. Memories of her persecutions early in life remained vivid in her mind. After watching a parade celebrating the fiftieth anniversary of the pioneers' arrival in the Salt Lake Valley, she recorded: "The old Pioneer waggons were almost too realistic. They brought back in a forcible manner the horrible journey across the plains. I only sat and cried while they passed."[30]

She drew strength from the blessings of Church leaders, many of whom were related to her by marriage. In 1894, Emily described her birthday celebration attended by Joseph F. Smith, then a member of the First Presidency:

> My children made me a birth day party. . . . I never enjoyed myself better before at a party in my life. . . . I wanted some of the bretheren to speak but told Carl not to ask them, for I wanted them to enjoy themselves in their own way. But Pres. Smith just before going, said he wanted to say a few words if we would excuse him for taking the liberty. I

26. Young, "Incidents," 13.

27. Young, Diary, November 16, 1878, p. 105.

28. Young, Diary, June 17, 1877, p. 33.

29. Young, Diary, November 3, 1883, p. 176.

30. Young, Diary, July 24, 1897, p. 255.

wish I could tell all that he said: He said a good many good words for me. . . . He blessed me and my family and all that was there; and I think we all [were] very much comforted and encouraged And I feel to live for those blessings. . . . Truly I am blessed above many for which I thank God.[31]

Gratitude for blessings was an important part of her life, as she recorded in her diary on Christmas Day:

Blessed be the day; but more blessed be He who gave us the day, with its many blessings and good gifts; and many friends with loving hearts and kind wishes. We here in the valleys of the mountains have great reason to rejoice, more than any other people upon the face of the whole earth. But do we appreciate the goodness of our God, can we always acknowledge his hand in all things; our trials as well as our blessings. . . . I feel very thankful for my blessings. I am thankful for motherhood. My children are more to me than all else."[32]

Another day she wrote: "The weather is beautiful and the birds are singing sweetly as I write this on my front porch. All is peace around and within me and Thank God that I am so blessed."[33]

Much of her ability to see the hand of the Lord came through her willingness to work hard and choose faith amidst her trials. At a young age, she struggled with the embarrassment of having to help her father in ways typical of a son, since her parents had five daughters before having a son who survived infancy. She recalled:

---

31. Young, Diary, February 28, 1894, p. 235. For another example, see Young, Diary, February 28, 1896, p. 246.

32. Young, Diary, December 25, 1893, p. 233.

33. Young, Diary, April 28, 1879, p. 117.

As fathers oldest children were all girls; my sister Harriet and I had to be his boys, and help him with his work; such as drop[p]ing corn, and potatoes after father had hoed the rows, and pick them up, when they were ready to dig, and going with him to the prarie to help load hay, and carry the chain for him when he surveyed the land. I sometimes felt a little plagued to have to do so much boys work. But I have, a great many times since had to do that kind of work, but have outgrown such silly, childish notions. Whatever is necessary to be done, I feel no shame in doing.[34]

She labored to raise her children and manage her household without the constant presence of a husband, sustained by spiritual commitment to restored truths:

July 15th [1877] The Gospel of Christ is the most liberal of any thing in the world. It provides for the happiness of evry being. . . . Happiness is what God designs for all his creatures, and the Gospel is what will give it to them, but mankind are so ignorant and shortsighted, they cannot trust their maker, so he places them in positions suiting their capacities . . . untill their minds shall devellop and grow in knowledge and wisdom when they will be able to apreciate blessings, and not abuse those precious gifts, God has in store for all that are worthy, and have been proven competent and trustworthy to receive them. Our Father with holds his most precious things, in mercy, because of ignorance, knowing they would prove our destruction, as a child handling a dangerous weapon, not knowing its danger it would destroy itself, so we see the necessity of seeking knowledge first, before we try to handle those things that are forbiden at the present time. Be patient and faithful, all will be well, be not over anxious, everything will be added in its time and

34. Young, "Incidents," 155–56.

season, do what is required keep pure and unspoted, and happiness and glory are sure.[35]

In the records she made, Emily fulfilled her wish "to use pen ink and paper as a trap, to hold [her thoughts] untill they can be used."[36] In a poem written shortly before her death in 1899, she expressed a wish for her posterity to know of her family's participation in the great events of the early days of the Church:

> *Now we are getting aged*
> *But why should we care*
> *Our children will read history*
> *And know that we were there.*[37]

Of perhaps greater importance than her record of events is Emily Dow Partridge Young's life testimony, preserved in her thoughts and commitment to restored truths. Her testimony still speaks:

> I am determined to move forward in the cause of righ[t]eousness though all hell oppose me; and all my powers of body and mind, shall be spent in the interest of the Kingdom of God. That shall be my life, my existence; I want nothing outside of it, Truth, as it exists with the Gods, is what my soul craves.[38]

---

35. Young, Diary, July 17, 1877, p. 39.

36. Young, Diary, 26.

37. Emily Dow Partridge Young, "Relics of Church History," Photocopy of typescript, p. 6, Church History Library.

38. Young, Diary, September 7, 1877, p. 58.

Chapter 30

"POWER FOR THE ACCOMPLISHMENT OF GREATER GOOD"

ZINA DIANTHA HUNTINGTON YOUNG (1821–1901)

Jennifer Reeder

BIOGRAPHICAL SKETCH

Zina Diantha Huntington was born on January 31, 1821, in Watertown, New York. The Huntington family was well known in the community; her father, William Huntington, a veteran of the War of 1812, and her mother, Zina Baker Huntington, worked to raise a family of ten children and build a profitable farm.[1]

In Nauvoo, Zina married her first husband, Henry Bailey Jacobs, on March 7, 1841; they had two sons, Zebulon and Chariton.[2] The marriage was not a happy one, and the two separated.[3] Zina was

---

1. William Huntington served with the Watertown Rifles, formed in 1813 in Jefferson County, New York. Martha Sonntag Bradley and Mary Brown Firmage Woodward, *Four Zinas: A Story of Mothers and Daughters on the Mormon Frontier* (Salt Lake City, UT: Signature Books, 2000), 6, 20–22.

2. Zebulon Jacobs (1842–1914) and Henry Chariton Jacobs (1846–1915).

3. Emmeline B. Wells wrote, "It was a most unhappy and ill-assorted marriage, and [Zina] subsequently separated from the husband who was so little suited to be

sealed to Joseph Smith as a plural wife. After Joseph's death, she married Brigham Young for time and became the mother of Zina Prescindia Young. She also raised the children of sister wife Clarissa Maria Ross Young—Mary, Maria, Willard, and Phebe—after Clarissa's untimely death.[4] Emmeline B. Wells observed that Zina had a "great mother-heart."[5]

The temple was important in Zina's life. She worshipped in the Kirtland Temple and participated in the choir, recording many spiritual manifestations there.[6] Zina received her endowment in Nauvoo, and she served in the Endowment House in Salt Lake City for many years.[7] She traveled to temples throughout Utah—St. George, Manti, and Logan—to perform sacred ordinances for the dead.[8] She

---

a companion for her through life. Joseph Smith taught her the principle of plural marriage for eternity, and she accepted it as a divine revelation, and was sealed to the Prophet for time and all eternity, after the order of the new and everlasting covenant." Emmeline B. Wells, "A Distinguished Woman: Zina D. H. Young," *Woman's Exponent* 10, no. 13 (December 1, 1881): 99; Augusta Joyce Crocheron, *Representative Women of Deseret: A Book of Biographical Sketches to Accompany the Picture Bearing the Same Title* (Salt Lake City: J. C. Graham, 1884), 12. Zina was sealed to Joseph Smith on October 27, 1841. Bradley and Woodward, *Four Zinas,* 114.

4. Mary Elizabeth Young Croxall (1847–1871); Clarissa Maria Young Dougall (1849–1935); Willard Young (1852–1936); Phoebe Louisa Young Beatie (1854–1931). Emmeline B. Wells described the situation: Zina "took them to her heart and cherished them as her own; the children returned her affection and grew up under her care and guidance." Emmeline B. Wells, "A Distinguished Woman: Zina D. H. Young," *Woman's Exponent* 10, no. 14 (December 15, 1881): 107.

5. Emmeline B. Wells, "Zina D. H. Young," *Young Woman's Journal* 12, no. 6 (June 1901): 257.

6. Crocheron, *Representative Women,* 12; Wells, "Distinguished Woman," *Woman's Exponent* 10, no. 13 (December 1, 1881): 99.

7. "Centennial of President Zina D. Huntington Young," *Relief Society Magazine* 8, no. 3 (March 1921): 134.

8. "Temple Workers: Sketch of Sister Zina D. Young, Worker in the Endowment House," *Young Woman's Journal* 4, no. 7 (April 1893): 294.

was the first matron of the Salt Lake Temple, acting in that capacity from 1893 until her death.[9]

Zina considered her relationships with the women around her to be sacred. She remained close to her mother, daughters, sister, sisters-in-law, and sister wives, as well as neighbors and fellow Church members. She joined the Nauvoo Relief Society on March 24, 1842, at its second meeting.[10] After that Relief Society disbanded, Zina continued to meet with the sisters in Nauvoo.[11] In Winter Quarters, she joined with friends to pray and exercise spiritual gifts.[12] She remained an important influence in the development of the Relief Society in Utah, serving as the third general Relief Society president from 1888 until her death in 1901.

Zina Diantha Huntington Young possessed the spiritual gift of healing. Her maternal grandfather, Oliver Baker, was one of the first physicians in New Hampshire.[13] Her mother, Zina Baker Huntington, "believed God would hear and answer prayer in behalf of the sick" and often was instrumental in healing others.[14] Zina Diantha studied obstetrics and nursing under Dr. Willard Richards

---

9. "Presidents of the Relief Society," *Relief Society Magazine* 7, no. 3 (March 1920): 132.

10. Nauvoo Relief Society Minutes, 1842–1844, March 24, 1842, p. 16, Church History Library, The Church of Jesus Christ of Latter-day Saints, Salt Lake City, Utah, hereafter cited as Church History Library.

11. For example, in her diary, Zina recorded on June 18, 1844: "I went to the Masonic hall with the sisters." Carol Cornwall Madsen, ed., *In Their Own Words: Women and the Story of Nauvoo* (Salt Lake City, UT: Deseret Book, 1994), 69.

12. Wells, "Distinguished Woman," *Woman's Exponent* 10, no. 14 (December 15, 1881): 107.

13. Emmeline B. Wells, "A Distinguished Woman: Zina D. H. Young," *Woman's Exponent* 10, no. 12 (November 15, 1881): 90; Edward W. Tullidge, *The Women of Mormondom* (New York: Tullidge and Crandall, 1877), 205.

14. Wells, "Distinguished Woman," *Woman's Exponent* 10, no. 12 (November 15, 1881): 91.

and attended several births and sickbeds.[15] She also participated in establishing the Deseret Hospital in Salt Lake City. Emmeline B. Wells described Zina as one of the "most powerfully gifted in faith of all the women in the Church. She seems to be specially endowed with this sacred gift, and in the exercise of it has had some wonderful manifestations of the power of God in healing the sick and afflicted. She has so distinguished herself among the sick and sorrowing, that she has gained with many the appellation of 'Zina, the comforter.'"[16]

One of Zina's unusual life experiences involved sericulture. In 1868, Brigham Young asked her to take charge of his large cocoonery and mulberry orchard at Forest Farm, on the outskirts of Salt Lake City, a few miles from her home. The tasks of raising silkworms was not a pleasant one for Zina; a birthmark in the shape of a curled-up worm in the palm of her hand and a mortal terror of worms produced nightmares as she worked to feed and cultivate the crops.[17] Despite her fears, Brigham Young asked the women of Relief Society to take the charge of producing silk, and Zina led the mission. She became the president of the Deseret Silk Association in 1875, traveling around the territory to train women how to produce silk.[18] She served as president of the Utah Silk Commission in 1896.

---

15. Emmeline B. Wells, "Our Beloved President: Zina D. H. Young," *Woman's Exponent* 30, no. 4 (September 1901): 29.

16. "Her sympathies are so keen, as to enter into the feelings of those who are suffering, and so appreciate their conditions as to render them that sympathy which is eminently helpful. She is also a natural nurse; her very touch is indicative of this quality, and her great tenderness wherever there is trouble, sorrow, or pain, is thoroughly genuine. She would have been an eminent woman physician, had she studied the art, but as it is, with her superior, natural ability in this direction and the experience she has gained in her long and useful life among the sick and distressed of all classes, she has won distinction beyond many who have graduated in the science, and her advice and help are often called for by physicians of skill and learning." Wells, "Distinguished Woman," 91.

17. Susa Young Gates, *History of the Young Ladies' Mutual Improvement Association* (Salt Lake City, UT: Deseret News, 1911), 23.

18. Chris Rigby Arrington, "The Finest of Fabrics: Mormon Women and the

Zina D. H. Young spent two of the last months of her life in Canada with her daughter Zina Prescindia Young Card, surrounded with grandchildren.[19] She passed away in Salt Lake City at the age of eighty on August 28, 1901, following a brief illness.

Life Experiences

Zina Diantha Huntington Young was connected to the Young Women organization from its beginning in 1869. Her daughter, Zina Prescindia Young, was one of the founding members. Zina D. H. Young traveled with Eliza R. Snow to promote and support fledgling Young Ladies' Mutual Improvement Associations throughout Utah Territory and outlying Church settlements, "Sister Snow's ringing challenge penetrating into the very depths of the girls' minds and brains, while Aunt Zina's loving appeal sank into their hearts and distilled upon their souls like the dews upon the thirsty hills around their valley homes."[20]

Zina continued to support the Young Ladies' organization when she served as general Relief Society president. Upon the request of editor Susa Young Gates, Zina wrote an account entitled "How I Gained My Testimony" for the *Young Woman's Journal*. The *Journal* was the official organ of the YLMIA under the editorship of Susa

---

Silk Industry in Early Utah," *Utah Historical Quarterly* 46, no. 4 (Fall 1978): 387.

19. Wells, "Our Beloved President," 28.

20. "They traveled thousands and thousands of miles, mostly in carriages or wagons, holding two and sometimes four meetings a day, organizing branches of the Retrenchment or Mutual Improvement Associations, meeting with the Relief Societies, 'preaching up' silk, or the loyal support of home industry; securing subscribers to the *Woman's Exponent;* urging the women and the girls to study well their responsibilities, as mothers, wives and daughters. Then, one meeting dismissed, the same audience would assemble while these two orators and organizers would call a session of the Suffrage Society, or, perhaps, a meeting of the children's Primary Associations. And in this taxing and yet glorious life this woman, these women, lived, labored, suffered, and passed to their rewards. God enrich their memory to all the readers of this history!" Gates, *History,* 25–26.

Young Gates.[21] The purpose of the *Journal* was to prosper and bless all young women "in your good works and noble desires to cultivate and improve yourselves, mentally and spiritually, that you may eventually be prepared to associate with the intelligences of heaven."[22] Zina's details of her conversion, written some fifty-eight years after the fact, reveal a rich testimony and lifelong commitment to the Church.

"How I Gained My Testimony of the Truth"

It was in the year 1831, and I was then but ten years old. There was some religious controversy in our neighborhood between the Presbyterians and the Congregationalists; the Presbyterians wanted to have their clergymen chosen and appointed by the clergymen themselves, and the Congregationalists wanted to have these appointments made by the people by vote themselves.[23] My father was a deeply religious man, and he was anxious to know which would be the right way to proceed in this matter. If he discovered which was right then he would join the sect which held the proper form of worship procedure in this delicate matter. So he said he would get out his own Bible and see for himself what was there said.

I can remember my father sitting quietly perusing the Bible, determined to find the right way, his firm lips closed

---

21. Kristin B. Gerdy, "Young Woman's Journal," in *Enyclopedia of Latter-day Saint History,* ed. Arnold K. Garr, Donald Q. Cannon, and Richard O. Cowan (Salt Lake City, UT: Deseret Book, 2000), 1387; Petrea Gillespie Kelly, "Young Woman's Journal," in *Encyclopedia of Mormonism,* ed. Daniel H. Ludlow, 4 vols. (New York: Macmillan, 1992), 4:1615–16.

22. General Superintendency of the Y.L.M.I.A., "Letter of the Presidency," *Young Woman's Journal* 1, no. 1 (October 1889): 19.

23. Zina wrote, "I was with all my Family raised strict Presbyterians . . . attended sabath school when quite young." Zina D. H. Young, "Autobiography," Holograph, p. 1, Zina Card Brown Family Collection, Church History Library.

with the determination to succeed if success was possible.[24] After many hours of study and reading, aided no doubt with hours of anxious prayer, father one day declared that none of the churches were right according to the way he read the Bible, for none of them had the organization peculiar to the primitive church. There were no prophets, no apostles, no spiritual gifts as were possessed by the ancient saints.

Nothing could shake him from this belief, and the more he thought and conversed upon the matter, the plainer and simpler it seemed to be presented to his understanding. While his mind was in this unsettled state the rumor reached us that there was a prophet in a distant country, who had found a new and golden Bible.[25] The very word "prophet" caught my father's ear and arrested his attention. He was anxious at once to go to this so-called "prophet" and test the strength of his claim.

A neighbor by the name of Joseph Wakefield, cooper by trade, was a companion of my father, and together they had discussed the matter of true and false religions for many an hour. When this rumor about the prophet reached us father and Mr. Wakefield had an earnest consultation as to which should go and see the man. That one should go was an accepted decision. After some talk, Mr. Wakefield thought he would be the better one to go, as he was not at work in the

---

24. One biographer wrote about "the religious spirit which always pervaded the home, and of how the practice of reading a chapter from the scriptures before morning prayers, was strictly observed." May Booth Talmage, "Past Three Score Years and Ten," *Young Woman's Journal* 12, no. 6 (June 1901): 255.

25. Watertown, New York, was about 130 miles from the Hill Cumorah, where Joseph Smith had received the gold plates, and 113 miles from Fayette, New York, where the Church was organized in 1830. In 1831, Joseph and most of the Latter-day Saints moved to Kirtland, Ohio, 375 miles southwest of Watertown.

winter season, and my father, who was a wealthy farmer, always had stock to attend to even in the winter.[26]

Mr. Wakefield, went at once to Seneca County, saw the boy prophet, received a convincing testimony of the truth, and returned with a heart full of zeal, bearing with him a copy of the new Bible, or as it is properly called, the Book of Mormon.[27]

I was going to school that winter, and so did not hear all the talk that was carried on at home after the return of Mr. Wakefield, but I knew in substance what report he had brought with him.[28] One day on my return from school I saw the Book of Mormon, that strange, new book, lying on the window sill of our sitting-room. I went up to the window, picked it up, and the sweet influence of the Holy Spirit accompanied it to such an extent that I pressed it to

---

26. Joseph Wakefield was born about 1792 and was a resident and property owner in Watertown, New York. As a cooper, or barrel maker, Wakefield would not have been working in the winter, whereas Huntington, a farmer, had animals to tend. Susan Easton Black, *Who's Who in the Doctrine and Covenants* (Salt Lake City, UT: Deseret Book, 1997), 323; Janet Peterson and LaRene Gaunt, *Elect Ladies: Presidents of the Relief Society* (Salt Lake City, UT: Deseret Book, 1990), 45.

27. Joseph Smith was well pleased with Joseph Wakefield, and Wakefield was called on a mission with Parley P. Pratt and later with Solomon Humphrey (Doctrine and Covenants 50:37; 52:35). Wakefield later became critical of Joseph Smith, concerned that Smith could engage in such holy work as translation and then immediately play with children. Wakefield became disaffected from the Church. George A. Smith, "Divine Origin of 'Mormonism'—Doings and Sayings of Early Opposers and Apostates," January 10, 1858, *Journal of Discourses*, 20 vols. (London: Latter-day Saints' Book Depot, 1854–1886), 7:112.

28. According to May Booth Talmage, "The child Zina was always delicate, and could attend school at intervals only, nor was she equal to the heavier household duties; but a wise mother saw to it that she was taught how the work should be done." Talmage, "Past Three Score Years and Ten," 255.

my bosom in a rapture of delight, murmuring as I did so, "This is the truth, truth, truth!"[29]

In the following summer Hyrum Smith and David Whitmer came to our house and stayed several days.[30] Father and mother had been baptized in the April of that same year, but neither myself nor my sister were baptized.[31]

David Whitmer persuaded me to be baptized while they were at our home, but some way I did not accept his offer. I had told my sister-in-law, Fanny Huntington, that when she was baptized I would go with her.[32]

The morning for the departure of these men from our house arrived, and I had not as yet become a member of the Church. That morning, a short time before they were to start, Hyrum Smith's cousin rode up with a message that they could not leave that day, as my brother Dimick and his wife Fanny, my dear sister-in-law, were desirous of being baptized.

The morning at prayers I had presented to me a heavenly vision of a man going down into the water and baptizing someone. So when this message came I felt it was a testimony that the time had come for me to receive baptism. Brother Hyrum Smith was mouth in prayer, and in

29. Zina later wrote: "I knew it had been brought forth by an angel's hand and the feeling that possessed me was one of supreme ecstasy. From that moment until the present I have never had a doubt of its divinity." Talmage, "Past Three Score Years and Ten," 256.

30. This mission of Hyrum Smith and David Whitmer was part of a larger proselytizing effort by all twelve apostles, who departed from Kirtland on May 4, 1835, for work in Pennsylvania and New York. Ronald K. Esplin and Sharon E. Nielsen, "The Record of the Twelve, 1835: The Quorum of the Twelve Apostles' Call and 1835 Mission," *BYU Studies Quarterly* 51, no. 1 (2012): 4–52.

31. William and Zina Baker Huntington were baptized in April 1835 by either John Smith or Joseph Smith Sr. Bradley and Woodward, *Four Zinas,* 44.

32. Fanny Maria Allen (1810–1894) married Dimick Baker Huntington on April 28, 1830. Her name is sometimes spelled Fannie.

my secret soul I had a wish that he should baptize me. I had refused the coaxing of Brother Whitmer, as I told myself, because mother and father were going away from home, and I had all the home cares on me, and I feared I would be tempted to speak crossly or say something I ought not to after so sacred an ordinance as that; but this strong testimony that the proper time had arrived I did not dare treat lightly.

As soon as I consented to go with my brother and sister-in-law David Whitmer began talking about performing the office for us. Happily for me, however, Brother Hyrum was chosen by the others to be the proper one and I added my preference to their words. Accordingly, we all went down to the water and were baptized by Hyrum Smith, and confirmed under the hands of Hyrum Smith and David Whitmer.

Soon after this, the gift of tongues rested upon me with overwhelming force. I was somewhat alarmed at this strange manifestation, and so checked its utterance. What was my alarm, however, to discover that upon this action upon my part, the gift left me entirely, and I felt that I had offended that Holy Spirit by whose influence I had been so richly blessed.[33]

I suffered a great deal in my feelings over this matter, and one day while mother and I were spinning together, I took courage and told her of the gift I had once possessed, and how, by checking it I had lost it entirely.

Mother appreciated my feelings, and told me to make it

---

33. Emmeline B. Wells described Zina's gift of tongues and interpretation: "She has, perhaps, as perfect a gift of interpretation of tongues as any person in the Church, for although her opportunities for education in language have been limited, and she is not a poet or rhymer, yet she gives the interpretation of hymns, psalms and sacred songs in the most musical and happy manner, without thought or hesitation. There is something divinely beautiful in thus rendering, by the gift of inspiration, words uttered in an unknown tongue." Wells, "Distinguished Woman," 107.

a matter of earnest prayer, that the gift might once more be given to me.

I walked down to a little spring in one of the meadows, and as I walked along I mused on my blessing and how I had turned away the Spirit of God. When I reached the spring, I knelt down and offered up a prayer to God and told Him if He could forgive my transgression, and give me back the lost gift, I would promise never to check it again, no matter where or when I felt its promptings.

I have kept this vow, but it has been a heavy cross at times, for I know that this gift is the least of all gifts, and it is oftentimes misunderstood and even treated lightly by those who should know better. Yet it is a gift of God, and should not be despised by him who receives it, but magnified to its extent, even as the lowest grade of the priesthood is the least of all, and yet it needs be magnified as earnestly as are the higher and greater offices.[34]

From the day I received the sweet testimony of the Spirit, when grasping the precious Book of Mormon in my hands to my breast, I have never doubted nor faltered in my faith. I know this is the Church and Kingdom of God, and I rejoice in putting my testimony before the daughters of Zion, that their faith may be strengthened, and that the good work may roll on. Seek for a testimony, as you would, my dear sisters, for a diamond concealed. If someone told you by digging long enough in a certain spot you would find a diamond of unmeasured wealth, do you think you would begrudge time or strength, or means spent to obtain that treasure? Then I

---

34. For example, on April 1, 1845, Zina recorded in her diary: "Went to Brother Brewer's to see Mother Brewer, the first time I have been there. Father Huntington came in the evening. He spoke in tongues. Henry also sung in tongues. It was very good. I interpreted the talk by the help of the Spirit of God. Had an agreeable visit." Zina D. H. Young, April 1, 1845, Zina D. H. Young Diaries, 1844–1845, 1886, and 1889, Holograph, Church History Library.

will tell you that if you will dig in the depths of your own hearts you will find, with the aid of the Spirit of the Lord, the pearl of great price, the testimony of the truth of this work.

ZINA D. H. YOUNG[35]

In 1881, Zina answered the Relief Society call to produce an autobiographical sketch for the Church's Jubilee Celebration in 1880. The following memoir outlines the principal events in her life and emphasizes her testimony. Along with contributions from seventy others, Zina's memoir was placed in a specially designed tin box as part of a time capsule. The box was opened fifty years later, in 1930, and the writings were dispersed to various living family members.[36]

Autobiographical Sketch, Jubilee Box

Salt Lake City March 30th 1881

To the Eldest female descendant of the Family of Zina Diantha Huntington Young Smith Born Jan 31st 1821 in Watertown Jefferson County New York Baptised by Hiram Smith Aug 1st 1835 sealed to Joseph Smith 1841.

Have been with the Church of Jesus Christ of Latterday saints in all its travels & expulsions except Jackson Co Mo Mother of 3 children Zebulon Chariton & Zina Step Mother to Mary Maria Pheba & William Young.

May Gods chosen blessings be uppon Israel and our decendants is my prayer.

---

35. Zina D. H. Young, "How I Gained My Testimony of the Truth," *Young Woman's Journal* 4, no. 7 (April 1893), 317–19.

36. Sarah M. Kimball, January 1, 1880, Relief Society Record, 1880–1892, Holograph, p. 52, Church History Library; "Zina D. H. Young Jubilee Box Contributions, 1878–1887," Holograph, Church History Library.

Salt Lake City, April 17 1881.

A brief sketch of Zina D. H. Young Smith's life.

I am the daughter of William and Zina Baker Huntington. I was born Jan. 31st 1821. Water Town Jeferson Co. St. of New York.

My parents were married Dec. 28th 1806 and lived in New York. My Father was a prosperous business man, and was noted for his temperance and Christianity. For years he had been looking for a church with prophets and apostles. In 1833 they heard the truth, and were baptised 1835 into the church of Jesus Christ of latter day Saints.

The next year they left New York and gathered with the saints in Kirtland, Ohio.^{37} My self together with my brother Dimmick B. Huntington and wife were baptised by Hyrum Smith the 1st day of August 1835. We witnessed many manifestations of the power of God, such as healing the sick, gift of tongues &c.^{38}

May 21st 1838 we left Kirtland for Missouri, and traveled 1000 mi. my father walking all the way. We traveled with ox teams, and the memory of the beautiful flowers and

---

37. On October 1, 1835, the Huntington family sold two hundred acres of land, their house, and barns at a great loss and departed to gather with the Saints in Kirtland. Young, "Autobiography," 4; Bradley and Woodward, *Four Zinas,* 51–52.

38. In Kirtland, Zina met Joseph Smith for the first time. She wrote, "When he was filled with the spirit of revilation or inspiration—to talk to the saints his countenance would look clear & bright & the witnesses of the book of mormon could never deny the spirit they received & witnessed." At the Kirtland Temple, Zina witnessed angelic singing: She heard "the singing one corner of the house seemed filled with music to sweet for earth the gift of tongs & healing the sick all our blessings faith & ordinances are in the new testament." Young, "Autobiography," 4–5. It was reported, "On one occasion in the Kirtland Temple [Zina] heard a whole invisible choir of angels singing, till the house seemed filled with numberless voices." Zina "was also at the memorable Pentecost when the spirit of God filled the house like a mighty, rushing wind." Crocheron, *Representative Women,* 12.

verdant grass of the pra[i]ries was some recompense for the severe storms and hardships we had to endure.[39]

We arrived at Far West where we found my brother Dimick.[40] My only sister Presendia B. Kimball Smith had gone on to Clay Co. My father and mother with my three brothers William Oliver and John with my self entered Adam ondiahman Oct. 1st and had the privilege of seeing the red sand stone altar where Adam once offered sacrifice to the living God.[41] We looked upon the valley of Grand River where his children rose up and called him blessed.[42] In all our triels in Misourri God sustained us.

We left Far West for Illanois in [18]39. We stopped in Quincy a short time, where we had the joy of seeing the Prophet Joseph again, he had just been delivered from prison.[43]

We arrived in Commerce or Nauvoo 14th of May of the same year. Here we had to pass through the sad trial of

---

39. According to William Huntington, the Huntington family was so destitute upon leaving Kirtland, due to the failure of the Kirtland Bank, that Oliver Snow lent them a pair of oxen to replace their mare. Bradley and Woodward, *Four Zinas,* 77.

40. The Huntington family stayed for a month with Dimick and Fanny Huntington, William and Diana's oldest son and daughter-in-law, before moving to Adam-ondi-Ahman. Bradley and Woodward, *Four Zinas,* 80–81.

41. Heber C. Kimball reported a conversation with Joseph Smith when he showed them "the ruins of three altars built of stone, one above the other, and one standing a little back of the other, like unto pulpits in the Kirtland Temple, representing the order of three grades of Priesthood. 'There,' said Joseph, 'is the place where Adam offered up sacrifice after he was cast out of the garden.' The altar stood at the highest point of the bluff. I went and examined the place several times while I remained there." Orson F. Whitney, *Life of Heber C. Kimball* (Salt Lake City, UT: Kimball Family, 1888), 210; Wilford Woodruff, *Wilford Woodruff, His Life and Labors,* ed. Matthias F. Cowley (Salt Lake City, UT: Deseret News, 1916), 481.

42. Doctrine and Covenants 107:53–54.

43. Joseph Smith, who had been imprisoned in Liberty Jail, was allowed to escape on April 16, 1839, during a change of venue.

burying our dear mother.[44] I was left to care for my father and three brothers. There was a great deal of sickness among the people at the time, and the kindness bestowed upon us by the Prophet Joseph and his wife Emma can never be forgotten, though we were afflicted yet was the Lord with us as was shown by the mericle of healing done among the Saints.[45]

My father married the widow of Bishop Edward Partridge, and they were very happy for six years.[46]

Through the mercy of God I accepted the pri[n]ciple of celestial marriage. I was taught it by Joseph Smith himself and have ever been thankful to God that I was thus blest, this was in 1841, and never have I spoken against the principle, though I have been a plural wife for forty years.[47]

The sceanes of June 27, 1844 need not be dwelt upon

---

44. Zina Baker Huntington died of malaria on July 8, 1839. Zina Diantha remembered: "Thus died my martyred mother! The Prophet Joseph often said that the Saints who died in the persecutions were as much martyrs of the Church, as was the Apostle David Patten, who was killed in the defense of the Saints, or those who were martyred at Haun's Mill. And my beloved mother was one of the many bright martyrs of the Church in those dark and terrible days of persecution." Wells, "Distinguished Woman," 99.

45. "The Prophet Joseph, with his characteristic sympathy for all suffering, showed [the Huntingtons] great kindness, doing all in his power to comfort them, and at one time made them tea with his own hands." Wells, "Distinguished Woman," 99.

46. William Huntington married Lydia Clisbee Partridge (1793–1878) on September 29, 1840, in Nauvoo. Lydia's first husband, Edward Partridge, the presiding bishop, had died in May 1840. William shouldered responsibility for the five surviving Partridge children. Bradley and Woodward, *Four Zinas,* 105.

47. Zina Young spoke publicly in defense of plural marriage at a mass meeting in Salt Lake City, November 16, 1878. She said: "The principle of plural marriage is honorable; it is a principle of the Gods, it is heaven-born. God revealed it to us among other things as a saving principle; we have accepted it as such, and we know it is of Him, for the fruits of it are holy." Emmeline B. Wells, "A Distinguished Woman: Zina D. H. Young," *Woman's Exponent* 10, no. 16 (January 15, 1882): 123.

by me. I was the wife of the Prophet Joseph and as a wife his death was mourned and loss severely felt.[48]

Two years later we started in the winter to find another resting place. Our enemies driving us from our homes in the dead of winter. We stoped at Mount Pisga, where my dear father died. This was in Aug. 19, 1849[6]. This was a heavy blow to me.[49]

Oct. 1st [1846] I started for Winter Quarter[s]. Our journeying from there to the Valley of Salt Lake is generally known. My brother Oliver drove my team and with my two sons Zebulon and Chariton we made the long tedious journey. We came in the next company after the pioneers and endured many hardships, but we rejoiced through it all for we were free to worship God as we had been directed by revelation, and God was with his people.[50] After we arrived I taught school for several months.[51]

---

48. Zina wrote, "My pen cannot utter my grief nor describe my horror. But after awhile a change came, as though the released spirits of the departed sought to comfort us in that hour of dreadful bereavement." Tullidge, *Women of Mormondom*, 326.

49. "My father was taken sick, and in eighteen days he died. Like my dear mother, who died in the expulsion from Missouri, he died in the exodus from Nauvoo. Sad was my heart. I alone of all his children was there to mourn. It was a solemn day at Mt. Pisgah when my father was buried." Wells, "Distinguished Woman," 107.

50. Zina and her two sons traveled with the 1848 Brigham Young Company in the care of her brother, Oliver Huntington. They left Winter Quarters on May 16, 1848, and arrived in the Salt Lake Valley on September 20, 1848. Oliver recorded that upon setting forth, siblings "Presendia, Wm, Zina and Oliver were all together once more upon the earth—and but a short time ago—a few months—and not one of Our Fathers family was with another and thousands of miles separated us. We were united and agreed, and felt to bless each other. . . . We had 2 joyful seasons of speaking in tongues, and much was said to our joy; and comfort." Oliver Boardman Huntington, May 16, 1848, Diaries, 1843–1932, Holograph, vol. 9, p. 88, L. Tom Perry Special Collections, Harold B. Lee Library, Brigham Young University, Provo, Utah.

51. Zina Young conducted school in her home in Salt Lake City from about

I am the mother of three Children Zebulon and Chariton Jacobs and Zina Young. In 1858 my husband, Brigham Young, wished me to take four of his children to raise whose mother, Clarissa Maria Ross was dead.[52] She had been one of my dear friends and her children, Mary, Maria Phebe and Willard by name, shared in my affections equally with my own.[53]

I have lived to see many changes. I have twelve grand-children, and am in good health.[54] I bear my testimony that this is the Kingdom of God, that we serve a just God, who

---

December 1848 to February 1849. She taught spelling, singing, and other topics to children and adults. Zina D. H. Young, December 11, 1848, "Diary 1848–1850," Zina C. Brown Collection, Church History Library, Salt Lake City, Utah; for a published version, see Marilyn Higbee, ed., "'A Weary Traveler': The 1848–50 Diary of Zina D. H. Young," *Journal of Mormon History* 19, no. 2 (Fall 1993): 91–100. According to one account, Zina taught several leading men in her private school. Talmage, "Past Three Score Years and Ten," 256.

52. Clarissa Maria Ross Young (1814–1858). Eliza R. Snow recorded tender experiences with Zina and Clarissa in Winter Quarters, describing their shared friendship: "This mor. take leave of the *female family* . . . we had a very interesting time to close my five day visit with the girls; for whom my love seem'd to increase with every day's acquaintance To describe the scene alluded to would be beyond my pow'r—suffice it to say the spirit of the Lord was pour'd out and we receiv'd a blessing thro' our belov'd Mother [Phoebe Ogden Ross] Chase & sis Clarissa, by the gift of tongues." Eliza R. Snow, *The Personal Writings of Eliza Roxcy Snow,* ed. Maureen Ursenbach Beecher (Salt Lake City: University of Utah Press, 1995), January 1, 1847, 151.

53. Zina Presendia Young affectionately remembered how "father asked mother to take charge of four of his little ones whose mother was dead. She consented, and this event entirely changed my after life; from being the pet and only child I now had to share with these motherless children. It was a trial in many ways, but my precious mother taught me to be unselfish and thank God for all His blessings and not complain, and I am thankful to say, following her advice without once alluding to the fact that my mother was not their own. Thus it proved to be the best lesson of my life, and a great blessing." Crocheron, *Representative Women,* 122–23.

54. This number of twelve grandchildren reflects those born prior to 1881, when this reminiscence was written, and includes the grandchildren born to Zina's

has spoken in this the last days of the children of men. That Joseph Smith was a true prophet and Brigham Young his legal successor. I have never doubted nor faltered but this testimony lives for ever. Now may we and must be ever faithful to our covenants is the prayr of Zina D. H. Young Smith.

Zina D. H. Young participated in the Relief Society from her early membership in Nauvoo in 1842 to her leadership in Utah. When the reorganization of Relief Society was begun in 1868, Zina served as treasurer of the Salt Lake City Eighteenth Ward's society.[55] She later served as first counselor to Eliza R. Snow, the general Relief Society president. Zina and Eliza worked closely together with Relief Society, Primary, and the Young Ladies' Mutual Improvement Association, as well as with efforts including retrenchment, home industry and silk manufacture, grain storage, and the Deseret Hospital. They often traveled together throughout the Territory and spoke at meetings.

Susa Young Gates described their relationship: "Some spoke of the two as the head and the heart of the women's work in Utah. Sister Snow was keenly intellectual, and she led by force of that intelligence. Sister Zina was all love and sympathy, and drew people after her by reason of that tenderness."[56] Zina was called to succeed Eliza R. Snow as general president of the Relief Society in 1888 and served until her death in 1901. During that time, the Relief Society celebrated its fifty-year jubilee in 1892, participated in the

---

four adopted children. In total Zina had nineteen natural grandchildren, plus twenty-three from Clarissa Maria Ross Young's family.

55. Until September 1, 1971, women paid annual dues to become members of the Relief Society. After that date, payment of dues was discontinued, and all Latter-day Saint women were enrolled in Relief Sociey. Jill Mulvay Derr, Janath Russell Cannon, Maureen Ursenbach Beecher, *Women of Covenant: The Story of Relief Society* (Salt Lake City, UT: Deseret Book; Provo, UT: Brigham Young University Press, 1992), 345–46.

56. Gates, *History,* 21.

Chicago World's Fair in 1893, supported the dedication of the Salt Lake Temple in 1893, and observed Utah's statehood and the return of woman suffrage in 1896.

As the third general Relief Society president, Zina coordinated the first general Relief Society conference on April 6, 1889, in the Salt Lake Tabernacle.[57] Her speech was recorded in the *Woman's Exponent* to allow women throughout the Church to read it and learn from their leader.

"First General Conference of the Relief Society"

The Relief Society, under whose auspices we have met together here to-night, to receive instruction, and advice in our several duties, was first organized nearly half a century ago, by the Prophet Joseph Smith; after the pattern of the Holy Priesthood, and under its direction, to dispense temporal blessings to the poor and needy: and to give encouragement to the weak, and restrain the erring ones, and for the better development, and exercise of woman's sympathies, and charities, that she might have opportunity to attain spiritual strength, and power for the accomplishment of greater good in the work of the redemption of the human family. . . . [58]

---

57. "One of the most notable features of the progress of the Relief Society was the inauguration of annual and semi-annual conferences for women, where special instruction peculiar to their work could be given by the President and her counselors and other experienced women, and where verbal reports are made by the Presidents of Stake and societies or their representatives. Each society through these privileges is enabled to receive the benefit of the combined wisdom and intelligence of the whole." Romania B. Pratt, "The Present Administration of the Relief Society," *Woman's Exponent* 20, no. 18 (April 1, 1892): 137.

58. Sarah Kimball remembered the organization of the first Relief Society in Nauvoo when Joseph Smith "declared the Society organized *after* the pattern, or order, of the priesthood." Kimball, "Relief Society Record, 1880–1892," 5. At the fifty-year jubilee celebration of the Relief Society, Zina Young declared, "As sisters

It is the privilege of the sisters, who are faithful in the discharge of their duties, and have received their endowments and blessings in the house of the Lord, to administer to their sisters, and to the little ones, in times of sickness, in meekness and humility, ever being careful to ask in the name of Jesus, and to give God the glory.[59]

Do not find fault with the Providences of God, it will not better our condition and only make our burdens heavier to bear; but rather be patient through all the trials of life, and speak not against the Lord's anointed. . . .

Sisters, let us be as one grand phalanx and stand for the right; let us be humble and firm, honor truth, and be valiant in sustaining it, not *presuming* it, but trust-worthy in all things.[60] Have we not shouldered the cross of the world's scorn, and braved its anathema with more valor, than the warrior the cannon's fury? Death with him, and then all is

---

of this organization we have been set apart for the purpose of comforting and consoling the sick and afflicted the poor and distressed, particularly those who love and fear God; to comfort one another in every trial of life, and cheer the depressed in spirit, on all occasions; this is our special mission, therefore keep this in remembrance. If we continue to do these things in the spirit thereof, the Lord, at the time when He comes to make up His jewels, will approve of us." "Relief Society Jubilee," *Woman's Exponent* 20, no. 18 (April 1, 1892): 140.

59. On such administrations by women in the early Church, see Jonathan A. Stapley and Kristine Wright, "Female Ritual Healing in Mormonism," *Journal of Mormon History* 37, no. 1 (Winter 2011): 1–85.

60. In 1861, John Taylor compared the priesthood to a phalanx, or organized body of infantry, united in a common purpose: "The Priesthood is placed in the Church for this purpose, to dig, to plant, to nourish, to teach correct principles, and to develop the order of the kingdom of God, to fight the devils, and maintain and support the authorities of the Church of Christ upon the earth. It is our duty all to act together to form one great unit—one great united phalanx, having sworn allegiance to the kingdom of God; then everything will move on quietly, peaceably, and easily." John Taylor, "Union—Human and Divine Government," April 6, 1861, in *Journal of Discourses,* 20 vols. (London: Latter-day Saints' Book Depot, 1854–1886), 9:14.

over, but we endure to live eternally. Purity, love and integrity, let these virtues live in our hearts; then the sunshine of a loving Father's smile will be ours. Do not doubt the goodness of God or the truth of the work in which we are engaged; but learn obedience, it is better than sacrifice; follow our file leaders and fear not.[61]

May we do a work acceptable to our Heavenly Father, and that will meet the approbation of our brethren, who are called upon to endure for the truth's sake, what the Ancients did, when seeking to establish righteous principles to benefit humanity. May we as women of Zion, ever know and honor our true position, and continue to grow in grace, and abound in good works, until He whose right it is to reign shall come.

---

61. 1 Samuel 15:22.

CONTRIBUTORS

LOWELL C. "BEN" BENNION received a bachelor's degree from the University of Utah, a master's from Syracuse University, and a PhD in geography from Syracuse University. He taught the subject for thirty-five years, first at Indiana University and then at Humboldt State University before retiring to Salt Lake City with his wife, Sherilyn Cox, in the year 2000. His publications include *Sanpete Scenes: A Guide to Utah's Heart* (coauthor Gary B. Peterson) and *Traveling the Trinity Highway* (coauthor Jerry Rohde).

ROSEANN BENSON earned a PhD in public and school health and a second master's degree in Ancient Near Eastern Studies. She is an adjunct professor at Brigham Young University and Utah Valley University. She teaches classes in religious education, nutrition, and drug education and has several publications on disordered eating. She also has several publications in the *Religious Educator* and one in the *Journal of Book of Mormon Studies*.

DAVID F. BOONE received a master's degree in American western history and a PhD in educational leadership, both from Brigham Young University, where he teaches religious education. David is married to Mary Farnsworth Boone, and they are the parents of eight children and grandparents of fifteen. A great-grandson of Lucy Hannah White Flake, he is transcribing and annotating her journals for publication.

CHRISTINE BANKS BOWERS received her bachelor's degree in sociology from the University of Utah and a master's degree in marriage, family, and child counseling from the University of Nevada–Reno. She has worked as a therapist and educator and volunteers as a public-speaking coach to young people in the Boys & Girls Clubs of Maui, Hawaii, where she lives with her husband, Daniel J. Bowers, a great-grandson of Mary Goble Pay. They are the parents of two children and grandparents of three.

JAY G. BURRUP graduated from Brigham Young University with a BA in history and an MS in library and information science. He is a certified archivist at the Church History Library of The Church of Jesus Christ of Latter-day Saints. Jay and his wife, Dorothy Anderson Burrup, live in West Valley, Utah, and are the parents of four daughters. Catherine Mehring Woolley is Dorothy Burrup's great-great-grandmother.

REBEKAH RYAN CLARK graduated from Harvard University with a bachelor's degree in American history and literature. After continuing her studies on Latter-day Saint women as a research fellow at the Joseph Fielding Smith Institute for Latter-day Saint History at Brigham Young University, Rebekah earned her law degree from the J. Reuben Clark Law School at BYU. Rebekah and her husband, Andrew, live in Highland, Utah, with their two daughters. She teaches history part-time for Brigham Young University–Idaho. She and her brother, Marcus Patrick Ryan, are coauthors of the story of their great-great-great-grandmother Janetta Ann McBride Ferrin.

TODD M. COMPTON received his bachelor's and master's degrees from Brigham Young University and a PhD in classics from UCLA. He presently works at a law firm in California in the Bay area. He is the author of *In Sacred Loneliness: The Plural Wives of Joseph Smith* and co-editor (with Charles Hatch) of *A Widow's Tale: The 1884–1896 Diary of Helen Mar Whitney* and (with Leland Gentry) *Fire and Sword: A History of the Latter-day Saints in Northern Missouri, 1836–39.* He and his wife, Laura, are the parents of two boys. He is writing a biography of Jacob Hamblin, which led to his interest in the life and writings of Mary Minerva Dart Judd.

DAVID R. COOK earned a bachelor's degree in chemistry from the University of Utah and an MBA from Westminster College in Salt Lake City. His career has taken him from laboratory science to public health. He is married to Kristin Carver, and they have four daughters. He is a family history researcher and a descendant of Susanah Stone Lloyd.

CRAIG C. CRANDALL attended Utah State University and graduated with a degree in agricultural technology. He resides in Chesterfield, Idaho, and owns and oversees ranching operations in southeast Idaho. He is married to Elizabeth Wright, and they are the parents of seven children. He is a great-great-great-grandson of Hannah Last Cornaby.

SHERILYN FARNES received a bachelor's degree in history teaching and a master's degree in history, both from Brigham Young University. After writing her master's thesis on Edward Partridge, she became an editor of the forthcoming *Let Zion in Her Beauty Rise: The Papers of Edward Partridge.* For the past year, Sherilyn has been working with the Joseph Smith Papers Project at the Church History Library.

EMILY B. FARRER received a bachelor's degree from Brigham Young University in school health and a minor in history. She and her husband, Evan Farrer, are the parents of four children. Emily enjoys reenacting pioneer life with her children at This Is the Place Heritage Park in Salt Lake City. She is the great-great-granddaughter of Margaret Condie Sharp.

ALISHA ERIN HILLAM holds a master's degree in antebellum American history from Purdue University, where she focused her research on the early history of The Church of Jesus Christ of Latter-day Saints. She taught Church history at the Purdue LDS Institute of Religion and earned a bachelor's degree in creative and professional writing, also from Purdue. She resides in Phoenix, Arizona, where she is a wife, a stay-at-home mother, and a freelance writer and poet.

CATHLEEN C. LLOYD has worked in the health information management field for the past twenty years. She is married to Wayne P. Lloyd, and they have two children and three grandchildren. In her spare time, Cathleen enjoys stitching reproduction school-girl samplers. She resides with her husband in South Jordan, Utah, and is a great-great-great-granddaughter of Hannah Last Cornaby.

JENNIFER L. LUND is the director of the Historic Sites Division in the Church History Department of The Church of Jesus Christ of Latter-day Saints. The recipient of a BA in English from the University of Utah and an MA in American history from Brigham Young University, she has worked with museums and historic sites for more than thirty years. She is married to Anthony F. Lund, a great-great-grandson of Sarah Ann Nelson Peterson.

CAROL CORNWALL MADSEN obtained bachelor's and master's degrees and a PhD at the University of Utah. She is a professor emeritus of history at Brigham Young University, where she was a senior research historian at the Smith Institute for LDS History before her retirement. Carol has written a biography of the public life of Emmeline B. Wells and is working on another biography of Emmeline's private life. Carol and her husband, Gordon, are the parents of six children and grandparents of twelve.

MARJORIE NEWTON earned her BA, MA (Hons.), and PhD from the University of Sydney. She is the author of *Southern Cross Saints: The Mormons in Australia* (1991), *Hero or Traitor? A Biographical Study of Charles Wesley Wandell* (1992), and *Tiki and Temple: The Mormon Mission in New Zealand, 1854–1958* (2012), as well as numerous articles. Her doctoral dissertation on Mormonism and the Maori is forthcoming from Greg Kofford Books. Marjorie is an Australian who was born in Sydney and lives in Hobart, Tasmania.

DEBORAH RICH OTTESON attended Ricks College and graduated with a bachelor's degree in secondary music education from Brigham Young University. Since that time, she has spent her career teaching music in elementary school using the Kodaly method of music education. She has endorsements in this method from the Hart School of Music in Hartford, Connecticut, and Intermuse in Provo, Utah. The past eight years she has taught music at American Heritage School in American Fork, Utah, and lives with her family in Draper, Utah. Emeline Grover Rich is Deborah's great-great-grandmother.

Madelyn Stewart Silver Palmer graduated from Wellesley College with a degree in psychobiology and then studied medicine at the University of Utah Medical School. She is married to James Palmer, and they are the parents of four sons. Madelyn practices medicine in Littleton, Colorado, and has written a historical novel about the wife of Nephi, the Book of Mormon prophet. Sarah Mariah Mousely Cannon is Madelyn's great-great-grandmother.

Jay A. Parry is a full-time writer and editor for the Church History Department of The Church of Jesus Christ of Latter-day Saints. He has published more than two dozen books, as well as many short articles in various periodicals. These publications include *Joseph Smith: The Boy, the Prophet; The Real George Washington: The True Story of America's Most Indispensable Man; LDS Women's Treasury: Insights and Inspiration for Today's Woman; Best-Loved Stories of the LDS People* (three volumes); *Everyday Miracles: True Stories about God's Hand in Our Lives;* and *Symbols and Shadows: Unlocking a Deeper Understanding of the Atonement.* Jay and his wife, Vicki Hughes Parry, are the parents of seven children and grandparents of nine.

Virginia H. Pearce was reared in Salt Lake City, Utah, the third child of Gordon B. and Marjorie P. Hinckley. She received a bachelor's degree in history and a master's degree in social work, both from the University of Utah. She has worked as a therapist, written several books, and lectured widely. Virginia served on the Primary general board and as a counselor in the Young Women general presidency. She and her late husband, James R. Pearce, are the parents of six children and grandparents of twenty-seven. Virginia is the great-granddaughter of Mary Goble Pay.

ANDREA G. RADKE-MOSS is a professor of history at Brigham Young University–Idaho. Her book *Bright Epoch: Women and Coeducation in the American West* was published by the University of Nebraska Press. She has published on Latter-day Saint women, higher education, school teaching, and material culture in the Great Plains and the American West. Andrea lives in Rexburg, Idaho, with her husband, Stephen, and their two children.

JENNIFER REEDER is a doctoral candidate in American history at George Mason University. She holds an MA in American history and a certificate in archival management and historical editing from New York University and a BA in humanities from Brigham Young University. The recipient of various fellowships, she is working on her dissertation, examining Mormon women and their cultural history, with a focus on material culture and the memory and commemoration of the Nauvoo Relief Society.

JENNIFER PRATT REIDHEAD received a bachelor's degree in international relations from Brigham Young University. She worked on Capitol Hill in Washington, D.C., and has worked part-time in the Human Resources Department of The Church of Jesus Christ of Latter-day Saints for many years. She and her husband, John Reidhead, live in Centerville, Utah, where they raised their three children. She is a great-great-great-granddaughter of Julia Sophia Raymond McKee.

TERESA S. RICH received bachelor's and master's degrees in microbiology from Brigham Young University. She has worked in a clinical viral reference lab, a general microbiology testing lab, a water bottling plant, and a dental research facility. During this time, she was involved in writing and editing articles for professional publications. She lives in Caldwell, Idaho, where she is an instructor of biology and microbiology at the College of Western Idaho. Teresa is a great-granddaughter of Emeline Grover Rich.

MARCUS PATRICK RYAN is an attorney in Dallas, Texas, where he is also the chapter chair of the J. Reuben Clark Law Society. He was a Gordon B. Hinckley Presidential Scholar at Brigham Young University, graduating in political science. Marcus received a JD from the University of Texas School of Law and lives in Texas, where he and his wife, Stephanie Crittenden, have three children. Marcus and his sister, Rebekah Ryan Clark, coauthored the chapter on Janetta Ann McBride Ferrin, their great-great-great-grandmother.

CHERRY BUSHMAN SILVER has degrees in English literature from the University of Utah (BA), Boston University (MA), and Harvard University (PhD). She and her husband, Barnard Silver, have two children and ten grandchildren. She has taught courses in American literature at BYU and at colleges in Washington State and California. With Carol Cornwall Madsen, she edited *New Scholarship on Latter-day Saint Women in the Twentieth Century* (2005). She is annotating the 1874–1920 diaries of Emmeline B. Wells and helps direct the Mormon Women's History Initiative Team, which promotes research and writing on Mormon women.

PATRICIA LEMMON SPILSBURY received a bachelor's degree in English and journalism from the University of Arizona and a master's degree in curriculum and instruction from the University of Nevada–Las Vegas. She taught second and third grades for twelve years and was a literacy specialist for eight years in Las Vegas, where she raised seven lively children. She is the grandmother of twelve and presently serves as a full-time missionary for The Church of Jesus Christ of Latter-day Saints, assigned to the Church History Library in Salt Lake City, Utah. Patricia is a great-great-granddaughter of Jane Cadwalader Brown Johnson.

STEVEN L. STAKER received a bachelor's and juris doctor degrees from Brigham Young University and a master's degree from San Diego State University. He is a past president of the William and Elizabeth Howard family organization. Steve lives in Columbia,

Missouri, with his wife, Avelina, and son, Samuel. Elizabeth Anderson Howard is his great-great-great-grandmother.

PATRICIA H. STOKER received a BA from the University of Utah. She has served as a member of Church curriculum writing committees and provided research for *To the Rescue: The Biography of Thomas S. Monson.* Patricia and her husband, Stephen, live in Salt Lake City and are the parents of seven children and have twenty-two grandchildren. Stephen is the great-great-grandson of Cordelia Calista Morley Cox, and Patricia is the great-granddaughter of Mary Goble Pay.

HEIDI S. SWINTON received a BA from the University of Utah in English and journalism and did graduate work at Northwestern University. She is the author of President Thomas S. Monson's official biography *To the Rescue* and has written several books and documentaries, including *Sweetwater Rescue, America's Choir, Sacred Stone, American Prophet,* and *Trail of Hope.* She has served on the Relief Society general board and on Church curriculum writing committees and conducts interviews for *Mormon Channel's* "Conversations." She served a mission with her husband, Jeffrey C. Swinton, formerly an Area Seventy, who presided over the England London South Mission. They have five sons and nine grandchildren. She is the great-great-great-granddaughter of Bathsheba W. Smith.

AMY TANNER THIRIOT graduated from Brigham Young University with a degree in history. She blogs at http://theancestorfiles.blogspot.com and is working on a series of biographies of early St. George women called "The Eminent Women of the St. George Temple." Amy also conducts research to document the slaves taken into Utah Territory before the Civil War. She and her husband, David Thiriot, live in Pennsylvania with their five children.

ROSALAND THORNTON graduated from Utah State University in nutrition and dietetics, interned at Massachusetts General Hospital, worked as a dietitian, and taught in hospitals in Portland, Oregon; Las Vegas, Nevada; and Salt Lake City, Utah. She served for many years as family historian of the family association of her great-grandfather Charles C. Rich, with special emphasis on the Emeline Grover Rich line. She and her husband, Troy, enjoyed their mission in Nauvoo, Illinois, which helped foster her interest and work in family history. They live in Bountiful, Utah, and have three children, ten grandchildren, and five great-grandchildren.

LAUREL THATCHER ULRICH did her undergraduate work at the University of Utah and then moved with her husband, Gael, to Massachusetts. While raising their five children, she completed a PhD at the University of New Hampshire, where she taught for many years. Since 1995, she has been a professor of history at Harvard University. She is the author of many books and articles on early American history, including *A Midwife's Tale,* which won the Pulitzer Prize for History in 1991.

ANDREA VENTILLA holds a master's degree in literature, linguistics, and education from the University of Pecs, Hungary, and is a PhD candidate in the History of Education Department at that institution. Her dissertation topic is Latter-day Saint women's education between 1875 and 1900. In her research, Andrea is focusing on women's participation in education as students. She lives in Rexburg, Idaho, with her husband and three daughters.

LAURA F. WILLES holds a BA in American studies from the University of Minnesota. She is the author of three books: *Minnesota Mormons, Community of Faith,* and *Christmas with the Prophets.* Laura served a full-time mission with her husband, Mark, as he presided over the Hawaii Honolulu Mission. She and her husband are the parents of five children and grandparents of twenty.

MARGARET BLAIR YOUNG earned a BA in university studies and an MA in English from Brigham Young University and teaches creative writing at that institution. For the past fourteen years, she has specialized in researching and writing on blacks in the west, particularly on black Latter-day Saints. She and Darius

Gray authored a trilogy of books on black Mormon pioneers and made a documentary entitled *Nobody Knows: The Untold Story of Black Mormons.* Margaret also wrote a play about Jane Manning James (*I Am Jane*),which has been performed throughout the nation. She and her husband, Bruce, have four children and three grandchildren.

INDEX